Conn Iggulden

# The DOUBLE DANGEROUS Book for BOYS

## Arthur & Cameron Iggulden

HarperCollins*Publishers*

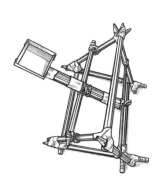

# The DOUBLE DANGEROUS Book for Boys

In this long-awaited follow-up
to his much-loved bestseller, written with his sons
Cameron and Arthur, Conn Iggulden presents a
brand-new compendium of cunning schemes, projects,
tricks, games and tales of extraordinary courage.

Whether it's building a flying machine, learning how to
pick a lock, discovering the world's greatest speeches or
mastering a Rubik's cube, *The Double Dangerous Book
for Boys* is the ultimate companion, to be cherished by
readers and doers of all ages.

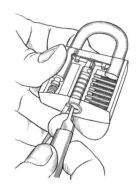

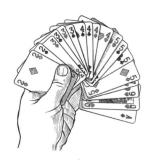

'Boys – you are here to study, and while you are at it, study hard. When you have got the chance to play outside, play hard. Do not forget this, that in the long run the man who shirks his work will shirk his play. I remember a professor in Yale speaking to me of a member of the Yale eleven some years ago, and saying: "That fellow is going to fail. He stands too low in his studies. He is slack there, and he will be slack when it comes to the hard work on the gridiron." He did fail.

'You are preparing yourself for the best work of life. During your schooldays, and in after-life, I earnestly believe in each of you having as good a time as possible, but making it come second to doing the best kind of work possible. And in your studies, and in your sports in school, and afterwards in life in doing your work in the great world, it is a safe plan to follow this rule – a rule I once heard preached on the football field: Don't flinch, don't foul, and hit the line hard.'

THE ADVICE OF US PRESIDENT THEODORE ROOSEVELT, GIVEN TO THE READERS OF *THE BOY'S OWN PAPER* IN 1903

# CONTENTS

HarperCollins*Publishers*
1 London Bridge Street
London SE1 9GF

www.harpercollins.co.uk

First published by HarperCollins*Publishers* 2019

1 3 5 7 9 10 8 6 4 2

Cover and internal design by Simeon Greenaway

The authors assert the moral right to be identified as the authors of this work

A catalogue record of this book is available from the British Library

ISBN 978-0-00-833298-3

Printed and bound at GPS Group

**MIX**
Paper from
responsible sources
**FSC**  **FSC™ C007454**
www.fsc.org

FSC™ is a non-profit international organisation established to promote the
responsible management of the world's forests. Products carrying the FSC
label are independently certified to assure consumers that they come from
forests that are managed to meet the social, economic and ecological needs
of present and future generations, and other controlled sources.

Find out more about HarperCollins and the environment at
**www.harpercollins.co.uk/green**

# ACKNOWLEDGEMENTS

Thank you to the brilliantly named Jack Fogg of HarperCollins, as well as Zoe Berville and Sim Greenaway. I thanked Bernard Cornwell in the first book, as he helped us out of a very tricky situation. That still stands. I'd like to thank Katie Espiner and Susan Watt as well, for everything they did. Victoria Hobbs, too, as my agent. I hope it's understood that strong women, like strong men, are a joy to heaven.

On that subject, I'd like to thank my daughters, Mia and Sophie, for all their help, despite the eye-rolling. I love you all more than you know. Not you, Bernard.

# ADDITIONAL CONTRIBUTORS

Thank you to all those who gave their time and knowledge when I needed it.

In particular: Johnny Ball, Andrew Snow, Helen Stone, David Iggulden, Daniel Martin, Shelagh Broughton and Ella Iggulden.

# INTRODUCTION

In 2006, there didn't seem to be many books of the kind I used to love. I wanted adventures, catapults, crystals, knowledge, history and craftsmanship. I wanted to read dozens of chapters, each different from the last. In short, I wanted a book I could hide in a treehouse – after I'd used it to build one. With my brother Harry, I worked for six months in a shed and wrote chapters on all the things that interested us – from cloud formations and astronomy, to juggling and tripwires. When it was finished, we sent it to the publishers. We didn't set out to write a bestseller. We just wanted to celebrate the wonderful, daft ideas of boyhood – when all doors are open, the future is unwritten and summers seem to last a really long time.

Thank you to all those who recommended it to friends and family. You made the publisher reprint that red and gold hardback over and over. You gave the book to a wider audience – to sons, grandsons, nephews, brothers and fathers. We said it would appeal to 'every boy from eight to eighty' and that was about how it turned out. If I am remembered for just one book, if my tales of Caesar and Genghis and the Wars of the Roses are all forgotten, I don't mind too much if someone dusts off the *Dangerous Book* in an attic and settles down to read with a smile.

I wrote this one with my two sons. One has become a young man since the original *Dangerous Book* came out. The other has reached the age of ten. He runs around like Huckleberry Finn and should wear shoes more often, probably. I thought for a while that I'd covered everything in the first book, but there's nothing like raising boys for surprising you.

Twelve years have passed since I first roughed out a chapter on conkers for a publisher. I wrote then, 'In this age of video games and mobile phones, there must still be a place for knots, treehouses and stories of incredible courage.' That's just as important today – though how we missed picking a lock, making an elastic-band gun and learning sign language, I'll never know. In the intervening years, I wrote down a good idea whenever I heard one. Perhaps I always knew I'd go back and do another book. These are all new chapters, from casting things in resin, doing table tricks and wiring a lamp, to learning strength exercises, the twelve Caesars, stress balls and ancient ruins. There is also a design for a paper aeroplane – and, yes, it's even better than the last one. The world is full of fascinating things. You'll see.

Conn Iggulden

# NOTES FROM THE TREEHOUSE

For us, this has been a chance to act like boys without consequences: to make catapults, build igloos and mix chemicals. We spent two days casting our grandfather's beans in resin to preserve them for ever, and who knows how many evenings playing cards with our family. We learned to make a paper frog jump and to polish shoes like the British Army.

Yet it was also a chance to show our dad some of the things we knew and he didn't. Those sunny afternoons the three of us spent learning sign language or struggling to teach him how to solve a Rubik's cube will be some we never forget. For all that, we are very grateful.

So when we have sons of our own and we pick up this book, what will stay in our minds and our memories will not be individual triumphs and disasters.

No. In the end, what matters most is that we did these things together.

Cameron Iggulden     Arthur Iggulden

# PICKING LOCKS

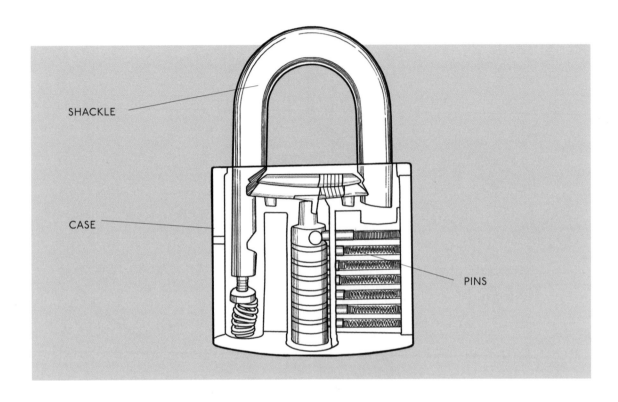

SHACKLE

CASE

PINS

To open a padlock or the cylinder lock of a door without a key, you need to have an idea of how that lock works. The process of picking the lock is actually fairly simple and involves just two tools. When we were young, all the spies and heroes on TV seemed to be able to do it in five seconds with a bent hairpin. It felt a little like a superpower. The truth is that it's a little trickier, but not that much. While researching this, we managed to open an old padlock – and that was one of the most satisfying moments of a lifetime.

Before we get to picks, look at all the illustrations in this chapter, preferably with a padlock in hand.

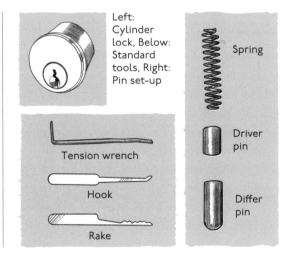

Left: Cylinder lock, Below: Standard tools, Right: Pin set-up

Tension wrench

Hook

Rake

Spring

Driver pin

Differ pin

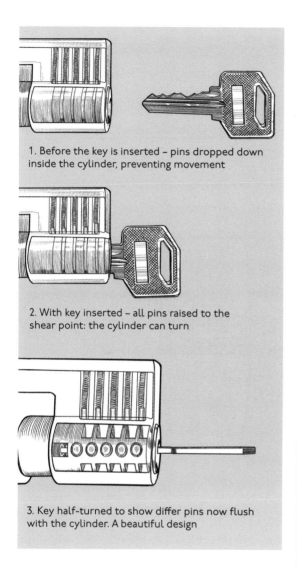

1. Before the key is inserted – pins dropped down inside the cylinder, preventing movement

2. With key inserted – all pins raised to the shear point: the cylinder can turn

3. Key half-turned to show differ pins now flush with the cylinder. A beautiful design

A standard padlock is identical in function to the cylinder lock on a front door. A cylinder – usually of brass – has to turn to release the lock. It cannot turn while a number of pins pass through it, blocking it from moving. Those pins come in two parts: a driver pin and a differ pin, with a spring pressing them down and the shape of the lock holding them in place. The different lengths of the differ pins match the key to the lock.

When the correct key is pushed in, it raises those pins, one by one, to a **shear point**. When the differ pins are raised to the shear point, the cylinder turns. The trick, then, is to copy the action of that key.

## LOCK PICKS

Slightly to our surprise, two pieces of wire might work. However, we discovered that only after purchasing four different sets of lock picks. The cheapest was £3 and fitted inside a fake credit card. The most expensive came with two Perspex locks and about twenty different lock picks. We don't usually recommend internet purchases. In this case, though, search for 'lock picks' and consider buying a Perspex lock or asking for one as a present. They're interesting things.

Although this chapter is not intended to make you into a professional locksmith, it is our hope that, with a bit of practice, you'll be able to open a padlock of your very own. Or your front door.

The first tool is called a **tension tool** or **tension wrench**. It keeps a slight turning force on the lock as you attempt to raise the pins. You'll need a stiff piece of metal – an ordinary paperclip would bend too easily. Examples can be seen below. Note that they all have a sharp bend in common.

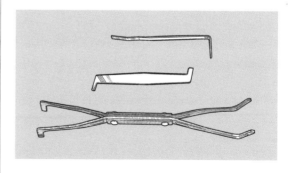

Types of tension tool

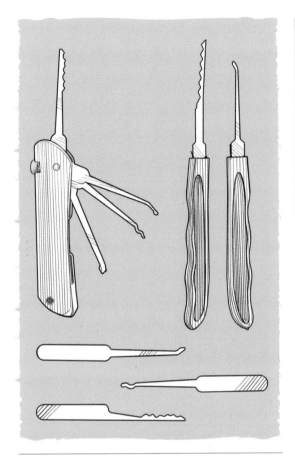

Some hooks and rakes

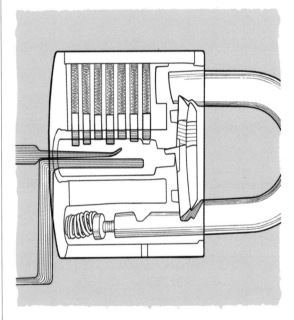

line one by one. That is why a stiff hairpin with a bent end can be used by a skilful locksmith.

Practise on a cheap padlock – as large as you can find, so that the pins are obvious. Begin by looking into the lock and seeing where the first pin sits.

When you are ready, insert the tension tool, moving it as far out of the way as you can. Put a little pressure in the direction the key would turn

The idea is to insert the tension tool into the lock and maintain a constant clockwise turning pressure as you insert the lock pick. That pressure strains the pins slightly so they remain in place as you adjust them. It also means that if something goes right and the lock is freed, it turns immediately. In practice, we got used to keeping gentle pressure on – beginners usually press too hard – until it suddenly turned, sometimes quite unexpectedly.

The second tool is the actual lock pick – a **hook** or a **rake**. The rakes might look a little like a key, while a hook is designed to raise pins to the shear

the lock. Then insert your lock pick. If it is the rake style, you'll have to fiddle it back and forth, getting a feel for the pins within. That action can result in lifting the pins into place, so try that first – just move the pick back and forth like a key a dozen times, while keeping that gentle turning pressure on. Alternatively, if your pick has a bend at the end – the one known as a hook – you'll want to reach right to the back and feel the ends of the pins, one by one, raising them up to the shear line.

The first time we tried this on a proper padlock, it took about two minutes. We decided there and then that we were lock-picking geniuses.

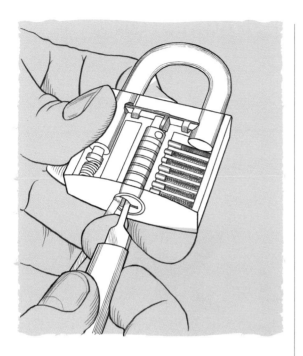

Unfortunately, that overconfidence led to the lock being snapped shut again. The second attempt took well over half an hour of constant fiddling with both a hook and a rake. It was harder than we'd realised, but the wonder of it was that it worked at all. For those of you, like us, who

have never understood how lock picks, or indeed cylinder locks, worked, this was a thing of awe.

In our research, we also came across the idea of a 'bump' key. These are keys for cylinder locks that

do the job of a rake and tension tool in one go. They are inserted into a lock and either wiggled back and forth like a rake or tapped. We've included an example to show what they look like, but we had no luck in using ours at all. Lock picks are clearly better.

The most satisfying combination was the padlock pictured, opened with a hook and a broad wire tension wrench.

Finally – enjoy the knowledge and the skill. One day, it might even come in useful.

# EXTRAORDINARY STORIES –
## PART ONE: ERNEST SHACKLETON

'For scientific discovery, give me Scott;
for speed and efficiency of travel, give me Amundsen;
but when you are in a hopeless situation,
when you are seeing no way out,
get down on your knees and pray for Shackleton.'

Raymond Priestley, part of Shackleton's *Nimrod* polar expedition
team as well as Scott's *Terra Nova* expedition

Born in Ireland to an Anglo-Irish family on 15 February 1874, Ernest Shackleton came to England at the age of ten and was educated at Dulwich College in London, of which more later. Along with a small group of elite explorers at the end of the 19th and the beginning of the 20th centuries, Shackleton chose to pit himself against the last truly unknown continent: Antarctica. When things went wrong, he called on depths of character and courage that still inspire today. Wherever leadership is taught around the western world, the name of Shackleton is spoken with quiet reverence.

Shackleton learned his seacraft in the Merchant Navy, joining at the age of sixteen. In 1898, aged just twenty-four, he passed as Master: a qualification to command a British ship anywhere in the world. When he was twenty-seven, he joined the 1901 *Discovery* expedition under Robert Falcon Scott, mapping the first part of the Antarctic continent. There, Shackleton fell ill and had to be sent to New Zealand to recover. He was bitterly disappointed.

Three years later, Shackleton returned as leader of his own *Nimrod* expedition – named after the ship. Shackleton and three companions made an attempt on the South Pole in horrific weather conditions. They came to within 97 miles of it, but by then they were dangerously low on food. Shackleton made the decision to turn back, though they had come closer than anyone before them. Wryly, he told his wife, 'I thought you would prefer a live donkey to a dead lion.' He came home a hero and was knighted by King Edward VII. However, the Pole remained unconquered – and Shackleton had caught the bug for the strange 'white warfare' of the south.

Antarctica has never had an indigenous population. It is a frozen wilderness larger than China. A range of mountains cross its heart and winds there can reach speeds of 200 miles an hour as they roar and scour in blizzards of astonishing ferocity. It has a good claim to being the most hostile place on earth. In 1911, Robert Scott launched his own ill-fated run at the Pole, reaching it in January 1912, only to discover the Norwegian Roald Amundsen had beaten them to it. Scott and his team died on the return journey. The story of that brave expedition and the extraordinary character of those men is told in the first *Dangerous Book*. It didn't seem possible to include two 'Extraordinary Stories' of Antarctic exploration at that time – but the world turns and here we are, with a story that deserves to be told.

As the Pole had been reached, Shackleton set his cap to be the first to cross the entire continent on foot. The plan was to sail as far as possible through sea ice, set out on foot to the Pole, then continue through to the other side. It was, to say the very least, a massive undertaking. It was simply impossible for his men to carry enough food to keep them alive over such distances, so Shackleton needed two ships. *Endurance* was a solid Norwegian three-master, designed in oak to smash through half-frozen seas. The captain would be a New Zealander named Frank Worsley. *Endurance* would land as far south as possible and, if necessary, provide a base during the first hard winter. The second ship, *Aurora*, would make key supply drops on the other side of Antarctica. It became the 'Endurance' expedition, a name taken from both the ship and his family motto: *Fortitudine Vincimus* – 'Through endurance, we conquer'.

The trip was mostly privately funded and Shackleton himself wrote to those who might donate. Public schools raised money for the dogs he would need and he named each dog after the school which had raised the funds for it. Given that he had seventy dogs, he ran out of

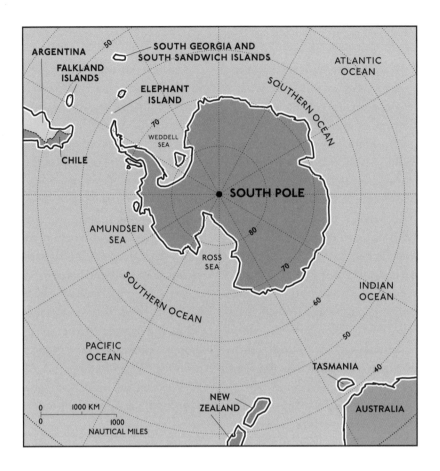

those names fairly quickly. After that, the dogs were called things like Satan, Bosun, Sally, Fluffy, Sailor and Shakespeare.

Shackleton also asked a wealthy cloth manufacturer named James Caird for a relatively small amount. In the end, Caird donated £24,000, a sum worth millions today. Shackleton had that effect on those he met, many times. In gratitude, one of three lifeboats was named *James Caird* in the man's honour, and a stretch of Antarctica is known today as the Caird Coast.

Shackleton advertised for men willing to endure years of harsh conditions. He wrote to *The Times* and almost five thousand hopeful replies came in, which says something about the age and culture.

In the end, he chose fifty-six, in two teams of twenty-eight. Preparations continued right into the summer of 1914 – and in Europe, Germany invaded Belgium and Britain declared war in response. World War I began.

Shackleton immediately sent a telegram, offering himself, his men and both ships to the war effort. Though he had spent years planning the expedition, he gave it all up the moment war was declared. However, the First Lord of the Admiralty understood there was more to life than war and sent them on. That was a young Winston Churchill. By such choices and such men, history is written – for good or ill.

Shackleton described the single-word order from Churchill – 'Proceed' – as laconic. Laconia was the region of Greece that gave birth to the Spartans, famous for their courage and never wasting words. When Philip II of Macedon threatened them, asking if he should march to Sparta as friend or enemy, they sent a one-word message: 'Neither.' Furiously, he tried again: 'You are advised to submit without further delay, for if I bring my army into your land, I will destroy your farms, slay your people and raze your city.' Their reply was once more a single word: 'If.' In the end, he did not threaten them further and the word 'laconic' came to be used to describe a dry, brief response.

In August 1914, *Endurance* set sail from Plymouth on the first leg, to Buenos Aires in Argentina, then headed to the active whaling island of South Georgia – the last piece of inhabited land before Antarctica. The plan was to make for the coast of Antarctica and spend the winter months in camp, growing used to the conditions and waiting for the few months of spring when a crossing might be possible. They set off from South Georgia in December 1914, taking *Endurance* into the Weddell Sea, a dangerous graveyard for ships. The sea froze in great sheets as they went further and further south. At times, it seemed as if they were sailing across white land, breaking ice as they went.

January 1915 was spent forcing *Endurance* through ice floes. The men used a system of semaphore to signal to the captain at the helm, dodging round huge pieces of ice and breaking through others. The whalers back at South Georgia had said the pack ice was unusually far out that season – and so it proved. After days of slow

progress searching for paths through, the ice grew so thick that even the reinforced hull of *Endurance*, combined with powerful engines, could not force the ship any further. *Endurance* was gripped in solid ice that froze hard, cracking and groaning against the timbers. Shackleton had no choice but to wait for spring. He had the sled dogs moved onto the surrounding ice and the men shot seals to feed them. They were at the 77th parallel of latitude, but moved north again as the ice floe they were on drifted, undoing all their labours. It was, in those months, the most isolated spot on earth.

To pass the time, Shackleton involved the men in races and competitions on the ice, binding them together in hardship. He dispensed with the normal ship's routines, understanding instinctively that he didn't need to enforce ship's discipline with men he had hand-picked for the expedition. To do this, he redesignated the ship as a 'Winter Station'. The crew kept their spirits up by hunting seals and training the dog teams. It was a bleak existence even so.

After months of unbroken darkness, the Antarctic spring in October brought hope – and then disaster. As the pack ice began to break up, vast pressures built against the hull of *Endurance*, crushing it remorselessly. Shackleton and the men tried to repair the broken beams, but the ship had to be abandoned. It sank from sight in November 1915, taking their hopes of crossing the continent with it. The men were left on the ice, with tents, dogs and supplies, but with no way of reaching their goal.

One reason Shackleton is held to be an example of a great leader of men is the decision he made then. Though everything he had dreamed of for years had been taken from him, he changed plan and accepted the new reality. He understood he could not complete the expedition – instead, his

task was to save his crew. Not a soul knew they were there, on floating ice, at the bottom of the world. Without extraordinary intervention, all that lay ahead were starvation and death. The men used planks taken from the *Endurance* to raise the Union Flag – to give them hope. They were in British territory, but utterly alone and impossibly far from help.

As the ice moved, the original camp proved too unstable and so they made another one further back. They began to ration food and burn seal blubber to cook and keep warm, while Shackleton planned a way out. They had kept the three lifeboats from *Endurance* – the *James Caird*, the *Stancomb Wills* and the *Dudley Docker* – and hauled them for seven miles to a more stable spot on the ice they named Patience Camp – while they waited for spring to advance.

In April 1916, the ice broke up and they took to the boats and the open sea, making for Elephant Island, an uninhabited flyspeck named after the enormous seals that rested there. The crew navigated and sailed the three small lifeboats for five days and nights in brutal cold, always wet and frozen by spray from the waves. When they were forced to row, the oars grew thick with ice. Yet when they reached the tiny island, they laughed and cheered and picked up pebbles from the shore – the first time they had set foot on true land for a year and a half.

Despite having reached solid ground, their predicament was still unknown. To get back to civilisation would require a much longer journey. Shackleton chose to make for the island of South Georgia. The Falkland Islands were closer, but the winds blew from that direction and the lifeboats were too frail to beat up against them. Though South Georgia was 800 miles away across wild and open sea, it lay with the winds. Shackleton knew the whaling stations there would put them in touch with civilisation – if he could reach them.

The *James Caird* was the largest and heaviest of the three lifeboats, so was chosen for the job. Shackleton needed Worsley for his skill at navigation. He asked for volunteers to form the rest of a crew of six. They would risk their lives to bring back a rescue party for those they left behind. They took supplies for just four weeks. It is difficult to imagine how it must have felt to watch that tiny boat set off. The men on the island had seal meat and could camp under the hulls of the other two boats, but Elephant Island was still a bleak and inhospitable place. They remained in polar waters, and the terrible cold, gales and hard conditions wore them down.

On 24 April 1916, Shackleton, Worsley, Tom Crean, Harry McNeish, Tim McCarthy and John Vincent set off in the *James Caird*. They had rigged canvas and wood to give a little shelter on the open boat – enough to allow them to use a primus stove. Each man took two-hour spells at the tiller or kept a four-hour watch, while the others tried to rest in sodden sleeping bags. For sixteen days they were never dry. Shackleton's account of that voyage remains one of the all-time great stories of seacraft and survival. They ran north into continuous gales and storms, so that the little boat climbed mountainous waves that made it look like a child's toy. When the rough seas opened seams in the boat, they had to bale at all hours, though the cold meant they were always exhausted. There was never enough fresh water, never enough food or sleep. The little boat grew sodden and heavy under the weight of ice and they had to spend hours each day chipping it away.

Worsley navigated using a sextant when there was sight of the sun or stars, as well as dead reckoning – a master sailor's estimate of speed, time and bearing to give distance and position. In that way, he brought them across open sea to South Georgia, though the winds were blowing a savage gale around the island and the sea was too rough to land at first. The men on the boat had grown weak and Shackleton decided he must land or see them die. He tacked back to bring the *James Caird* onto the south of the island, the only place he could reach.

With the boat leaking and the seas still running high, Shackleton knew how lucky they had been to make safe landfall. Some of the six were not doing well. Vincent and McNeish were weak from exhaustion and frostbite. Shackleton ordered McCarthy to stay and look after them. The waves were far too rough to consider venturing out into

The *James Caird*

them again, even if the boat had not been leaking and made fragile by the constant battering. Shackleton knew that he had been fortunate to survive the extraordinary journey. So instead of trying to sail around South Georgia to the north side, he made a decision to cross the island on foot. It was a risky choice. The island had never been explored and no one knew what lay in the interior. Shackleton set off with Captain Worsley and Second Officer Crean on Friday 18 May.

These three men crossed the mountain range of South Georgia, walking doggedly on with the fate of the twenty-two on Elephant Island and their three boat companions on their shoulders. They walked and climbed to the point of complete collapse, but kept going. Shackleton asked nothing more from the others than he gave himself and, by his uncomplaining endurance, inspired the others to the same.

On the morning of 20 May 1916, they climbed the last ridge and sighted the whaling station below. They had marched for thirty-six hours, though they had barely recovered from the sea journey. Yet the odyssey was at an end. Pausing only to shake hands, the three men climbed down a frozen waterfall to get close enough to signal the astonished whalers. Filthy and bearded, they were not recognised at first by those who had met them on the way out.

They picked up the three on the other side of the island, as well as the *James Caird* that had brought them so far. Yet winter had come again – and the sea to the south had begun to freeze into the same pack ice that had trapped and crushed *Endurance*. Shackleton made four attempts to reach the men on Elephant Island, but each one was defeated by savage winter conditions.

In August 1916, the sea ice began to break up once more – and Shackleton set out in a small steamship he had borrowed from the Chilean government. The ice had thinned enough for him to get through and he reached Elephant Island at last, desperate for some sight of those he had left behind.

When the waiting men saw the ship, they lined up on the shore. On board, Shackleton counted them aloud in joy, one by one. They had four days of food left and had been so certain 'The Boss' would return that for weeks they'd begun each day by rolling up their kit for a quick rescue. They had never lost faith that Shackleton would come for them – and he did.

In 1917 they returned to a world that was still at war – and a world that had discovered how terrible war can be. Most of his men signed up to fight and, of course, some of them did not make it home again.

Shackleton was brutally honest and blunt about the expedition being a failure. Yet the rescue of his men is still one of the great tales – of endurance, courage and honour. He did not let them down.

Shackleton wrote his account of it in the book that forms the main source for this chapter, still in print as *South: The Endurance Expedition*. He gave the copyright of that book to his creditors to pay debts and tried to live simply with his wife. Yet he was unhappy in the real world, away from the ice. It was not long before he was planning a return.

In 1921, Shackleton sailed back to the southern continent as commander of the *Quest* scientific expedition. With Antarctica in sight, he had a heart attack and died. When news reached his wife, she sent back the instruction 'Bury him where he was happiest.' His grave is on South Georgia, where he knew at last that he had reached civilisation – and saved his men.

As a postscript, the *James Caird* lifeboat was brought back to England. Shackleton gave it to an old school friend in exchange for him sponsoring the *Quest* expedition. It was then donated to the school both men had known: Dulwich College in London. It can be viewed today, with prior appointment, on any Tuesday. It is a small, frail boat that has known the howling gales and vast swells of the Antarctic oceans.

# OLD BRITISH COINS

Each generation loses some old knowledge – and learns something new. Along with death and taxes, this is one of life's certainties. Over passing centuries or millennia it can lead to great shifts in 'general knowledge'. What was once known to all can become the knowledge only of specialists – or lost for ever.

Our task is not to preserve the past for its own sake. There are many thousands of books and plays that refer to the pre-decimal coinage of Britain. We include a brief sampler here of those coins. It would not feel quite right if no child today knew that there were once twelve pennies in a shilling, or two hundred and forty pennies in a pound.

The first coins to circulate in Britain were gold **staters** from ancient Gaul, imported around 150 BC. The designs suggest they were influenced by Macedonian coins of King Philip II, father to Alexander the Great. Coin production in Britain began some fifty years later, around 100 BC. These ancient coins, like those of Rome, were made of gold, silver or bronze. The three metals seem to form the basis of all ancient coin systems. Gold is eternal – it does not rust – so has always been a symbol of perfection and high value in almost every human society. Silver is attractive, but goes black very easily. Like bronze, however, silver has a relatively low melting point and is easy to mine and work. That probably explains its popularity, along with tin and copper. Those metals are all soft enough to be hand-stamped with a hammer. In the early British coins, the images stamped on them were very varied. They included horses, helmets, faces, stags, wreaths and a host of other pictures without words. Most people could not read, after all.

From the first Roman invasion in 55 and 54 BC, Britain came into the orbit of the Roman world. After AD 45, Roman coins circulated as well as native ones. The metal itself had value, so could be exchanged for others with a different design or origin. The Cantii tribe in Kent produced their own coins, as did the Trinovantes, the Catuvellauni and the Iceni in Norfolk under Boadicea, who led an uprising against the Romans in the 1st century AD.

The Roman empire produced many coins – not only for all its emperors, but also to mark military successes and key festivals. As well as gold **aureus** coins, they issued silver **denarius** coins (denarii in the plural: den-**ar**-i-eye) and **sestertius** coins (sestertii: sest-**ur**-tee-eye) in silver or brass. There was also a bronze coin called an **as**.

After the Roman legions left Britain and their last officials were expelled in AD 410, coins were still minted north and south – the silver **penny** became virtually the sole coin in common use for at least five centuries. It was still referred to as a 'denarius', or 'd' for short. Though it became a copper coin in later centuries, the habit of labelling a penny as '1d' continued right up to decimalisation in 1971.

Rulers of small kingdoms such as Mercia or East Anglia would issue their own silver coins, as did established Viking invaders around York. By the 10th century, King Æthelstan, the first king of England and Scotland, organised the mints and closed down a lot of fake coin shops.

After 1066, King William of Normandy maintained the Anglo-Saxon regional mint system, but over time it became more centralised. Coins that could be cut into halves and quarters were a brief experiment, but not popular. In 1180, Henry II put his name 'Henricus' and 'Rex' (king) on his coins, though it did not become standard practice for his sons Richard and John.

Short-cross coin of Henry II, issued 1180–1189

By the 13th century, under King Edward I, the minting of coins had become a royal activity and was restricted to London, Canterbury, Durham and Bury. In 1279, new coins were produced: the first **halfpenny**, a '**farthing**' quarter-penny and a **groat**, worth fourpence. The name of 'Edward' appeared on them all.

A fourpenny piece – the 'groat'

In the 14th century, during the long reign of Edward III, gold coins made a return, with the introduction of the gold **florin** and the gold **noble** and **half-noble**. Intricate designs could be stamped on gold and they were still the symbol of great wealth. Silver pennies, halfpennies and farthings also continued to be issued. Those were the main denominations up to King Henry VI, Edward IV and the Wars of the Roses, when the wonderfully named gold **angel** and **half-angels** were also issued – a reference to the design of the Archangel Michael killing a dragon stamped on the coin.

The gold 'angel'

As the first Tudor, King Henry VII made changes in 1489. A pound by weight of sterling silver had been a unit of measurement for centuries, but no pound coin had ever been issued. Henry Tudor issued the first – and as the design included the king on a throne, called it a **sovereign**. Double- and even triple-weight sovereigns were also issued. Sovereigns have been issued by every monarch since then, a practice that continues today. They are still made of gold and are very valuable.

The first pound coin – the 'sovereign'

The first **shillings**, coins worth twelve pennies, were produced by Henry VII and known then as 'testoons' or 'head-pieces' – as they had his head printed on them. He and his son Henry VIII debased the level of silver in the coins, a practice that was just too tempting. Mixing

silver with cheaper metals meant two coins could be produced for the same amount of silver – or four, or twelve . . . The history of coins is also the history of forgery and cheating. Queen Elizabeth I recalled many of these cheap coins and reissued higher-quality ones.

The explosion of commerce in the Elizabethan age required sixpence and threepence coins marked with a rose, as well as the shilling, groat, penny, halfpenny and farthing. She also issued crowns, worth five shillings, and half-crowns, worth two shillings and sixpence. They were issued from the brief reign of her older brother Edward to 1967.

Elizabethan shilling – a very modern coin

In 1660, King Charles II was restored to the throne after the years under Cromwell. In 1663, the first machine-produced coins were made, consigning hand-stamping to history. Coins could then be milled with great precision. Some even had the words 'Decus and Tutamen' cut into the edge – 'an ornament and a shield' – to protect them from being clipped. The gold used in these coins came from Guinea in Africa, so they became known as the first **guineas**. Originally, they were worth twenty silver shillings. Later, they became worth twenty-one shillings, or a pound and a shilling. Guineas are still used in some racehorse auctions, where it is possible to bid a thousand pounds and have the bid raised with the word 'guineas' – one thousand and fifty pounds. Charles II also issued copper coinage for the first time and tin/copper coins to help the Cornish tin industry.

In 1797, the government issued copper pennies, though when copper became scarce, they changed to bronze around 1860. Still called 'coppers', bronze halfpennies, farthings and even third-farthings were issued as the 19th century went on.

At the start of the 20th century, the currency was stable and produced by a royal mint. King Edward VII and then King George V had their image on coins ranging from a third of a farthing up to a five-pound gold coin. Over time, smaller coins began to be less useful. The 'inflation' of currency meant that prices went up and money was not worth as much. Farthings were dropped around 1960.

Queen Elizabeth II began her reign in 1952 with a currency based around the number twelve, with a history stretching back to ancient Rome. When the symbols for pounds, shillings and pence were written, it was always '£, s and d' – the last, as we've seen, for denarius. In 1970, Britain still used the halfpenny, the penny, the threepenny bit, the silver sixpence, the shilling, the florin (two-shilling piece), the half-crown (two shillings and sixpence), the crown (five shillings), the half-sovereign (ten shillings), the sovereign (twenty shillings or £1) – and the guinea of twenty-one shillings. My mother told a story of when she was a young girl and found her father asleep in an armchair. Kneeling beside him, she whispered, 'Can I have a half-crown?' into his ear. When there was no response, she crept around to the other side and whispered, 'Can I have a crown?' into that ear. There was silence for a time, then without opening his eyes, he murmured, 'Go back to the half-crown ear.'

In 1971, the government of Prime Minister Edward Heath formally abolished the old coin values and went to a decimal system (based on the number ten). He hoped to modernise Britain, breaking those ties to the ancient past. New coins were issued, with the five-pence piece referred to as a shilling to help with the transition. A pound was redesignated as 100 pennies, so that the 5p piece was still one-twentieth. New green one-pound notes were issued, replaced in 1983 by the first pound coins. Later, two-pound coins were issued for normal use. Some special-edition five-pound coins are produced each year and gold sovereigns are still minted. The bank notes at the time of writing are for five, ten, twenty and fifty pounds.

It is worth noting that these are artificial systems. Whether a pound (or a dollar) has a hundred pennies or 60, 240 or even 360 is a matter of choice. We chose to keep 60 minutes in an hour, 360 degrees in a circle and 24 hours in a day. Yet some numbers are just more useful than others. 240 has 1, 2, 3, 4, 5, 6, 8, 10, 12, 15, 16, 20, 24, 30, 40, 48, 60, 80, 120 and 240 itself as factors – 20 in all. In comparison, 100 has 1, 2, 4, 5, 10, 20, 25, 50 and 100 itself – just nine factors. In that way, 240 is more useful than 100, both in trade and in teaching maths.

The history and stability of a country can be read in its currency – and knowing the road behind can be useful in judging the road ahead. Of course, it is possible that before the 21st century comes to an end, all transactions will have become digital and coins will have gone the way of the dinosaurs. That would be a shame – there is something comforting about a handful of change clinking in a pocket – along with two thousand years of history.

# FLYING MACHINES

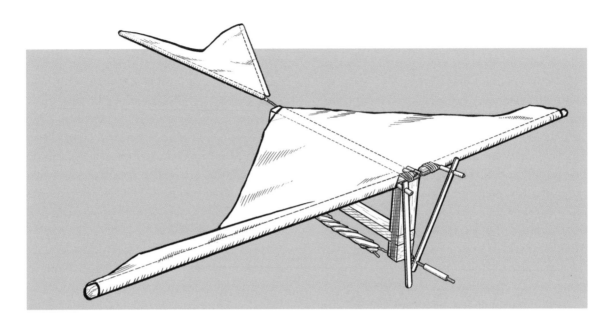

Rubber-band aeroplanes are as old as, well, rubber bands. You could use the skills in this chapter to make a simple one, with a propeller. That's part of the reason why we've put this in the book: it's astounding what you can do with balsa wood, superglue and ordinary thread. The other reason is that an 'ornithopter' flaps its wings. They've been around since the 19th century as toys, but they're still impressive. You can buy a kit or a complete plastic one easily enough, but it is immensely satisfying to make. At the time of writing, the world record for indoor rubber-band-powered flight is 21 minutes, 44 seconds, held by Roy White of America. Our ornithopter will fly for just a few seconds, but it's still worth it.

## YOU WILL NEED

- Needle-nose pliers
- Superglue
- Thread
- Elastic bands
- A razor blade or art knife
- Tissue paper or a supermarket plastic bag
- Wire. Paperclips will do, but we used ¹⁄₁₆in brass

rod, because it felt a little stronger
- Electrical wire (for the plastic covering)
- Oil or grease
- ⅛in aluminium tubing
- A few coffee-shop wooden stirrers (or ice-lolly sticks)
- A hard plastic bead
- Spars of balsa wood

Note: 'Super' or 'crazy' glue refers to the group of fast-setting cyanoacrylate glues. Although it is apparently a myth that they were developed to close battlefield wounds, they are sometimes used in that way today, to seal cuts where it would be difficult to stitch. In other words, superglue sticks well to balsa wood, but it sticks amazingly well to skin. In the course of making this ornithopter, we stuck our fingers together many times – and our fingers to other things, including the tube of glue itself. Acetone is your friend when it comes to removing superglue, but please try to avoid pulling your fingerprints off. They do grow back, however. There is clearly potential for injury here, so find a dad and make him help, but don't let him do all the tricky bits. Remember: scars are fine. Having to go through life attached to a superglue tube is not.

In balsa wood, you'll need a couple of spar pieces to act as the body and a couple of thin spars to form the backbone of the wings. Hobby shops sell balsa in all shapes and sizes. It's not expensive stuff, so you should be able to get a selection for a few pounds. The point of having more than you need is (a) for when you tread on a wing spar and snap it, and (b) because, as you'll see, balsa is really useful. It won't be wasted.

We formed the main body with four pieces. The thin spars are ⅛in thick, ½in wide and 7in long (4mm × 13mm × 17.5cm). The thick ones are ½in × ½in square and 2in long (13mm × 13mm × 50mm). We added blocks of ½ × ½in batten beneath as well, to hold the rubber band later.

Up to this point, it's all symmetrical. Choose an end to be the front and cut three pieces of aluminium tube. You could use brass or plastic. It should be the right size to allow your wire to pass through.

With a razor blade or a hacksaw, we cut all three tubes the same length – ⅝in (16mm). As a general principle, it's worth sanding the rough edges. Two tubes go on the top, parallel to one another, while the third goes at the bottom. It's vital they don't come loose, so we cut a groove for the bottom one, glued them all in place, then wound cotton thread around the entire assembly. Cyanoacrylate glues essentially form a hard plastic as they set, with a little heat given off. The result is impressive and incredibly strong. Honestly, the application of superglue on balsa was very satisfying. Once or twice when fiddling, a crack was heard. A dab of glue on the hairline crack, good as new.

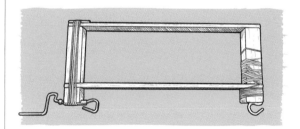

The crank is the only tricky part of making this, so here it is. The rubber band will be held by one end and wound at the front. (We did try a rear-winder on the first attempt, with a cork attached. That actually worked pretty well, but we'll keep this simple.)

The problem is how to turn that rubber band rotation into an up-and-down motion for the wings. A spinning disc doesn't work – it's impossible to get the wings to act together. What works is a staggered crank, which lifts two rods at slightly different times.

The wire comes out of the bottom tube, leaving enough room for a plastic bead (fake pearls work well). With the needle-nose pliers, make a 90-degree bend to the left, looking at it from the front. It should be as sharp as you can make it – you do not want that bead to work its way around the corner. After ¼in (6mm), make another 90-degree bend, heading away from the main body. Leaving enough space for a small wooden batten – say ¼in – turn back in a 90-degree bend, parallel with the first bend.

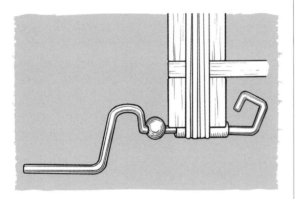

So far so good, but that upside-down 'U' has to be twisted to create an angle of 60 or 70 degrees. Looking down the crank, it will look like this:

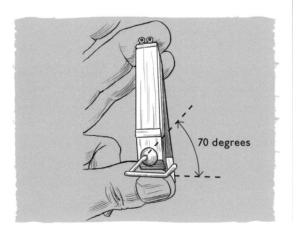

If you bend it the wrong way, the wings will not work together, no matter what you do. It took us a ridiculously long time to figure that out.

On to the wings. You'll need two narrow 8in (200mm) balsa spars for this. We've heard of one built entirely of wooden coffee stirrers, which isn't a bad idea, though balsa is perfect. Lightness is crucial – the less weight the better.

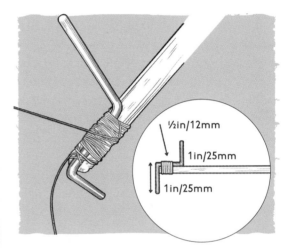

The two wing wires are bent twice at 90 degrees. One end will go into the twin tubes from before, as shown below. More thread and glue will keep the wires stable. We cut the wires so that a little bit poked out at the back of the tubes. With the pliers, you can twist those ends up a fraction. It stops the wings falling out all the time.

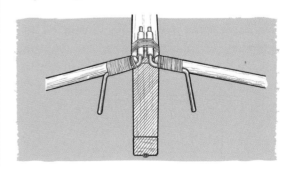

That is the hardest part over with, believe it or not. There might be some fiddly bits to finish, but the main job is done.

## JOINING THE CRANK AND THE WING SPARS

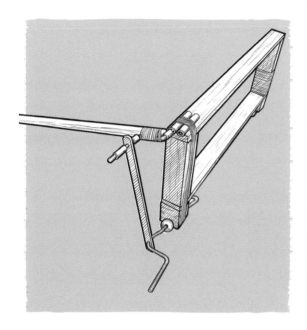

This is where the wooden coffee stirrers or ice-lolly sticks cut lengthways come in. You'll need to drill a tiny hole at each end. Remember to use scrap wood underneath. Our first stick had holes 2¾in (70mm) apart for the inner batten, with a fraction more – 72mm – for the outer one. The plastic stoppers are vital to stop it all falling apart. Cut a piece of electrical wire and use pliers to tug out the copper core, leaving only the plastic sheath. You can then cut that into small pieces and wiggle them on.

The inner batten sits at the bottom of the 'U' on the crank – the first position. Line up the highest position of the crank with a wing position of no higher than 40 degrees up from horizontal. Any higher and it can be unstable. Mark your holes and drill. Once attached, you should be able to turn the crank and watch one wing rise and fall through its entire motion. If for some reason it doesn't work – which happened to us on the second run-through – the problem will lie with the length between the holes or the angle of the wire crank. Adjust – half of making something is fiddling around when the thing just refuses to work and you can't see why.

Once you have one wing rising and falling on the crank's turn, you can attach the second. This outer batten sits on the part of the crank furthest from the main body – the second position. You'll need more bits of electrical plastic sheath to hold it in place. Line up both wings so that they're symmetrical at the midpoint of the sequence, mark your holes and drill. Be prepared to drill a line of holes and try each one if it doesn't quite work. Keep your temper. You will be proud you did – and ashamed if you didn't.

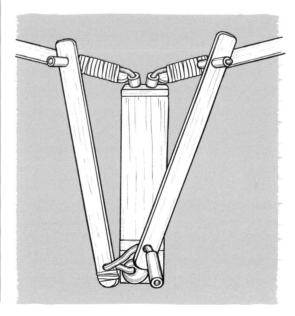

Once you have the wings moving smoothly, you'll need to attach a hook at the back to hold the elastic band. The crank will wind it, so this is just a piece of wire, held with thread and glue. Something like this:

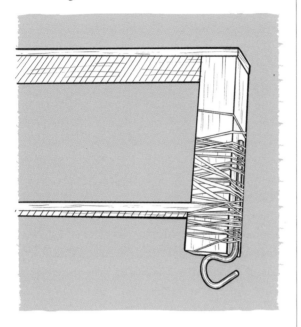

For the tail, we first tried a short wide one, which was completely useless. This bird is front-heavy, so it needs a long tail to give it a chance of stability in the air. With a main body 7in long, our best tail was 8in (20cm). We bent a narrow wire into a shape of an isosceles triangle with an apex of 45 degrees, and fixed coffee stirrers to it with glue and a few turns of thread. The top wire was then fixed with glue and thread to the main body. It's trickier to wind the thread with the wings attached, so the tail should go on first.

To cut out the tail, just put the plane on a flat surface upside down, use sticky tape to hold the plastic in place, mark it with a felt-tip pen and cut it. Superglue will hold the tail to the wooden struts.

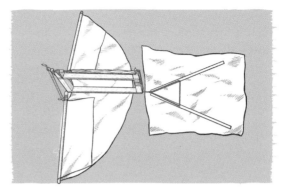

Our first wings were made from white paper, which looked fantastic, like something Leonardo da Vinci might have dangled from his workshop ceiling on a thread. If you're after a model, that will look great. The trouble is that the paper tore really easily – and even though they were easy to fix, with strips of more paper and a dab of glue, we ended up cutting up a supermarket plastic bag and making a new tail and wings out of that instead. Fiddling and improving is the key here.

## THE WINGS

We tried two wing shapes – curved and later a triangle. Both seemed to work. They should be taut, however. Leaving them to flop about just leads to rips.

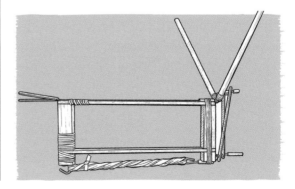

The first wings were formed as a big semicircle of 16in radius (40cm). We used a circular tray to trace it on tissue paper. We then cut out a smaller semicircle at the centre point, to keep the mechanism clear. When you are finished, it is a thing of beauty and enormously satisfying to use. Photograph it immediately, before you snap it in two.

When you wind the elastic for the first time, it's quite possible it will jam. The band pulls tight on the front assembly and friction is the enemy. The plastic bead on the outer side of the crank will help, but a drop of oil on every moving part is vital.

The elastic is two bands doubled and doubled again. We tried various kinds, but thin ones seemed to provide better power than thick ones. Buy a box of them and put oil on the bands to ease friction.

That's it. Wind it up forty or fifty turns, find a high place and let it fly. Fetch it back, raise the tail a little and let it fly again. If there is a bad landing, be prepared to fix it on the spot with superglue and thread. The mechanism is a wonder to behold – it moves a little bit like the mandibles of an insect. Making a rear winder is easy enough, with a cork to help turn the wire and a groove to lock it, ready for take-off.

## FINAL THOUGHTS

After half a dozen flights, our first ornithopter snapped almost entirely in half while we were wrestling with the crank. One of the wing spars broke at the same time. The amazing glue-and-thread combination restored it all well enough to flap again! No damage is so great that it means the end – though it will get heavier.

One bead works better than two. Flapping speed is vital, so you might consider purchasing a range of rubber bands.

Remember, the purpose of this is to build a flying machine, yes, but also to introduce you to the combination of balsa, thread and glue. Using the same set-up, you could get a small plastic propeller from a model shop and glue it to a hook instead of a crank. An epoxy glue would be more suited to holding the propeller in place. If you add a fixed wing made from either balsa sheeting or paper, it shouldn't be too hard to make a small prop plane. Pictures of planes you have made can be sent to the authors care of the publishers – and are very welcome. Good luck.

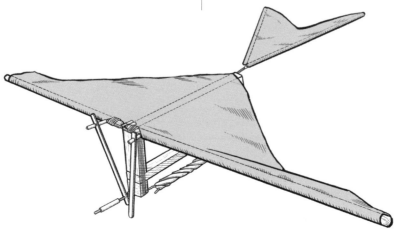

# QUESTIONS ABOUT
# THE WORLD – PART ONE

The first *Dangerous Book* asked and answered a number of questions: Why is a summer day longer than a winter day? Why is it hotter at the Equator? What is a vacuum? What is latitude and longitude? How do you tell the age of a tree? How do we measure the earth's circumference? Why does a day have twenty-four hours? How far away are the stars? Why is the sky blue? Why can't we see the other side of the moon? What causes the tides? How do ships sail against the wind? Where does cork come from? What causes the wind? and What is chalk? Could there possibly be any questions left unanswered? Well, yes.

1. What is the tallest mountain on earth?
2. Why does the earth have a magnetic field?
3. Where are the hottest and the coldest places on earth?
4. What was Pangaea?
5. Is the earth slowing down?
6. What are the longest rivers?

## 1
## WHAT IS THE TALLEST
## MOUNTAIN ON EARTH?

Hawaii. Mauna Kea on the island of Hawaii is the tip of a much larger mountain. From the sea floor to that mountaintop is over 33,000 feet (10,203m). In comparison, Mount Everest on the Nepal/Tibet border is just over 29,000 feet (8,848m). Of course, at the bottom of Mauna Kea, pressure is crushing, so the mountain may never be climbed.

If you measured all the peaks from the centre of the earth, the mountain known as Chimborazo in Ecuador is furthest out. It lies almost on the Equator. As an actual bottom-to-top measurement, though, Hawaii's Mauna Kea is No. 1.

(The deepest spot on earth is the Mariana Trench. Everest could be dropped into it.)

## 2
## WHY DOES THE EARTH HAVE
## A MAGNETIC FIELD?

The earth's magnetic field deflects charged particles coming off the sun, known as the 'solar wind'. We suspect it is a key requirement for life to exist, so it's something we look for in the solar system and further out.

It is generated by the rotation of liquid metal at the earth's core. The forces involved are almost beyond imagination, but that much molten iron/nickel moving at that speed produces a huge magnetic field. In comparison, Mars has a very weak magnetic field – and one problem of Mars colonisation would always be that lack of protection from solar particles.

By measuring the strength of gravity at the surface (scientists jumping up and down, mostly), we are able to estimate the mass of the earth – it's around 5.9 sextillion tonnes. Nothing on the surface is heavy enough to produce the gravity we can observe, which means the centre has to be a dense metal able to produce a magnetic field. Iron and nickel are the best candidates – both dense

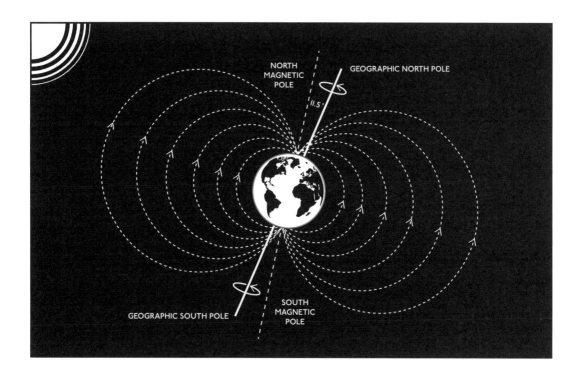

enough to explain gravity and a magnetic field.

A number of planets in the solar system have magnetic fields. Yet when it comes to future exploration, our best bet might be the only moon that does – Ganymede, a moon of Jupiter. Dwarfed by the largest planet in the solar system, Ganymede is a respectable size – about two-thirds the size of Mars. Although its magnetic field is relatively weak, it should mean it has a liquid core, which suggests a source of heat to tap for future explorers.

---

### 3

## WHERE ARE THE HOTTEST AND THE COLDEST PLACES ON EARTH?

The hottest air temperature ever recorded was in Death Valley, California, in June 1913, of 134°F (56°C). (There was actually a temperature of 136°F recorded in Libya in 1922, but that's considered dubious due to problems with the instrumentation.) Either way, temperatures of over 110°F (43°C) are common in Death Valley each year from May to October, which makes it all the more extraordinary that long-distance races are run across it. The Badwater Ultramarathon is run across Death Valley in summer each year – 135 miles (217 km) from the lowest point in California to the foothills of Mount Whitney. The runners tend to use the white lines in the middle of the road. If they run on black tarmac, their shoes melt. Human beings can be extraordinary.

The coldest place on the earth is Antarctica. This measurement is complicated by wind chill, which can make a low temperature much, much lower. However, in still air, the coldest temperatures recorded in Antarctica are –135°F (–93°C). The Antarctic Ice Marathon has been run every December since 2006. It takes place at 80 degrees south latitude, at the foot of the Ellsworth Mountains. Although it is run during the Antarctic 'summer', temperatures of –20°C (–4°F) are common, with winds of 10–25 knots.

(Note: Centigrade/Celsius (C) is used almost universally in Britain, influenced by its wide adoption in European countries. Fahrenheit (F) used to be the British standard and is still more common in America. The best idea, it seems to us, is to use Fahrenheit for hot days (It's 80 degrees!) and Centigrade for cold days (It's –5!) There's no particular reason to choose Fahrenheit (German/Polish/Dutch) over Celsius (Swedish), but using both underlines that they are utterly artificial and man-made.)

---

**4**

## WHAT WAS PANGAEA?

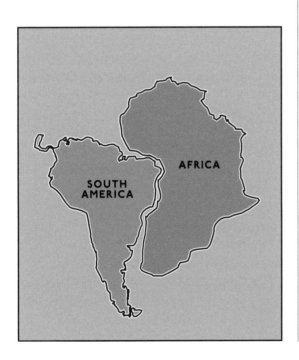

Alfred Wegener (1880–1930) was a German scientist and the first to notice that the continents of earth look as if they might fit together. Africa and South America share a suspiciously similar-looking coastline, for example.

Wegener's theory was that continents drift on enormous plates – and if time could be wound back, they would creep towards one another. The original land mass would have been a single super-plate that slowly broke up to form modern continents. Later measurements of drifting plates and similarities in fossil records have borne out the theory. The name 'Pangaea' was coined to describe that single land mass of 'all the earth'.

---

**5**

## IS THE EARTH SLOWING DOWN?

The short answer is yes. This is measurable by the length of the day, which is getting longer. That much is certain – 2017 was the fourth year in a row that we measured a decrease in the earth's spin. The reasons for this are still a matter of conjecture, of course. One theory is that the moon exerts a braking effect on the earth. That is a good possibility. We know tides are created by the moon's gravitational pull. It makes sense that this might exert a slowing effect.

However, the effect is incredibly small. It would take millions of years to get to the point of a 28-hour day, for example.

---

**6**

## WHAT ARE THE
## LONGEST RIVERS?

There are two possibilities. The Nile is usually given as the longest river system on earth, providing water to eleven countries and stretching 4,200

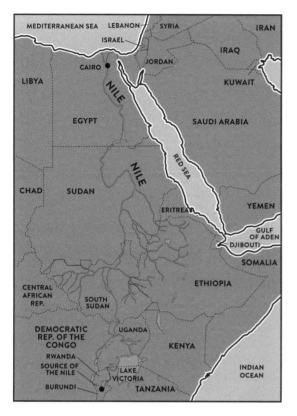

miles (6,700 km) across Africa. However, until every tributary and source has been mapped and measured, we can never know for certain.

The river rises in the great lakes of central Africa and flows north until it reaches Egypt and the Mediterranean Sea.

The Amazon in South America is the other candidate. Usually described as the second-longest river in the world, it too has its champions and it is true that more water passes through the Amazon than the Nile each day. It begins in Brazil – or Peru, depending whom you ask. Rivers can run underground, which is one of the reasons it's not always easy to measure their length and pin down the exact source. Still, these are by far the two longest – the Amazon is just over 4,000 miles (6,400 km).

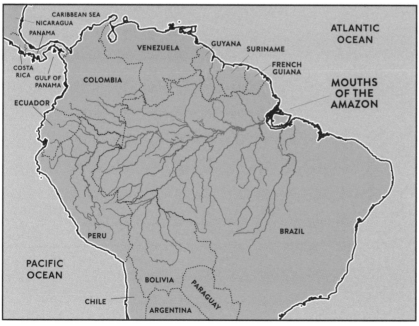

# TYING A
# WINDSOR KNOT

Every boy learns a basic tie knot in school – the 'four-in-hand' or 'schoolboy' knot. You can probably do it in your sleep. However, that's no reason to go through your whole life tying the same knot. The Windsor knot is just as easy to do – and it's a neat, symmetrical knot. In *From Russia, With Love*, Ian Fleming writes that a Windsor knot is too flashy – a knot that rouses James Bond's suspicions. If that was ever true, it isn't now. The Windsor is used by the Royal Air Force and the armed forces of Canada and the United States. It suits a wide collar. Tie it a dozen times. Chances are, you'll never go back to your primary-school knot again.

There is a 'wide end' and a 'narrow end' to a tie. That's pretty much it for terminology.

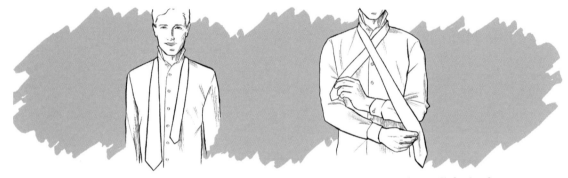

1. Begin with the wide end ten or twelve inches longer than the narrow end. You'll find a first position that works for you – and you'll learn which shirt button (fourth or fifth) you prefer to align with the narrow end. Cross the long wide end over the narrow end.

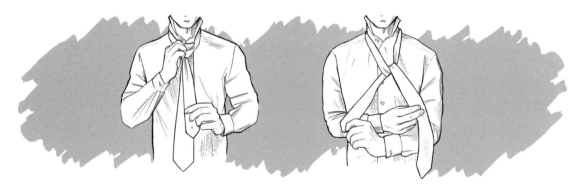

2. Bring the wide end up underneath on the left side of the narrow end, pulling it through.

3. Take the wide end around the back of the narrow end and then over the right-hand side of the knot, pulling it through.

4. Completing the knot is very similar to the schoolboy knot. Take the wide end across, then up behind the knot. Poke it under the top layer and pull taut. Adjust as you would for the knot you know.

The result is pretty magnificent – a triangular, symmetrical knot – and simpler than most people realise. Left, right, across and under. Worth learning.

# ADVICE FROM FIGHTING MEN

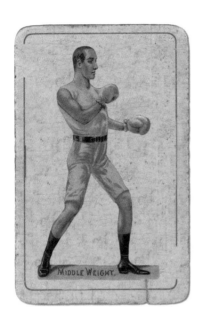 

'Boxing is the first necessity for a gentleman, unless he wishes to be imposed upon whenever he comes into the company of rough men, stronger than himself. It is necessary, if he wishes to be able to protect a lady from insult, a position in which a man often finds himself.'

Colonel T.H. Monstery, *Self-Defense for Gentlemen and Ladies*

'Everybody has a plan, until they get punched in the face.'

Mike Tyson, former world heavyweight boxing champion

Many years ago, a friend of the authors got into an altercation with a group of six men outside a pub in London. The friend was young and fit, but he knew he couldn't possibly take on so many. As the leader went for him, he sprinted away – and, of course, they followed, howling, in his wake.

Men run at different speeds. When he risked a glance over his shoulder, he noticed they had begun to string out over distance. The slowest were quite far back, while one keen young greyhound was right out in front of the rest. Our friend slowed just a touch to let the man in the lead catch all the way up. He waited until his pursuer was almost on top of him, then stopped suddenly. The one chasing was not ready for the move. As he skidded to a halt, our friend hit him twice in the face and knocked him down. The ones behind were closing at high speed by then, so he set off again, sprinting away into the night.

Some time later, the same beads-on-a-string effect could be observed, with a different pursuer in the lead. Our friend knew he'd be less likely to surprise them a second time, but it had worked once and, frankly, had delighted him.

In short, it worked again. He stopped, hit the man rushing at him – and then raced away. The rest of them gave up the chase. Now, our friend couldn't possibly have survived a battle with six opponents. There are few men alive who could. Yet with tactics and a steady nerve, he surely won that battle, and lived to tell the tale.

Years passed between hearing that true story and meeting a 5th Dan Aikido master named Stuart Akers – perhaps the deadliest man I have ever encountered. Stuart trained for long, gruelling sessions every day, working with weapons and multiple opponents. He and I discussed the beginnings of an idea that fighting techniques, as told by truly dangerous men, might make an interesting and unusual book. We'd have to travel around the country and interview a range of trained people to see what advice they would offer. We lined up serving members of the SAS and the Brigade of Gurkhas, a former British boxing champion, Tae Kwon Do and Karate masters, and even experienced nightclub bouncers. The question – some variant of 'What advice would you give to someone in a fight?' – was for the most experienced, for the ones who had survived dozens or hundreds of violent events. We also thought that there was a good chance there would be many stories like the one above, just on general principles.

The problem revealed itself very quickly. Regardless of the particular martial art or even war experience, the advice was very similar. Over and over again, we kept hearing the same things. It became obvious that there just wasn't enough material for a book. It was possible, however, that there might be enough for a short chapter.

Here is what we were told. It is offered, not as an instruction manual on how to beat someone up, but as an insight into self-defence that you might one day find useful. A boy – or a man – should be able to defend himself to a degree, as a matter of pride and self-respect. After all, one simple truth of being a boy is this: you will be punched in the mouth at some point in your life. Possibly just once, possibly many times. How you react to that event will be something you chew over in your memory for years afterwards – in humiliation and regret, or enormous satisfaction. So try to get it right.

Please note: We do not recommend any of these comments for use. They are for academic interest and nothing more.

The first point is this: men who knew they could fight and win, who were not insecure about themselves, kept responding in the same way: 'First thing is, I'd walk away, if I could.'

Every fight involves some risk, and the recovery from injury is painful and takes for ever. No matter how confident you might feel, you could still slip on a bit of mud and lose. So if there is an opportunity to get clear without fighting, take it. You might also consider that walking away will remove an opponent from his place of choosing, and perhaps also from those who might support him, but in the main, it removes you. I cannot stress enough that this wasn't cowardice. One of them called it: 'turning the other cheek, but from a position of strength'. This was the most common first response from men who had fought a hundred times and who had nothing to prove.

An unexpected response was the reluctance to use kicks of any kind. The advice was: unless you are actually a martial-arts black belt with hundreds or thousands of hours of sparring behind you, you must not raise your leg above knee height in a fight. What worked for Bruce Lee does not work in the real world. There's just too great a chance of an opponent grabbing the leg – and once they have a leg, it's all over.

One old boy, who'd received World War II commando training, was still keen on a short, sharp kick at the other man's knee as he rushed in. Bear in mind that he was in a war and his opponent would have been trying to kill him, but the idea was that he could maintain eye contact with the enemy, while lashing out very low down. As he put it: 'Worst case you'd just cause him to stumble, but a good strike to the knee will ruin his day.'

Another friend of ours used to enjoy fighting in pubs. Red-haired and well over six feet tall, he preferred to end a Friday or Saturday evening with a massive battle and someone calling the police. There was never any malice in it, though it is true he spoiled a wedding or two in his time. He tells of one incident in his youth when he was jostled by a stranger. Our friend was around eighteen at the time. Without a thought, the red-haired one hit a man in his thirties twice in the face: one-two. The man was driven back a step and went down to one knee. He raised a hand to his lips and examined the smear of blood. He nodded, looked up at our friend and said, 'OK, son, you've shown me what you can do. Now I'm going to show you what I can do.' As you can imagine, what followed was a beating the likes of which he had rarely known.

In summary, then, the advice was that if all else fails, if an attack cannot be avoided, don't muck about. The best defence then becomes a steadfast and determined offence.

If an opponent falls over, or quits the battle to lie down and quietly consider his life choices, the advice varied as to whether it was ever acceptable to continue the fight after that. In such a situation, we'd like to think the calibre of our readers means they would do the decent thing. We would like to believe in a world where no one ever 'puts the boot in' to a fallen opponent.

Spite should certainly be resisted, especially in moments of high emotion. Try to imagine your father standing at your shoulder and act accordingly – unless he would be trying to kick the fallen man himself, obviously.

Practice is key. Our red-haired friend got into fights almost every week for years and years, so he was actually pretty good at it. Yet as a rule, a trained man does not fear an untrained man, that's just the truth of it. If you want to survive or win, visit a boxing or kick-boxing class and be honest – say that you don't know how to fight and you'd like to learn. Or take up a martial art – every single one involves sparring, and though they are rarely as aggressive and fast as a real-life encounter on the street, they'll help you to stay calm for those vital few seconds. Honestly, a lot of it is resisting the urge to freeze up after a blow. The first reaction is absolutely the wrong one – it holds you in place for the follow-up punch. So always keep moving.

A martial art will also improve your fitness, and that is no small thing. Fighting is the most exhausting activity known to man, though chopping wood is a close second, for some reason. One reason most fights last less than ten seconds is that untrained men are usually exhausted by then. If you're not exhausted after ten seconds of adrenaline-fuelled scrambling, you will be in a pretty good position to make them regret ever starting it.

As a final point, if you ever see a group beating up just one person and you call to a crowd something like: 'Come on, lads, let's lend a hand,' check they are actually coming with you before you arrive as guest of honour to your own beating.

Another friend of ours once joined four others in a car to drive to where they had been challenged by a gang in Harefield, England. When they arrived at the designated spot and time, they were dismayed to find perhaps a dozen young men waiting for them. Full of youthful enthusiasm, our friend leaped from the car – and then watched in amazement as it was driven away without him. He chased that car – and the gang of lads chased him – for a long, long way. So choose your friends carefully as well.

# KINTSUGI

Kintsugi is an ancient Japanese art form that means 'golden joinery'. It is also called kintsukuroi – 'golden repair'. Whether you ever try it or not, it is a fascinating thing. In essence, it's repairing broken pottery, but not in order to hide the cracks. Instead, the cracks are filled with gold or silver dust and made as obvious as possible. The result is a spiderweb of bright colour across the original surface – as beautiful, or even more so, than the original.

The idea is that broken things can still be valuable, even wondrous. Perhaps there is a lesson in kintsugi about scars and how we see ourselves. It is not difficult to imagine a bowl or vase with special value – the gift of a loved one, for example. Allowed to drop, it would break into pieces and seem impossible to fix. Yet perhaps, a dozen quiet evenings later, something beautiful might emerge.

There are pieces of ceramic that are masterworks in themselves, of course. For such a fragile material, it's amazing they survive for the centuries they do. You might see iron bands worked into one of those to hold an old break together. This is not that practical solution – kintsugi is an art form in itself.

Now, obviously we can't manage the expense of gold dust, silver or platinum. Ours was strictly a cheaper project. Our white vase came from Hobbycraft, as did the glitter and glue. Make sure you get a glue that can handle a ceramic break. The Japanese use resin or lacquer.

For the purposes of testing it for this chapter, we thumped the vase once with a club hammer and broke off a piece. If you have shattered a vase into forty different pieces, don't despair. It will take a long time to complete a job that has to wait for glue to dry at each stage, so bear that in mind.

If we simply reglued the broken piece, even with glitter mixed into the glue, it would form a hairline and be almost invisible. The idea is for the break lines to be as obvious as possible. Take a steel file and remove the edges of the broken piece and the rest of the jug. Try not to break it or send anything flying across the room. The idea is to widen those cracks. You might try refitting the piece every now and then to check your progress.

When you're ready, mix up a batch of glue and glitter. PVA glues will dry clear, leaving the glitter visible. However, our best result came from a pre-mixed glitter paste. Slather the stuff on liberally and replace the broken piece. Of course, as you've filed away the edges, you might find it doesn't stay in place any longer. Having a roll of masking tape around is extremely useful.

Wipe as much of the glitter-glue away as you can while it's still wet – it's trickier to remove when it's dry, especially if the piece of pottery isn't glazed. Try not to get too much of the glitter on you as well. This is a fairly messy process, but the results can be rather lovely. The most valuable thing you will ever own is your time. Using some of it to make a thing of beauty cannot be a bad thing – and reminding yourself that broken things can be fixed is always worthwhile.

# THE FASTEST LACES
# IN THE WEST

We all learn a simple way to tie shoelaces when we are kids. This technique – sometimes called a butterfly knot – is at least twice as fast. You appear to tie the knot in one quick movement, which impresses onlookers. It might look tricky, but it's one you can learn very quickly. Once you have done it a few times, you'll never go back to the old loop-loop-knot method again.

Note: This is much easier to do than to describe! Follow these instructions while you try to tie the knot on an actual shoe. Just as when you first learned to tie a shoe – it gets much easier.

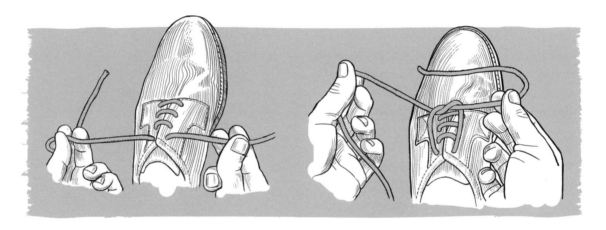

1. Begin with the traditional cross-over. Regardless of how you tie your shoes, you might want to put one lace through a second time. It forms a triple, which has more friction and so locks every knot in place. Your shoes will come untied less often if you take nothing but this away.

2. Note and practise the finger positions in the next pictures until they are second nature. Thumb and middle on the right hand, index and middle on the left. The idea is to form and bring both loops together in the same movement, completing the knot in one swift tug.

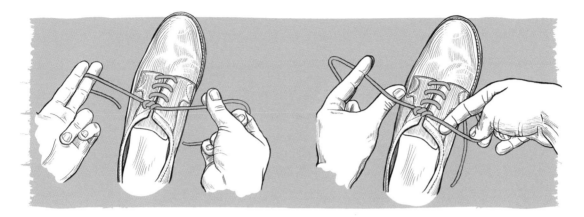

3. Rotate each hand – the left clockwise to bring the thumb underneath, then anticlockwise to form an upside-down U or open loop.
4. The right hand moves anticlockwise to bring the second/index finger up underneath, then clockwise to form an upside-down U or open loop.

This probably seems impossibly complex at this point. Just remember – there is nothing wrong with complexity. If something is hard, we don't give up. We grab it by the throat and throttle it until it's easier. In this case, that might mean sitting with a shoe on a table and the book propped open next to you for ten minutes, but the principle is clear enough.

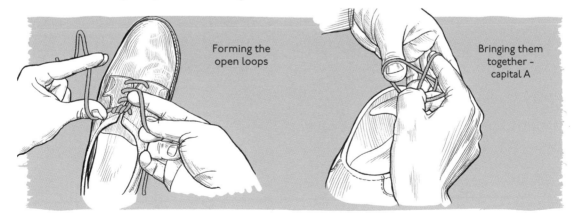

Forming the open loops

Bringing them together - capital A

5. It helps to form exaggerated open loops when you are learning. Bring them together, right hand over the left hand, holding the four points taut – the two bends and two grips.
6. When the right-hand lace is brought over to the left hand, it forms a capital letter A.

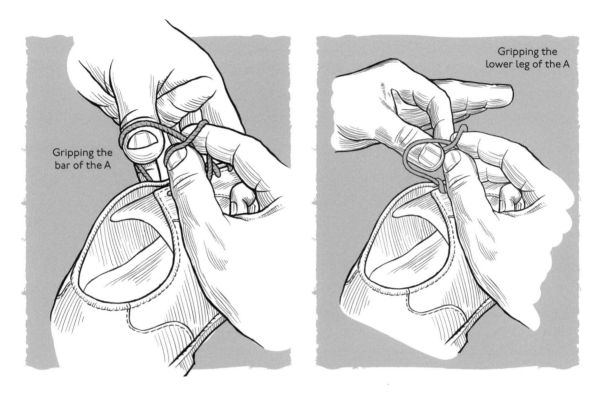

Gripping the
bar of the A

Gripping the
lower leg of the A

7. With the thumb and forefinger of the right hand, grasp the crossbar of the A.
8. With the thumb and forefinger of the left hand, grasp the lower left leg of the A.
9. Pull gently – and the familiar twin loops will form.

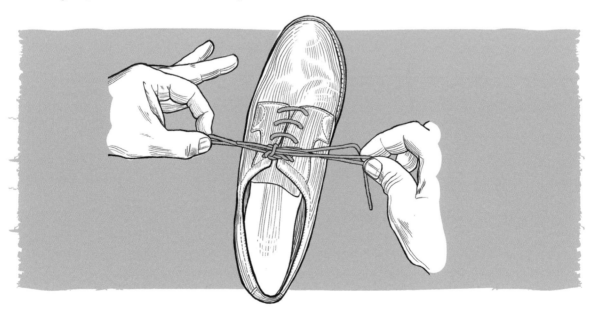

# FINDING THE HEIGHT OF A TREE

I f you want pinpoint accuracy, there are laser devices on the market that will give you precision in a split second. This is more for those who want to know if a tree will hit their roof when it blows down. Or just because the basics of trigonometry are interesting.

### YOU WILL NEED

- A protractor
- A pencil
- A bit of Blu Tack
- A calculator

Trigonometry has to do with triangles. It's the branch of mathematics that examines the relationships between the lengths of the sides and the angles. You probably already know that the internal angles of a triangle always add up to 180°. That is one of the first things you learn – so if we know one angle of a triangle is 40° and another is 80°, the last has to be 60°, because 40 + 80 + 60 = 180.

So whether it's an equilateral triangle, where all the sides and angles are equal:

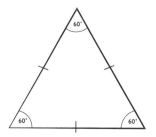

Or an isosceles triangle, where at least two sides are equal:

. . . the internal angles always add up to 180°. You might also be interested to know that angles along a straight line also add up to 180°. If you think about it, 180° is half a circle of 360°.

If you drew a straight line and crossed another through it, you would have two right angles of 90° – for a total of 180°. Four right angles, or 4 × 90 = 360 – the full turn.

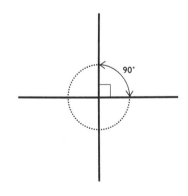

That means, just as a matter of interest, that if you know any internal angle of a triangle, you can extend a straight line and also know the external angle. That might come in handy one day.

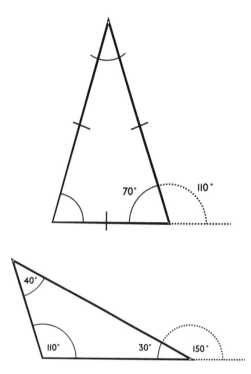

Sadly, there isn't space enough here to cover all the interesting aspects of triangles. We'll concentrate on one very specific task – finding the height of something using trigonometry – a word that means 'triangle measuring'. It might be a tree or a building. In theory, it could be a person, though this is more a method for big objects.

First, pace a distance from the base of your object. Use a little common sense and pace out a fair way – 30, 60 or 90 yards. Those are not accidental choices. One problem with metres is that they have no physical reality, whereas a yard is a man's

pace. It's possible to pace out a field in yards, for example, but not metres. However, a metre is – as near as makes no odds for our purposes – 3ft 4in. That means that 10ft (3 × 3ft 4in) is very close to 3m. So we chose a distance from the tree that could be expressed fairly easily in both yards and metres. Sixty yards is 180ft, or 18 × 3m = 54m.

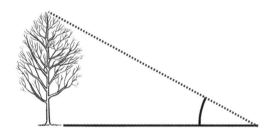

You now have the base of your triangle. You are still missing the height of the tree, the hypotenuse (the longest side diagonal) and the angles. Where the tree touches the ground is 90°, which is what will make this work. The next part works for all right-angled triangles – triangles with a 90° angle in them.

Now, part of trigonometry lies in recognising the relationship between the lengths of the lines and the angles. If you lengthen a line in a triangle, the angles change. We express that relationship with the words 'sine', 'cosine' and 'tangent'. On a calculator, they are usually written as Sin, Cos and Tan.

Each one of those three expresses a relationship between two of the triangle lines and an angle. The mnemonic for all three is SOH-CAH-TOA (pronounced so-car-toe-a). The letter 'O' is for Opposite, 'H' is for Hypotenuse and 'A' is for Adjacent – the side closest to the angle.

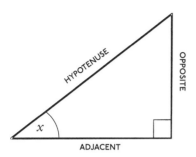

Sine is the relationship or ratio between the Opposite and the Hypotenuse. You find the sine of the angle *x* by Opposite/Hypotenuse. The most famous example is the 3–4–5 triangle. (Pythagoras used it to prove the relationship between the sides on a right-angled triangle was $a^2 + b^2 = c^2$, where c is the hypotenuse.) In this case that would be $3^2$ $(3 \times 3) + 4^2 (4 \times 4) = 5^2 (5 \times 5)$.

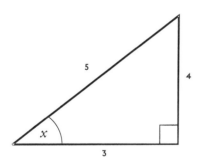

In this example, if we wanted to find the angle *x* and had all three side lengths, we could use Sin, Cos or Tan to do it.

Sin = Opposite divided by Hypotenuse = 4/5 = 0.8

Cos = Adjacent divided by Hypotenuse = 3/5 = 0.6

Tan = Opposite divided by Adjacent = 4/3 = 1.33 recurring

It is possible to work out which angle would produce each of those ratios, but it's pretty advanced. Before calculators, schoolboys used log books, where the answers had been worked out and could be checked or confirmed. Today, you'll probably use the $Sin^{-1}$ button – inverse sine – to turn that ratio back into an angle.

Sin *x* = 0.8
*x* = inverse sin ($Sin^{-1}$) of 0.8 = 53°

Now that we've covered the basics of trig – back to our tree. We have the base of the triangle. However, we don't know the height of the tree, nor the hypotenuse. We need to know an angle. For this, we use a protractor, a pencil and a blob of Blu Tack.

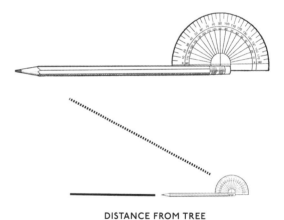

**DISTANCE FROM TREE**

Lie on the grass and get as low as you can with the protractor. (We found we couldn't lay it right on the ground because we couldn't get an eye low enough to look along the pencil and see the top of the tree.) Holding it steady and just off the ground, raise the pencil until the tip points at the top of the tree. Read off the angle – in our example it was 50°.

**HEIGHT OF TREE**

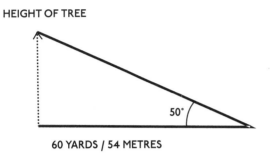

**60 YARDS / 54 METRES**

We still couldn't use sine or cosine (Sin or Cos) as we didn't know the hypotenuse. However, we could use the Tan ratio to discover the missing height.

Tan 50° = Opposite (h for height) divided by Adjacent (60)
Tan of 50° is 1.19 (to two decimal places), which we can plug into the equation:
1.19 = h/60

To get h alone, we still have to do something about that 'divided by 60'. You may know that an equation means two sides that are equal. You can double one side and, as long as you do the same to the other side, it's still equal. So 2x = 4 is the same as 4x = 8.

If we multiply both sides by 60, that will make the 'divided by 60' disappear – and leave just h: the height of the tree.

1.19 × 60 = *h*
So 71.4 = *h*

That figure of 71.4 is in yards, of course. We'd multiply that by three to put it in feet – a mature Douglas fir that turned out to be 214ft tall.

Just to be clear, 60 yards is approximately 54m. (It's actually 54.864m, so a little over.) To prove it works, we'll use the metre figure here. If we plug that into the same equation, the answer comes out in metres.

Tan 50° = Opposite (h) divided by Adjacent (54.864)
1.19 = h/54.864
1.19 × 54.864 = h (in metres)
h = 65.288m

Or in feet: 1.19 × 180 = h
h = 214ft tall

Now, this wasn't as precise as we'd have liked – that angle will always be a best estimate and it's a key number. However, the basic idea – pace off 60 yards, estimate the angle and use Tan *x* = Opposite divided by Adjacent to find a height you can't reach otherwise – is not beyond you.

Finally, you could estimate the key angle by kneeling and raising an outstretched arm. Remember to tell those around you that it's not a Nazi salute. That could be really important.

# HOW TO START A FIRE
# WITH A BATTERY

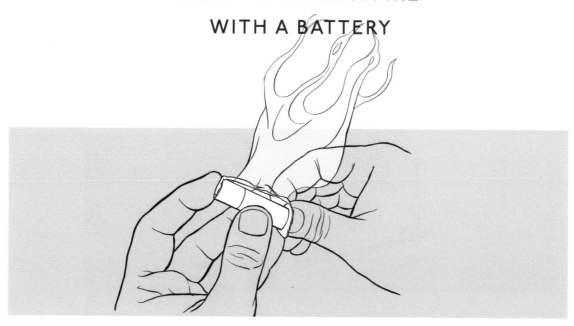

Quick and easy, this one. You'll need a packet of chewing gum, a battery and ideally a pair of scissors, though at a pinch you could tear it carefully.

Chewing gum usually comes wrapped in a piece of paper-backed foil. You'll have to try this a few times before you find the width that works, but you want to cut or tear the foil into this sort of shape. Foil on one side, paper on the other.

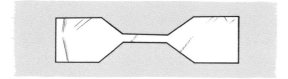

The electricity in an ordinary AA battery cannot overwhelm the full width of foil – but it can set a narrow strip of paper on fire, where it is in contact with the foil. Test it a few times first, then assemble something flammable, such as a shred of tissue paper or, you know, a small piece of firelighter.

Attach one end of the foil to either terminal of the battery, put it in position and touch the other end to the second terminal. With a little luck, it should burn through the paper layer. Alternatively, try a little wire wool rubbed across the terminals of a 9v battery. We teased out a bit of Brillo Pad.

You may be thinking, with some justification, that if you have the foresight to bring a battery and some chewing gum or steel wool with you, you might as well just bring a box of matches. Wire wool can be lit with those matches to help you start a fire, after all. However, that would be missing the point entirely. The nice thing about this is that you will have learned something interesting. The actual lighting of the fire is fiddly and secondary. And you never know, there might come a time when all you have is a battery and a bit of wrapper – and perhaps a firelighter. That is worth a little forward planning. This page is that forward planning.

# QUESTIONS ABOUT THE LAW – PART ONE

1. Can the Queen be charged with a crime?
2. Is treason still a crime?
3. When can the police stop and search you?
4. What is the highest court authority in Britain?
5. Can you be tried twice for the same crime?

Ignorance is no defence under the law, so it isn't enough to say, 'I didn't know it was illegal!' If you don't know *anything* about the laws of the land, there will be times when you are effectively helpless. Not everyone has the time or capacity to learn all the ins and outs of the law and its procedures, of course. That is why solicitors and barristers exist – as experts in their field.

In recent years, attempts have been made to make the law more accessible, by replacing Latin terms such as 'plaintiff', 'writ' and 'in camera' with 'claimant', 'claim' and 'in private'. As you might guess, we think that's a shame. Yet regardless of the language used, there will always be a need for expert defence and prosecution.

It seems to us that we should all know a few basics. Our usual explanation in this book is that some knowledge is 'a joy to own for its own sake'. Yet knowledge of the law might be worth rather more, in the right circumstances.

---

## 1

## CAN THE QUEEN BE CHARGED WITH A CRIME?

It is a fairly well-known principle that the Queen cannot be prosecuted with a criminal offence. She also cannot be arrested, interviewed in a police station or even stopped by the police and spoken to. She is quite literally above the law, and for good reason. As well as being our monarch, Her Majesty Queen Elizabeth II is also our head of state (and head of state for many other countries). It is very common that heads of state enjoy immunity from prosecution, one of the primary reasons being to protect the country from scandal and embarrassment.

The only sitting monarch to be charged with a crime was Charles I, in 1649. He was famously charged with crimes against his own people and executed, following the end of the English Civil War. Parliament established the High Court of Justice to try Charles I for treason, the justification being that the king had made war and a secret pact with the Scots, which had led to great loss of life. The trial was prosecuted by the first solicitor general of England, John Cook, who came from a Leicestershire farming family.

Following the English Restoration of 1660, which saw Charles II (Charles I's son) take the throne, a new law was passed that condemned the revolution and its protagonists. Brilliantly named the 'Indemnity and Oblivion Act', this piece of legislation delegitimised the entire period following Charles I's execution up until the Restoration. John Cook, alongside all those who had officiated over the trial of King Charles, was named by the Act as traitor and convicted of regicide. The penalty for such a crime? Cook was hanged, drawn and quartered. He is, however, peerless in legal history as the first lawyer to prosecute a head of state, an event seen by many as the foundation stone of modern international criminal law.

The closest any modern monarch has come to a brush with the courts was King George V (our current Queen's grandfather), who in 1910 was accused of bigamy by a republican newspaper. He sued the paper for libel and was apparently prepared to give evidence. However, the attorney general advised that it would be unconstitutional and that put an end to it. The journalist, Edward Mylius, was convicted regardless and sentenced to twelve months in prison.

Unfortunately for them, the Queen's wider family do not enjoy the same untouchable status as Elizabeth II. Her daughter, Anne, the Princess Royal, was once summonsed to appear at Slough Magistrates' Court for speeding. In the absence of a revolution, however, it is almost unimaginable that we will ever see the Queen anywhere near a courtroom.

Parliament could, of course, change the law in this area if they wished, although they would need the Queen's assent to pass the Act, so that's not very likely either!

---

## 2

## IS TREASON STILL A CRIME?

Treason is a crime committed against the Crown and is one of the most infamous and serious crimes a person can face. The original common-law offence was brought into law by the Treason Act 1351. One of the oldest laws still in force in the UK today, it defines treason as:

> *Compassing the Death of the King, Queen, or their eldest Son; violating the Queen, or the King's eldest Daughter unmarried, or his eldest Son's Wife; levying War; adhering to the King's Enemies; killing the Chancellor, Treasurer, or Judges in Execution of their Duty.*

Perhaps the most famous traitor in British history is Guy Fawkes, who was brutally tortured and then executed in 1606 for his part in the Gunpowder Plot. The event is still marked today on 5 November, Bonfire Night. The last person to be hanged in this country for the offence of high treason was a man called William Brooke Joyce (aka Lord Haw-Haw), in 1946, for 'adhering to the King's enemies' by spreading Nazi propaganda during WWII. This was despite Joyce being an American citizen at the time and therefore technically not one of the King's subjects.

The introduction of the Crime and Disorder Act 1998 reduced the maximum penalty for an offence of treason in the UK to one of life imprisonment. The offence of 'high treason' has not been used since the war and more recent high-profile prosecutions for behaviour that the public might consider 'treasonous' have tended to rely on other offences of a similar nature, such as breaching the Official Secrets Act.

One of the most famous cases of recent times was that of the former British spy George Blake, who worked as a double agent for the Soviet Union between 1953 and 1961, after being taken prisoner during the Korean War. He was caught and sentenced to forty-two years in prison, the longest sentence in British history at the time – said to represent a year for the life of each MI6 agent he had given up to the Russians. Blake managed to escape from Wormwood Scrubs prison and fled to Russia soon afterwards.

However, despite the range of modern sentences available, if a British subject made a direct attempt on the Queen's life today, then he or she could very well expect to be charged and convicted with the offence of high treason.

## 3

## WHEN CAN THE POLICE STOP AND SEARCH YOU?

The main powers of the police come from the Police and Criminal Evidence Act 1984, normally referred to as PACE. Section 1 of PACE confers powers on police to stop and search any person where they have a 'reasonable suspicion' that the person may be carrying a weapon, illegal drugs or stolen property. They can even search you for perfectly legal items such as a crowbar or screwdriver, if they have grounds to suspect that it is intended to be used in a crime (referred to as 'going equipped'). In the year up to March 2017, the Metropolitan Police carried out over 137,000 stop and searches in London alone and it remains an effective tool in the fight against drug-related violent crime.

A police officer may stop you in the street and ask you what your name is and where you are going, and there is nothing to say that you must stop and answer him. If you choose not to, and there is no other reason to suspect anything is wrong, then the police have no right to search you. However, refusing to answer these questions may give the police 'reasonable suspicion' that you have some criminal reason for not wanting to speak to them. It is therefore normally advisable to cooperate with the police, unless of course you really are hiding something. Perhaps it's also worth pointing out that the police do a very difficult job, during which they often deal with angry, rude and violent people. It doesn't hurt you to be courteous and polite when dealing with a police officer – and it might help.

## 4

## WHAT IS THE HIGHEST COURT AUTHORITY IN BRITAIN?

For centuries the highest court in Britain was the House of Lords. Sometimes confused with its namesake, the parliamentary House of Lords, this was in fact the supreme court in Britain until 2009. It was originally a court intended to try peers of the realm (lords who had been charged with crimes), as well as being a court of last resort in the UK and across the Commonwealth. In 2009, many of the judicial functions of the House of Lords were transferred to the new Supreme Court of the United Kingdom, which is the highest court authority for anything governed by English, Welsh and Northern Irish law, as well as for any matters in Scottish civil law. The 'Judicial Committee of the Privy Council' remains the highest appellate court for a number of Commonwealth countries and Crown dependencies (such as the Falkland Islands).

While the Supreme Court is the highest court in the land, Britain has been a member of the European Economic Community (later the EU) since 1973 and has therefore been subject to the rulings of the European Court of Justice (ECJ). However, the supremacy of the European Courts has always sat uneasily with the UK's unique, largely unwritten constitution and the doctrine of parliamentary sovereignty. Many have argued that being subject to the ECJ fundamentally undermines a central tenet of the British constitution, while others point to the fact that Parliament could, ultimately, withdraw the UK from the EU at any time, thus preserving its sovereignty. At the time of writing, it is impossible to say whether EU law will still apply in the UK after 2019.

## 5

## CAN YOU BE TRIED TWICE FOR THE SAME CRIME?

For centuries a legal principle existed in the UK that prevented a defendant being retried for the same offence, or a similar offence arising out of the same facts, if he or she had already faced trial and been acquitted. However, that rule was removed by the Criminal Justice Act, introduced in April 2005, which allows the Crown Prosecution Service to reopen cases where 'new and compelling' evidence comes to light. There have been several cases where defendants acquitted of serious crimes, such as murder or involvement in organised crime, have given interviews to the press and even written books in which they appear to admit their crimes. However, this evidence is often inadmissible in court, so cannot be used to reopen old cases. The development of DNA techniques, however, as well as other digital forensic investigation tools, means that prosecutors can now re-examine serious cases in which they suspect a miscarriage of justice, such as the murder of Julie Hogg by her boyfriend Billy Dunlop in 1986. Dunlop was acquitted after two juries failed to reach verdicts, meaning that he could not be prosecuted again for the crime. Knowing this, Dunlop confessed to having killed Hogg to a prison guard while serving a sentence for assault. He was also reported to have confessed the crime to Judge Michael Taylor during a closed family hearing following the criminal trials. The double-jeopardy principle meant that he could only be prosecuted for perverting the course of justice at his original trial, for which he received a six-year sentence. Following the introduction of the Criminal Justice Act, however, Dunlop became the first person ever to be convicted of an offence in the UK having previously been acquitted.

# CHESS OPENINGS

A chess opening is a pattern of moves that has been proven over time to create a strong attack or defence. The idea is both to control the centre of the board and to create an opportunity to castle. Which opening you use depends on the responses of the opponent, with nearly infinite variations. The idea here is to learn and practise four or five of them, so as to be able to develop any opening position. That said, former world champion Bobby Fischer began every white game with pawn e2-e4. He considered that the perfect opening move.

There was a chapter on the basics of chess in the first *Dangerous Book*. Unfortunately, with the constraints of space, the only classic opening we were able to include was 'The King's Indian'. For that reason, we have not included it here.

We'll use the standard modern description of a board, with 'a' to 'h' across from the left and 1–8 up. (Always begin with a white corner in the bottom right.) So 'e2-e4' would mean the fifth white pawn from the left, moving forward two places. (A lot of chess books use shorthand such as 'e4' to describe the same move.) As both knights and kings begin with the letter 'k', knight moves are usually written with an 'N' such as 'Nf3' or 'Nc6'. For those, there will be only one knight that can reach the square

## RUY LOPEZ

One of the quickest and easiest openings in three white moves.

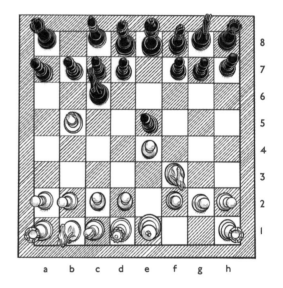

1. *White opens with pawn e2-e4. Black counters with pawn e7-e5.*
2. *White moves knight Nf3, attacking the black pawn. Black responds with Nc6, protecting the pawn.*
3. *White brings out the bishop to b5, to attack the black knight on c6. That's it.*

The Ruy Lopez (pronounced 'Roy') is a favourite of Garry Kasparov. It does, however, usually lead to the exchange of knight and bishop.

## THE ENGLISH OPENING

Most openings begin with the white pawn move e2-e4 or d2-d4. That's because those moves begin to control the central four squares and open a path to move a bishop – allowing you to castle on king or queen side. Set up a board and have a look at the opportunities that come from each move.

The English Opening is so named because it was a popular first move among English players in the 19th century, including Howard Staunton. You are probably using a set with pieces named after him as they are now the standard design. However, it is not a weak or old-fashioned opening. It was used by Fabiano Caruana in round ten of the 2016 world championship, to defeat former world champion Viswanathan Anand.

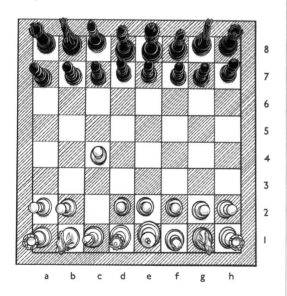

*1. Pawn c2-c4 – that's it. One move.*

In the Caruana vs. Anand game, Anand as black replied by going for the centre squares with pawn e7-e5.

White brought up a knight Nc3, which was echoed by black with Nf6.

White Nf3, black Nc6 – all knights out.

White (Caruana) then brought up another pawn at g2-g3 – and the game develops. The English Opening has the advantage of surprising opponents who are not used to a flank attack on the centre.

Back almost two hundred years ago, Staunton also tended to bring out his knight behind the c4 pawn and develop the pawn on g2 to g3.

## THE QUEEN'S GAMBIT

This is one of the most popular openings because of its quick attack and then constant pressure on black. It is an opening for players who like to play white aggressively.

1. *Pawn d2-d4, answered by black's pawn d7-d5. So far, nothing too shocking.*
2. *White moves pawn c2-c4 – allowing it to be taken by the black pawn.*

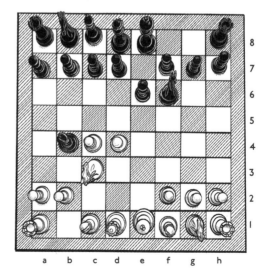

The idea is to develop white rapidly, at the expense of a pawn, while black loses a move of its development to take that pawn: 'Queen's Gambit Accepted'. It's a trade-off and it's risky. White will then reply by moving the pawn on e2-e3, which defends the pawn on d4 and attacks the black pawn. It's not easy for black to protect that pawn and it mucks up his whole development trying.

However, black can also defend that pawn on d5 with a pawn to e6. White can then exchange pawns. The Queen's Gambit is an interesting opening and well worth including in your range.

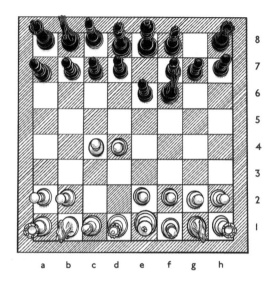

Indian Defence

## THE NIMZO-INDIAN DEFENCE

So far, we've dealt with white openings, but, of course, there are also black openings – defences. The Nimzo-Indian Defence (developed by Aron Nimzowitsch 1886–1935) is a good example of the class of black openings known as 'Indian' defences. They were first developed by Moheschunder Bannerjee in the 19th century. The Nimzo-Indian, Bogo-Indian and Queen's Indian are all in response to a pawn d2-d4 opening by white.

1. *Pawn d2-d4 by white. Black responds with Nf6 – knight to f6.*
2. *Pawn c2-c4 by white. Black moves pawn e7-e6.*

Those two exchanges are the opening moves of all 'Indian' defences. The Nimzo variation looks a little bit like the Ruy Lopez attack.

3. *If white moves Nc3 – knight to c3 – black can bring the bishop across to pin the knight. The white attack has been disrupted. Black usually takes the knight on c3, for the advantage of doubling white's pawns.*

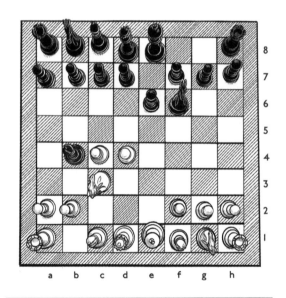

Nimzo-Indian Defence

## THE SICILIAN DEFENCE

This defence begins from an e2-e4 pawn opening by white. Instead of the standard response of e7-e5, black responds with c7-c5, attacking from the c file.

This is known as the Dragon Variation, as the black pawns are said to look like a dragon.

1. *Pawn e2-e4, Black responds with c7-c5.*
2. *White knight moves: Nf3. Black moves pawn d7-d6.*
3. *White moves pawn d2-d4. It is taken by black's pawn: c5 x d4.*
4. *White takes the black pawn: N x d4. Black is still developing and moves: Nf6.*
5. *White moves up second knight: Nc3. Black responds with pawn g7-g6.*

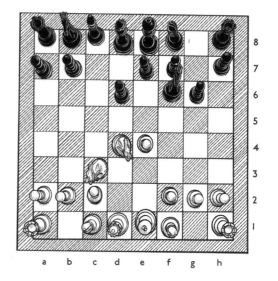

Further developed: five moves

The Najdorf Variation of the Sicilian Defence was one often used by Bobby Fischer. It is exactly the same until move five, when instead of the g7-g6 pawn move, a pawn is moved a7-a6 instead. There is also an attack on the foremost white knight with the black pawn move e7-e5.

You get better at chess by playing, but also by learning successful strategies. Get to know these. Use them as often as you can and enjoy the games that result.

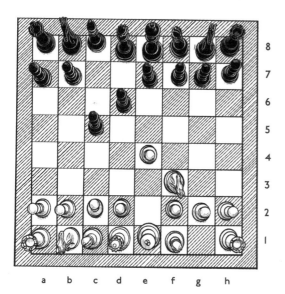

Sicilian Defence after two opening moves

# GREAT BRITISH TREES

Yew

There is a chapter on trees in the original *Dangerous Book*, but despite astonishing variety, we managed to include only eight: the oak, the lime, the hawthorn, the silver birch, the beech, the horse chestnut, the sycamore and the ash. They are good ones, but space prevented the inclusion of more – something we can remedy with another six here, bringing the total to fourteen. With thanks to the Woodland Trust, a charity that protects ancient woodland and plants new ones.

## YEW
*Taxus baccata*

Evergreen and extremely long-lived, with dense foliage that can be shaped into a hedge. Highly poisonous and traditionally believed to ward off evil spirits, which is one reason why they are often planted in churchyards. Ancient yews are slightly eerie to encounter. The most famous use of their wood is in the longbows of English and Welsh archers, so they have a powerful historical association.

## WILLOW

Not only are cricket bats, baskets, fences and chairs made from flexible willow, but its bark contains salicylic acid, which is better known as aspirin. It was the world's first painkiller and anti-fever agent. For that alone, it would be a wonder – but also, see cricket bats. The two most common varieties are the crack willow (*Salix fragilis*), which has twigs that break with a crack sound, and the white willow (*Salix alba*), which has pale undersided leaves and more flexible twigs. Usually found near water.

*Willow*

## LONDON PLANE

Worth including here as it is found in every London park and places such as Berkeley Square, though few other places. It is not a native breed, but a hybrid of the Oriental plane (*Platanus orientalis*) and the American plane (*Platanus occidentalis*) – imported in the 16th and 17th centuries respectively. Distinctive speckled bark. Planted in huge numbers in the 19th century to help soak up pollution. Sometimes called the 'lungs' of London.

*London plane*

## ROWAN
*Sorbus aucuparia*

Known to the Greeks and sacred to the druids, this ancient British tree hangs heavy with red berries when all else has gone to winter. The berries are inedible in large quantities to humans, but loved by birds. The trees have been associated with protection and magic for thousands of years. They were often planted near houses to keep witches away. One friend of ours has rowan trees on three sides of his house, but cannot prevent his aunties getting in through the front door.

*Rowan*

## SCOTS PINE
*Pinus sylvestris*

Ancient pine with blue-green needles. Native to Scotland and found mainly in the Highlands. Adopted as the official tree of Scotland in 2014, they can grow to 120ft tall (36m). They are home to red squirrels, wildcats, pine martens, owls and capercaillies – the largest member of the grouse family. As with oaks, each mature tree is a village.

*Hornbeam*

*Scots pine*

## HORNBEAM
*Carpinus betulus*

An ancient hardwood tree, native to south-east England. The name means 'hard tree'. Looks similar to beech, as the bark is smooth and grey, though hornbeam leaves are double-toothed, spikier, with much more pronounced ridges. Grows surprisingly quickly for such a hard wood, and so densely it also makes a good hedge, though unlike a beech hedge, it loses all leaves in winter.

Top: hornbeam; middle: hornbeam leaves; bottom: beech (left), hornbeam (right)

# HANGING TOOLS ON A WALL

One day, with a little luck, you'll have a workshop to call your own. It might be a shed, with a workbench, a vice and a range of tools, or the wall of a garage perhaps. You'll use the space for little jobs – it is amazing how vital a single vice can be. You'll plane a pine shelf in there, or rewire a plug, or repair the base of a door where it went rotten and had to be cut out. Each job will require its own tools and slowly you'll build up a collection. You'll get a set

of chisels and find you use the half-inch one for almost everything. You'll buy a massive hammer and discover it's too big for knocking in small tacks. Piece by piece, you will put together a set capable of handling most jobs.

Here is a list of the tools you'd hope to find in any workshop set: tenon saw, coping saw, jigsaw (powered), rip saw, hacksaw; inch, half-inch and quarter-inch chisels; sharpening stone and sharpening jig to hold the chisel steady;

G-clamps in varying sizes, sash clamps, grip clamps that can be fastened with a pumping action; sander (powered), as well as a box of sandpaper in various grades; two or three Phillips or cross-head screwdrivers; two or three flat-bladed screwdrivers in different sizes; a wooden mallet and a couple of different-size hammers up to 23oz; a wood and steel try square, a metal ruler, spirit levels – short and long; needle-nosed and blunt-nosed pliers; pincers, a punch; marking gauge, planes long and short; drill (powered) and various drill bits; box of miscellaneous screws; carpenter's pencils for marking wood; kneepads to wear while kneeling on the floor. Also, a socket set will be useful for a thousand jobs. That's a decent start. Altogether, it costs a fortune, but, of course, they are built up in single purchases over many years. High-quality tools are also often inherited. They should be kept oiled, clean and in the open, so they're not found rusted and ruined years later.

Warning: If a man buys a pair of first-class boots, he will pay more than for the cheapest ones, but be warm and secure for ten or twenty years. The man who bought the cheapest boots will have to replace them as they break apart – over and over and over. In the end, he will spend more on bad boots than the first spent on good ones – and he'll have wet feet. Good boots are an investment – and so are good tools. There are *very* cheap tools out there, made of such poor metal alloys that they can bend or even snap. This is an area – to be delicate – where better results can be found when buying an adjustable spanner made in England in the 1900s rather than some modern ones. The concept of cheap, replaceable items is an invention of the second half of the 20th century. Bear that in mind. Good-quality tools can be found in car-boot sales or auctions for very little. If you need new, go for better-quality brands like Stanley, Crown, Vaughan or Lie-Nielsen. The tools will cost more than the cheapest possible alternatives, but they will last a lifetime. As with the boots, that is cheaper in the end.

Some of these tools come in their own plastic boxes. These can be fussy and annoying to open. The best system of storage is still to hang the tools on a flat wall in plain sight and arm's reach. There must be hundreds of different ways to do it. In America, for example, boards with metal pins are very popular, as well as being easy to attach and set up. There is nothing wrong with that. This chapter aims to give some ideas about hanging tools using bits of pine and brass screws. Making the holders does, of course, involve sharp tools like chisels, so this might be a job for dads. Each piece took a while to shape and hang, but the results look pretty good, and frankly there is something satisfying about seeing them in place. (We use the word 'satisfying' a lot in this book, because it is a feeling not of joy or excitement, but of a craft learned or a job well done. That is worth something.)

All of the holders are attached to a sheet of five-ply. It's cheap and easy to shape. We bought a large sheet and sawed it into two pieces. Those were attached to a brick wall. (Drill holes with a power drill and a masonry bit. Insert plastic Rawlplug. One screw in each corner will hold immense weight. In this case, we also used white plastic cuffs on the screws for the look of the thing.)

## THE SAWS

Four of the five saws in the picture (on page 63) are held with some sort of oval shape attached to the wall with a single screw. (Note that all of these screws were 'countersunk', that is, the original holes were drilled, then a new drill bit was swapped in to widen the top. That meant the screw could sit flush, and frankly it looks neater. It's time-consuming to keep swapping the drill bits, but we think it's worth it.)

The ovals had to be cut to fit the saw. We did this quickly and crudely. Laying the saw on a pine plank, we put a pencil through the handle onto the wood and drew the oval. As it was a curved shape, we used an electric jigsaw to cut out the oval – and an electric sander held upside down in a vice to sand the edges.

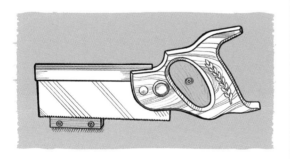

Please note that a jigsaw is one of the most dangerous tools in a workshop. You're cutting a line in a sheet of wood, but you often can't see beneath it. You'll need clamps to hold the wood steady – and you need to be sure you don't send one of your fingers flying into the air.

Once the oval was formed, we put a small pilot hole through into the plywood sheet behind. We then countersunk the hole and screwed in a brass screw. (Get one colour of screw for this. It looks better.)

Some of the saws were left hanging down, but for the look of it and to save space, we wanted to keep this one horizontal. To do that, we cut a rectangle of pine. Two countersunk holes straight into the plywood would hold it in place. The only extra work was the trench for the saw blade. We held the piece in a vice and made two shallow cuts with a tenon saw, then chiselled it out. Strictly speaking, it would have been fine without that trench, but it's . . . satisfying to take time and get it right.

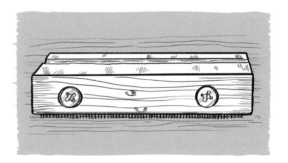

## THE MALLET

To hold the wooden mallet in place, we used three pieces of pine. All these pieces were made using the same cheap planking. For each one, we'd just cut whatever we needed, usually with a tenon saw or the jigsaw.

In this case, we sawed off two short pieces, which then had countersunk pilot holes drilled in them. Pine can snap really easily along its grain, especially near the edge. In many ways it's a terrible wood, but it's cheap and it does work.

The main bar was just a simple rectangle, with a trench cut in it for the hammer handle. We placed the handle up against the piece of pine and drew a pencil line on it to show where to saw, then chiselled out the trench. Sandpaper was always on hand to smooth rough edges –

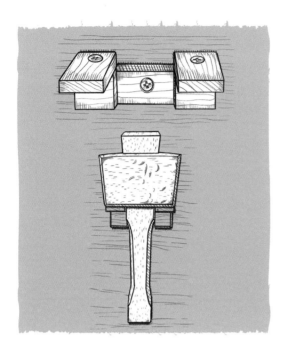

its length. To make it, we cut a narrow strip of pine, sawed it across to make a short piece, then sanded the edge to a curve by holding it against an electric sander.

another thing that is a lot easier with pine than, say, oak.

We attached the two top pieces to the main bar before putting the holder onto the wall. Glue would work, of course, though screws are faster than waiting for glue to set. Held by single screws, they can obviously still move. That's fine. If the screw is tightened, they'll remain in place without needing adjustment.

## THE SPIRIT LEVEL

We used a similar set-up to hold one of the spirit levels. For this, though, we decided the central tab shouldn't move. We used two pieces to build out a 'shelf' to the right width to hold the level, then attached the final tab using a shallow trench chiselled out, so that it couldn't turn. It's probably a bit fussy, but it's an old spirit level and we didn't want it to fall off just because someone slammed a door.

## THE TRY SQUARES

These tools – used for measuring and scribing angles – are held by two pieces. The first is a narrow bar of pine, held in place with two screws. In the centre, we cut and shaped a little tab of pine. On a single screw, the idea was that it could be moved open and shut if necessary, to remove the tool. That worked surprisingly well, though we had to take great care not to snap the thing along

## COPING SAWS

Coping saws are useful. They cut around corners and are excellent for delicate work such as dovetail joints. (The narrow blades do snap, though, so keep spares. There's nothing worse than having your last blade snap on a Sunday afternoon, with no shops open.)

For these, we cut a piece of pine as you can see in the cross-section image. Hold in a vice and make two saw cuts that meet. Leave enough room for a couple of screws to attach it to the wall and you have a nice wooden lip.

## THE HAMMER AND RIP SAW

The big 23oz hammer and the rip saw are held with pegs. For this we went to a DIY store and bought pine dowel, then sawed it into pieces. We needed a much bigger drill bit to put the holes in the plywood sheet. We held the saw to the wall

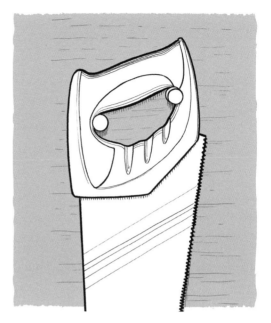

and marked the positions where the pegs would go – using a spirit level to make sure the saw hung straight down as well. With a little sanding and shaping, we glued the dowel pegs in place, tapping them in gently with the wooden mallet – and then hitting them really hard when 'gently' had no effect whatsoever.

## THE CHISELS

The most complicated holder is the one we made for the chisels. We shaped two opposite side pieces with a jigsaw. We cut a trench in each one to support the shelf, but had no screws long enough to go through the wide bottom section, so added a lower bar. We were able to attach that with screws at both ends and then also attach it to the plywood behind.

The chisels drop down into square holes we marked at regular intervals. A lot of careful marking, measuring and pencilling was required

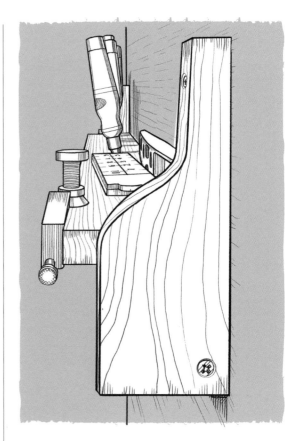

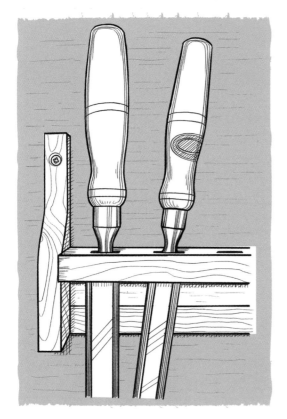

to make these. Pleasingly, we used the chisels themselves to cut their own slots.

We also tapped a few nails in. Hammers can have a small hole drilled in the wooden shaft and be hung from a nail. Rulers and spirit levels usually come with a hole to hang them. None of this is expert-level carpentry. It's all pretty rough and ready, but the results work. The tools are all within reach, exactly where we left them last time. It makes life easier.

Finally, we attached a shelf of pine on another wall with about twenty holes drilled in it, to hold pliers and screwdrivers. It's enormously useful and it helps to keep clutter off the workbench from the original *Dangerous Book* – still going strong.

# INTERESTING CHEMICAL REACTIONS

Chemical reactions can be extremely dangerous. Read these for interest, but either don't try them or get an adult involved and accept that trying them comes with risk. You should wear goggles, masks and gloves when using potentially toxic chemicals.

One difficulty of writing the first *Dangerous Book* was getting hold of chemicals. Even for something simple like growing crystals, finding a reliable source for copper sulphate or potassium permanganate was almost impossible. Since then, the website eBay will supply all sorts of interesting chemicals – for a price.

As a test, we bought pieces of sodium and potassium. These metals react so violently with water that they have to be kept under oil – just the moisture in air will cause them to combust. You may have seen them used in school chemistry labs: tiny pieces dropped into a bowl of water to fizz around and glow purple or orange. In comparison, dropping a large piece into a drinks bottle half-full of water will cause it to explode after two or three seconds. Do not try that. If you do try that, make sure you run a long way and are safely behind something; learning about the properties of sodium and potassium is interesting, but it should not be at the expense of eyes or fingers. Please be clear about this: the man who invented the stunt kite became a recluse when he heard a boy had been carried off a cliff by one of his kites – a death that would not have happened if not for his invention. If in doubt, don't do it.

Without resorting to the internet, some things found around the home can also be made to react in interesting ways. Of course, sometimes a reaction is just setting something on fire.

————————( 1 )————————

## FLAMING BUBBLES

This first one **should not** be tried without adult supervision. It involves large bursts of flame and, frankly, of the eight or ten times we tried it for this

chapter, we almost set the house on fire twice and actually did burn all the hair off our fingers and forearms. It was spectacular, but come to think of it, just do not try this inside. Or at all.

We used a kitchen bowl half-filled with water, some liquid soap, a box of matches and some butane gas of the sort that refills cigarette lighters. It's available from any supermarket.

Upturn the butane gas in the water and press the nozzle against the bottom of the bowl. The gas will form large bubbles in the soap – exactly like a bubble bath, but, you know, filled with highly flammable gas.

Wet your hand in cold water. **<u>Do not forget to do this.</u>** Move away from the bowl. On the two occasions we nearly set fire to the kitchen, it was when we forgot to move clear of the bowl and the butane-filled spatters of foam on the kitchen counter.

Touch a match to the bubbles. The flame burns bright and large, but if you remembered to wet your hand, you won't be burned before the flame is out. Probably.

## 2

## MATCH AND MATCH, OR MATCH AND CANDLE

This is fiddly, but nice when it works. When you blow out a candle or a match, a line of smoke rises in a curling grey/white line. That line can be set on fire, so that the flame travels back down and relights the candle or match below.

This could easily take half a dozen attempts. We suggest you never try this on a date, or at a formal dinner table. Not because of fumes or setting something on fire. It just might suggest you are not completely focused on the event.

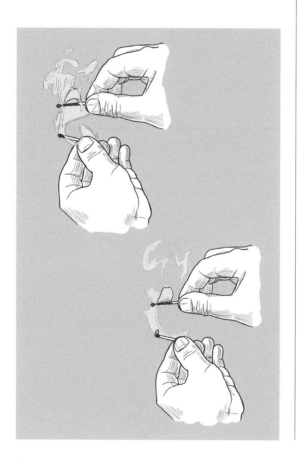

## 3

## THE FIRE SNAKE

This next one is pretty spectacular, though the main ingredients can be found in most kitchens. Now, it *can* be done indoors, in theory. It smells quite pleasant, like burned sugar or toasted marshmallows. It does involve flame and considerable heat, however, so there is always a chance you will burn the house down. Outdoors on a windless day might be a better idea. You may have seen versions of it in indoor fireworks sets. We'll call it the Ram's Horn, or possibly the Dragon's Tail. Or the Fire Snake.

You'll need some ordinary sand, lighter fluid and a kitchen cereal bowl. The bowl will get hot, so stand it on something solid, like a piece of tile. We used an old wooden chopping board.

Fill the bowl almost to the brim with the sand and pack it down. Scoop out the centre, or mould the sand so the centre is lower than the edges. Take 10g (⅓oz) of bicarbonate of soda (ordinary baking soda) and mix it with 40g (1⅓oz) of ordinary white sugar. Use a cup or any container for the mixture.

Squirt lighter fluid onto the sand until it is dark and wet with it. Be generous – it's not easy or advisable to add more later. When you have drenched the sand in the bowl, pour in the mixture of baking soda and sugar – doing your best to keep it to the centre of the bowl. The ideal is a cone shape. Narrower cones will create longer snakes – or horns. Or dragon's tails.

With a match, touch a flame to the lighter fluid. There is no going back from this point. What happens will take up to half an hour. The heat will ignite the mixture. A snake (or possibly a ram's horn) of thick black ash rises slowly out of the bowl and begins to curl on itself. The ash is actually cool to the touch, but the bowl is not, so be careful not to get burned poking at it.

You'll be able to get different widths of snake (or tail) with different cone diameters of the baking powder/sugar mix, but keep the same ratio of 1:4 as it works well.

The ash is formed from carbon dioxide released when the baking soda is heated – the burning sugar caramelises and creates the ash, while the baking powder inflates it. When the flames have gone out, you can usually lift the entire snake (or dragon's tail) away from the bowl. Take it outside if you are overcome with the desire to squish it, however.

After half an hour, the bubbling comes to an end. By then, the ash should be about eighteen inches to two feet long (45–60cm). It is a thing of awe.

# REGIMENTS
## of the
# BRITISH ARMY

It seems to us that there is a certain quiet pleasure in knowing things. Whether it is that the United Kingdom has 102 counties: from Cornwall to Antrim in Northern Ireland; or that the UK has 48 police forces, including the British Transport Police and the Civil Nuclear Constabulary. The accumulation of knowledge is one of life's subtle joys. Here, for that reason, is a list of British Army regiments, correct at the time of writing. These things do change, of course. Most of these regiments were formed from one or more older ones, either to reduce costs or to answer modern requirements of warfare, reconnaissance, defence and peacekeeping roles. For reasons of space, we have been able to include only a few of the cap badges and mottos. For those who would like more information, we recommend Charles Heyman's excellent *British Army Guide*, which is produced each year.

The total for Army, Navy and Royal Air Force is approximately 150,000 serving men and women. Of these, 84,000 are in the British Army.

## CAVALRY

### THE HOUSEHOLD CAVALRY
Life Guards, and Blues and Royals. Formed in 17th century by King Charles II. Current Commander-in-Chief: Queen Elizabeth II. (On operations, they become the Household Cavalry Regiment and the Household Cavalry Mounted Regiment – armoured fighting vehicles.)

### 1ST THE QUEEN'S DRAGOON GUARDS
Light armoured cavalry vehicles. Amalgamated from two 1685 regiments in 1959.

Dragoons were originally mounted infantry who would dismount to fight, but became light cavalry units. The origin of the name could be from *draconarius*, a Roman standard-bearer. Alternatively, they were named after the short muskets, or 'dragons', carried by horse soldiers.

### THE ROYAL SCOTS DRAGOON GUARDS
Formed in 1971 by amalgamation of ancient regiments. Through one of them, the Royal Scots Greys, this is the oldest cavalry line regiment in the British Army. Victorious at Waterloo against Napoleon.

### THE ROYAL DRAGOON GUARDS
Formed in 1992 from the 4th Royal Irish Dragoon Guards, the 5th Dragoon Guards, the 6th Inniskilling Dragoons and the 7th Dragoon Guards, regiments dating back to 1685–1689. Served in Iraq and deployed to Afghanistan in 2010. Motto: QUIS SEPARABIT – 'Who shall separate us?'

### THE QUEEN'S ROYAL HUSSARS
Formed in 1993 from the Queen's Own and the Royal Irish. Challenger 2 tanks. Winston Churchill joined the Hussars as a young man.

### THE ROYAL LANCERS

(Queen Elizabeth's Own). Raised in 1715, they are the last regiment to retain the word 'Lancers' – referring to the ancient weapon of armoured knights. Today, they are a modern armoured cavalry reconnaissance regiment, using tracked fighting vehicles. Motto: DEATH OR GLORY.

### THE KING'S ROYAL HUSSARS

First raised in 1715. Modern armoured regiment, using Challenger 2 tanks and Scimitar reconnaissance vehicles to seek out and destroy the enemy.

### THE LIGHT DRAGOONS

Uses Jackal 2 armoured vehicles. Originally formed in 1759 as a fast, light cavalry unit. Took part in the Charge of the Light Brigade in the Crimean War.

### 1ST ROYAL TANK REGIMENT

Formed when tanks were invented by the British in WWI, this is the oldest tank regiment in the world. Uses Challenger 2 tanks as well as Scimitar reconnaissance vehicles.

---

### INFANTRY

The five Foot Guard regiments all have a dual role – active service in war, and protection and guard duty in royal palaces in London and Windsor. They wear red uniforms and the famous bearskin hat – taken from Napoleon's Guards at the Battle of Waterloo.

### THE GRENADIER GUARDS

Active from 1656. Motto: HONI SOIT QUI MAL Y PENSE – 'Evil be to him who evil thinks'.

### THE COLDSTREAM GUARDS

Formed 1650. The oldest continuously serving unit in the British Army. Captured New York in 1776. Motto: NULLI SECUNDUS – 'Second to none'.

### THE SCOTS GUARDS

Mechanised infantry. Uses Mastiff and Jackal vehicles. Motto: NEMO ME IMPUNE LACESSIT – 'No one attacks me with impunity'.

### THE IRISH GUARDS

Formed in 1900 by Queen Victoria. Light and fast infantry as well as the guarding role. Motto: QUIS SEPARABIT – 'Who shall separate us?'

### THE WELSH GUARDS

Formed in 1915 by King George V. Motto: WALES FOREVER. They wear a metal leek as a cap badge. Sniper rifles, machine guns and Foxhound vehicles.

### THE LONDON REGIMENT

A Reserve regiment formed in 1908 that provides reinforcements to the five Foot Guard regiments. Sniper, heavy machine gun, mortar, assault rifle.

### THE ROYAL REGIMENT OF SCOTLAND

Formed in 2006 from ancient Scottish regiments stretching back to 1633.

**1ST BATTALION:**
The Royal Scots Borderers
**2ND BATTALION:**
The Royal Highland Fusiliers

**3RD BATTALION:**
The Black Watch
**4TH BATTALION:**
The Highlanders –
mechanised infantry
**5TH BATTALION:**
The Argyll and Sutherland
Highlanders
**6TH BATTALION RESERVE:**
52nd Lowland
**7TH BATTALION RESERVE:**
51st Highland

## THE PRINCESS OF WALES'S ROYAL REGIMENT

– 'The Tigers'. Formed in
1992 as an amalgamation of
regiments going back to 1572.
Warrior and Bulldog vehicles.
Mortars and machine guns.

## THE ROYAL REGIMENT OF FUSILIERS

Modern regiment created in
1968. Originally raised in 1674,
named after the 'fusil' musket.

## THE ROYAL ANGLIAN REGIMENT

Light infantry. Formed in 1964

from regiments that went back
to 1685. Based in Woolwich,
London, and Cyprus.

## THE DUKE OF LANCASTER'S REGIMENT

– 'Kingsmen'. Raised in
1680 by Charles II. Modern
regiment formed in 2006.
Uses Jackal 2 vehicles, as well
as mortars, grenade machine
gun and heavy machine gun.
Note red rose of Lancaster.

Motto: NEC ASPERA TERRENT
– 'Nor do hardships terrify',
or alternatively 'Difficulties be
damned'.

## THE YORKSHIRE REGIMENT

Originally raised in 1685.
Close combat and urban
operations. Uses Warrior,

Foxhound and Bulldog
armoured vehicles. Main
weapon SA80 A2 assault rifle.
Motto: FORTUNE FAVOURS THE
BRAVE. Note white rose of York.

## THE MERCIAN REGIMENT

Formed in 2007. Recruits from
the English counties of the
ancient kingdom of Mercia.
Warrior vehicles, sniper rifles,
mortars, machine guns. Motto:
STAND FIRM AND STRIKE HARD.

## THE ROYAL WELSH

Recruits primarily in Wales.
Original regiments raised
in 1689. Modern regiment
formed in 2006. Warrior
vehicles. Sniper rifles, mortars,
machine guns. Motto: GWELL
ANGAU NA CHYWILYDD –
'Death before dishonour'. Also:
ICH DIEN – 'I serve'.

## THE ROYAL IRISH REGIMENT

Recruits primarily in Ireland.
Raised in 1689. Modern
regiment formed in 1992.
Motto: FAUGH A BALLAGH
– 'Clear the Way'. Uses

LII8 field gun of the 3rd Regiment Royal Horse Artillery

vehicle-mounted grenade machine guns as well as SA80 assault rifles. Land Rover and Foxhound vehicles.

## ROYAL ARTILLERY – 'THE GUNNERS'

### 1ST REGIMENT ROYAL HORSE ARTILLERY
Uses AS90 self-propelled artillery and armoured multiple rocket launchers.

### 3RD REGIMENT ROYAL HORSE ARTILLERY
– 'The Liverpool and Manchester Gunners'. Uses L118 field gun.

### 4TH REGIMENT ROYAL ARTILLERY
– 'The North-East Gunners'. Uses L118 field gun.

### 5TH REGIMENT ROYAL ARTILLERY
– 'The Yorkshire Gunners'. Current role includes Surveillance and target acquisition.

### 7TH (PARACHUTE) REGIMENT ROYAL HORSE ARTILLERY
–'The Airborne Gunners'. Uses L118 field gun. Serves in Air Assault Brigade.

### 12TH REGIMENT ROYAL ARTILLERY
 – 'The Lancashire and

Cumbrian Gunners'. Uses STARstreak high velocity missiles.

### 14TH REGIMENT ROYAL ARTILLERY
Provides training and support.

### 16TH REGIMENT ROYAL ARTILLERY
– 'The London and Kent Gunners'. Equipped with Rapier surface-to-air missiles.

### 19TH REGIMENT ROYAL ARTILLERY
– 'The Highland Gunners'. AS90 self-propelled and multiple-armoured rocket launchers.

A Thales Watchkeeper Unmanned Aerial Vehicle (UAV)

### 26TH REGIMENT ROYAL ARTILLERY

– 'The West Midland Gunners'. AS90 and rocket launchers.

### 29TH COMMANDO REGIMENT ROYAL ARTILLERY

– 'The Commando Gunners'. Provides artillery support to 3 Commando Brigade.

### 32ND REGIMENT ROYAL ARTILLERY

– 'The Wessex Gunners'. Unmanned aerial vehicles: war drones.

### 47TH REGIMENT ROYAL ARTILLERY

– 'The Hampshire and Sussex Gunners'. They operate the Thales Watchkeeper unmanned surveillance and target acquisition system.

### THE KING'S TROOP ROYAL HORSE ARTILLERY

Ceremonial regiment, based at Woolwich, London. Provides royal gun salutes on celebratory occasions. Uses 13lb WWI-era field guns.

## OTHER UNITS

### THE RIFLES

Formed in 2007 from much older regiments dating back to 1685. First to wear camouflaged uniforms. 117 Victoria Crosses won. Five battalions, and three more in reserve.

### THE ROYAL GURKHA RIFLES

Recruits only in Nepal. Modern regiment formed in 1994, amalgamating four

that served the Crown for two hundred years. Based in Brunei and UK. Motto: KAATAR HUNNU BANDA MARNU RAMRO – 'Better to die than be a coward'.

### THE PARACHUTE REGIMENT

– 'The Red Devils'. Formed in 1942. Airborne assault infantry. Motto: UTRINQUE PARATUS – 'Ready for anything'.

## THE SPECIAL AIR SERVICE (SAS)

Special Forces. Founded in 1941. Small team and covert actions. Snipers, stealth and combat. Motto: 'Who dares wins'.

## THE SPECIAL RECONNAISSANCE REGIMENT (SRR)

Special Forces. Formed 2005. Surveillance and reconnaissance. Counter-terrorism.

## THE CORPS OF ROYAL ENGINEERS

Combat engineers or 'Sappers' provide support to the rest of the Army in war and peacetime. Duties include bomb disposal, bridge building, diving, communications and maintenance of armoured vehicles. The regiments are: 21st, 22nd, 23rd, 24th Commando, 26th, 32nd, 33rd, 35th, 36th, 39th and 42nd.

## THE ROYAL CORPS OF SIGNALS

Formed in 1920, signals regiments deploy wherever the main army or special forces go. They are responsible for communications, digital security and electronic warfare. The signals regiments are: 1st, 2nd, 3rd, 10th, 14th, 15th, 16th, 18th, 21st, 22nd, 30th.

## THE ROYAL LOGISTIC CORPS

The logistic corps provides ammunition, parts, rations, food, water and whatever else the rest of the army needs to function. The regiments are: 1st, 3rd and 4th Close Support Regiments; 6th and 7th Force Logistic Regiments; 9th Theatre Logistic Regiment; 10th Queen's Own Gurkha Logistic Regiment; 11th Explosive Ordnance Disposal Regiment; 13th Air Assault Regiment; 17th Port and Maritime Regiment; 27th, 29th Regiments. They use heavy transport vehicles like the Mastiff.

## ARMY AIR CORPS

Combat air support is provided by helicopters and fixed-wing planes. The regiments are 1st, 3rd, 4th and 5th, and they use Apache helicopters as well as the Lynx.

## THE CORPS OF ROYAL ELECTRICAL AND MECHANICAL ENGINEERS

Six battalions. They maintain all equipment, including tanks and helicopters. Motto: ARTE ET MARTE – 'By skill and fighting'.

## ROYAL ARMY MEDICAL CORPS

Six regiments. Formed in 1898. Non-combatant, though they may use their weapons in self-defence. Provides vital surgery for the wounded. Maintains the health of the rest of the army. Regiments are: 1st, 2nd, 3rd, 4th, 5th, 16th. There are also three field hospitals: 22nd, 33rd and 34th.

There are a number of other corps and services in the Army, as might be expected to administer so many, often far from home and under extreme conditions. These are: **Queen Alexandra's Royal Nursing Corps** (nursing), **Adjutant General's Corps** (administration), **Intelligence Corps** (intelligence), **Royal Army Veterinary Corps** (animals, mostly dogs), **Small Arms School Corps** (small arms training), **Royal Army Dental Corps**, **Royal Military Police**, **Military Bands** and

'There is no beating these troops, in spite of their generals. I always thought them bad soldiers, now I am sure of it. I turned their right, pierced their centre, broke them everywhere; the day was mine, and yet they did not know it and would not run.'

French Marshal Soult, commenting on the British infantry as he retreated in 1811

the **Royal Army Physical Training Corps** – Motto: MENS SANA IN CORPORE SANO – 'A healthy mind in a healthy body'.

Finally, there is a **Royal Gibraltar Regiment**, defending the British Overseas Territory of Gibraltar. In Bermuda, the **Royal Bermuda Regiment** defends the British Overseas Territory of Bermuda. This is not part of the British Army but can request training and operational support if needed. The Commander-in-Chief is the Bermudan Governor General.

Around another 30,000 soldiers can be counted in various reserves, such as the **Scottish and North Irish Yeomanry**, or the **Royal Wessex Yeomanry**, always available to be called up.

## RANKS IN THE BRITISH ARMY

## 'OTHER' OR NON-COMMISSIONED RANKS

**PRIVATE** – Trooper, Gunner, Sapper, Kingsman etc., depending on regiment.
**LANCE CORPORAL** – in charge of four soldiers.
**CORPORAL** – in charge of more soldiers and equipment.
**SERGEANT** – senior role, often second in command of thirty soldiers.
**STAFF OR COLOUR SERGEANT** – senior role, managing 120 soldiers.
**WARRANT OFFICER CLASS 2** (Company Sergeant Major) – senior adviser to the Major in command of the unit.

**WARRANT OFFICER CLASS 1** (Regimental Sergeant Major) – senior adviser to the Commanding Officer, responsible for up to 650 men.

## OFFICER OR COMMISSIONED RANKS

**OFFICER CADET** – rank held while training at Sandhurst.
**SECOND LIEUTENANT** – first rank on being commissioned.
**LIEUTENANT** – in command of around thirty soldiers.
**CAPTAIN** – second in command of 120, equivalent to Roman optio.
**MAJOR** – in command of 120, equivalent to Roman centurion.
**LIEUTENANT COLONEL** – in command of 650.
**COLONEL** – staff rather than field rank.
**BRIGADIER** – commands a brigade.
**MAJOR GENERAL** – commands a division, and Sandhurst Military Academy.
**LIEUTENANT GENERAL** – very senior role, commands a corps.
**GENERAL** – highest rank available to serving officers.
**FIELD MARSHAL** – highest honorary rank.

# MAKING A BOARD GAME

Many of us have looked at Monopoly or Cluedo and thought, really, how hard can it be to make something like that? The answer is a little like chess: easy to begin but hard to master. Anyone can make a board game. The question is, will you be able to persuade your family or friends to learn the rules and actually play it? Still, that's exactly how Scrabble and Trivial Pursuit started. Those remain hugely popular today. In a world of smartphones and first-person shooter games, there still seems to be a place for a small group to sit around and compete with one another for fun. In this chapter, we aren't going to try and invent a new form of chess, go or draughts. We'll concentrate on classic board games, like The Game of Life, Sorry! or Risk.

## THE CONCEPT

The basic concept should be simple – even Snakes and Ladders has its fans, and that has no structure or tactics *whatsoever*. As it is almost two thousand years old, though, that makes a bit of sense. They hadn't invented Chance cards then.

Snakes and Ladders has the aim of reaching a particular square, while in Monopoly players go round and round the board as difficulty increases, until someone runs out of money. We think the second form is a better model – no 'goal' square, but gaining money from a finite pot. People like collecting wads of cash.

Pick a concept your family or friends might

possibly enjoy. This is important: as soon as you decide the game is called 'Ninja Castle', ideas will pop up. Can you win Ninja equipment? Is the basic idea to climb through the levels? Will you need a fighting system when players encounter guards? Are you an assassin, or is that too dark for a board game – and so on. If you call it, say, Poker Master, you'll have to work out how to incorporate poker hands into a board game. Will there be betting? Will someone have to be the dealer?

You may have a lifelong interest in orchids, but will your hobby make a good theme for a board game? Probably not – though now we're wondering if an orchid hunt through a jungle board might just be the best idea we've ever had.

## MONEY

Consider the use of money. In Monopoly, money is used to purchase tokens (houses and hotels) that make life harder for the other players. Your game 'Orchid Adventure' (all right, we're just running with it now) might involve the purchase of rare flower bulbs. You could then win breeding tokens and cross-breed them to form rarer and more expensive orchids, with the aim of producing truly rare specimens that would allow you to finally build your own glasshouse in Orchid Manor.

However, as fun as that is beginning to sound, you also need a way to disadvantage the other players. In our example, you might be able to purchase 'Root Rot' cards or, better still, tokens, to be left on the board like a booby-trap, or deployed against another player at a crucial moment. (That attack might be limited further by the use of a six-sided die: roll 1 or 2, the attack succeeds; 3 or 4, no result; 5 or 6, rebounds on you. That is a 1/3 or 33.3% chance of success. Learn percentages –

they're really useful for this sort of thing.)

Money, then, is not an end in itself, but a means to an end in the game. Whatever they start with, it should be possible for a player to take some from the others – perhaps at the end of each circle of the board – and then to buy something useful with it. The Monopoly hotel piece is the model for that – a token earned or won that ruins another player's day when he or she lands on it. In a Ninja game, you might have caltrops made from paperclips, for example.

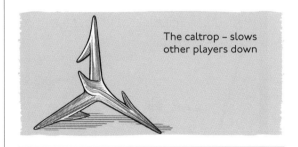

The caltrop – slows other players down

## DISASTERS AND REWARDS

The game shouldn't feel too arbitrary. People like to develop tactics. Our Orchid Adventure idea has scope for any number of disasters – jungle spiders, chased back down the board by local tribes, etc: all variants of the snake in Snakes and Ladders. Yet if we are to go round and round the board (with possible trips through the jungle interior for extra risk/reward), you'll need to incorporate small successes and failures into the game. As a side note, we learned recently of the unpleasantly large camel spider found in desert locations, which follows moving shadows, so appears to hunt people. A soldier we met described how he had to use a handgun to shoot a particularly aggressive one. The idea of a spider token that pursues a player – perhaps beginning a few squares back, with a 50/50 die roll to bring it closer or not each move – feels like a good one. Another alternative might be to have some

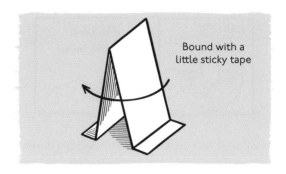

Bound with a
little sticky tape

aggressive tokens on a particular square – ghost ninjas, say, that might choose to follow any players that go past – if a 6 is rolled. Or an odd number.

The classic board-game penalty square is either one with something unpleasant printed on it – 'Quicksand. Miss a go' – or a symbol to take a card from a pack, with either disasters or rewards in them. A third possibility is a card or die roll that allows you to take something of your choice from another player.

In The Game of Life, players begin at Infancy and end at Happy Old Age. It's a variation on Snakes and Ladders, with good and bad squares for players to land on as they go. The original had squares for 'Poverty', 'Gambling' and 'Ruin', as well as 'College', 'Truth' and 'Matrimony' – there was also a 'Suicide' square. Fun for all the family.

## PLAYER PIECES

A proper game company can produce all sorts of shapes in plastic or metal, of course. You could use pieces of bent card for your tokens, but this is an area you shouldn't dash off. In fact, the more care you take with this, the more seriously people will take it. If you have access to a grinding wheel, for example, you could fashion different pieces from wood or metal, whatever you can find. Keep the tips of your fingers in ice, by the way, or pop them into a bag of frozen peas on the way to hospital.

The tokens don't all have to be the same – as the iron and dog of Monopoly show. They could easily be Lego characters, with different hats. Look out for them in charity shops, where you can pick them up for very little. In those same shops, you might also buy another game to use its tokens in your prototype. You'll need at least four for the players, ideally six to have a couple of spares.

## THE BOARD ITSELF

The design of the board is the key to the whole thing, of course. Will your players all begin on the same spot, or on four different corners? As soon as we wrote that last sentence, the idea of a pursuit aspect popped up. Can we have rewards for passing the next player, or lose orchid bulbs for being passed? Choose what you think might work and begin to rough out a board on scrap paper. Preparation is key. Producing something that works is like writing a book. There will be editing and changes and going back over it all again from the beginning. No one gets it right first time.

To some extent, your board will depend on your theme. Will you have a line around the outside, like Monopoly, or wiggly lines through the whole board, like The Game of Life? Will there be teleportation squares – to a hidden prison from which you must

throw a 4, 5 or 6 to escape, or to unexpected rewards? If you run round the outside, you can still fit a central cross – like Trivial Pursuit. In that game, the choice to go through the centre is down to the player's whim, but you could include other dice-based factors.

Example: Underwater game, where every player has to find a surface square at intervals or drown, called something like 'Surface Tension'. (We like that even more than Orchid Adventure.) You reach a U-bend. Roll 1, 2, 3 or 4 to pull yourself out with no ill-effects; 5 or 6 takes you into a side-tunnel, pulled by a strong current.

It occurs to us that the Chance and Community Chest cards in Monopoly – 'You have won second prize in a beauty contest. Collect £10.' – are similar in a way to a Dungeon Master in Dungeons and Dragons – 'You see ahead of you a dark pit. The air is warm and moves as if something is breathing . . .' There is no reason why a board game couldn't have its own 'Cave Master', 'Orchid Master' or whatever works, though not every group has someone willing to run the show. Otherwise, written cards can fulfil the same role. Be careful not to include too much script that could slow the game down. Players don't mind waiting for others to complete their go, as long as it doesn't take an age.

## TESTING

So by now you have your theme – Underwater Adventure, or Ninja Orchids. Perhaps you've looked at the Paper Box section of this book and made thirty or so complete cubes that can be stacked as some element of skill or game progression. Or ruined a few cheap packs of cards to glue winning poker hands together. You've designed your characters and found tokens from an old charity-shop game of Ludo. You've written rules for pursuing Ghost Ninjas, Enemy Divers or Victorian Orchid Collectors intent on stealing your life's work. You have decided on what a 'win' is – getting the most money, reaching a destination before a ticking egg timer goes 'ding', or assassinating the head of another Ninja clan.

When you have all that, you'll need to do a run-through. The first time has to be on your own, honestly. If you run the game for the first time with other people, someone is going to ask something you haven't considered, such as 'What happens if I just keep all my Orchid cards until the end?' You'll try to make something up to keep the game going, and that won't really work. So: plan everything. Write the rules. Create the board, the pieces and any tokens you might need. Run through on your own at least once. Adjust the rules if you have to – perhaps having to roll sixes slows the game down too much. Finally, try it on those who love you enough to give it a go just because you want to.

If it turns into a family favourite, or you get a request from Aunty Emma for another set, because they enjoyed it so much when they came over . . . consider sending it to a board-game company. Not the whole thing! They don't want a mass of paper, card and strange pictures of orchid bulbs to come through the post. Look up the address. Call them to find out if a particular person handles submissions. Send just the outline of the game – the concept and the rules, with printed pictures of the board and the options available. Every single board game in existence was once invented by someone. Why not you?

'If history were taught
in the form of stories, it
would never be forgotten.'

Rudyard Kipling

We tend to think of the record of all human activity in terms of sweeping movements and wars. Yet it is also a collection of interesting single events. In historical order, here are just a few of many, many more. They are true stories, though we cannot say for certain if every part of them is true. Sometimes there is only a single source – and no way to go back and confirm. One or two are the sort of stories we tell to create our sense of who we are. Yet they are all fascinating glimpses into the past.

IN 660 BC, THE CITY OF LOCRI in southern Italy had a Greek administrator named **Zaleucus**. He is said to have created the first Greek code of written laws. There were very few of them – and the punishments were always severe. No man was allowed to enter the senate house armed, for example, on pain of death. However, once the law code was in place, Zaleucus worried that future lawmakers would add more and more, constraining freedom and interfering with his perfect creation.

His great idea was that anyone proposing a new law would have to make his case with a noose around his neck, ready to be hoisted up and strangled if it did not pass a vote. It is said that no new laws passed for almost three hundred years. Sadly, Zaleucus did not survive to see the success of this. He forgot to remove his sword on entering the senate house. When this was pointed out to him, he threw himself on the sword immediately.

IN 333 BC, ALEXANDER THE GREAT was marching an army of conquest through Anatolia – part of modern Turkey. His men came across strange cults and temples, and some of the stories told are fascinating. One of the most famous was at

Gordium, the capital of ancient Phrygia. There, Alexander was shown the chariot of the city founder, Gordias. The yoke of the chariot was attached by a large and astonishingly intricate knot. So cleverly tied was it that no ends showed at all. It sat like a swarm of bees, a perfect ball upon the wooden beam. Alexander was told of an old legend, that whoever untied the impossible knot would rule all of Asia. Alexander immediately drew his sword and cut the Gordian knot in half. He went on to prove the prophecy true.

## JULIUS CAESAR (c. 100-44 BC) WAS AN ASTONISHINGLY INTELLIGENT MAN.

In his career in the senate and particularly on the battlefield, he established a reputation for original thinking and cunning traps. In a civil war against the Roman Gnaeus Pompey, for example, Caesar discovered an extraordinary technique. Perhaps the first time was an accident, but faced with Roman legions on the field, Caesar offered to spare them all – to exact no punishment for taking the field against him – if they would lay down their weapons. He asked only that they give their word they would not take arms against him again. Bearing in mind that they too faced veteran Roman legions led by the greatest war general of the day, they agreed to this and surrendered. It was common practice then to slaughter a helpless army, but Caesar kept his word and allowed them to leave the field. Very few dared to return to Pompey, of course, who certainly would have had them executed.

Enraged, Pompey sent more legions against Caesar – but the word was out. If they surrendered, they would be spared. Some of them hardly reached the battlefield before they laid down their weapons. Julius Caesar spared them all. Only once did he attack, when he identified a legion standing against him as one he had already pardoned – and even then, he pardoned the survivors. It was an astonishing tactic for a civil war, and Pompey never understood what was happening. His response was to impose more and more brutal punishments on his men. In the final battle between them at Pharsalus in Greece, Pompey had only the core force – his most loyal legions – remaining. Caesar then outmanoeuvred and outfought his Roman enemy, using cavalry like no other Roman commander and forcing Pompey to flee for his life.

Pompey took a boat across to Egypt, hoping to recover there, perhaps to gather new forces. Caesar chose to follow him with just a small boatful of men, leaving all his armies behind.

He arrived on the docks at Alexandria and, to his surprise, was met by the courtiers of the pharaoh, who presented him with a clay urn. Inside were Pompey's head and his ring. They had listened to the man's tale and decided they did not want Roman armies rampaging through their ancient land – so had executed him. Julius Caesar looked into the urn and wept, for a great and noble Roman brought low.

IN AD 870, VIKING INVADERS controlled almost all of England except the south-west – the kingdom of Wessex. The embattled King Æthelred and his brother Alfred fought together for years to drive the Vikings back, including a great victory at the Battle of Ashdown in 871. Even that was not a crushing victory, and the strain took its toll on the brothers. Æthelred passed away the following spring and Alfred became king over a troubled realm. He bought time by making a peace treaty with the Danes, though in truth they were too varied and independent a group of raiders for one treaty to bind them all.

That peace lasted until AD 878, when a Viking named Guthrum launched a massive attack on Wessex. Alfred's heartland of Chippenham was taken, and some of the English surrendered and swore allegiance to their new masters.

Along with just a few friends and loyal servants, Alfred was forced to flee deep into the wetlands of Somerset. He had lost everything and it was the low point of his life. Despairing, he dismissed the last of them and went off on his own. Wet and cold, he asked for shelter in a cattle herder's hut on the island of Athelney in Somersetshire, deep in the marshes there. The man's wife did not know Alfred, and when she had to leave for a time, she asked the king to keep an eye on some cakes cooking on the fire. Safe and warm, Alfred was both exhausted and preoccupied with the problems that beset him. He forgot to check the cakes and they were burned. When she returned, she scolded him most unkindly, saying he was more ready to eat than work.

Despite that poor start, he remained with them for six months – until fortune smiled on Alfred once more. The Danes had continued their destruction, heading into Wales and Devonshire, part of Wessex. One of their leaders attacked Kenworth Castle, judging correctly that it could not be defended. Unfortunately for him, the English inside it were of the same opinion. They

sallied out, killed him and routed his men before he had time to mount a proper defence. They also took the famous raven standard (war banner), which was considered a good-luck charm.

Alfred took hope from that small victory. He called his people and they gathered once more in Selwood Forest. There is a tale told that Alfred spent several days as a harper in the Danish camp, learning their weaknesses. There is no way to know if that is true, however.

Once he had gathered a good-sized army, Alfred attacked and routed the main Danish forces at Edington in 878. That crushing victory led to the Treaty of Wedmore, dividing England between Alfred and Guthrum – the Dane still seething at his losses. It was not a perfect arrangement, but the country remained at peace for several years until 893, when a lesser group of Danes broke off raiding northern France and landed in Kent. Alfred forced them to run for it when they saw the size of the army he brought to repel them.

The Danes ravaged France and returned to England in 894, led by a Viking adventurer by the name of Hastein. By this time, Alfred had created a navy to take the fight to them rather than see them vanish over the horizon, only to return later. He is credited with the creation of the first English navy. Alfred smashed them on land and at sea, driving them back to France – and for a while all the way to Italy, where Hastein sacked the town of Luna by pretending to be dead. His coffin was allowed in with a large group of 'mourners', until the moment he leaped out of it and began looting the town. Hastein was very disappointed to discover it was Luna, apparently, as he'd thought he was attacking Rome.

The last battles between Alfred and the Danes took place in 897, mostly at sea – and once on a river he dammed and diverted, leaving their ships stranded on the mud. He was fifty-two when he died in AD 899, having lived a life of almost constant war. Yet he preserved Wessex from being conquered – and Wessex was the seed that became England. His grandson Æthelstan is the official first king of England – and has a good claim to being the first king of Britain as the Scottish king, Constantine, swore fealty to him as feudal lord.

Queen Elizabeth II is descended from Alfred and rules England, Scotland, Wales and Northern Ireland – as well as the friendly nations of the Commonwealth that have her as head of state. Alfred is the only king in that history ever to be given the name 'The Great' – and appears to have deserved it.

IN AD 1016, ENGLAND WAS CONQUERED by King Canute – sometimes written Cnut. He was a Danish prince – son of Sweyn Forkbeard and grandson of Harald Bluetooth – so, possibly the most Danish prince in all history. He and his father Sweyn invaded England in 1013 and drove out King Ethelred. Sweyn Forkbeard then died, meaning Canute succeeded him as king of Denmark – and was acclaimed king of England as well. It was a sudden rise: too sudden for the English council. Ethelred came home and Canute was driven off. He returned with a massive Viking army in 1015. By then, Ethelred was too ill to fight, and instead his son went out – known as Edmund Ironside and no weakling. Over a year of brutal war followed, with London captured and Northumbria attacked. Ethelred died in 1016 and, tragically, Edmund Ironside followed him just seven months later. Canute was triumphant in the end and ruled for almost twenty years. He became renowned for his wisdom and intelligence, which is why one version of the famous holding-back-the-waves story makes more sense than the other.

The original story goes that Canute was so overcome with his own power that he put a chair in the shingle on a beach and commanded the waves to retreat. The tide came in despite his command and he got very wet.

A second version gained in popularity a few decades ago – that it was Canute's flattering courtiers who suggested he had such power even the waves would retreat from his command. To show his courtiers what he thought of that, he put a chair in the shingle and commanded the waves to retreat. When the tide came in anyway, he had taught the courtiers a valuable lesson about the limits of his authority – and what he thought about greasy flatterers.

What little we know of Canute does suggest that he was a man of drive and high intelligence, making the second version of the story much more likely to be true. However, it also serves to illustrate the difficulty of historical tales. Sometimes, without knowing all the details, it's very easy to misinterpret a story. Yet stories like these are who we are – they reinforce our values. We like cleverness and courage. We despise bragging and cowardice. Our stories reveal us and are important for that. Of course,

no modern historian can make a name for himself or herself by confirming the old tales. To make a splash, they must say, 'Ah, but Canute *didn't* try to hold back the waves.' In that case, the alternative is as interesting as the original, but if it means the story is no longer told, that would be a terrible loss. Stories have power.

EDWARD III WAS ONE OF THE GREATEST KINGS England ever had. He ruled for fifty years – from 1327 to 1377 – an astonishing reign for a man of the 14th century. From the lines of his sons would come battle kings like Henry V and the great houses of York and Lancaster. As well as his personal courage during victories against the French such as Crécy and Sluys, he also established one of the oldest and most prestigious orders of chivalry in the world.

The word 'chivalry' comes from the Latin and French for 'horse', so is associated with mounted knights. The central idea was self-control and restraint by the strong – the opposite of the cruel tyrant or bully. Today, it might be used to describe behaviour when a man has come to the aid of a woman. 'That was chivalrous of you', or 'Chivalry is not dead, I see.' It is not used the other way around.

In 1348, Edward was a victorious battle king, at the height of his power. While dancing with the young Countess Salisbury at a ball in Calais – then English territory – one of her garters slipped down her leg and was left behind on the floor. In those days, there was no elastic, so garters – a ring of cloth tied with laces to hold up stockings – would often come loose. There was laughter and some rude comments from the knights and noblemen present, embarrassing the lady. Edward saw her blushing and picked up the garter, putting it on his own leg. The formal court language then was French and so he said aloud, '*Honi soit qui mal y pense*' – 'Evil be to him who evil thinks.' In other words: shame on you for thinking the worst. It became the motto of the Order of the Garter.

The order began with a great feast and a joust. The original membership was King Edward and his son the Prince of Wales, with twelve members, or 'Knights Companion', each. Twenty-six 'poor knights' were also appointed, to pray for the Knights Companion. In later centuries, their name was changed to the Military Knights of Windsor – all older military men. The Garter membership was expanded in the 18th and 19th centuries, to allow other members of the royal family, as well as 'Stranger, or Extra Knights', who were usually the heads of foreign nations, to be granted membership as an honour. During World War II, the crest of Emperor Hirohito of Japan was taken down from St George's Chapel, Windsor. Holders of the Order of the Garter are appointed at the discretion of the monarch and use 'KG' after their names. They are also knighted by the monarch. Knights of the Garter rank above all other orders. It is an immense honour.

As a young woman, Queen Elizabeth I gave a ring to the dashing Lord Essex. The story goes that she loved the handsome courtier, but knew well her own temper. She told him to send it to her if he ever found himself in distress – that the sight of it would remind her of how she had once loved him and she would rescue him. Many years passed and Essex was part of a disastrous and foolish rebellion against the Crown. Condemned to death and awaiting execution, he realised it was time to collect on that old promise. He tossed the ring from his cell window to a passing boy to get it to the queen. The boy handed it to the Countess of Nottingham – and she kept it.

Elizabeth waited and waited for Essex to send her the ring. When he did not, she thought he was too proud and signed his death warrant. He was beheaded in 1601, in private. She mourned him.

When the Countess of Nottingham was on her deathbed, she asked Elizabeth to come to her and confessed what she had done, handing back the ring. Elizabeth was enraged enough to strike and shake her, saying, 'May God forgive you, because I never shall.'

Some modern historians doubt the story, though the ring certainly existed as a gift from Elizabeth to Essex. These are the tales that made us. They should be known to all – and of course, we are not at the end or even the midpoint of history. No, we are at the beginning.

# MAKING A
# STINK BOMB

Classic stink bombs have an iconic status – from the characters of Dennis the Menace and Bart Simpson, but also every joke shop that sells plastic flies in sugar cubes, chewing gum that snaps at your fingers and, of course, fake dog poo. (That last created a misunderstanding that led to a real 'dog poo fight' with Stephen Connell in Warrender Park. We flung them at each other. Honestly, it is astonishing we didn't catch some awful disease.)

---

Warning: As with all chemicals, don't get anything in your eyes or swallow any. Also, don't throw poo at each other.

---

In those days, our parents kept bantam chickens in a suburban garage in Eastcote, Middlesex. (That garage became so encrusted with bird muck, it could have been mined for phosphate fertiliser.) The chickens would lay eggs in any quiet spot – and of course we wouldn't always find them. On one occasion, an entire clutch of eggs had gone completely rotten. One of the authors made the mistake of throwing one against a wall in the garage and that was that: we couldn't enter for the rest of the year. That smell was the worst he had ever known. In a way, rotten eggs are too awful to use.

The classic stink bomb found in joke shops has the distinctive odour of hydrogen sulphide, though the words 'rotten-egg smell' are only used by those who have not experienced the real thing. However, unlike a real rotten egg, reasonable stink bombs can be created with two easily available ingredients: non-safety matches and household ammonia. The sulphur in the matches reacts with the ammonia. The result is acrid and extremely unpleasant. It's not quite the smell of hydrogen sulphide, but it's pretty close for home-made.

Cut the heads off a whole box of matches – scraping them off with a knife into a bowl works well. Pour these into a dry and empty plastic bottle and add two or three tablespoons of household ammonia. Note that we don't mean bleach, which often contains chlorine. Swirl the bottle around and put the top on. For best results, let it rest for at least a day, but you'll be able to smell the ammonium sulphide gas in a couple of minutes. Once smelled, never forgotten. Enjoy.

# GODS OF GREECE AND ROME

The ancient world lasted from the dawn of history to the fall of the western Roman empire about 1,500 years ago. Emperor Constantine was the first Christian emperor – and helped to spread that faith across Europe. He built a city on the Bosphorus strait to be his second eastern capital, on the site on an old Greek fortress named Byzantium. That city of 'Constantinople' remained as a library of Greek and Roman thought until it fell in 1453, to be renamed Istanbul. The greatest works of philosophy were smuggled back to Italy, where they helped to create an explosion of art, invention and philosophy that became known as the 'Renaissance' – the rebirth. The influence of ancient Greece is simply extraordinary.

Before Alexander the Great, the Greeks fought mostly among themselves – in a hundred and fifty city-states, the most famous of which were Athens, Sparta, Thebes and Corinth. They had a few colonies in southern Italy, Marseilles in Gaul and some cities in Thrace (modern-day Bulgaria), but their 'empire' was primarily the islands and cities of Greece. Every four years, they would have a formal truce so that athletes from far and wide could travel to Olympia for contests in running, jumping, wrestling, and throwing shields and spears – sports with clear warlike applications. The victors were crowned with a wreath of olive leaves.

Alexander the Great united those Greek city-states and then spread the Greek language to many other nations, as far off as Egypt, which he conquered in 332 BC. The New Testament of the Bible was written in Greek because the language was so well known at the time.

On Alexander's death, his general Ptolemy took Egypt as his fiefdom and became pharaoh there. (His descendant, Queen Cleopatra, who still spoke Greek, would bear a child to Julius Caesar

IONIC     DORIC     CORINTHIAN

– Ptolemy Caesarion. Sadly, that child did not survive the Roman wars.)

In short, there is a golden thread from one culture influencing another. The Romans conquered Greece, but they admired its culture above all others. That can be seen in the columns of ancient Greece, Rome and Britain, with modern examples in places as far apart as Australia and America.

The oldest column style is the simplest, 'Doric', used in the Parthenon of Athens and also the Lincoln Memorial in the United States. The 'Ionic' style is used in the Jefferson Memorial. The Romans used the Corinthian style more than the others – for the Pantheon in Rome, for example – and it can be seen in St Paul's Cathedral in London today. The distinctive capitals of Corinthian columns feature acanthus leaves. In ancient Greece, these were a symbol of immortality, which seems appropriate.

It is not correct to say the Romans had no gods before they encountered the Greek ones. It was more that overlapping systems merged. The Roman goddess Venus, for example, was a patron of fertility. Young women might pray to her if they hoped for a child. The Greek goddess Aphrodite was more associated with love – and over time, they became two faces of the same concept. The Romans were open to influence. If they came across a foreign city with temples to a god or goddess they had never encountered, they tended to ask questions. The Greeks were a hugely successful culture: who knew if that success wasn't in part because of their gods? In such a way, Rome took on attributes of other cultures, such as the ancient Etruscan goddess 'Menrva'. Remodelled by Rome, she became Minerva.

There are twelve major gods and goddesses in the Greek pantheon. They were said by the early Greek poet Hesiod to be descended from an even mightier group known as the Titans – the twelve children of Gaia (earth) and Uranus (the sky – the planet Uranus is named after him). It is quite possible that Hesiod padded out the Titan group for pleasing symmetry. One or two are interesting, so we've included them here.

## TITANS

| BROTHERS<br>*Oceanus, Coeus, Crius, Hyperion, Iapetus* | SISTERS<br>*Themis, Tethys, Phoebe, Theia* |
|---|---|
| **CRONUS** – *a dark and frightening figure. He overthrew his father Uranus and was himself father to six: Zeus, Hades, Poseidon, Hera, Hestia and Demeter.*<br><br>*The Romans named Cronus Saturn – and accepted him as the father of Jupiter/Zeus.*<br><br>*Saturday (Saturn's day) and the planet Saturn are named after him.* | **RHEA** – *wife of Cronus, mother to Zeus, Hades, Poseidon, Hera, Hestia and Demeter.*<br><br>**MNEMOSYNE** – *goddess of memory. Her name shares the same root as 'mnemonic', a device to remember something, such as 'Richard Of York Gave Battle In Vain' for the colours of the rainbow: red, orange, yellow, green, blue, indigo, violet.* |

Having overthrown the rule of Uranus, Cronus was in turn overthrown by his own children, led by Zeus. There is a deliberate lesson here about the rise and fall of empires.

## THE TWELVE OLYMPIANS – AND THEIR ROMAN EQUIVALENTS

| GREEK | ROMAN |
|---|---|
| **APHRODITE** – *goddess of love.* | **VENUS** – *goddess of fertility/love.* |
| **APOLLO** – *god of the sun, music, healing.* | **APOLLO** – *god of the sun, poetry, prophecy.* |
| **ARES** – *god of war.* | **MARS** – *god of war (also Bellona, a female equivalent).* |
| **ARTEMIS** – *goddess of chastity, the hunt and the moon.* | **DIANA** – *goddess of the hunt and virginity; originally separate from Artemis, the two became blurred together over time.* |
| **ATHENA** – *goddess of wisdom and warfare. Founder of Athens.* | **MINERVA** – *goddess of wisdom (influenced by Menrva, the Etruscan goddess).* |
| **DEMETER** – *goddess of fertility and the harvest.* | **CERES** – *goddess of the harvest, from whom we have the word 'cereal'. (I'm sure this terrifying goddess would be delighted.)* |

| | |
|---|---|
| **DIONYSUS** – *god of wine, madness and 'Ec Stasis': 'stepping outside oneself', from which we take the word 'ecstasy'.* | **BACCHUS** – *god of wine, pleasure and insane frenzy. Wine was revered and feared in Greece and Rome.* |
| **HEPHAESTUS** – *god of fire, patron of blacksmiths. Creator of divine weapons and armour.* | **VULCAN** – *god of fire, the forge, metal and volcanoes. Creator and crafter of wonders.* |
| **HERA** – *queen of the gods. Goddess of marriage and birth. Wife and sister to Zeus.* | **JUNO** – *queen of the gods. Goddess of marriage and birth. Wife and sister to Jupiter.* |
| **HERMES** – *god of trade, thieves and athletes. Messenger to the gods.* | **MERCURY** – *god of merchants and travellers. Messenger to the gods. Quick and nimble, the closest planet to the sun is named after him.* |
| **POSEIDON** – *god of the sea, sailors and storms. It makes sense for such a seafaring nation to have a specific god to pray to during a storm.* | **NEPTUNE** – *god of the sea and patron of sailors. For Romans too, the deep oceans were dark and terrifying, with most voyages along a coast.* |
| **ZEUS** – *the head of the gods. Husband to Hera. Always unfaithful; half the stories of Greece seem to begin with Zeus courting a young lady and fathering a demi-god, such as Heracles.* | **JUPITER OR JOVE** – *the head of the gods. Husband to Juno.* |

These are the twelve major gods said to live on Olympus. The most powerful of those who did not was the Greek Hades, known to the Romans as Pluto. He inhabited the underworld – a grey hell, guarded by a river and a three-headed dog named Cerberus.

The rest of the stories usually involve a child of the original twelve, such as Pan, the half-goat pipe-playing son of Hermes; or Persephone, daughter of Demeter, who was taken into the underworld by Hades and had to be rescued; or Aeneas, son of Aphrodite – and ancestor to Romulus and Remus, the legendary twin founders of Rome.

It's easy to suspect that some might have been real people – ancient kings or heroes, whose deeds were first exaggerated in stories, then explained through the attribution of supernatural powers. Even if Heracles was never an enormous young warrior strolling with a mastiff through the markets of ancient Greece, even if he was just a fantasy about determination and strength, his tales – and all of the others – reveal something about us. They are worth knowing for that alone, but the Greek and Roman cultures still influence the languages, stories and even the architecture of today – just as we will influence those who look back two thousand years to us.

# BALLOON DOG
# AND SWORD

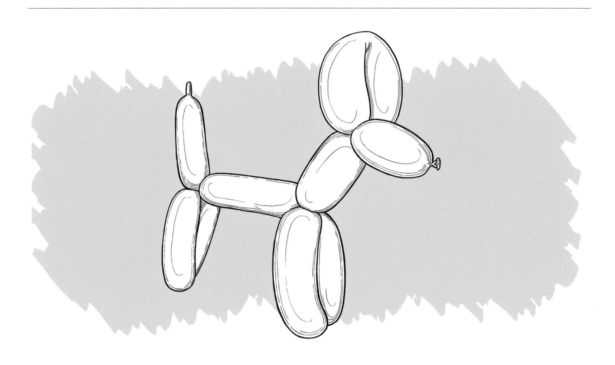

Not the hardest thing in the world, but we think every boy should be able to do this, not least because that boy will one day be a parent and grandparent. Balloon animals are just fun.

You'll need long thin balloons. 'Modelling' balloons are the best, though harder to blow up than some. We bought half a dozen for 15p each and then almost popped a lung out trying to inflate just one of them. It's hard to imagine a grandparent managing it without a trip to the Emergency Room. It's worth getting hold of a hand pump if you can, honestly. We'll cover the two classic shapes here – dog and sword. The giraffe is also popular, which is just the dog with a longer neck.

## THE DOG

Inflate and tie a thumb knot in the end. You'll make the ears as a double fold, so go back a little and make your first double twist – the nose. Sometimes, the balloon will pop, of course. Generally, though, they seem to survive being made into a shape. After the nose, make a second twist a couple of inches back – and fold the balloon back on itself, making a third twist. Those doubled ears can be twisted into the first to hold them. Don't worry: this is much easier to do than it is to describe.

Make another twist at the neck and then repeat the ears to make the front legs – you can adjust

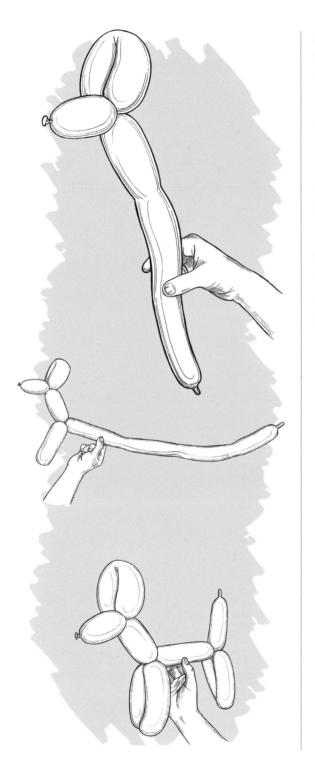

the way they lie as you go. Leave a few inches for the body and then repeat the third doubled-over section for the rear legs. You'll be left with a tail without any effort.

## THE SWORD

A balloon sword is easier – with the same folds. Pick one end as the hilt and fold a doubled section, like the dog's ears or legs. Twist them around and fold over another on the other side to make your hilt. There will be enough balloon left to be the blade. This takes a few seconds and can be given to young children – unless you have burst a major vein trying to blow them up. Hand pump. Seriously.

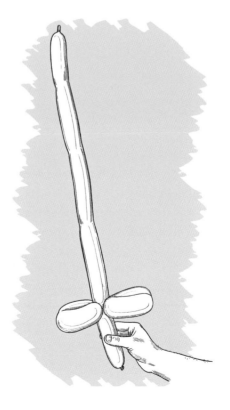

Johnny Ball is a British national treasure. For three decades he was a mainstay of children's television, in programmes such as *Think of a Number*, *Think Again* and *Johnny Ball Reveals All*. From 1977 to 1994, he introduced entire generations to a love of puzzles and a fascination with numbers. He writes today with the same enthusiasm for the subject. We are delighted he agreed to produce a selection of puzzles for this book. Without reservation, we commend his body of work to you. The answers are at the end of the chapter, but try each one first. Some are classics you may have heard before; others will be completely new.

## OODLES OF POOZLES

Sometimes I wonder why we stick to the same words for things when, with a little imagination, we can come up with words that are much more fun. When my son Nick was three, he called the thing that keeps the rain off an 'Underbarella' – brilliant. It describes how you use it perfectly. Now I wouldn't call one anything else.

I love puzzles but always want to call them poozles, as they can be very poozling and some are real stinkers. But don't ever be put off by a poozle or puzzle appearing to be difficult. The reason puzzles were invented was to help teach us something. Puzzle study is rather like a crash course in maths, and anything that makes maths easier is surely a great thing.

Once you know the solution to a puzzle, you have just a little more armour, a little more brain power, and next time you meet a similar problem, your experience will come into play – and play is always more fun than work – so always treat your work as play. OK?

Now here is a collection of puzzles, most of which have been around for a long, *long* time. For me they are like old friends. I hope you'll grow to like them too. Enjoy.

①

## HOW OLD WAS DIOPHANTUS?

Diophantus lived in Alexandria around AD 50, or possibly some 200 years later. No one is sure. What we do know, or think we know, is how old he was when he died, as a remarkable riddle has survived the ages. It was found in an old Greek anthology of puzzles and says:

This tomb holds Diophantus and tells the measure of his life: God granted that he be a boy for a sixth of his life, and added a twelfth part where his cheeks were cloaked with down. He married after a further seventh part and after five more years he had a son. Sadly, after attaining half his father's age, the son died. Diophantus grieved on alone for four more years and then sadly also died.

So, what was the measure of Diophantus' life?

## TRUTH OR LIAR?

Indiana Smith was lost and he came to a fork in the road. It had been dropped by two fellas who were having a picnic, at the very spot where the road forked. Smith's super-intuition told him that of the two chaps, one always told the truth, but the other always lied. However, his intuition didn't tell him which was which.

So he dreamed up one single question to ask either of them, so that from the answer, though he would still not know which man was which, he would know which road led to safety.

What was that question?

## CROSSING THE RIVER WITH A WOLF, A GOAT AND A CABBAGE

This puzzle dates back some 1,200 years and is credited to the monk Alcuin of York, who travelled to Europe, where he invented lower-case letters (like those you are reading now) to make copying of ancient manuscripts far quicker and easier.

A chap has a wolf, a goat and a cabbage. He has a small boat that will take him and just one of the three. How can he get them all safely across the river? If he takes the cabbage, the wolf will eat the goat. If he takes the wolf, the goat will eat the cabbage. So how can he get them all across the river safely?

This is the oldest of the many crossing puzzles. Question 4 is another crossing puzzle, but it is slightly trickier.

## THE THREE HUSBANDS AND THEIR NEW BRIDES

Long ago, three young husbands were travelling with their new brides and they needed to cross a river. There was a boat, but it would only take two people. Now, this was in an age of lawlessness and distrust. No husband would leave his bride in the presence of either of the other two men, even for a moment. How could they all cross the river safely?

## THE QUICKEST WAY HOME

Here we have a young girl with a water pot, her home some distance away, and a straight river full of beautiful fresh water. Her mother has phoned and asked her to come home as quickly as she can, but to fill the water jug on the way. So what is her quickest route home? She could take the shortest route to the river, fill the pot and then go straight home. Or she could go to a point on the river nearest to her home, fill the pot and then go straight home. But there is a route that is quicker than both of those. What is it and how would she find it?

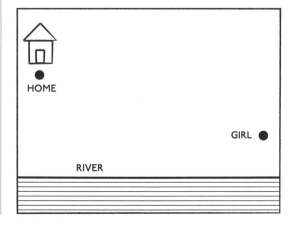

---
## 6

### GOING STRAIGHT
### FOR THE JUGULAR

There are many puzzles involving jug pouring. This is the most well known. You have three jugs that each hold 8, 5 and 3 pints of water. With the 8 jug full, can you now divide the water exactly into two measures of 4?

---

## *Answers*

---
## 1

### HOW OLD WAS DIOPHANTUS?

We need to split his life into small proportions as fractions or years: a sixth as a boy, a twelfth before he shaved, a seventh more still single, five years married, then half of all that as a father. Then another four years till he died. So we can write this as ⅙ + ¹⁄₁₂ + ⅐ + 5 years + ½ + 4 years.

The fractions of 6, 12, 7, 2 all divide into 84 – the lowest number they have in common. Converting into 84ths we get – 14 + 7 + 12 + 42 = 75. Now add the 5 and 4 years, and we get 75 + 5 + 4 = 84. So Diophantus lived to be 84 years old – or so the story goes.

---
## 2

### TRUTH OR LIAR?

Indiana Smith asked one chap, 'If I were to ask the other chap which was the right way home, what would he say?' The liar would say that the other fella would say the wrong way, while the truth-teller would say the liar would say the wrong way. So, either way, the answer he gets has to be the WRONG answer and he needs to do exactly the opposite.

---
## 3

### CROSSING THE RIVER WITH A WOLF,
### A GOAT AND A CABBAGE

First the man leaves the wolf (tied to a tree?) and the cabbage and crosses with the goat. He leaves the goat and comes back, and this time takes the wolf – or the cabbage. At the other side, he brings the goat back. He next takes the cabbage or the wolf across. He then comes back and takes the goat across. Luckily the wolf doesn't like cabbage.

---
## 4

### THE THREE HUSBANDS
### AND THEIR NEW BRIDES

This is a tricky river-crossing puzzle but the answer is not too hard to find. We might call the couples A, B and C.

So couple A cross first and the husband brings the boat back. Now the two wives B and C cross and wife A comes back to join her husband. Now both men B and C cross. But this time (and this is the trick) a couple come back – either couple B or C. Now the two men leave their wives and cross and the third woman comes back, leaving all three brides safe, but on the bank where they started. Any two cross and the husband of the remaining bride comes back and takes his wife across. At no time has any bride been in the presence of another man without her husband being there to protect her. Phew.

--------- 5 ---------

## THE QUICKEST WAY HOME

To find the quickest route home, the girl has to imagine that the river is also a mirror. If it were, she would see the reflection of her home in the mirror. By heading straight for that mirror image till she reaches the river, then filling the pot and going straight home, she will have taken the shortest possible route.

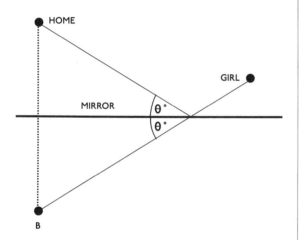

This puzzle was featured by Heron of Alexandria when he was trying to work out how our eyesight works and discovered that light always travels in straight lines, taking the shortest possible route.

--------- 6 ---------

## GOING STRAIGHT FOR THE JUGULAR

There are two answers to this jug-pouring puzzle, depending on which way you start.

From the 8 jug, fill the 5 jug. Now from the 5 jug fill the 3 jug. Pour that 3 back into the 8 jug. You have 2 measures still in the 5 jug. Pour that into the 3 jug. From the 8 jug, fill the 5 jug. From that, add 1 measure to the 3 jug to fill it. You now have 4 measures in the 5 jug. Pour the 3 jug into the 8 and you have 4 measures in there as well. Success!

The other way – from the 8 jug fill the 3 jug. Pour the 3 into the 5 jug. From the 8, fill the 3 jug again. Pour from the 3 to fill the 5 jug. That will give you 5 in the 5 jug and 1 in the 3 jug. Pour the 5 back into the 8 jug. Pour the 1 in the 3 jug into the 5 jug. From the 8 jug, fill the 3 jug and pour that into the 5 jug. You now have 4 measures in the 5 jug and 4 in the 8 jug.

Both are equally successful, but the first took seven pours while the second took eight.

Note: This puzzle assumes the jugs are juglike, with curved sides and a handle. If the jugs are regular cylinders, then the solution is far simpler.

From the 8 cylinder, pour into the 5 cylinder until the water surface line in the 8 cylinder reaches from the lip at the pouring end to the top of the base at the far end. At that very moment, the water in the 8 cylinder is exactly half its volume, or 4 measures, and there must be 4 measures in the 5 cylinder – and you have completed the task in a single pour.

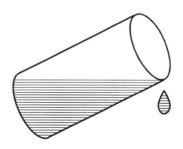

# FAMOUS HORSES

For thousands of years, horses have played a part in the development of mankind. They have pulled ploughs, carried messages and, when it came to warfare, carried charging warriors, thundering along in formation at thirty miles an hour.

In ancient Greece, Spartan warriors ran alongside horsemen, holding the tails of the horses, to give them extra range. Horses were then mainly for messengers and for officers, allowing them a view of the battle denied to those on foot, with dust thick in the air. Royal messengers of Persia were famous for the distances they could cover in short times, changing horses at royal stables along roads that stretched across an empire.

Crossing from BC into AD, Roman legions marched on foot, yet legion horses carried the *equites*, a high-status group of knights, as well as messengers and senior officers. A light force of men known as *extraordinarii* were also used as fast mounted scouts, the forerunner of light cavalry.

A thousand years later, Genghis Khan's hordes had stirrups and high-pommel saddles made of wood. These inventions gave stability in the saddle, a vital requirement for cavalry attacks. They moved vast distances on their Mongolian ponies, bred uniquely for endurance over strength or size. The warriors of Genghis trained to shoot with a bow and arrow while hurtling along at full gallop, an extraordinary skill. Warriors on horseback could flank an enemy or provide reinforcements at a key point in a battle.

The use of cavalry reached its peak on the battlefields of the 18th and 19th centuries, playing a vital part against Napoleon at Waterloo in 1815, for example. The massed charge of armoured men and animals was a fearsome thing to behold, never mind to have thundering towards you. They continued to be used into the 20th century, but the end of the massed charge came about with the creation of the machine gun, though it took some horrific slaughters to bring that message home. Winston Churchill rode in one of the final cavalry charges, at the Battle of Omdurman in 1898, but the last one is usually said to have been the absolutely insane charge of an Italian cavalry group – the Savoia Cavalleria – riding with swords and hand grenades against Russian forces equipped with mortars and machine guns in 1942. Against all odds, the Italians overran the Russian position. It was an extraordinary action – the Italian Charge of the Light Brigade. If they'd had a Tennyson to write a poem about it, it would surely be as well known today as it deserves to be.

In the 21st century, cavalry regiments command tanks and armoured vehicles, though they ride horses in parades and for ceremonial occasions. Horses are also still employed by the police in riots, which is as close to warfare as any of them come. Beyond that, horses seem to have become the much-loved companions of strong young ladies. Yet there was a time when they galloped through shot and shell, when they showed control under thunder and fire, to somehow bring their masters through.

The relationship has always been a special one. In English, the word 'cavalier' can mean arrogant and dismissive. Its root lies in the Latin *caballarius* – horseman – seen also in the Spanish *caballero*. After all, cavalry have always tended to think of themselves as superior to those who fought on foot. A warhorse brings speed, range, height and status. This chapter is dedicated to a few of the finest.

① 

## BUCEPHALUS – THE HORSE OF ALEXANDER THE GREAT

Bucephalus, or 'Ox-head', was a freak of nature – a massive black stallion, originally presented for purchase to Alexander's father, King Philip II of Macedon. The price asked was thirteen talents, an unimaginable sum. In bright sunshine, the enormous horse kicked, snapped and fought the merchants trying to show him to the king. Despite his obvious strength, Philip decided he was unrideable and waved the animal away. His young son Alexander spoke up in protest. Amused, the king allowed the boy to approach the wild horse.

Alexander had seen how Bucephalus was spooked by the movement of shadows on the ground. He approached the horse gently and turned his heavy head towards the sun so its shadow fell behind. Bucephalus then allowed him to mount. The king presented his son with the horse and they were inseparable from that point.

Alexander rode Bucephalus in every campaign of his life – through Greece and Persia, all the way to India. It is said that Bucephalus would neither let Alexander mount another horse, nor allow any other man to ride him. On one occasion, when his master was away from his camp, Bucephalus was captured, stolen in a raid by an enemy ruler. When Alexander discovered what had happened, he sent a message promising that he would lay waste to the entire region if his horse had been hurt. Bucephalus was quietly returned to him.

Bucephalus finally died around 326 BC, of old age or a battle wound. Alexander built a tomb for him, said to lie on the bank of a river near Jhelum in Pakistan. He also named a city Bucephala after him. The location has since been lost.

---

(2)

## COPENHAGEN – THE DUKE OF WELLINGTON'S HORSE

If Bucephalus is the best-known horse in history, Copenhagen is probably the second. Unusually, he was not enormous, but only fifteen hands – one inch taller than a pony. Neither was he sweet-natured; he was known to lash out around him with enormous violence and no warning. Stallions are often aggressive, but Wellington was a strong and experienced horseman.

Originally a racehorse, Copenhagen was sold to the Duke of Wellington in Spain, quickly becoming his favourite mount. Wellington rode Copenhagen at the Battle of Waterloo, in 1815, where Napoleon's rapacious conquests were finally brought to an end. The horse retired to the Stratfield Saye estate near Reading, where he lived in happy retirement, being fed chocolate creams and Bath buns until he died, aged twenty-eight. He was buried in the grounds of that estate – the gift of a grateful nation to his master. An acorn was planted by Wellington's housekeeper on that day – and it is now a great oak, towering over the headstone.

The duke himself was buried in St Paul's, next to Nelson and lying under the centre point of the great dome. Of Copenhagen, he said, 'There may have been many faster horses, no doubt many handsomer, but for bottom and endurance I never saw his fellow.' One of the hooves was made into an inkwell and remains today in the ownership of the family.

### 3

## MARENGO – THE HORSE OF NAPOLEON BONAPARTE

Marengo was the horse that carried Napoleon Bonaparte for sixteen years, through his most famous battles. He was named after the Battle of Marengo, where Napoleon rode him for the first time. Smaller even than Copenhagen, this stallion of just fourteen hands was both fast and enduring. Though he had never owned a horse as a child in Corsica, Napoleon was a fearless rider, well known for galloping at high speed without thought to his safety. When he was just seven, a family bailiff brought two horses to his home to show to the family. Napoleon leaped up on one of them and galloped away, laughing.

Marengo was the horse that carried him through his most perilous marches and campaigns. Despite taking eight

wounds through the years, Marengo never ran shy of battle gunfire. The horse was eventually captured by British forces at Waterloo and returned to England. After a long retirement, Marengo died at the age of thirty-eight in 1831. His skeleton can be viewed at the National Army Museum in Chelsea. Two of his hooves were removed after his death and made into gold and silver snuffboxes. One of them was presented to officers of the Brigade of Guards, St James Palace. The other was retained by the owners.

### 4

## SIR BRIGGS – THE HORSE OF CAPTAIN GODREY MORGAN

Godfrey Morgan was a 22-year-old captain in the 17th Lancers when the Crimean War began. Britain, Turkey and France were allied against Russia in a war that would become a byword for disaster. Morgan's personal mount, Mr Briggs, carried his master safely through the Battle

# 'Into the valley of Death Rode the six hundred . . .'

Tennyson

of Alma. Then, on 25 October 1854, came the most famous action of that ill-advised war: the Charge of the Light Brigade.

Orders had come to prevent Russian guns from being removed from the battlefield, but there was some confusion as to which guns were meant in the orders. Led by Lord Cardigan, a British force of 670 light cavalry charged into a valley with Russian forces on three sides. The air filled with grapeshot, cannon shot, rifle fire and exploding shells. It was a terrible error, though the discipline and courage they showed in assaulting an impossible position made it the most famous cavalry action of all time.

Morgan found himself galloping straight at a Russian artillery piece – and saw the gunner touch the fuse to the barrel. The shot killed the man next to Morgan. He exchanged sabre blows with Russian gunners, though his horse fell when another mount crashed into them. One of the Russians struck Mr Briggs on the head with his sabre.

Having achieved their objective, the Light Brigade had nowhere to go. They wheeled round and began to race back through the valley – and the guns opened up behind them and on either side once again. Somehow, Morgan survived, and when he examined Mr Briggs he found a single sabre wound on his head. Quietly, Morgan knighted the animal on the spot and referred to him as 'Sir Briggs' ever after.

Man and horse both survived to return to Wales, where Captain Morgan inherited his father's title and became Lord Tredegar. Sir Briggs enjoyed a long and happy retirement, where he met and was fed sugar by the grandfather and great-grandfather of the authors, one John Iggulden. The horse was buried in the grounds of Tredegar House in Newport, Wales, the spot marked by a monument that can be visited today.

The inscription reads, 'In memory of Sir Briggs, a favourite charger. He carried his master, the Hon. Godfrey Morgan, Captain 17th Lancers, boldly and well at the battle of Alma, in the first line in the light cavalry charge of Balaclava, and at the battle of Inkerman, 1854. He died at Tredegar Park, February 9th 1874, aged 28 years.'

There are other famous horses: Incitatus, owned by the Roman Emperor Caligula, who threatened to make the horse a consul; Bayard, which carried King Edward I in battle; the Byerley Turk, which was captured by a British officer in 1686 – one of three Arabian horses from which all modern thoroughbreds are descended; Black Bess, the mare that carried the 18th-century highwayman Dick Turpin; Comanche, sole survivor of the Battle of Little Bighorn, where General Custer was killed; Reckless, a Mongolian mare used by the US military in the Korean War to carry supplies and evacuate soldiers (she did so well that she was promoted to 'Sergeant Reckless'). Man's relationship with horses has been a long one. Yet it would be a strange list that didn't include a racehorse, in this case the greatest of them all.

## RED RUM

Steeplechase racing began between country riders who would sight a church steeple in the distance and go flat out for it, leaping fences, hedges and anything else that got in their way. It was both extremely dangerous and exhilarating, and it

involved a lot of the skills that would be vital in warfare. The greatest modern steeplechase is the Grand National, run every year at Aintree, Liverpool. It has been run from 1839 and is 4 miles, 514 yards long (around 7 km) – two laps and sixteen huge fences, some of which are famous in their own right, such as Becher's Brook and The Chair. The prize money is over £1 million.

Red Rum was born in Ireland in 1965. His name was created from the last three letters of the names of his dam (mother), Mared, and his sire, Quorum. Despite many great racehorses in his bloodline, he was born with weak hooves and showed no early promise. The trainer Ginger McCain bought him in 1972. He ran him on sand and took him swimming in the sea to build up his strength. It worked, and Red Rum won his first Grand National in 1973, showing an extraordinary desire to win. This was not a horse that enjoyed being second in anything. In 1974, he beat 11–1 odds and did it again, only the second horse to win back-to-back Grand Nationals. In 1975 and 1976, he came second, but at the age of twelve, in 1977, ridden by Tommy Stack, he ran the race of his life and came from behind to win by an enormous distance, beating the best horses in the world. Red Rum retired in 1978 and lived right up to 1995, aged thirty. Like others in this list, he was loved by many. He is buried at the winning post of Aintree racecourse.

# THE RULES OF ULTIMATE FRISBEE

One summer, with a few family friends in a local park, the authors found themselves involved in a game of Ultimate Frisbee. It turned out to be enormous fun and we made a mental note to include it as a *Dangerous Book* chapter. We covered cricket, rugby and football in the first one. Obviously, we could have gone for hockey, rounders and netball in this – but they're not personal favourites. Ultimate Frisbee (unlike Frisbee golf, which will get you thrown off a golf course) can be played on any open field, with teams as small as two or three, and up to around seven. It's the perfect game for sunny afternoons: puffing, middle-aged men and women (with a slight advantage of height) – and young kids running rings around them. Honestly, it is worth a go.

There is no Ultimate Frisbee world cup, leagues or accredited organisations on the scale of FIFA, say. The rules of rugby are called 'laws'. These, though, are more in the nature of guidelines.

The playing field can be marked with jumpers. You need two rectangular goal zones at the ends of a long, narrow rectangle: 70 yards long and 40 yards wide (paced out by any man or tall woman). We've seen variations in the length of the field, depending on how fit you are – up to 120 yards.

If you are a team of fit university athletes, you might make your goal zone 40 yards across and 25 deep. Ours was smaller than the main field, at 6 yards across and 4 deep. There is no goalkeeper in Ultimate Frisbee, so it required a tactical shift to reach the end of the field and then manoeuvre into the goal.

With the field marked out, the two teams line up across opposite ends. Toss a coin to see who gets the first throw. The Frisbee is thrown to the defenders, just as a rugby game begins with the ball kicked to the opposing side.

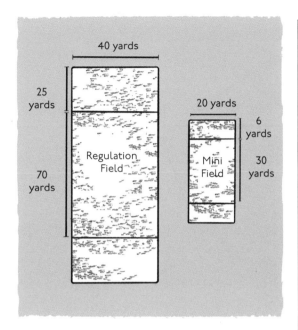

40 yards

25 yards

70 yards

Regulation Field

20 yards

6 yards

30 yards

Mini Field

The aim of the game is to advance up the field and complete a pass in the goal zone to score.

The Frisbee can be thrown to team-mates in any direction, including backwards, though as in netball, players have to stand still when they are holding the disc. They have a maximum of ten seconds to make a pass.

If the Frisbee touches the ground, goes out of bounds or is intercepted, the other team immediately takes possession, with no stoppage of play. Whoever is closest picks it up, essentially.

Ultimate Frisbee is a non-contact game. If contact does occur, that is a foul. The team with possession retains it and play continues. You could have the opposing team member take a step or two away as a penalty.

Tactically, the game begins with a great rush forward, chasing down the thrown disc. It will either reach the opposing team or touch the ground for

them to pick up. Once they have it, they will pass back and forth, moving the disc down the field and attempting that final pass to someone standing inside the goal zone – or over the goal line, depending on how you've set up the field.

There are no umpires. Emphasis is on friendly and good-natured play. The lack of stoppage time makes this a game for fit people, but if you have a decent Frisbee, it's a lot of fun on a sunny day.

A note on Frisbees – famously named after a pie tin. There is really only one kind good enough to make this game work: the Aerobie Pro. It costs around £12 and lasts pretty much for ever, or until the dog gets it. We don't usually recommend specific products, but this is such an extraordinary thing, it's worth doing. The first one we had was a gift from an American and, honestly, we've never looked back. We've spent hours throwing one in triangles or squares of people, just seeing how many successful throws we can get before someone drops it. As it has a hole in the middle, you can catch it by putting your hand through, which is enormously satisfying.

# SOLVING THE RUBIK'S CUBE

More than 400 million of these have been sold since they were invented by Hungarian architect Erno Rubik in 1974. They remain a fascinating challenge – a mixture of physical dexterity and quick thinking. There are far, far too many quintillion combinations to ever be solved randomly. All solutions use some sort of pattern, though at high speeds it becomes a little like playing the piano – no one is thinking about individual notes at that point. The actor Will Smith can complete one in less than a minute – as can one of the authors. The world record is less than five seconds, which is simply extraordinary.

It might help to know there is *no* combination that takes more than twenty moves to solve. Most take between fifteen and nineteen. However, that number assumes perfect knowledge, which we don't have. What follows allows any position to be solved in around five minutes. There are much faster techniques, but this is a good starting place. Please note: if this is the first time you are trying to solve a Rubik's Cube, it will seem laborious and unbelievably difficult at first – especially 'finding the cross', which can be maddening. It gets easier and easier and easier. 'Use makes master' – so practise and don't give up.

## THE BASICS

Look at the cube. It is made of twenty-six smaller cubes. There are six sides and six colours – and each colour has a central square that never changes position. So if you see a green square in the centre, that is the green side. This is important to know.

As well as six **centre squares**, there are eight **corner squares**, which have three colours, and twelve **edge squares**, which have two colours. Identify a few of these. Find the blue/white edge square as an example. Make a few moves and see how the centre squares always remain in the centre. When you're ready, try these instructions. Go slowly and be patient.

## NOTATION

First: names commonly used for the sides. The pattern of moves to solve a cube is called an **algorithm**. Part of it might look like this – R F R´ – so we need to agree terms for the cube faces. You'll need to know only five: **Front (F)**, **Back (B)**, **Right (R)**, **Up (U)** and **Down (D)**. As with anything, these will seem clunking and slow at first, then become obvious and second nature.

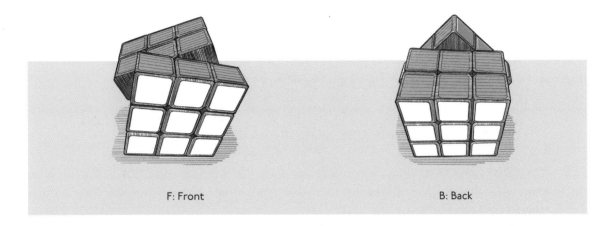

F: Front                                                B: Back

Whichever side of the cube faces you is the Front or F side. The Back layer is the furthest away. You will decide on a new front any number of times during this process, turning it as you go.

R: Right                        U: Up                        D: Down

The Right layer is to the right (we tend not to use left). The Up layer is the top, the Down layer is on the bottom. That's it for names of layers. When you are instructed to turn one, it's clockwise *as you look at the layer*. A prime symbol (´) is used when it's a reverse turn – anticlockwise as you look at it.

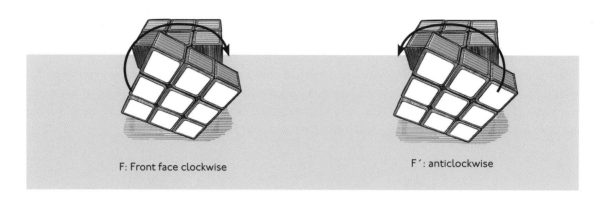

F: Front face clockwise                    F´: anticlockwise

The final move instruction is to note a lower-case letter: **f.** Lower case represents turning two layers rather than one. This is equivalent to rotating the opposite side backwards.

## STAGE ONE: FORMING A CROSS

Pick a colour. Make sure it's white so these instructions work. The first stage is to form a white cross on the bottom of the cube, then fill in the corners to make a complete side. In some ways, this is the trickiest part for beginners. It takes time.

Put the side with a white square in the centre facing down. That one has to be the white side. Your aim here is to bring down the four white 'edges' to join it – the four two-colour cubes of white and another colour. There are only four edge pieces with white on them, so you should have to do this only four times.

Find a white edge (white–green, for example), and twist the sides until it is on the 'top' layer – the layer furthest from white. This layer can twist freely **without interfering with any lower levels**. So once the white–green edge is on the top layer, twist it so that the edge sits above the corresponding coloured centre (in our case: green).

From here, there are two possible situations, and two ways to deal with these situations.

1. The edge has white on the top.
   In this case, make sure the coloured centre (for us: green) is facing you, then rotate it twice (**F2**).

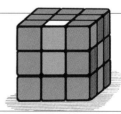

2. The edge has a colour on the top.
   In this case, also make sure the coloured centre is facing you, then perform the following algorithm: **F D R´ D´**.

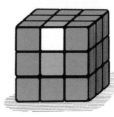

You should now have two white squares next to each other on the bottom, and two coloured squares on one of the faces, as shown. To form the full cross, this needs to be done three more times.

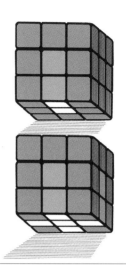

As you move other white edge pieces to the top layer, manoeuvre them over the correct coloured centre (a white–red edge needs to be above the red centre, for example). If a white edge piece is out of place, put it on the right and rotate it up to the top. (If it's in the middle layer: **R U R′**, on the bottom layer: **R2**.)

## STAGE TWO: THE WHITE CORNERS

The next step is to fill in the white corners around the cross. This will end with a fully completed white side.

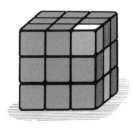

There are four white corners with two other colours on them. Locate one on the top layer, and twist it so that the corner is positioned directly above where you want it to go. There are two other colours on that white corner, so the cube must sit in between these two colours. If the corner is white–red–green, it must sit in the corner position in between the red and green centres, as shown.

There are only three possible positions for the corner to be in at this point, so put this corner on the right-front side, and then perform the following algorithms:

1. The white square is on the top: **R U2 R′ U′ R U R′.**

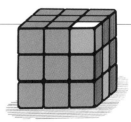

2. The white square is on the right: **R U R′.**

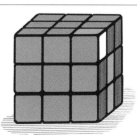

3. The white square is on the front: **F′ U′ F**.

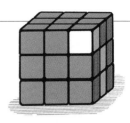

That will put each white corner into place, creating a completed white side and finishing the first layer. It should look something like this:

(If it *doesn't* look like this, mix it up and begin again – at this stage. You'll find it easier to adjust an unusual result as you get more experienced.) The cube is a third finished. Take some deep breaths. Show it to trusted family members. Take a walk or have a lie-down or something. Come back refreshed for the next bit.

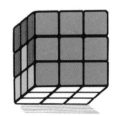

## STAGE THREE: THE SECOND LAYER

The second layer can be completed by inserting the missing four edge pieces. To begin, find an edge piece with no yellow. As an example, we used a red–blue edge. Just as with the corners, it is easier to find an edge that is already on the top layer.

First, align the colour not on the top with its centre colour. This step is often forgotten, and may be the reason it doesn't work. In our example, blue was on the top of the edge piece, and red was not, so we placed the edge above the *red* centre.

Place the side that has the edge (in our example, the *red* side) on the right. There are then only **two** possible situations. In both, the top colour needs to move towards its coloured centre:

1. The edge needs to move 'back'. In this example, the edge has blue on the top, so to put it in place, it must be rotated backwards, towards the blue centre: **R′ U′ R′ U′ R′ U R U R**.

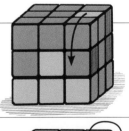

2. The edge needs to move 'forwards'. In this example, the edge has green on the top, so to put it in place, the side must be rotated forwards, towards the green centre: **R U R U R U′ R′ U′ R′**.

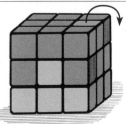

This should insert the edge into the correct place. Now repeat this for all the other edges on the top layer that don't have yellow.

It is possible that the whole of the first two layers can be completed like this, yet sometimes an edge will be in the correct place, but with the colours reversed, as shown. We need to remove this edge from where it is, then reinsert it correctly. To do this we insert another edge that is not useful to us in place of the one we need. So we use the same steps as above to insert an edge with yellow on it into the place of the reversed edge.

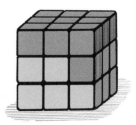

In our example, we put the red side on the right, and performed the first algorithm: **R′ U′ R′ U′ R′ U R U R**. This removed the red–blue edge, and inserted another random edge. At this point, we can follow the steps above, aligning the red–blue edge with the correct side and using the algorithms to insert it.

With a little luck, a few false starts and redos – and a lot of patience, you now have two sides finished. That leaves just eight pieces to get into the right place. Final parts coming up.

## STAGE FOUR: FINDING THE YELLOW CROSS

We now turn to the top (yellow) face and approach it in a similar way to the original white face. There are numerous patterns you may find on the top, but usually two distinct ones appear, and both can be solved with algorithms. Often there are other yellow squares scattered around, but these patterns can almost always be found and will allow you to make the yellow cross. Make sure to rotate the cube so that the patterns face exactly in this way:

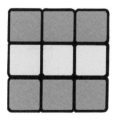

F R U R′ U′ F′

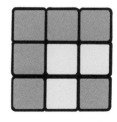

f R U R′ U′ f′

(Remember: small 'f' means to rotate the front two layers in a clockwise turn.)

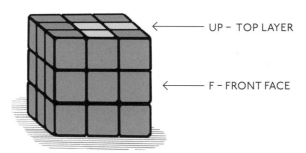

UP – TOP LAYER

F – FRONT FACE

If something goes wrong, don't panic. Try to reverse the algorithm. If that doesn't work, or makes it worse, go back to an earlier part of the sequence and fill in the gaps again.

If neither of these patterns initially appear, repeat the first algorithm from any side until one does (**F R U R′ U′ F′**), then repeat the steps above: rotate the cube so that those patterns can be found, and complete the algorithms. This will complete the yellow cross.

## STAGE FIVE: COMPLETING THE YELLOW CORNERS

This stage will finish the top yellow side by filling in the corners. There are three possible situations you will come across, but only one algorithm to perform: **R U R′ U R U2 R′**. If it doesn't resolve at first, repeat the process.

1. There are no corners filled in.
   If this is the case, rotate the top layer of the cube until the left-front corner has a yellow square on the left side. This may sound confusing, so refer to the diagram. The front-most left corner needs to have yellow on the left, as shown. Perform the algorithm: **R U R′ U R U2 R′**.

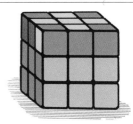

2. There is only one corner filled in.
   This is a similar case. Rotate the top layer so that the left-front corner has a yellow square on the top side. The one square that is filled in will sit in the left-front spot. Perform the algorithm: **R U R′ U R U2 R′**.

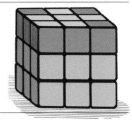

3. There are two corners filled in.
   Two possible patterns have two corners. Both have been depicted. Just as before, rotate the top layer so that the left-front corner has a yellow square on the front side. With that yellow square as your F side, perform the algorithm: **R U R′ U R U2 R′**.

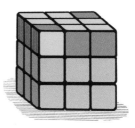
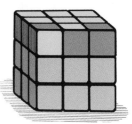

## STAGE SIX: COMPLETING THE TOP LAYER

First, you need to find '**headlights**'. These are two squares on the top layer which are the same colour with another in between. We have used green headlights as an example. Place these headlights at the back, then perform the following algorithm. It is the hardest of all of them, so it may be tricky to follow. If there are no headlights, do the algorithm on any side to reveal them.

Here it is: **R′ F R′ B2 R F′ R′ B2 R2**.

(Remember: 'B' is back – the rearmost layer. As it's a double turn, it doesn't matter if it's clockwise or anticlockwise.)

## STAGE SEVEN: FINISHING THE CUBE

The previous algorithm will create a top layer which will have 'headlights' on three or four sides. Line up the headlights with their correct colour side.

If there *is* a fully completed side, place it at the back and perform the final algorithm below.

If there isn't a completed side, pick any side as 'F' and perform the algorithm to reveal it. This pattern circulates the four top edge squares.

Here it is: **R U′ R U R U R U′ R′ U′ R2**.

There are faster methods. With practice, this will solve the cube in around five minutes or less. We found that the more times we did it, the more an understanding of how to achieve a move set in. However, begin by memorising these stages and algorithms. Completing a cube – especially one you thought you would never complete – is a special moment.

# GREAT RUINS

SANDAL CASTLE,
WAKEFIELD

It's not just that there's something oddly fascinating about the remains of great castles, with the battlefields that lie around them. Visiting such places is often the only way to understand why the events of history unfolded in the way they did. One of the authors, writing historical fiction, has found great insight into the past by visiting spots where it actually happened. If you have the chance, you should go out of your way to stand in these places and imagine how it must have been. You will not be disappointed.

Note: While it is true that pyramids count, none of the authors have been to Egypt, so we didn't include them here. These are ruins we have visited – with the stories that made them.

## SANDAL CASTLE

In December 1460, Richard Plantagenet, Duke of York, and his friend Earl Salisbury were engaged in a fight for the crown of England against the House of Lancaster. This was part of a series of battles between 1455 and 1485. The symbol of the House of York was a white rose and the symbol of Lancaster was a red rose, so they are known today as the Wars of the Roses.

The Duke of York and Earl Salisbury heard that a great Lancastrian army was being gathered in the north. They wanted to stop it forming before too many lords and their men arrived on the field, so they raced north from London with around seven thousand men. They hoped to catch the House of Lancaster by surprise.

It was a terrible mistake. By the time York and Salisbury arrived in the area, at least eighteen thousand men had assembled to face them. Outnumbered almost three to one, York cast about for a safe place to rest and call for reinforcements. The closest refuge he owned was Sandal Castle, near the town of Wakefield. It was a small fortress in what were then deep woods. As well as the outer walls, it had been constructed with a massive inner moat and tower as a final retreat for the family. If you visit, you will be amazed that York and Salisbury crammed seven thousand soldiers into it. Inside the walls, they slept on the frozen ground that night and ate everything in the fortress stores. It wasn't far off Christmas and the temperatures would have been bitterly cold. No doubt it was a miserable night.

In the morning, Earl Salisbury decided to lead a small party into the woods around the fortress to hunt deer – to bring food back for the exhausted and starving men who had marched from London. He was not aware that his army had been spotted the day before. The army of Lancaster, which included Queen Margaret, wife to King Henry VI, had crept up through the woods in the night.

Earl Salisbury came under attack and, in Sandal Castle, York heard alarm horns being blown. The keep at Sandal rises far above the outer walls. The men who kept watch up there would have been standing around a brazier, half-frozen, but they saw movement in the woods below and called warnings to York. He was a brave and experienced soldier, and he ordered his men out immediately to save Salisbury. Yet Sandal Castle was designed for defence and the only way in or out was over a walkway just six feet wide. It was simply impossible

to deploy seven thousand men quickly through that pinch point. York's men were overwhelmed, and both he and Salisbury were killed. The Wars of the Roses might have ended there – and the design of Sandal Castle would have been the cause as much as anything else. Yet as it happened, the lords of Lancaster could not have known what they had done by killing York and Salisbury. Both men had sons and they too were great friends. One of them was six foot four and a terrifying warrior. He would go on to be King Edward IV. The other was known as Earl Warwick – and he would become known to history as the 'Kingmaker'. In killing the fathers, the house of Lancaster had unleashed the sons.

---

2

## PEMBROKE CASTLE

This castle in Wales is perhaps most famous for being the birthplace of Henry Tudor, who went on to be King Henry VII of England, father to Henry VIII and grandfather to Elizabeth I. It was Henry Tudor who would end the Wars of the Roses when he defeated King Richard III of York at the Battle of Bosworth. He spent part of his youth in Wales and then escaped to France with his uncle Jasper – before he came home to challenge for the throne

THE ACROPOLIS, ATHENS

on the field of battle in 1485. Although Henry was of the House of Lancaster – the red rose – he married the daughter of King Edward IV of York, and so joined the red and white together in what would become the Tudor rose.

Pembroke is far better preserved than Sandal Castle, with the outer wall and entire sections still intact. Like Sandal, it has a massive central keep, for the inhabitants to seek refuge in when all else failed. Yet Pembroke was never taken and remains today one of the great castles in Britain. It has two huge kitchens and at the back of one is a small door that leads down and down through the hill on which Pembroke stands – to a vast cave far below. The cave, known as the Wogan or Hogan, is a secret entrance to the castle and opens onto the river below. It is a completely natural wonder and may be the reason a castle was originally built in that spot.

## 3

### THE ACROPOLIS OF ATHENS

An 'acropolis' is a combination of 'acron', or high point, and 'polis', city. It fulfilled essentially the same role as the keep at Sandal Castle – the most fortified part of a Greek city, to which the inhabitants could retreat in the event of an attack. There is more than one acropolis in Greece, but when someone says 'The Acropolis', they mean the one in Athens. It stands on a steep limestone hill above the rest of the city and so is visible to all. In ancient times, it was both a refuge and a holy place, with temples to many gods.

As a naturally defensible rock, there have been inhabitants on the Acropolis for many thousands of years. Yet the Parthenon and the temples that remain today were built during the extraordinary

5th century BC – the golden age, when Greece produced Socrates, Euripides, Pericles, Hippocrates and dozens more: thinkers, playwrights, soldiers, doctors and leaders. Democracy, mathematics, perspective and the theatre all have roots in this unbelievably creative cluster.

You'll have to buy a ticket to climb up, but after that you're on your own. It's hot, but the geography is a wonder. The views are breathtaking, not least because of those names from antiquity who looked out on the same hills and distant temples. From the heights, you can gaze down onto a theatre where the first plays were produced. Not just ancient plays – the very first ones. If you're interested in such things, you might also note that the sight lines on the Parthenon were constructed with a curve that makes them look straight. They were designed with a visual effect in mind – and that is incredible.

Oddly, you'll hear a lot of Italian voices as well. If you've ever wondered where Italians (who are, after all, blessed with sun, beaches and great food) go for a holiday, the answer is Greece. You might also note that the sea is noticeably darker than the Mediterranean. The Greek writer Homer described the Aegean as the 'wine-dark sea' – one of his most famous lines. The strange thing is that now that you have read that, the phrase will pop back into your head the first time you see the Aegean. It will be worth it.

Greece is the birthplace of empires. The Romans modelled themselves on Greek culture. British schoolchildren learned Greek and Latin and revered great thinkers like Aristotle, Plato and later, ·Cicero. America today has a senate, speaks English and has a number of neoclassical buildings, from Union Station in Washington to the White House itself. Each culture forgets or rejects some of what has gone before, but retains some of the best parts.

There were other influences over the last two thousand years, of course – human beings love a good idea wherever they find it – but the Acropolis in Athens is where the West began.

## SPARTA

The city-state of Sparta is on the Peloponnesus, in Greece – a peninsula linked to the Greek mainland by a narrow isthmus. On one occasion, the Spartans blockaded that land bridge while they assembled, then sallied out against their enemies. Unlike almost every other city from the 6th to the 3rd century BC, the city had no walls and no monuments because, as the Spartans said, *they* were the walls; *they* were the monuments.

The Spartans lived in the valley of the Eurotas river in the region known as Laconia, surrounded by mountains and hostile terrain. It was a dry place, without the good soil of other cities. Perhaps that was one of the reasons the Spartans raised warriors instead of crops. Allowing no weakness and through constant training, they became the most feared warriors in the world, capable of extraordinary feats. We described Thermopylae and the Three Hundred in the last *Dangerous Book*. Some eighty years after that, around three

thousand Spartans moved at will through a Persian army at Cunaxa as part of the Ten Thousand. Each one was a master of four weapons – sword, spear, shield and the kopis, a very nasty long knife, not a million miles from a modern Gurkha's kukri.

The city of Sparta exists today, though it is a fairly sleepy place. Just outside the Greek streets is a running track. Up a hill behind it are the Spartan acropolis and ruins going back over two thousand years. Many different periods mingle there in stone, but the essential landscape is the one King Leonidas would have known. It is worth a visit for that alone. Compared with Athens, Sparta is not easy to reach – though in a way that is part of its magic. This is literally the land of legend – and the greatest warrior state in history.

---

### 5

## THE FORUM IN ROME

The city of Rome is a wonderful destination in itself, for the Colosseum, St Peter's, the Sistine Chapel, statues by Bernini, the Trevi Fountain and so on. It is also a fairly small city – compared with, say, Shanghai, New York or London – so it's possible to see a lot of it in a single afternoon. The Forum is an extraordinary place. Some parts, such

as the house on the Palatine Hill that belonged to Emperor Augustus, are so well preserved that you'll be able to see the use of eye-tricking perspective on walls painted two thousand years ago.

The Forum, like the Greek agora (open space, or market) before it, was where the business of Rome was conducted – which included speeches, letters read to crowds, triumphant parades and even riots. It sits below the level of the modern city around it, so there are many places where you can stand and look over the past. Sometimes a great arch or just a few columns hint at old glories – or the Temple of Vesta, or a senate house that is the third or fourth to stand on that spot.

Today, you can stand in the ruins of Pompey's theatre and walk up over Capitoline Hill and down into the Forum – exactly as the assassins of Julius Caesar did in 44 BC. They held out their bloodied hands to show they were not ashamed of what they had done, though they should have been. In the end, not one of them would escape punishment, and Brutus threw himself on his own sword rather than be captured.

Rome is full of stories, so a good guidebook is useful. It's worth going in January or February, when there are fewer crowds, but the sky can still be an aching blue. Honestly, it is a miraculous place that deserves the name 'eternal city'.

---

### 6

## POMPEII

There is only one place in the world like Pompeii – and that's Herculaneum, the other city buried in the same eruption of Vesuvius in AD 79. Famously, Pompeii was preserved in thick ash and Herculaneum was smothered in superheated mud that set like rock. The destruction left doorways and even tables intact, with mosaics and clay pots exactly as they were in that terrible year. The people themselves are upsetting figures. The original archaeologists realised there were many human remains, reduced to bones over time. They injected plaster into the cavities left by the bodies. As a result, figures of bone and plaster survive as they were in the moment of their death – mothers curled around their children, fathers who died protecting their families. There is unbearable tragedy here.

In Pompeii, you will be able to walk streets built at the time of the Roman empire. The wheel ruts of wagons are still visible where they were worn in stone, with the remains of lead pipes showing where they brought water in to fountains. It is worth paying for a guide, by the way. You'll fly to Naples airport and probably get a room somewhere on the Amalfi Coast. With that base established, Pompeii is half an hour and a day trip away. Herculaneum, near Pompeii, is smaller, though in some ways more tragic. Before the eruption it was a seaport for wealthy Romans. When boiling mud and ash began to rain down, they ran for the sea, just as you would. Yet the sea boiled. Herculaneum was much harder to excavate than Pompeii and at least half of the ancient city is still hidden – not least because modern housing has been built over it. Yet the hard mud meant that the level of preservation is, if anything, even better than Pompeii. Colours are preserved and even some carbonised furniture. You will need another guide, but leave time simply to walk in silence. Julius Caesar's father had a holiday home in Herculaneum. Using computer imaging, it has been possible to recreate some of the burned scrolls found there.

Finally, if you wish, it is usually possible to walk up Vesuvius, perhaps on a different day. The approach is a long and very winding road. When you park, the path is not particularly arduous and the views are magnificent. You will still see steam issuing forth from the crater. It remains an active volcano, so there is a very small chance you won't be coming down again. The past is all around you, for those with eyes to see.

# THINGS TO DO: TWO TABLE TRICKS

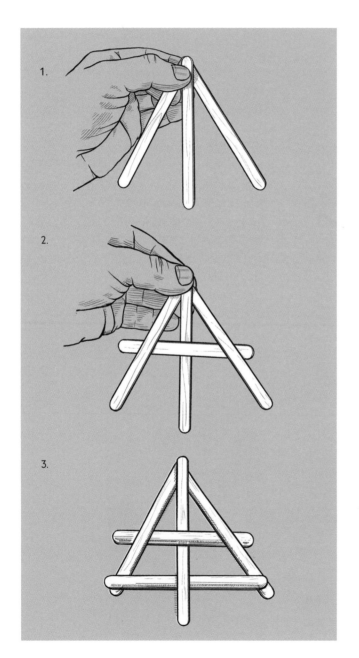

1.

2.

3.

These are just interesting to know. Each one takes a few minutes to learn, but then you'll have a trick you can do for the rest of your life.

## LOLLY-STICK SPINNER

Simple, but it works – and it's not immediately obvious how to do it.

Take three lolly sticks and hold them as you see here. The middle one should be on top.

Holding the three steady, insert a middle bar across, as in Fig. 2. It goes under-over-under.

Finally, insert the last one – over-under-over. The opposing forces will hold it all together.

Now you *could* add a few drops of superglue to stop them springing apart, but that sort of defeats the point. Throw it in the open somewhere. When it comes apart, remake it.

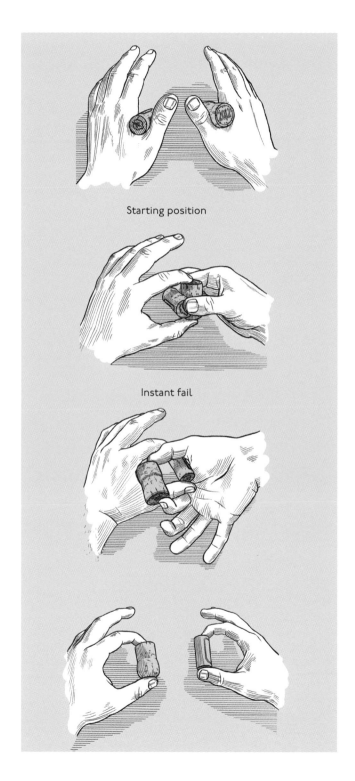

Starting position

Instant fail

## 'UNCLE MAZ CORKS'

A family favourite, thanks to Mario Arpino, who infuriated us with these for many years.

Take two corks and hold them in the crooks of your thumb and first finger, as you see here.

Using ONLY your thumbs and first fingers, the aim is to swap the corks over to the other hand. The first attempt will usually go wrong – some version of the second picture. The fun part of this is that you can show exactly how it's done, over and over, but very few people will be able to reproduce the action. You show them, you hand over the corks. They fail, so you show them again. They watch you carefully. They ask for slow motion – and they still won't be able to do it.

The trick is to turn only one hand, though you can make it look like you are turning both when you have the knack of it.

For practice, keep your left hand upright and steady, and turn your right hand so the palm is towards you. You should be able to take hold of both corks then as you see here, using only finger and thumb. Gently move them apart, un-twisting your right hand as you go – it makes it harder to see how you did it. The final position is pictured on the left.

# THE ENDLESS CARD

ike the paper hat, boat and water bomb in the first book, this is fairly easy to do and pleasing to be able to make. For a birthday card, you can draw on each panel to personalise it – which takes a bit of time and effort. Such things are always appreciated.

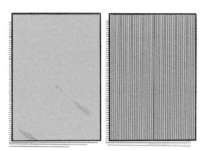

Begin with two pieces of A4. We found thin card worked best, though you can do it with paper. You might prefer to use two white pieces, though we made this one with blue and green.

Make each one into a square by folding one edge over onto itself and tearing off a rectangle.

Fold both those squares in half lengthways, then open them up and cut along that central crease. Not the diagonal.

You should now have four smaller rectangles. You need fold lines at the quarter, half and three-quarter points – one that folds both ways. The easiest way to do this is to fold it in half and then fold each half along a quarter line.

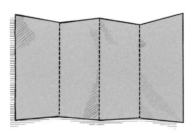
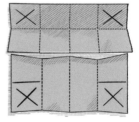

Lay two of the rectangles together, as if to make the original square once more. With Pritt Stick, dab a square in each corner. The best results will come from gluing the whole of each square marked with an

X in the diagram. Lay the other two on top in the opposite direction. So if the first ones lie east and west, put the other two north and south.

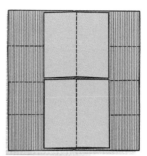

It's worth taking a moment to glue those four squares more securely before you go on. (If it's floppy, it's probably because you haven't glued those squares properly.)

Holding the card like a book or a window, it should be possible to open up the top layer and fold them back to reveal the layer underneath. Press it all flat the first time.

Each time you 'open' and fold back the card to reveal another surface, you have to rotate it 90 degrees – a quarter turn. Doing that along the seam should reveal another stage:

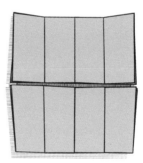

. . . and back to the beginning. Choose different scenes for the card – perhaps opening curtains on the first part, with something more personal inside. The card does stand up – and whoever you give it to is going to know you spent some time on it. That is never a small thing.

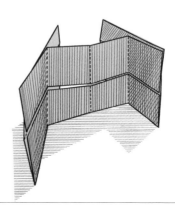

# THE COMMONWEALTH

In the first *Dangerous Book*, we included a short chapter about the Commonwealth, an alliance of fifty-three nations and 2.4 billion people. In May 2018, at the royal wedding of Meghan Markle and Prince Harry in Windsor, the bride wore a veil embroidered with fifty-three flowers or symbols of those countries. So it seems the right time to devote a little more space to that extraordinary group, bound by history, culture and, essentially, goodwill. Sixteen Commonwealth countries have Queen Elizabeth as head of state. In 2018, the Commonwealth leaders confirmed that her son Prince Charles would be the next head of the Commonwealth. With a third of the world's population, the Commonwealth has an economy bigger than the European Union and contains some of the world's largest, smallest, richest and poorest nations. All fifty-three nations have a voice in this, the oldest political association of states.

### ANTIGUA AND BARBUDA

Three tropical islands (including Redonda) in the eastern Caribbean. There are 365 beaches on Antigua alone.

### AUSTRALIA

Its own continent. Capital: Canberra. Founder member of the Commonwealth and the largest island in the world, at 3 million square miles (7.6 million sq km).

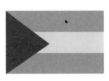

### THE BAHAMAS

Around 700 islands just south-east of Florida, of which 30 are inhabited. The main towns are the capital, Nassau, and Freeport.

### BANGLADESH

Borders India and the Bay of Bengal, and has a vast water-transport network. Capital: Dhaka.

### BARBADOS

Subtropical Caribbean island. Capital: Bridgetown, a deep-water port. Hotels and white beaches.

### BELIZE

Once home to the Mayans. Borders Mexico and Guatemala, with an east coast overlooking the Caribbean. Capital: Belmopan.

### BOTSWANA

Borders South Africa, Zimbabwe, Zambia, Angola and Namibia. Capital: Gaborone. Contains the Kalahari Desert. Almost a fifth of the country is either national park or game reserve.

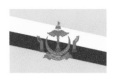

### BRUNEI DARUSSALAM

Wealthy state, with oil reserves, ruled by a sultan. Borders Malaysian territory on the island of Borneo, with its coast on the South China Sea. Capital: Bandar Seri Begawan.

### CAMEROON

West coast of Africa. Borders Nigeria, Chad, Central African Republic, Congo, Gabon and Equatorial Guinea, as well as a sea coast onto the Gulf of Guinea. Capital: Yaoundé. Oil, timber and vast natural resources.

### CANADA

Founder member in 1931. Second-largest country in the world after Russia. Borders America and three oceans: Arctic, Pacific and Atlantic. Capital: Ottawa. Freezing to temperate climate – ideal for ice hockey.

### CYPRUS

Mediterranean island with 9,000 years of history. Invaded by Persians, Franks and Romans. More recently, Turkish soldiers invaded in 1974 and are still there in the northern third of the country.

### DOMINICA

Lush volcanic island in the Caribbean. Capital: Roseau. Visited by Columbus in 1493. Tourism, bananas and offshore finance.

### ESWATINI

African monarchy formerly known as Swaziland. Landlocked, Eswatini is bordered by South Africa and Mozambique. Subtropical to temperate climate. Capital: Mbabane. Wood pulp, textile, canning, clothing and sugar-cane industries.

### FIJI

North of New Zealand, Fiji is a volcanic Pacific archipelago of around 300 islands. The climate is tropical and they play rugby there. Exports sugar cane, as well as gold and clothing. Capital: Suva.

### THE GAMBIA

Left the Commonwealth in 2013; rejoined 2018. Smallest country in West Africa. Borders Senegal and the Atlantic. Capital: Banjul.

### GHANA

West Africa, with coast on the Gulf of Guinea. Borders Togo, Burkina Faso and Côte D'Ivoire. Tropical climate. Capital: Accra. The Black, Red and White Volta rivers all meet to form the man-made Lake Volta. Exports aluminium and electricity.

### GRENADA

Volcanic-formed archipelago of Caribbean islands and a major exporter of nutmeg. There is a symbol of a nutmeg clove on the flag. Capital: St George's, a deep-water port. Beautiful tourist destination.

### GUYANA

Mainland South America. Borders Venezuela, Suriname and Brazil, with an Atlantic coast. Heavily forested. Exports gold and bauxite, an ore of aluminium. Capital: Georgetown.

### INDIA

Borders Nepal, China, Pakistan, Bhutan, Bangladesh and Myanmar (previously Burma). Capital: New Delhi. Population of over 1.3 billion. Very hot climate, with monsoon rains and cooler mountains.

### JAMAICA

Caribbean island south of Cuba. Tropical at sea level, subtropical or cooler in the hills. Lush and spectacularly forested tourist destination, with many beaches. Capital: Kingston.

### KENYA

East African country on the Equator. Borders Tanzania, Somalia, Ethiopia, South Sudan and Uganda. Vast national parks and grass savannas. Capital: Nairobi. Exports tea, coffee. Manufacturing hub.

### KIRIBATI

(Pronounced: Kiribas.) Vast archipelago of coral atolls in the Pacific. Thirty-three main islands. Capital: Tarawa.

### LESOTHO

Tiny landlocked country surrounded by South Africa – a mountain kingdom. Capital: Maseru. Manufactures clothing, shoes and textiles, and encourages tourism.

### MALAWI

Landlocked African country, though Lake Malawi runs two-thirds of its length. Borders Zambia, Tanzania and Mozambique. Capital: Lilongwe. Economy: tea and agriculture.

### MALAYSIA

Lies just north of Singapore and south of Thailand. Capital: Kuala Lumpur. Tropical climate. Forest and mountains, down to plains, mangrove swamps and beautiful beaches. Exports tin, rubber, oil, gas, palm oil and manufactured goods.

### MALTA

Archipelago of six islands in the Mediterranean. Capital: Valletta. The nation was awarded the George Cross in 1942 for courage and aid given during WWII – the cross visible on the flag. Beautiful islands and warm climate. Shipbuilding, tourism, finance and business services.

### MAURITIUS

Isolated island nation east of Madagascar in the Indian Ocean, off East Africa. Capital: Port Louis. Coral beaches. Handles shipping of sugar, oil, cement and wheat.

### MOZAMBIQUE

South-east Africa. Borders South Africa, Eswatini (formerly known as Swaziland), Zimbabwe, Zambia, Malawi and Tanzania, as well as the long east coast on the Mozambique Channel – an area of Indian ocean between the mainland and the island of Madagascar. Capital: Maputo. Key ports for this region. Exports gas and coal.

### NAMIBIA

South-west Africa. Borders South Africa, Botswana, Zambia and Angola, as well as the Atlantic Ocean. Capital: Windhoek. Arid climate, as it contains part of the Kalahari and Namib deserts. Mining and fishing industries.

### NAURU

Pacific island with a small population. No official capital. The main town is Yaren. Tropical paradise, with a history of phosphate mining that is coming to an end. Tourism welcomed.

### NEW ZEALAND

East of Australia. Founder member of the Commonwealth in 1931. Capital: Wellington. From personal experience, places like Waiheke Island are close to paradise. Beautiful place. Well worth a visit. Agriculture, fishing, tourism and manufacturing.

### NIGERIA

Huge and populous West African country. Borders Cameroon, Chad, Niger and Benin, with a coast on the Gulf of Guinea. Capital: Abuja. Very hot climate. Exports oil and gas, as well as manufactured goods.

### PAKISTAN

Borders India, Afghanistan, Iran, China and the Arabian Sea. Capital: Islamabad. There is a disputed territory between India and Pakistan that also shares a border with Tibet. The climate is varied – from freezing peaks of the Himalayas to great heat. Natural gas, manufactured goods, cotton and financial industries.

### PAPUA NEW GUINEA

Just north of Australia – 600 Pacific islands. Capital: Port Moresby. Shares one land border with Indonesia. Gold, timber, oil and gas resources. Hot, humid climate, with a vast variety of flora and fauna.

### ST KITTS AND ST NEVIS

Beautiful volcanic two-island nation in the Caribbean. Capital: Basseterre. Sugar, tourism and ship-registry industries.

### ST LUCIA

Volcanic-origin island with sandy beaches. Caribbean tourist destination. Capital: Castries. Tropical, with dry trade winds. Manufacturing, bananas and offshore finance industries.

### ST VINCENT AND THE GRENADINES

Volcanic-origin Caribbean islands just south of St Lucia. Capital: Kingstown. St Vincent has mostly black sand beaches, while the Grenadines have beaches of white sand. Heavily forested, tropical climate, with dry trade winds. Bananas, manufacturing, call centres and tourism industries.

### SAMOA

The name means 'sacred centre of the universe'. Tropical Pacific islands of volcanic origin. Rugby-playing paradise. Fish and coconuts are the major exports. Capital: Apia.

### SEYCHELLES

Indian Ocean archipelago of around 115 islands, east of Kenya. Tourism and tuna are major industries. Very popular destination. Capital: Victoria.

### SIERRA LEONE

Portuguese for 'Lion Mountain'. West coast of Africa. Borders Guinea and Liberia. Capital: Freetown. Natural resources: diamonds, aluminium, titanium and gold.

### SINGAPORE

'City of the Lion' in Sanskrit. Just south of Malaysia. Hot and humid climate, but friendly people and great shopping. Manufacturing, pharmaceuticals, financial services. Powerhouse economy.

### SOLOMON ISLANDS

Archipelago in the south-west Pacific. Mountains, coral atolls and reefs. Capital: Honiara. Two active volcanoes and a few dormant ones. Tropical, humid climate. Fishing, logging and gold industries.

### SOUTH AFRICA

The southernmost tip of Africa. Biggest economy of the region. Climate varies, but allows vineyards. Cape Town is very beautiful. Kruger National Park is unimaginably vast. Inventors of magnificent biltong. Capital: Pretoria. Manufacturing, telecoms, energy, tourism and banking industries.

### SRI LANKA

Island just off the coast of southern India. Most famous for its tea plantations, Sri Lanka (formerly Ceylon) also has manufacturing, banking and textile industries. Administrative capital (including parliament): Sri Jayawardenepura Kotte.

### TANZANIA

Borders Kenya, Uganda, Rwanda, Burundi, Democratic Republic of Congo, Zambia, Malawi and Mozambique. Lake Victoria lies in the north and the east coast is on the Indian Ocean. Capital: Dodoma. Tropical to temperate climate, which includes Mount Kilimanjaro, the highest peak in Africa. Exports gold, diamonds, coffee, tea, fish and tobacco.

### TONGA

Polynesian Pacific monarchy – an archipelago of 172 islands, of which some 36 are inhabited. Four active volcanoes and a rugby team. Hot, humid climate. Tourism industry. Mainly agricultural, exports squash and fish. Unhurried and unspoilt. Capital: Nuku'alofa.

### TRINIDAD AND TOBAGO

Two islands, of which Trinidad is the larger, off the coast of Venezuela in South America. Tropical climate made gentler by trade winds. Oil, gas, manufacturing and tourism industries. Capital: Port of Spain.

### TUVALU

Group of islands north of Fiji. One of the world's smallest democracies. Main town: Vaiaku on Funafuti island, which also has an airfield built with Commonwealth assistance. Warm climate. Small-scale fishing and tourism.

### UGANDA

Landlocked African country, bordered by Sudan, Kenya, Tanzania, Rwanda and Democratic Republic of the Congo. Uganda shares part of Lake Victoria with Kenya and Tanzania, and has a number of other lakes. Capital: Kampala. Tropical climate. Exports coffee, tea, tobacco and gold.

### UNITED KINGDOM

Islands off the coast of western Europe. Capital: London. Temperate climate. Banking, financial services, energy, manufacturing industries, authors.

### VANUATU

Group of volcanic-origin islands in the south-west Pacific. Capital: Port Vila. Ships sail from here to New Caledonia and Auckland, New Zealand. Fishing, tourism and offshore finance industries.

### ZAMBIA

Landlocked towards the southern end of Africa. Bordered by Botswana, Zimbabwe, Mozambique, Malawi, Tanzania, Democratic Republic of the Congo, Angola and Namibia. Capital: Lusaka. Exports cotton, cobalt, copper, gemstones.

'The Crown is the symbol of the free association of the members of the British Commonwealth of Nations . . . no law hereafter made by the Parliament of the United Kingdom shall extend to any of the said Dominions . . . otherwise than at the request and with the consent of that Dominion . . . It is hereby declared and enacted that the Parliament of a Dominion has full power to make laws . . .'

Taken from the 1931 Statute of Westminster

# STRESS BALLS AND ROLLERS

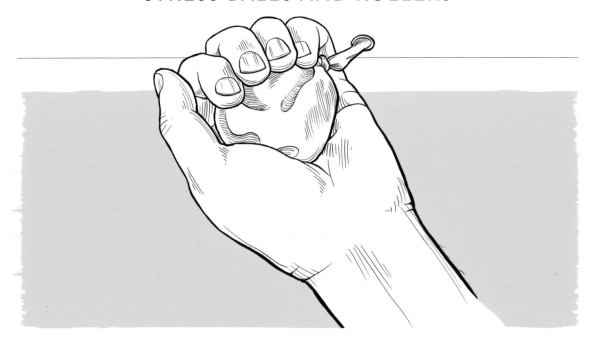

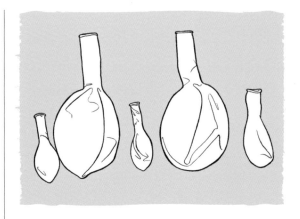

S tress is what people feel if they can't see a way past the tasks that lie before them. It's not just working hard, or even working hard every day and feeling exhausted and in need of a weekend. If we've learned one thing over a lifetime – two things, actually – it's that if something is overwhelming, it helps to go to sleep. In the morning, the problem will be exactly the same, but it will seem smaller because you'll be better able to deal with it. The other thing we've learned is that exercise is really important. In the meantime, this is a quick and easy way of making something to squeeze.

## STRESS BALLS

We bought a range of balloons. Generally, you want them to be as big as possible. Big ones will burst less often. We went to a party shop, which

was nowhere near as much fun as it sounds. We also overdid it with the size of balloons and ended up with two £5 ones that were frankly enormous and far too big for the job.

When we tried this as kids, the great benefit seemed to be that the 2lb bag of flour in the cupboard was apparently free. It isn't, of course, though it's cheap stuff to buy. Cornflour works

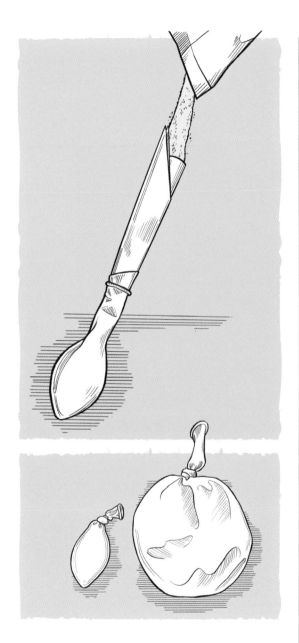

You can't force the balloons to inflate by putting flour in – and any attempt to blow them up partway with air will end in absolute disaster. Just spoon or tap flour into them until they feel full – and tie a simple thumb knot to close it off. I don't suppose anyone can say if they really help with stress, but they are enjoyable to squeeze and they last until the rubber perishes. Our enormous ones ended up looking like medical waste. The blue one put people in mind of a dog-poo bag.

## ROLLERS

It's difficult to know why some things work. This is the easiest, simplest thing in the world, but we enjoyed making it as kids and we enjoyed it again on the kitchen floor this time. Take a little aluminium foil and wrap a piece of it around a cricket ball. It should be loose enough to allow the ball to turn easily. Fashion a tail out of the same piece and trim with scissors. Roll it along a hard floor. It moves as if it's alive. If you've ever seen the film *ET*, it also moves a little bit like ET running with a blanket on his head. Race your friends.

as well. You'll need to make a paper funnel, by twisting it into a tube wider at the top than the bottom and made secure with sticky tape. Make sure that everything is dry – this is going to be a little messy and it's impossible to avoid spreading flour everywhere.

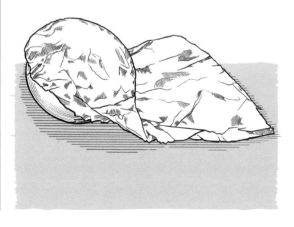

# THREE GREEK LEGENDS
# EVERY BOY SHOULD KNOW

Some stories are so well known that they become culture and blur the edges of history. In the French Revolution, when Queen Marie Antoinette was told the peasants had no bread, did she really say, 'Let them eat cake'? (In French, 'brioche'.) It is unlikely, but it served as an example of arrogance, no matter how unfair to her personally. Did someone really predict Caesar would be killed on the Ides of March, or was it added later to give an epic quality to his death? Did Sir Walter Raleigh truly cover a puddle with his cloak for Queen Elizabeth I? Did William Webb Ellis ever pick up a ball and run with it at Rugby School, and so invent the game? No one can be certain. History is written in stones – and in stories.

We tell it as grand tales, but what shines through are the heroes and villains – and our shared values. There isn't a Great Wall between history and myth – mythology always carries seeds of truth. There is a golden thread in all of them – of real lives, or parable and metaphor: from a world of strange beasts and sea creatures (like squid, whales and Komodo dragons, perhaps), to Prometheus stealing fire and being punished – or to put it another way, learning the joys and the burdens of knowledge.

Without those shared references, we lose the things that make communication easier. For example, if one person describes a task as 'Sisyphean', the audience needs to know that Sisyphus was someone given a task by Zeus, to push a stone to the top of a hill only to see it roll down again – over and over for eternity. His task was endless and heartbreaking.

There are many good books of Greek legends – and they should form part of your general knowledge. One thing is for sure: you will never regret learning them. Here are just a few of the best known.

—————————————— 1 ——————————————

## HERACLES

This early Greek hero was the child of Zeus and a mortal woman. The boy was named Heracles – pronounced '**Hair**-a-cleez'. The Roman version is Hercules ('**Her**-queue-leez'), and that's the more common spelling and pronunciation today.

We can't know if Heracles was based on some real-life ancient warrior, though it does seem likely. With his famous club and lion skin, in a sense, he's one of the first superheroes – extraordinary strength being his power. Yet first and foremost, he was a tragic figure – a touch of realism that makes us suspect he really lived, once.

The earliest play about Heracles was written by Euripides in Athens, around 417 BC. Heracles was already a figure of worship by then – his is a much older story. Rome then retold the tale with a play by Seneca, called *Hercules Furens* – 'The Fury of Hercules', in the 1st century AD. We know the main story from the *Bibliotheca* by Apollodorus – a 1st- or 2nd-century collection of all the myths and legends of ancient Greece. There are other sources, but because this was copied and recopied through the centuries, much survives. It opens with: 'Draw your knowledge of the past from me and read the ancient tales of learned lore. Look neither at the page of Homer, nor of elegy, nor tragic muse, nor epic strain. Seek not the vaunted verse of the cycle, but look in me and you will find all the world contains.'

## THE TWELVE LABOURS

The Greek god Zeus was not a faithful husband, not even slightly. His wife Hera was enraged to discover he had fathered yet another child, by the name of Heracles. At first, she sent snakes to kill the newborn in the crib, but Heracles was already strong and strangled them. Later, she cast a glamour on Heracles as a young man. He saw his wife and sons as enemies – and killed them all. Heracles was overcome with grief and horror once he realised what he had done.

Seeking a way to atone, he went to the Oracle at Delphi – a key engine of many of the stories of ancient Greece. There is no doubt it existed – the oracle involved priestesses and a temple built over sulphurous mists of volcanic activity. Delphi was an eerie place and it was common for Greeks to go there looking for predictions of the future or an answer to a problem. The oracle sent Heracles to his cousin, King Eurystheus – and he was given twelve tasks to perform, the famous Twelve Labours. (Originally, he was given ten, but Eurystheus disliked the decimal system and added two more at the end.)

1. **TO SLAY THE NEMEAN LION.**
   Wild lions used to exist in Greece and Europe. They are now extinct.
2. **TO KILL THE MANY-HEADED HYDRA** – a monster that became a metaphor. Every time Heracles cut off a head, two grew back. Eventually, he had to use fire to cauterise each stump – and buried one immortal head under a stone.
3. **TO CAPTURE THE GOLDEN HIND** – a deer, but also the name of Sir Francis Drake's ship that went around the world between 1577 and 1580. A golden hind was the crest of Drake's patron – influenced of course by this Herculean labour.

4. **TO CAPTURE THE ERYMANTHIAN BOAR** – involving side adventures with centaurs and drunkenness.

5. **TO CLEAN THE AUGEAN STABLES** – a task that has become another metaphor. Referring to something as the Augean ('or-**jee**-an') stables or a task 'of Augean proportions' is to suggest it is a mountain of filth. Heracles diverted a river to run through the ancient, poo-filled stables.

6. **TO SLAY THE STYMPHALIAN BIRDS.** Stymphalia was just a region of Greece, but the birds were man-eating. Heracles shot them with arrows dipped in Hydra blood.

7. **TO CAPTURE THE CRETAN BULL** – a monstrous white bull running mad. Though terrifying, this is one of the least mythical tasks. Bulls, like rogue elephants, can be territorial and violent. It's not difficult to imagine one becoming a public menace.

8. **TO STEAL THE MARES OF DIOMEDES.** Everyone forgets this one. Heracles had to steal four man-eating horses. He managed it, after feeding the original owner to his pets.

9. **TO STEAL THE GIRDLE OF HIPPOLYTA.** (Hip-**ol**-it-a), queen of the Amazons. The magical belt was duly stolen by Heracles, either peacefully, or leaving dead Amazons behind him, depending on the version.

10. **TO STEAL THE CATTLE OF GERYON** – a monster with three heads. Heracles went to him, killed his dog, killed his herdsmen and eventually shot Geryon with a Hydra-blood arrow. There were side adventures with the cattle, but Heracles brought them back eventually.

King Eurystheus claimed that neither the Hydra nor the Augean stables counted because Heracles had been helped both times – the second time by a river, which seems a bit weak. Either way, the king added two more demands:

11. **TO STEAL THE APPLES OF THE HESPERIDES NYMPHS** – somewhere near Portugal, probably. They might also have been oranges. Either way, he took them.

12. **TO STEAL CERBERUS** – the dog belonging to Hades, god of the underworld. We can be reasonably sure Heracles was not meant to come back from this one. However, he found an entrance, went down and brought the three-headed dog back, having strangled it a bit to teach it some manners.

After parading Cerberus around Greece – it's not difficult to imagine a powerful warrior with something like an enormous mastiff, later remembered in more heroic terms – Heracles returned the dog to the underworld and went for a drink and a lie-down.

The Twelve Labours is a story of penance – paying a terrible price for a great sin. It's also a terrific tale of survival and victory against enemies, great odds and a really angry goddess.

## JASON AND THE ARGONAUTS

In Thessaly, Uncle Pelias took the throne that belonged to Jason's father, killing all claimants and putting his own royal brother in a dungeon. The newborn Jason was spared when his mother convinced the king he had been still-born. Jason was then spirited away by servants. When Pelias consulted an oracle, he was told he would lose his throne to a man wearing one sandal.

Years later, Jason returned as a grown man, though he had lost his sandal on the road. He was announced to Pelias, but his uncle wasn't willing

to just step down, no matter what the oracle had predicted. He agreed to give up the throne if Jason brought him the Golden Fleece – the skin of a legendary ram, sacrificed to Zeus centuries earlier. Undeterred, the heroic Jason set about assembling a group of fifty heroes – Heracles, Orpheus and Theseus among them. He hired a ship called the *Argo*, so they became Argonauts, as they set out to look for the object of their quest.

What follows is a series of adventures, mostly involving island-hopping with monsters or strange women. Vengeful or angry women seem to pop up quite a lot in Greek myths.

The Argonauts fathered children on one island, defeated some giants on another, lost the crewmember Hylas to nymphs when they drowned him, left Heracles behind by accident when he went looking for Hylas, accidentally killed one friendly host king and saved another by killing Harpies – savage bird-women, whose name became a description for an unpleasantly screeching type. The Argonauts survived clashing rocks by rowing quickly through them and finally reached Colchis, where the fabulous fleece had its home with King Aeetes.

King Aeetes was also a wily ruler. He promised to hand over the fleece if Jason completed a task. Luckily, Jason had the help of the king's daughter – a powerful enchantress named Medea, then young and beautiful and somewhat in love with Jason. The task was to plough a field with fire-breathing oxen. Medea gave him ointment to protect against the heat and he managed it without being burned.

Astonished, King Aeetes decided to make an end of Jason. He gave him another task – to sow a field with dragon teeth. If you ever get the chance to see the old film with stop-motion animation by Ray Harryhausen, this is a great scene. When Jason planted the teeth, they sprouted up as warriors. Medea told him to throw a rock into their midst. They were clearly very touchy dragon-teeth soldiers, as they all immediately killed one another.

The furious king was forced to tell Jason he had permission to retrieve the fleece. Yet as soon as Jason went off, King Aeetes gave orders to kill the Argonauts. However, his daughter and Jason were too quick for him. Medea made the dragon sleep, and Jason took the fleece and ran for the ship. The Argonauts made it out.

Knowing her father would pursue them, Medea killed her own brother and spread the pieces around to slow him down. You will appreciate, this was quite an extreme act. Medea was not the delightful young lady she had seemed at first. Her relationship with Jason would become a dark tragedy in the years ahead.

On the way home, the Argonauts were blown off course by storms sent by Zeus. They passed the island of the Sirens, irresistible women who drew men to their deaths on the rocks with their songs. However, Jason had Orpheus in his crew, who played so well on his lyre that his music ruined the spell. They sailed then to Crete, where a bronze giant threatened them. Medea cast a spell to make him sleep, and then removed a plug in his ankle so that his molten bronze bled out and he died.

When they returned the fleece to King Pelias, he was not thrilled to see them and was still unwilling to give up the throne. Medea persuaded his daughters that she could invigorate their aged father, and make him youthful and strong again. She demonstrated by cutting up a ram, then making it leap alive and younger out of a cauldron. Delighted, the daughters waited till the old man was asleep and chopped him up, putting him into the cauldron. At that point, Medea just walked away. Medea was a monster – and her story is not finished yet.

Jason and Medea were married, but were banished by one of Pelias' sons, so he didn't become king – because this is a Greek legend and not one written by Disney.

---

### 3

## THESEUS

Before we get going on young Theseus, we have to mention Medea and Jason. They had a number of children, but did not live happily ever after. Jason abandoned Medea for Glauce, daughter of a king. Medea's rage was so savage that she sent poisoned items to Glauce and her father, bringing about their deaths, then *murdered her own children* to hurt Jason, before fleeing to Athens. There is an old proverb: 'Hell hath no fury like a woman scorned', but the example of Medea got there first.

In a small Greek town, a young lad grew up to be a strong young man. His father had passed through the area years before – a king who had spent time with a local woman and thought she was pregnant. The king's name was Aegeus, and he left a sword and a pair of sandals underneath a

great rock, telling Theseus' mother that if one day the boy could lift it, he should come to Athens.

When Theseus was grown, his mother took him to the rock and told him about his father. He lifted it and threw it into the woods, took up the sword and sandals, and set off to Athens to meet King Aegeus. He chose to walk, as he was afraid of nothing. As a result, he was involved in a number of fights and adventures. He took part in the *Argo* expedition and helped Heracles with a couple of his Twelve Labours.

Interestingly, Theseus was clever as well as strong. Unlike Heracles, he preferred to win by tricking his enemies. One example shows his style. He was threatened by a man carrying a big club he claimed was made of solid brass. Theseus said he doubted that. He suggested it could only be a sheet of brass over wood. The enraged man handed it over for Theseus to examine – and Theseus knocked him out with it.

When Theseus reached Athens at last, he was introduced to his father, King Aegeus – and his new wife, the sorceress Medea. Medea had already borne a son and heir to Aegeus, and had no desire to see a previous heir appearing at court, especially not one who had known her in the Argonaut adventure, so had a pretty good idea of her past.

Medea put poison in a cup for Theseus, but the old king recognised the sword Theseus carried and dashed it from her hands before his son could drink. Medea left the court then, rather than be killed for her wickedness.

Theseus was content for a time in Athens, until a ship appeared with black sails. It had come from Minos in Crete, demanding a terrible tribute. A savage beast known as the Minotaur roamed a maze beneath the palace on Crete. The king of Minos was a powerful man with a huge fleet and army. He demanded that Athens feed his monster with fourteen young men and women each year.

Theseus persuaded his father to let him go as one of the victims – with the intention of killing the fearsome beast that was said to be half-bull, half-man. King Aegeus agreed reluctantly, but made Theseus promise that if he survived to return to Athens, he would change the black sails for white ones, so the old man could stand on the cliffs and know he had not lost his beloved son.

When he arrived in Crete, Theseus made a good impression as a dashing young prince of Athens. The daughter of King Minos, Ariadne, was very taken with him. Just as Medea had done with Jason, Ariadne offered to help Theseus in return for a promise of marriage. When he agreed, she gave him a ball of thread that he could unwind as he went through the labyrinth under the palace and so find his way back. It's possible he was expecting something more impressive.

The next morning, Theseus and the other thirteen were herded into the maze as food for the Minotaur. Theseus tied the thread to the door and unwound it as they searched for the beast. They found him asleep and Theseus tore off one of his horns. As the Minotaur woke enraged, Theseus jammed it into his neck, killing the monster.

Taking loyal Ariadne with him, Theseus sailed back to Athens. On the way, the god Dionysus appeared and said Ariadne was already promised to him – and that Theseus should abandon her on an island. He did so and sailed off without her. It is difficult not to wonder if Theseus the trickster had intended to do that all along, making up the whole bit about Dionysus afterwards.

Either way, his punishment came quickly. He forgot his promise to take down the black sails, so when his ship approached Athens, his elderly father believed Theseus had been killed by the Minotaur. King Aegeus leaped from a cliff into the sea and was drowned. From that point, the sea was known as the Aegean.

As well as the longer legends, you probably should know that Pandora opened a box/jar that let all the world's evils fly out – a metaphor today for doing something awful that can't be undone. Perhaps you should also know that Narcissus was a youth who fell in love with his own reflection and starved to death looking at it. There is a flower called a 'narcissus' that grows next to rivers and so looks at its own reflection. We also use the word 'narcissist' to mean someone in love with themselves.

You might be interested to learn that the goddess Athena became patron of Athens rather than Poseidon because though he brought the sea, she planted an olive tree – and for Greeks then and today, olives are life. Or that the word 'arachnid' comes from Arachne, who thought she was a better weaver than Athena and was turned into a spider as a punishment, to weave webs for ever. Or that Icarus flew too close to the sun, or . . . a hundred other examples.

These are tales with origins lost so far back they are mingled with mythical elements – men of bronze, strange singing Sirens. These are the stories – and the heroes – known to the playwrights of Athens, the soldiers of Sparta and Thebes. When the Roman empire reached its height, the stories of Zeus had become tales of Jupiter, but there was Hercules, there was Jason and Theseus, still. They have influenced all that came after. In that way, they are the thread that leads through the labyrinth, bringing us home.

With a good-sized group of people of all ages, these can be a lot of fun. The trick with the first is not to sneeze.

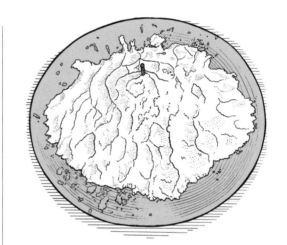

## ① FLOUR AND MATCHSTICK

You'll need a large plate, a packet of white flour and a box of matches. Pile the flour into the centre of the plate, forming a cone. Stand the matchstick up in the cone.

Using ordinary kitchen knives, take it in turns to slice away a piece of the flour. Each slice can be as small or large as you like. You'll want the first slices to be quite large, then get smaller and smaller as you reach the area around the match. Whoever makes the matchstick fall has to put their hands behind their back and pick up the match in their teeth. This usually results in a faceful of flour. Reset with a new match and go again.

(2)

# SPOONS/PIG

These two are so similar, we've kept them as one choice, though both have their supporters.

For 'Spoons', you need a pack of cards, and one spoon less than the number of players. You can play this one with a larger group – six or eight is fine.

Prepare by selecting as many sets of four cards as you have people. If you have six at the table, you might select four queens, four kings, four jacks, four aces, four tens and four nines. Put the rest of the pack aside and shuffle only these sets of four together.

All these cards are dealt, so that each player has four. The aim of the game is to collect four of the same card. If you were given an ace, two kings and a nine, you might decide to concentrate on kings and discard the ace or the nine.

Each player keeps three, puts one face down on the table and waits to begin. This should be as fast as possible. Choose a speaker to say '1, 2, 3 . . . pass'. On the word 'pass', each player slides the card they don't want facedown to the left, and picks up the one that is pushed towards them. They examine that new card and consider whether to keep it or discard it – aiming always to get a set of four.

This '1, 2, 3 . . . pass' routine goes on at speed, until someone at the table gets a set of four cards. That person immediately picks up a spoon and touches it to their nose. They can do this obviously or subtly. When the other players notice, a mad scramble follows as everyone else rushes to snatch up the remaining spoons. One person will be out.

That person continues to play and pass cards, but does it without looking at them and cannot get back into the game.

In this way, player after player is eliminated until there are only two left. At this point, they have to sit on opposite sides of the table, facing each other, with a single spoon on the table before them. The cards should be split in two. Each half of the pack is put on the outside of the two players, so that they have to turn their heads to see both of them.

To the chant of '1, 2, 3 . . . turn', the top card of each of the packs is turned over by two other players. Each of the final pair has to look left and right to see both cards. When they are the same, they grab the last spoon to find a winner. 'Pig' is exactly the same, except instead of spoons, the player who collects four of the same card first puts their finger to their nose and pushes up to make a pig expression. This is harder to detect than the sudden grab for spoons. Both versions are a lot of fun.

# EXTRAORDINARY STORIES –
# PART TWO: MOUNT COOK, 1982

Sir Edmund Hillary climbed this peak in 1948, as part of his preparation for Everest. Also known as 'Aoraki', it is the highest in New Zealand and lies in the Mount Cook National Park. It remains an intensely dangerous challenge today. Each year, around 150–200 people climb it, either with guides or, just as often, without. Rather wonderfully, there is no requirement to register a climb, so exact numbers are unknown. Over the last century, something like eighty climbers have died in the attempt – and sixty remain in the high crevasses or buried in the ice. It is an extraordinarily harsh environment that punishes the smallest mistakes, claiming the lives of many strong, fit and expert climbers. Yet the rewards clearly outweigh the appalling risks. For those rare few who can reach such places, the beauty and isolation are awe-inspiring. The chance to test themselves to the limits is clearly an irresistible lure. It may be the same deep urge that has raised human beings to cross vast oceans and build skyscrapers.

In 1982, Mark Inglis and Philip Doole were climbing a route on the Middle Peak section of Mount Cook. Both were extremely experienced and in fact had previously been part of the Mount Cook search-and-rescue team. They were as familiar with the mountain as anyone in the world, so when they failed to return the first day, those who knew them were not immediately worried. However, the weather was getting worse and a serious storm was on the way.

Don Bogie had also been part of the search-and-rescue team the summer before. He literally wrote the book on Alpine rescue techniques in the Mount Cook National Park. He had himself spent a night on the mountain in poor conditions more than once. The storm was reducing visibility to nothing, but he knew Inglis and Doole would dig a snow cave and rest in it, waiting for the storm to pass. In blizzards and howling gales, shelter is the key to survival.

Up on the Middle Peak, Inglis and Doole had found an alcove not far from a thousand-foot sheer drop. They hacked out a tiny shelter, barely protected from a brutal wind and plummeting temperatures. They ate a little food and settled in for a night on the mountain. They thought they would climb down in the morning, but when the light returned and they tried to leave, the gale was much worse, like a live thing trying to pull them to their deaths. It would have been suicide to climb in those conditions, so they huddled back into the tiny snow cave. Frostbite was an immediate danger as sweat froze in their socks and remained as ice in contact with flesh.

The storm worsened, the wind a constant howl. Visibility was at zero and all they could do was hold on. They ate a single biscuit each day and some drink mix, using body heat to melt snow to drink. By the third day, frostbite had damaged the feet of both men, making them swell. On the fourth day, Inglis knew they would not be getting out on their own. They had to be rescued – and they had no way of communicating with the rescue teams, even to tell them where they were. Inglis attached a red jacket to an ice screw in the hope that it would flap around and be spotted by a search-and-rescue team or a helicopter.

In the village below, the storm made any chance of a rescue impossible. Nothing could fly safely, though rescuers and friends took off anyway in a helicopter, searching for the missing pair. The rescue team knew Inglis and Doole had no sleeping bags and no stove, so as each day passed, the chances of finding them alive dropped further and further.

On the seventh day, the storm lifted long enough to fly search runs in the helicopter. At around seven in the evening, pilot Ron Small spotted the red jacket waving in the wind. The wind made it impossible to land and take them down, a heartbreaking realisation for Inglis and Doole. Frostbite had eaten into them and they were starving and exhausted.

Ron Small managed to drop bags of vital supplies to them. For the first time in a week, they had food, a stove, sleeping bags – and a radio. They began communicating with the rescuers, but had to conserve battery power, clicking once for yes and twice for no. Even so, it was an enormous relief to hear the voices of the others and to know that their families had been told they were alive. On the ground, Don Bogie began to prepare plans to drop climbers close to the pair. Spirits rose, only to be dashed once more.

Don Bogie and the Iroquois helicopter

That night, the storm grew worse again, stealing hope of a rescue. Finding the men was one thing, getting them down quite another. The gale-force winds continued and thick frozen mist made it impossible to get back to the area. Inglis and Doole remained where they were, growing weaker and weaker as each day passed. They were too damaged by then to get out on their own. All they could do was wait, at the mercy of the elements. Inglis developed a chest infection he could not treat. On day ten, the radio batteries died – their precious link to the outside world. At this point, all of New Zealand was following the story on television, waiting to hear if the men would survive.

On day thirteen, a New Zealand Air Force Iroquois helicopter joined the team to help ferry climbers to a position on the Empress Shelf, around 1,500 feet below Inglis and Doole. Conditions were poor and the whirring rotor blades threw up a white-out of snow. The pilot was unable to see and his tailplane touched the ice, flipping the helicopter over. Those inside bailed out onto the snow, with part of the helicopter hanging over the Empress Shelf. No one was hurt, but it meant Ron Small had to fly a run to rescue the crew, bringing them down safely.

Day fourteen – 29 November 1982 – opened with clearer skies. A team that had been landed on the Empress Shelf with a doctor and emergency medical equipment prepared to see what state the two men were in. It began to snow and a white mist descended. The decision was made to go, and Ron Small flew his helicopter over the position and dropped another radio. The new rescue plan, based on a system developed by Canadian rescue teams, involved taking off with a rescuer dangling on a rope below. Don Bogie had practised the technique and was the man for the job.

Bogie landed and scrambled into the tiny snow cave, where the two men greeted him in delight. They asked about the Iroquois crew and were desperately relieved no one had been killed rescuing them. Inglis was in worse shape than Doole. The two men were airlifted out and taken to hospital.

With Christmas on the way, both Inglis and Doole were told gangrene had set in – the frostbite had killed the flesh of their feet and lower legs. To save their lives, the doctors had to amputate. The operation was set for Christmas Eve. When Inglis and Doole woke on Christmas morning, both men had paid a terrible price – both legs removed below the knee.

Inglis returned to Mount Cook – and reached the summit in 2002. With prosthetic legs, and ice spikes attached to the feet, Doole tried four times. He made it in 2006.

In the same year, Inglis went on to climb Everest. A fall during that climb of the world's highest mountain led to one of his carbon-fibre legs snapping, so that a spare one had to be brought up from base camp. When that new one was attached, he carried on, becoming the first double amputee ever to reach the peak. He also won a silver medal for cycling at the Sydney Paralympics in 2000.

Such men are extraordinary. As well as Joe Simpson of *Touching the Void* fame, we put Douglas Bader in the first *Dangerous Book*. They overcame difficulties greater than most of us will ever know. That determination and courage is inspiring – and puts the trials and petty irritations of ordinary life into some sort of perspective.

*Adapted from* No Mean Feat *by Mark Inglis, published by Random House New Zealand.*

# MAKING PERFUME

It is surprising how many of us once tried to make perfume as a gift for Mother's Day. It felt like a stroke of genius at the time – and cheap, which was an added bonus. The roses were taken from our garden and yes, all right, quite a few other gardens in the local area. A mass of petals and water was boiled on the kitchen stove and left to simmer for hours. It was then strained through paper towels into quite an attractive old perfume bottle – and presented.

The problem was, it looked like brown water. If it had smelled magnificent, that would have been a minor problem. Unfortunately, the smell wasn't great either.

That has rankled for a long time – and we can put it right here. There is a French farmhouse process named 'enfleurage' – roughly, 'putting in the flowers'. It is a way to make a long-lasting perfume that, with a decent bottle, might actually make a good gift. That said, it might be worth asking if the person likes the flower in question, something like, 'Don't these roses smell nice?' Hearing, 'No, I hate roses!' will save you a lot of time and effort.

## ———— YOU WILL NEED ————

- White lard, available from any supermarket.
- Fragrant flower petals of your choice. We used wisteria this time, as they were in bloom here when we started. You'll need access to at least one good plant. This won't really work in winter.
- Perfumer's alcohol. You will probably need an adult to buy this online. Perfumer's alcohol is almost odourless. How much you get depends on how much you intend to make, but it comes in 250ml bottles.
- A small bottle of aromatherapy oil – ambergris or bergamot.
- A sealable Kilner jar and possibly a nice bottle of some kind. It could be an old perfume bottle.
- A small plastic funnel to help pour from one bottle to another.

Melt the lard in a pan at low heat. Some people begin with beef suet and scoop off the fat that rises to the top as part of a purifying process.

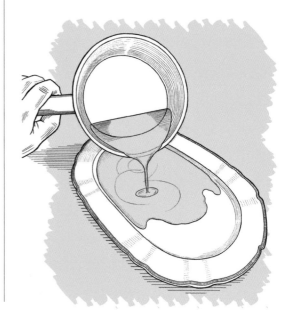

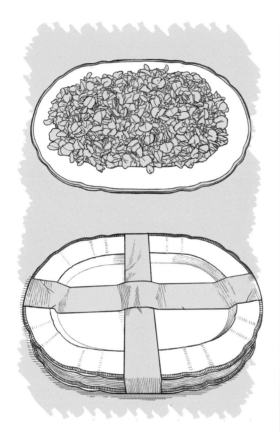

We think that is madness. Lard is already as pure as it gets – and cheap. Half a pound of the stuff cost us 59p in the local supermarket.

Pour the thick liquid lard over a plate and score the surface as it begins to harden. Press an inch-thick layer of petals into the lard and put another plate on top – tape them together. Leave for a day or two. The aim is to fill the lard with the odour of the flowers.

After two days, take the petals out and replace them with new ones – do this two or three times over a week or so. At room temperature in summer, this was a fairly messy business. The wisteria blossoms had to be picked out of the soft lard using fingers and a fork.

When you have removed the flower petals for the third time, we suggest putting the plate briefly in the freezer to harden the lard. This will make it easier to chip it into pieces.

Half-fill your first Kilner jar/bottle with pieces of the lard. If the opening is narrow, push the pieces in with something like a fork handle. Top up with the perfumer's alcohol. Close it up. If you can find some masking or electrical tape, it helps to wrap the lids. You don't want the alcohol to evaporate.

Leave for three months in a cool, dark place. Shake it occasionally if you want, but generally don't worry about it. Try not to forget about it completely until you have left home.

When the three months is up, the alcohol should have taken on the scent from the lard. Strain through cloth into the final bottle. Use a funnel if the opening is small. The alcohol still tends to evaporate, so you'll need to add a few drops of oil, which should help to make it stable and long-lasting. Those aromatherapy oils do have a scent, but it shouldn't overwhelm the odour of the original blooms.

# EMPIRES OF GOLD

Far-called, our navies melt away;
On dune and headland sinks the fire:
Lo, all our pomp of yesterday
Is one with Nineveh and Tyre!

Rudyard Kipling, 'Recessional'

From the beginning of recorded time, mankind has sought control over large swathes of land and sea. Early leaders and city-states desired the wealth, power and security that could only come by conquering other cities and the populations within.

Some empires lasted for just a single lifetime, others for centuries. If each one was given a different colour and speeded up, they would look like flowers opening and closing over millennia. They are interesting for the glorious tendency of human beings to reach beyond their grasp, over and over. Empires and landing men on the moon can be mentioned in the same breath because they spring from the same engine, an engine that will eventually take us to Mars and beyond.

The pattern is often the same: a young and aggressive culture conquers the tribes around it. They expand for a time, using the resources from each victory to go further and faster. Together, they become rich and powerful – a plateau period, during which great art is often produced. Over time, they grow complacent and less willing to defend all they have won – until one day they meet another group of young soldiers. 'Who are you to challenge us?' they ask. 'We are Persians,' comes the reply, or 'We are men of Rome.' That happened to the ancient empire of Carthage when they first encountered Roman soldiers in Sicily. For the merchants of Carthage, Sicily was a distant outpost of an empire. For the Romans, it was a stepping stone to much more – including the lands Carthage ruled. Roman legions destroyed the city of Carthage so thoroughly that it was lost to the knowledge of man for over a thousand years before the ruins were discovered in modern-day Tunisia. Perhaps there are lessons to be learned from these maps. Or perhaps it's just a 'Best Empires of All Time' chapter – a sort of Top Trumps of Conquest.

---

①

## MESOPOTAMIA/SUMERIA
### (c. 2500 BC)

The armies and kingdoms of the area around Mesopotamia (modern-day Iraq) have been giving each other the chop for many thousands of years – from long before the invention of writing. As a

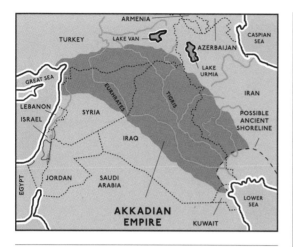

The Akkadian Empire

result, records are scarce, but Sargon of Akkad is one name that has survived. He ruled Mesopotamia around the 24th century BC. (Note that some modern web pages and even some books have begun to use BCE and CE instead of BC and AD. This doesn't stand for 'Before Christian Era' and 'Christian Era', but 'Before Common Era' and 'Common Era' – a meaningless term. It still uses the birth of Christ as its origin point in Year Zero, so it's actually a little bit silly.)

Sargon of Akkad is worth a mention because he conquered the city-states of Sumeria and established a dynasty lasting around a century – an achievement similar to that of Genghis Khan, three thousand years later. Sargon is also credited with the first – or one of the first – multi-nation empires. His memory was revered right into the Persian empire of 400 BC, but we don't know his real name, only the name he chose when he became king. Even that royal name was lost until it was rediscovered in 1870. The British archaeologist Sir Henry Rawlinson came across records of 'Great King Sargon of Akkad' while

excavating Nineveh – the ancient city in Iraq now known as Mosul.

The extent of territory once enjoyed by Sargon of Akkad can only be a rough estimate. Even the location of his capital is unknown – somewhere on the Euphrates. We do know he came from humble beginnings – cast adrift on a river as a baby and saved by a court water-carrier. He became the trusted cup-bearer to a king and eventually rose to conquer Sumeria and the lands around Mesopotamia. He may have reached as far west as Cyprus, the island in the Mediterranean conquered by almost every empire that ever existed.

Sargon built roads, standardised weights and measures – and created peace, once the Sumerian city-states had stopped fighting him. Empires always seem to begin in terror and savagery, but if they survive, they can see a golden period that would surely never have existed without them. Science and the arts flower in empires – which is no small thing to understand.

***

2

## PERSIA – THE ACHAEMENID DYNASTY
### (*c.* 550–330 BC)

The Achaemenids were the ruling house in the first great flowering of the Persian empire that stretched, almost unbelievably, from the western coast of Turkey, Libya and Egypt all the way east to the borders of India. It was the first major empire in history – a superstate, with extraordinary bureaucracy and vast armies. The modern motto of the US Post Office – 'Neither snow nor rain nor heat nor gloom of night stays these couriers from the swift completion of their appointed rounds' – was originally a translation from the Greek Herodotus, writing about the Persian couriers who raced horses up and down the wide royal roads of this empire.

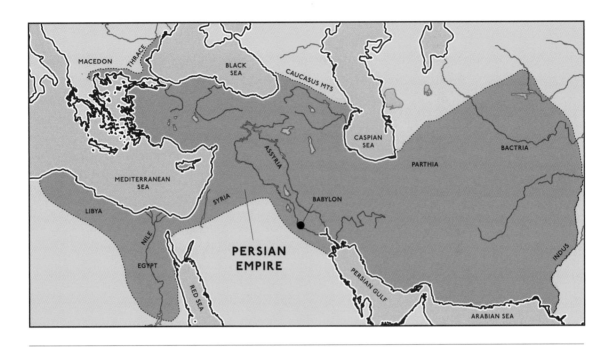

Persia around 500 BC

To grow to such a vast size took generations of constant warfare. All the previous empires and peoples of the area, such as the Babylonians, Medes and Assyrians, were conquered one by one. This was an empire that grew in leaps and bounds from smaller ones that went before it. Only the city-states of Greece stopped the armies of Persia – both at sea and on land. Alexander the Great arrived around 334 BC and crushed the Persian armies on their own territory, which is just as astonishing as it sounds.

---

**3**

## ALEXANDER THE GREAT
### (356–323 BC)

Anyone who could take on and beat the Persian empire deserves a mention. Alexander was a brilliant and charismatic leader, whose armies must have been the best led, equipped, trained and motivated on earth at that time. He could go anywhere he wanted. As he died young, it was the briefest flowering. He left a number of cities named after him, though only Alexandria in Egypt retains the name today. His body was displayed in a glass case in Alexandria. Julius Caesar visited it, as he revered Alexander. Caesar's great-nephew, Emperor Augustus, also went to Egypt and leaned too close over the mummified remains, accidentally breaking the nose. Later, Emperor Caligula visited the tomb and stole Alexander's breastplate. The body was lost in the centuries that followed and no one knows where it is today.

Apart from Alexander's conquests, the extraordinary cultural shift that occurred around the 5th century and 4th centuries BC in Greece did not lead to empires of the ordinary sort. Sparta had no interest in conquering new territories,

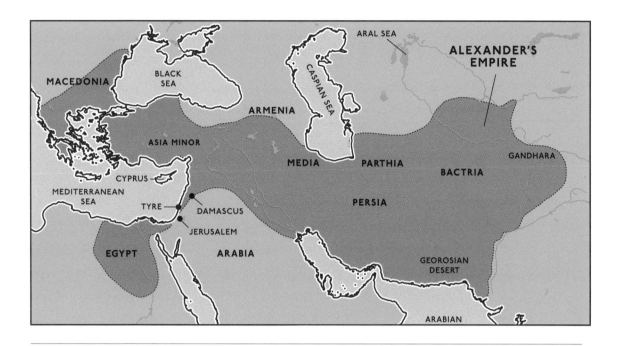

Alexander's Empire

though they hired themselves out as mercenaries. Athens was more interested in trade. The Greeks fought among themselves for centuries, but they did take over some islands and establish a few colonies around Naples in southern Italy. They also invented democracy and philosophy, for which we have reason to be thankful.

----

4

----

## THE MAYAN EMPIRE
### (c. AD 250–900)

The Mayan civilisation stretches the definition of 'empire' a bit. It was more a collection of city-states and a monoculture than an empire. It certainly wasn't one of the largest – though there is a Mayan temple on the island of Java, thousands of miles west and across the entire Pacific, which is interesting. The Mayan territory of Central Amer-

ica stretched from what is today southern Mexico down into Nicaragua. Early settlements were there as early as 2000 BC, but the founding of cities and

The Mayan Empire

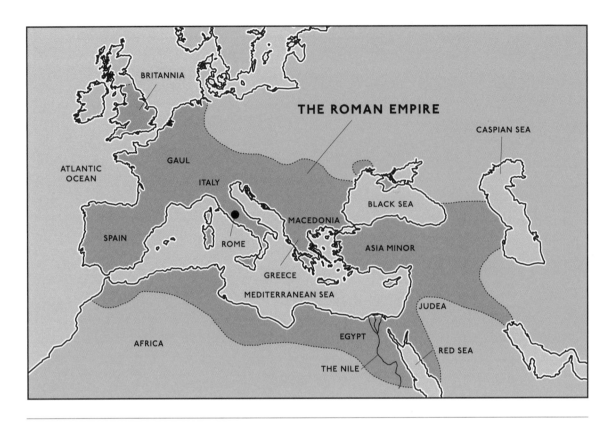

The Roman Empire

building of temples generally took place around the 3rd to 6th centuries AD – though the culture continued right up to the arrival of the Spanish in the 16th century.

---

5

## THE ROMAN EMPIRE
### (c. 300 BC – c. AD 1500)

Estimates vary, but the civilisation that began on seven hills around the single city-state of Rome and ended with the fall of its eastern capital of Constantinople – Istanbul as it is known today – lasted for around 1,800 years. Influenced by Greece, the Romans were magpies of culture,

taking on gods, foods, technology and military techniques – anything they could find that was useful or interesting. They achieved total military dominance in the professional legions created by Julius Caesar's uncle Marius – and then put those up against the wild mobs in Gaul, Spain and Britain with a great deal of success. There were disasters – the chapter on the Twelve Caesars will tell some of them. Yet they established a *Pax Romana* – 'a peace of Rome' – across the continent that allowed science and the arts to flourish for centuries. Echoes of Greek and Latin can be heard in Shakespeare and Milton, as well as half the root words of modern English, French, Spanish and Italian.

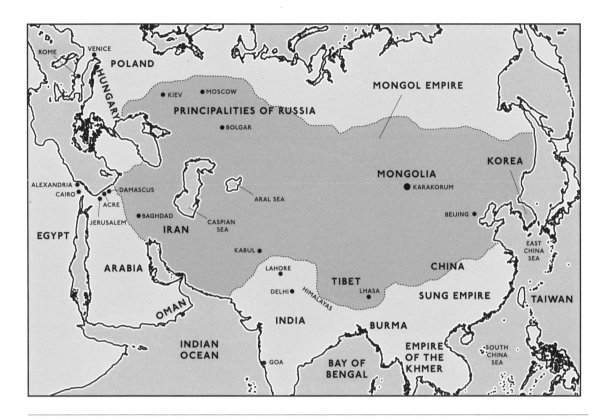

The Mongol Empire

## 6

### MONGOL EMPIRE (c. 1210–1360)

Genghis Khan was born around AD 1160. His father was the leader of a small nomadic tribe in Mongolia, but when he was killed, his family was abandoned and left to die: the mother and six children down to a babe in arms. They were left on the plains of Mongolia, one of the harshest environments on earth. The young boy named Temujin went from utter poverty, almost starving to death, to ruling all of Mongolia and creating the largest single land-mass empire in history. He was certainly a ruthless enemy, but he was a good brother and father to his sons and grandsons. His grandson Kub-

lai Khan ruled all China and was the richest and most powerful man alive. At one point, Mongol master archers and horsemen went deep into Russia in winter, conquering Kiev. They reached through Hungary, where they met and battered armoured knights for the first time. They had no equal on the field of war and only luck – the heart attack of a khan that pulled the armies home again – stopped their advance into the west as well as the east.

The Yuan dynasty of Kublai Khan was a short one, though the name is still used for Chinese currency today. The story of Genghis Khan and those who followed him is simply the greatest rags-to-riches story in human history and a demonstration of how a single life can change the history of the world.

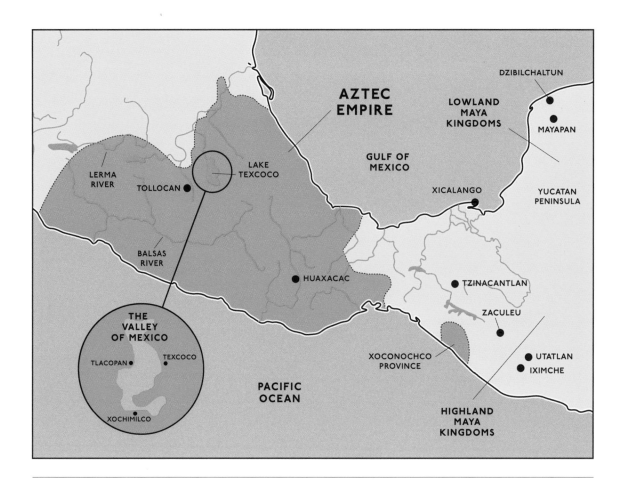

The Aztec Empire around 1520

## THE AZTECS
### (13TH – 15TH CENTURIES)

In a similar way to the beginnings of Rome, the spread of Aztec civilisation began with competing city-states in central Mexico. Constant war forced them to form alliances, which could then attack other, weaker groups. For around three hundred years, larger and larger territories came under the control of a single throne – just as Persia was put together. Once that single dominant culture was established, art and buildings flourished. The Aztecs built enormous temples and developed trade and agriculture. They worshipped a pantheon of gods such as Quetzalcoatl, the feathered serpent, and Tlaloc, the god of rain. By the 16th century, the capital city, Tenochtitlan, had at least 200,000 inhabitants. Like the Mayans, the Aztecs did not survive the shock of meeting the Spanish, a culture with ship and weapon technology so advanced it must have seemed like magic. The culture collapsed when the capital was brutally sacked and destroyed by the invaders.

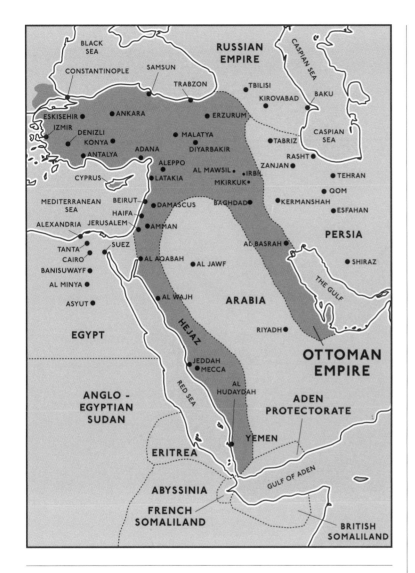

The Ottoman Empire in 1914

and including all of Turkey. It reached its height of power and influence in the 16th and 17th centuries – from 1520, when the Sultan Suleiman came to rule just as the Spanish arrived in Central America. Very much a military leader, Suleiman conquered territories in Hungary, then turned his attention east. He was a lover of poetry and, once again, after all the conquering came a period when art and building flourished. The empire he had built was still a major force at the outbreak of World War I, but it came in on the side of Germany. After some initial successes, the empire came under attack by Russia, France and Britain. Constantinople was occupied by Allied troops, including the Italians, which must have been historically interesting. The Ottoman empire came to an end by fire and the sword – the crucible from which modern Turkey was created. It is also remembered today for the methodical massacre of 1.5 million Armenians.

8

## THE OTTOMAN EMPIRE
### (13TH – 19TH CENTURIES)

With ancient Byzantium/Constantinople as its capital city, the Ottoman empire could be seen as a second throw of the dice for some of the old Persian territories, extending to the Middle East

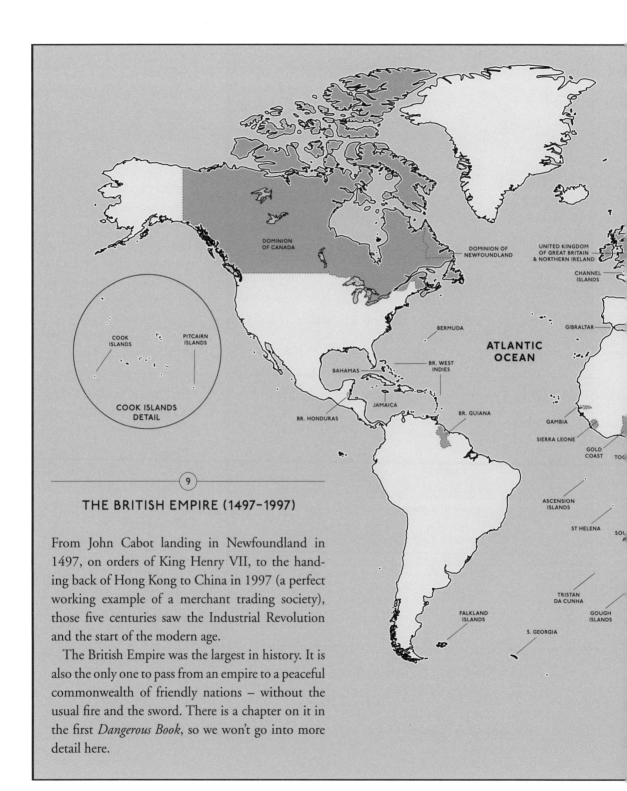

**9**

## THE BRITISH EMPIRE (1497–1997)

From John Cabot landing in Newfoundland in 1497, on orders of King Henry VII, to the handing back of Hong Kong to China in 1997 (a perfect working example of a merchant trading society), those five centuries saw the Industrial Revolution and the start of the modern age.

The British Empire was the largest in history. It is also the only one to pass from an empire to a peaceful commonwealth of friendly nations – without the usual fire and the sword. There is a chapter on it in the first *Dangerous Book*, so we won't go into more detail here.

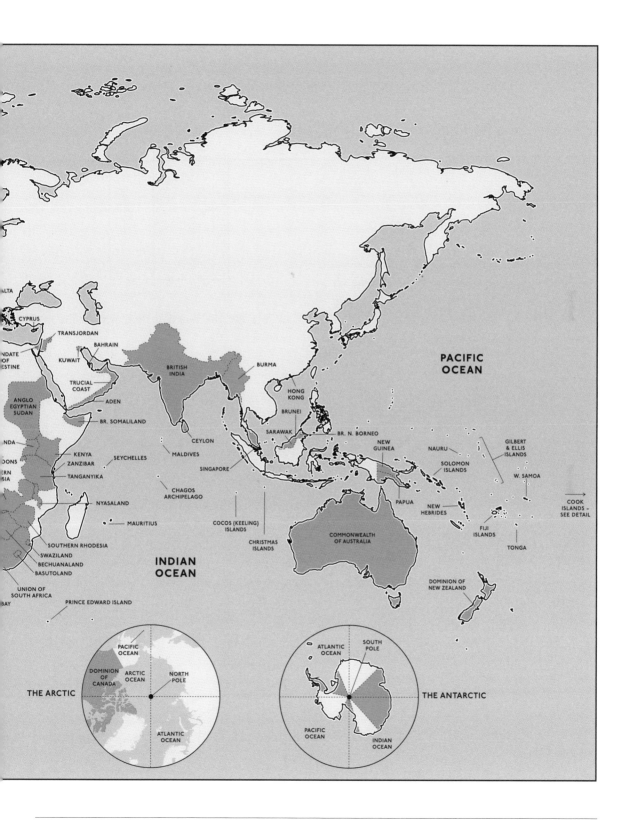

ALTA

CYPRUS

TRANSJORDAN

BAHRAIN

NDATE
OF
ESTINE

KUWAIT

TRUCIAL
COAST

ADEN

ANGLO
EGYPTIAN
SUDAN

BR. SOMALILAND

NDA

OONS

ERN
SIA

KENYA

ZANZIBAR

TANGANYIKA

SEYCHELLES

BRITISH
INDIA

BURMA

HONG
KONG

BRUNEI

SARAWAK

CEYLON

MALDIVES

SINGAPORE

CHAGOS
ARCHIPELAGO

NYASALAND

MAURITIUS

SOUTHERN RHODESIA

SWAZILAND

BECHUANALAND

BASUTOLAND

UNION OF
SOUTH AFRICA

BAY

PRINCE EDWARD ISLAND

INDIAN
OCEAN

COCOS (KEELING)
ISLANDS

CHRISTMAS
ISLANDS

BR. N. BORNEO

NEW
GUINEA

PAPUA

NAURU

SOLOMON
ISLANDS

NEW
HEBRIDES

FIJI
ISLANDS

COMMONWEALTH
OF AUSTRALIA

PACIFIC
OCEAN

GILBERT
& ELLIS
ISLANDS

W. SAMOA

COOK
ISLANDS –
SEE DETAIL

TONGA

DOMINION OF
NEW ZEALAND

THE ARCTIC

PACIFIC
OCEAN

DOMINION
OF
CANADA

ARCTIC
OCEAN

NORTH
POLE

ATLANTIC
OCEAN

THE ANTARCTIC

ATLANTIC
OCEAN

SOUTH
POLE

PACIFIC
OCEAN

INDIAN
OCEAN

Here are six more – answers at the end.

## THE DAMAGED CHESSBOARD

A chessboard has 64 squares, but this one has two opposite corner squares missing and only 62. Albert has 31 dominoes that will each cover two squares perfectly. So the question is, can he cover the broken board entirely with his 31 dominoes?

## STRICTLY FOR SQUARES

Here we have a square array of 64 squares, just like a chessboard.

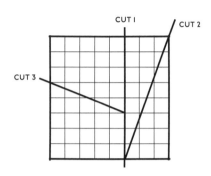

Now let's cut the board in two with a cut five squares across: Cut 1.

That gives two rectangles – one 5 × 8 squares = 40, and one 3 × 8 = 24. The squares still add up to 64.

Now let's cut the 3 × 8 rectangle along the diagonal: Cut 2.

Finally, let's cut the 5 × 8 rectangle on a sloping line three squares down on the left and five squares down on the right: Cut 3.

We now have two triangles and two four-sided shapes. We can easily arrange them to form a rect-angle. But this rectangle is five squares high and thirteen squares wide. 5 × 13 = 65 squares. So the question is, where did the other square come from?

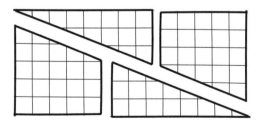

---
9
---

## A WEIGHT ON YOUR MIND

You can weigh anything. You could even weigh a whale – take it to a whaleway station. But this puzzle involves placing weights on either side of a balance scales. In fact, using this method, you can balance any weight from 1 to 120 units. The question is, what are the five weights that would enable you to do this?

---
10
---

## A ROPE AROUND THE EARTH

A chap once put a rope around the earth – I heard it on the noose, but it could have been fake noose? The rope would have to be 40,000 km long, as that is how far it is around the earth.

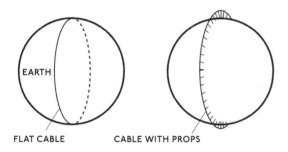

FLAT CABLE          CABLE WITH PROPS

However, conservationists pointed out that the rope impeded snails, slugs, tortoises and all kinds of small animals, as they might not be able to crawl over it. So the man decided to raise the rope on posts, all the way around the earth, so the impeded creatures could crawl under it.

He decided to make the posts all one metre high. The question was, how much longer would the rope now need to be, to still reach around the earth on the one-metre posts?

---
11
---

## THE STRANDED GIRL
## AND THE DASHING PILOT

A young girl sits sadly on her suitcase at an airport. Someone has stolen her purse, money and credit cards. How is she going to get home? A dashing young man stops dashing and slows down to ask her what the trouble is. When she tells him her story, he says, 'Don't worry. I'm a pilot. Where I am going, I can drop you off at your destination without going out of my way!' So the question is, where is he going?

---
12
---

## THE BEAR FACTS

A fella goes hunting with his camera, in the hope he can spot and photograph a bear. So he leaves his camp and walks 5 miles due south. No bears to be seen, so he turns and walks 5 miles due east, where he sees a bear. But the bear sees him and charges towards him. So he turns due north and runs 5 miles with a bear behind him, except that after a mile or so the bear gives up. But the man completes the 5 miles north and is amazed to find that he is back at his camp. So the big question is, what colour was the bear?

*Answers*

## THE DAMAGED CHESSBOARD

No he can't. The two missing squares are both the same colour, and if you try it, you'll see no domino can cover two squares of the same colour. If you take out two white squares, you'll always be left with two uncovered black diagonals – and one domino. So, covering the 62 squares with 31 two-square dominoes is, in two words, Im – Possible.

## STRICTLY FOR SQUARES

The mystery is solved by closely examining the diagonal lines in this diagram. If you make a model of the original 8 × 8 array and cut it carefully, when you assemble the 5 × 13 diagram, you will notice the pieces don't quite fit. There is a very narrow gap across the diagonal line. The area of this gap would exactly equal the one extra square.

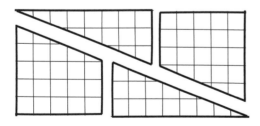

## A WEIGHT ON YOUR MIND

The weights need to be 1 unit, 3 units, 9 units, 27 units and a massive 81 units. Together they add up to 121 units and you can balance any weight from 1 unit to 120 with these five and a simple balance scale with two pans. Here are a few examples.

2 units are weighed with the 3 on one side and the 1 on the other. The difference is 2 units.
7 units are balanced with 9 + 1 on one side and 3 on the other. 10 – 3 = 7
90 units can be balanced using just the 9 + 81 on one side.
100 is balanced with 81 + 27 + 1 against 9 on the other.
105 is 81 + 27 – 3.

So you can measure any number of units from 1 to 121, using just these five weights.

---10---

## A ROPE AROUND THE EARTH

The 40,000km rope, to still fit around the earth on posts one metre high, would need to be 40,000 km long plus approximately another 6.28 metres. It is all to do with $\pi$ (pi).

If you look at a ball from any angle what you see is a circle. When you think about it, there are only two things you can measure with a circle – the distance across it, and the distance around. But no matter how big your circle, the distance around it is approximately $\pi$ times the distance across it. $\pi$ is 3.14159 . . . The decimal places go on for ever, but a usable approximation for $\pi$ is 3 1/7 or 3.14.

Our rope-wrapping chap, to raise his rope one metre all around the earth, needs to make that circle two metres wider. So the extra rope needed would be 2 × 3.14 or 6.28 metres – that is all the extra rope he would need. As they say in film and TV, that's a wrap.

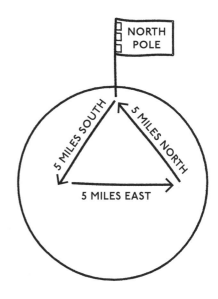

---

### 11

## THE STRANDED GIRL
## AND THE DASHING PILOT

He is either going to a point exactly opposite where they are on the globe, or he is going right around the earth and back to where they already are. Either way, wherever on earth she might be going, he can take that direction, drop her off at her destination and then continue around the globe till he is home again.

---

### 12

## THE BEAR FACTS

The bear has to be white as it must have been a polar bear and the man must have built his camp right at the North Pole. If he walked 5 miles south, then 5 miles east and then 5 miles north, he would be back at the North Pole, where any bears would have to be polar bears.

Now here is an extra question. Could his camp have been somewhere else? In fact, could the man have seen, not a polar bear, but a penguin? Think about this one before you read the answer below.

The answer is his camp could be in an infinite number of places, all quite close to the South Pole. Imagine a circle around the South Pole exactly 5 miles in length. It would be approximately 1.6km from the South Pole. Now, if his camp was at any point 5 miles north of that circle, he could walk 5 miles south, once round the circle 5 miles east or west and then 5 miles north and be back at his camp. But there are an infinite number of such points.

*It's just as well Polar Bears live near the North Pole while Penguins live near the South Pole. Polar Bears hate Penguins. They don't know how to get the silver paper off.*

# TWO GREAT CARD GAMES

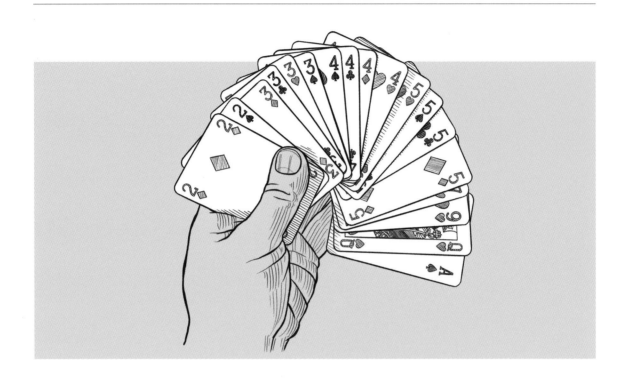

## NOMINATION WHIST

Nomination whist is a brilliant game and easy to learn. It works best with four people, with each player given thirteen cards – a quarter of the fifty-two-card pack. If you play with five or six, you have to adjust the number of cards to ten or eight each – and agree to leave out a few low-value cards.

Begin with a sheet of paper, listing the names of those present across the top and the suits down the side. In a friendly game, these can be chosen beforehand – at random, as it makes no difference.

| | JOHN | JANE | MUM | DAD |
|---|---|---|---|---|
| ♥ | | | | |
| ♦ | | | | |
| ♣ | | | | |
| ♥ | | | | |
| ♠ | | | | |
| | | | | |

Choose the first dealer and deal four hands. It's good manners not to touch the cards before they have all been dealt. It distracts the dealer.

Before anyone picks up and looks at their cards, agree the suit for the hand – say, hearts. These will be 'trumps' – the most powerful suit that beats all others. Now, this explanation might seem complicated at first, so just breathe slowly, read slowly and go over it again. Perhaps it does feel hard when it's new, like almost everything. Part of learning is recognising the strange frustration that steals over us when we are soaking up new information – and ignoring it to get to the point where we can hardly remember how difficult we once thought it was. We'll 'talk' you through a hand in a bit – and it will become obvious.

## 1. PREDICTING TRICKS

Each player picks up their cards and usually shuffles them into suits, trying to work out how many 'tricks' they might take.

You win a trick by putting down the highest card. Aces often win, but if you have a queen, say, you'll know there is at least a king and an ace out there to beat it. Part of the game, then, is to watch which cards are played, to know if you have a better chance to play yours.

Quick example: you have the ten of clubs. First trick, someone plays the ace and the other players put the king, the queen and the jack on it – all complaining. Your ten is now the highest club out there, but it still might not make a trick. Any of those other players might have run out of clubs and can then play a trump to beat your ten.

There are thirteen tricks in all when playing with four people, ten with five (two cards left over) and only eight tricks with six people (four cards left over).

Before the first card is laid down, players must say aloud how many tricks they think they can make. Starting to the left of the dealer, they say a number and the dealer (or anyone else) marks it in the little box next to their name. A player with the ace and king of trumps knows those cards are guaranteed tricks. If the rest of his hand is strong, he might say 'Five' – a confident prediction. Most will content themselves with three, two or even zero. Throwing away high cards to hit a target of zero is a skill in itself.

The last person to predict the tricks they will win is the dealer again – with one problem. They are not allowed to choose a number that adds up to the number of tricks out there: thirteen, ten or eight. That is the slight disadvantage of dealing. If you have the worst hand in the world but the other three have predicted five, five and three – thirteen between them – you can't say 'Zero'. In that case, you would choose 'one' and hope someone else makes a mistake or has overestimated their hand.

Once all the predictions are written down, the game begins. So it's a simple process: label and draw out the sheet, deal the hands, predict the tricks and start.

## 2. PLAYING

The person to the dealer's left puts down the first card. If hearts are trumps, nothing will beat the top hearts, so there's no point putting them down early. Non-trump aces might take an easy trick at the beginning, or get trumped immediately.

As each trick is won, the collection of cards is gathered up and laid down next to the person who won it, usually across each other for easy counting – and to show the other players how many tricks they have. The tactics of remembering who has won their tricks and doesn't want to win another is a vital part of this. In our family, we have to constantly ask the question 'How many tricks did Arthur want, again?' The paper is consulted and we nod and sneer suspiciously at each other.

The essence of it is a memory game – remembering which cards have been dealt, how many trumps are still out there and so on. Obviously a lucky hand is always possible – and quite a joyous event. Being given a hand full of trumps and predicting you'll take all the tricks is fun, but just luck. The skill comes in both getting your own target and denying someone else theirs.

One tactic might be for someone to lead a low trump to draw out the high cards. If you have a four, a nine and a jack of the trump suit, you might lead the nine to try to force the ace, king and queen out of hiding. If someone has only one in that suit, they must play it, after all. There are few things more upsetting in this game than having to lay a high trump on an even higher one – wasting it.

If someone leads a suit you don't have, you can put a trump on it. This will usually take the trick, except for the rare occasions when someone else does the same and puts a higher trump on. However, you don't have to. If you've predicted a low target for yourself, or if you've already reached your target, you'll want to throw away remaining high cards. Leaving high cards or trumps in your hand right to the last few tricks is dangerous – it's too easy to win one of those by accident and then, when you're leading, to win the last couple as well. Few things are more disappointing than predicting four tricks and ending up with six – see scoring.

As with almost everything in life, the game gets better and easier with practice. When you have a family or group of friends who all know nomination whist, you can have a fairly raucous time – for all ages, pretty much. Watching someone else playing a seven, say, when they have all the tricks they need, only to see everyone else put a two, three and five on it – forcing them to take the trick and ruining their entire plan . . . well, it's pretty satisfying, unless it happens to you.

## 3. SCORING

At the end, the tricks are added up and compared against the nominated targets. If the target has been met, ten points are added to the score. So a target of three, with three tricks won, would give a score of thirteen. A target of zero, with no tricks won, would give a score of ten.

If the target was missed, the player just gets one point per trick won. So a target of four, with six tricks won, would get six points.

Consistency is vital here. The player who drops the fewest rounds is most likely to win, at least in our games. On the scoresheet, add the totals as you go along for easy comparison. So if 'David' gets thirteen points in the first round and eleven in the second, write down twenty-four.

That's pretty much it. We usually play four or six

| | JOHN | | DAVID | | MUM | | DAD | |
|---|---|---|---|---|---|---|---|---|
| ♥ | 0 | 10 | 3 | 13 | 2 | 12 | 1 | 0 |
| ♦ | 1 | 21 | 1 | 24 | 3 | 14 | 1 | 11 |
| ♣ | 1 | 32 | 2 | 25 | 2 | 26 | 3 | 24 |
| ♥ | 0 | 42 | 2 | 37 | 4 | 40 | 0 | 34 |
| ♠ | 2 | DOUBLE 44 | 0 | POINTS 57 | 4 | ROUND 68 | 1 | OF DOOM 56 |
| | 4TH | | 2ND | | WINNER | | 3RD | |

hands and often do a final 'Double-Points Round of Doom', which can change a whole game. Nomination whist is a simpler form of the game of bridge and we recommend it.

①

2

## CHEAT

Despite the name, this is a great card game for all the family. The rules are incredibly simple, but this is, hands down, the noisiest card game we know.

Shuffle and deal the cards out. Give the players a moment to arrange them – suits are not important, so number order is the usual way. Whoever is to the left of the dealer will begin.

The aim of the game is to get rid of all your cards. Going round in a circle, each player can lay one, two, three or four cards face down. As they do so, the player must say what they are aloud – 'Two queens', for example.

The next player is then limited to putting down the same card, the one below it or the one above. So in this example, they could lay down queens, jacks or kings. If someone plays an ace, the next player will have to lay aces, kings or twos. If they don't have any of those cards, they are going to have to lay down another and lie aloud about what it is. A common tactic is to put just one card onto the pile if you don't have the right one. The table might believe 'One four', but 'Three fours' is much harder to sell – especially if someone else is looking at two of them in their hand.

As each card or cards is put down and announced, there is a brief moment when someone can say 'Cheat!' It has to be before the next card is dealt – and of course the next player is keen to get a move on and get rid of their own cards. When a cheat is called, the player who laid down the last card/s has to turn them over and reveal them to the table. If their 'Three jacks' turn out to be two sevens and a four, they take all the cards in the pile back into their own hand. This can result in huge

collections of cards and the nickname 'Big Pack', as in 'Come on, Big Pack, it's your turn.' If the 'Three jacks' actually turn out to be three jacks, the person who called 'Cheat!' has to take all the cards on the table into their own hand – so calling out a cheat always comes with a risk. The aim is a fast-paced game, going quickly round the table: 'Two fours . . . Three fives . . . One five . . . Two sixes . . . Three sevens . . . Cheat!'

One form of cheating is putting down three cards and saying 'Two jacks' – ignoring the third card. However, most of it comes when a player has to follow, for instance, a four with threes, fours or fives, but has none of them in his hand. You get a situation then, when a few hands have been picked up, when one person might have all the possible cards – and so waits with delight for a cheat they know *must* come.

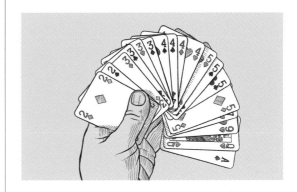

# THE PAPER BOX

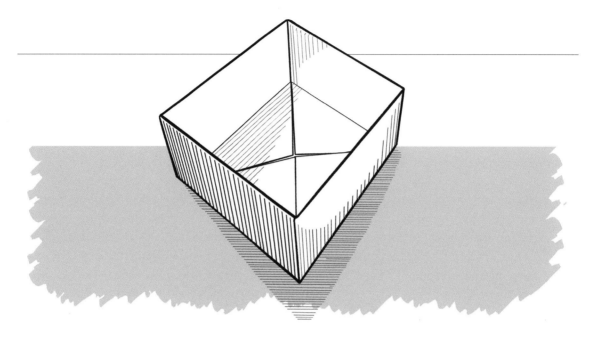

A part from the obvious – it can be used to hold things and it will float for a while, at least as well as the paper boat from the first book – this has no earthly use whatsoever. It's difficult to explain to someone who doesn't see the point. Like Mount Everest, these things are just 'there'. That said, if you make two – and fit one inside the other, it will work brilliantly as a gift box. In short, it's worth learning. You'll need a sheet of A4 and a pair of scissors. That's it.

First turn your A4 rectangle into a square by folding one corner over on itself. Use the scissors to cut the strip away – precision improves the result enormously.

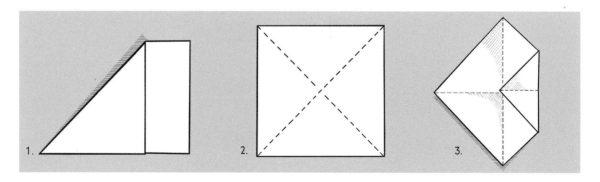

Once you have your square, fold the extra diagonal into it, then fold each corner into the centre. Crease everything tightly. Sharp lines are good.

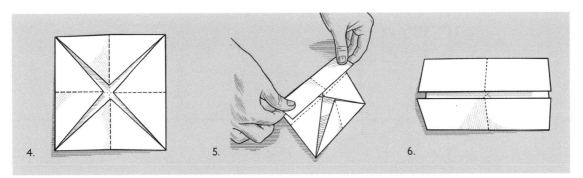

You'll have made a shape similar to Fig. 4. After that, fold a rectangle in from the outer edge to the centre on both sides.

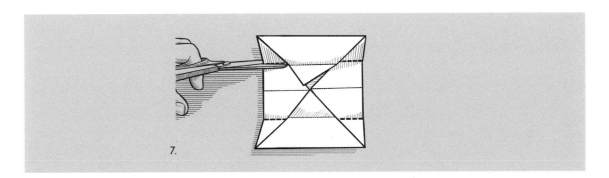

Open it up again and, with the scissors, make four cuts. We've included dotted lines to show where they go, though you don't have to. Each cut should be straight and just far enough in to cut the triangle. This is the only tricky part, honestly. The rest is just folding.

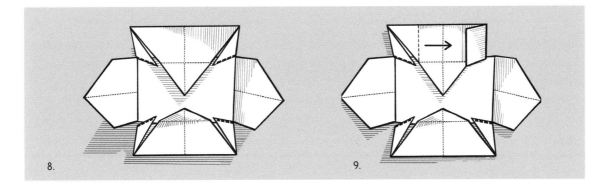

These four cuts allow you to open it up as you can see here. Now fold a tab in towards the centre line, as you see in Fig. 9. Follow that with three more: its opposite and the ones on the other side.

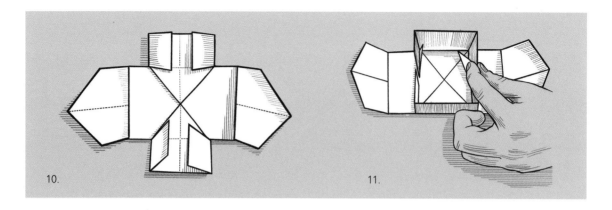

Bring those four tabs upright and allow them to open out. You should see the basic structure of the box now, as in Fig. 11. Nearly finished.

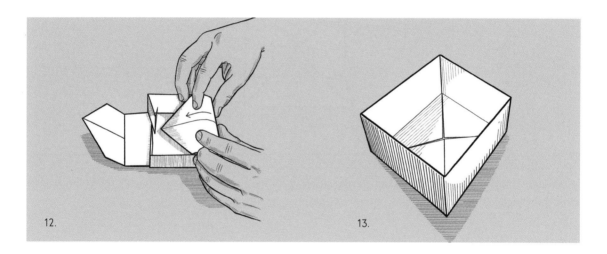

While holding the tabs together, fold over the side piece, pressing it down to hold the whole thing securely. This is a little fiddly. Repeat with the other side. Do your best to pinch and crimp every folded seam, to make it as sharp and neat as possible.

When you have finished admiring a very impressive box, make another one and wiggle it into place as a lid. This is an enormously satisfying thing to be able to make from just a couple of pieces of paper.

# FIVE GREAT SPEECHES

There is something in mankind that responds to the right words. Throughout history, orators have stood before crowds – to inspire new action, to mourn, to call for vengeance. Constraints of space prevent more than short extracts here, but the purpose is for you to read them aloud – and not just to read, but to declaim: to stand with head up and shoulders back, speaking the words clearly and slowly, pausing on each comma and full stop – in short, to fill the room.

1

## 'FRIENDS, ROMANS, COUNTRYMEN'

This funeral oration for Julius Caesar, spoken by Consul **Mark Antony**, is from the Shakespeare play, but Mark Antony actually did address the crowds in Rome after Caesar's murder. The common people of Rome mourned a great man. Mark Antony not only showed them the torn and bloody toga Caesar had worn, but also a wax effigy of his body, with twenty-three wounds visible to all. Slowly, Mark Antony turned the mob against the assassins. Up to that point, men like Brutus and Cassius claimed to have saved Rome from a tyrant. After this speech, they had to run, before the crowd tore them to pieces.

Friends, Romans, countrymen,
lend me your ears.
I come to bury Caesar, not to praise him.
The evil that men do lives after them;
The good is oft interred with their bones.

So let it be with Caesar. The noble Brutus
Hath told you Caesar was ambitious.
If it were so, it was a grievous fault,
And grievously hath Caesar answered it.
Here, under leave of Brutus and the rest—
For Brutus is an honourable man,
So are they all, all honourable men—
Come I to speak in Caesar's funeral.

He was my friend, faithful and just to me.
But Brutus says he was ambitious,
And Brutus is an honourable man.
He hath brought many captives home to
Rome,
Whose ransoms did the general coffers fill.
Did this in Caesar seem ambitious?
When that the poor have cried, Caesar hath
wept.
Ambition should be made of sterner stuff.
Yet Brutus says he was ambitious,
And Brutus is an honourable man.
You all did see that on the Lupercal
I thrice presented him a kingly crown,
Which he did thrice refuse. Was this ambition?
Yet Brutus says he was ambitious,
And sure he is an honourable man.
I speak not to disprove what Brutus spoke,
But here I am to speak what I do know.
You all did love him once, not without cause.
What cause withholds you then to
mourn for him?
O judgement, thou art fled to brutish beasts,
And men have lost their reason! Bear with me.
My heart is in the coffin there with Caesar,
And I must pause till it come back to me.

Note the power of repetition! Four times Mark
Antony says Brutus is an honourable man, until
it is finally clear he means the complete opposite.

----------- (2) -----------

## QUEEN ELIZABETH I
## AT TILBURY DOCKS

In 1588, a terrifying armada of Spanish ships was
clustering along the French coast, about to invade
England. **Queen Elizabeth I** addressed her troops
at Tilbury docks. With a hostile army assembling
at Calais and the Spanish fleet ready to bring fire
and the sword, the situation was desperate.

My loving people, we have been persuaded
by some, that are careful of our safety,
to take heed how we commit ourselves to
armed multitudes, for fear of treachery; but I
assure you, I do not desire to live to distrust
my faithful and loving people. Let tyrants fear!
I have always so behaved myself that, under
God, I have placed my chiefest strength and
safeguard in the loyal hearts and good-will of
my subjects; and therefore, I am come amongst
you, as you see, at this time, not for my
recreation and disport, but being resolved, in
the midst and heat of the battle, to live and die
amongst you all; to lay down for my God, and
for my kingdom, and my people, my honour
and my blood, even in the dust.

I know I have the body of a weak and feeble
woman, but I have the heart and stomach of
a king – and of a king of England too, and
think foul scorn that Parma or Spain, or any
prince of Europe, should dare to invade the
borders of my realm; to which rather than any

dishonour shall grow by me, I myself will take up arms; I myself will be your general, judge, and rewarder of every one of your virtues in the field. I know already, for your forwardness you have deserved rewards and crowns – and we do assure you in the word of a prince, they shall be duly paid you. In the meantime, my lieutenant general shall be in my stead, than whom never prince commanded a more noble or worthy subject; not doubting but by your obedience to my general, by your concord in the camp, and your valour in the field, we shall shortly have a famous victory over those enemies of my God, of my kingdom, and of my people.

Neither the Spanish nor their French allies were allowed to land. They were scattered by fire, ship, storm and Sir Francis Drake.

3

## THE GETTYSBURG ADDRESS

Standing in the cemetery at Gettysburg in 1863, President **Abraham Lincoln** was only too aware of the loss of life that place had seen just a year before, when more than fifty thousand perished in one of the most brutal battles of the American Civil War.

Four score and seven years ago, our fathers brought forth on this continent a new nation, conceived in liberty, and dedicated to the proposition that all men are created equal.

Now we are engaged in a great civil war, testing whether that nation, or any nation so conceived and so dedicated, can long endure. We are met on a great battlefield of that war. We have come to dedicate a portion of that field, as a final resting place for those who here gave their lives that that nation might live. It is altogether fitting and proper that we should do this.

But, in a larger sense, we cannot dedicate – we cannot consecrate – we cannot hallow* – this ground. The brave men, living and dead, who struggled here have consecrated it far above our poor power to add or detract. The world will little note, nor long remember what we say here, but it can never forget what they did here.

It is for us the living, rather, to be dedicated here to the unfinished work which they who fought here have thus far so nobly advanced. It is rather for us to be here dedicated to the great task remaining before us – that from these honoured dead we take increased devotion to that cause for which they gave the last full measure of devotion – that we here highly resolve that these dead shall not have died in vain – that this nation, under God, shall have a new birth of freedom – and that government of the people, by the people, for the people, shall not perish from the earth.

[*Make holy]

---

4

## 'BLOOD, TOIL, TEARS, AND SWEAT'

Among a few other achievements, **Winston Churchill** is one of the most famous orators in British history. His was the voice that inspired the British Empire to keep fighting, even when all seemed lost. These were his words to Parliament in 1940, after taking over as Prime Minister:

In this crisis I hope I may be pardoned if I do not address the House at any length today. I hope that any of my friends and colleagues, or former colleagues, who are affected by the political reconstruction will make all allowances for any lack of ceremony with which it has been necessary to act.

I would say to the House, as I said to those who have joined the government, 'I have nothing to offer but blood, toil, tears and sweat.' We have before us an ordeal of the most grievous kind. We have before us many, many long months of struggle and of suffering.

You ask, what is our policy? I will say it is to wage war by sea, land and air, with all our might and with all the strength that God can give us; to wage war against a monstrous tyranny never surpassed in the dark and lamentable catalogue of human crime. That is our policy.

You ask, what is our aim? I can answer in one word: victory. Victory at all costs, victory in spite of all terror, victory, however long and hard the road may be, for without victory there is no survival.

Let that be realised. No survival for the British Empire, no survival for all that the

British Empire has stood for, no survival for the urge and impulse of the ages, that mankind will move forward towards its goal. But I take up my task with buoyancy and hope. I feel sure that our cause will not be suffered to fail among men.

At this time I feel entitled to claim the aid of all, and I say, 'Come, then, let us go forward together with our united strength.'

---
5
---

## 'WE CHOOSE TO GO TO THE MOON'

In this extract from a much longer speech in 1962, President **John F. Kennedy** announced that America would reach the moon before the decade was over. At the time, it was an astonishing assertion. Kennedy would not live to see his dream realised. He was assassinated just over a year later. Yet Neil Armstrong and Buzz Aldrin stepped out onto the moon in 1969.

We choose to go to the moon. We choose to go to the moon in this decade and do the other things, not because they are easy, but because they are hard, because that goal will serve to organise and measure the best of our energies and skills, because that challenge is one that we are willing to accept, one we are unwilling to postpone, and one we intend to win, and the others, too.

. . . Many years ago, the great British explorer George Mallory, who was to die on Mount Everest, was asked why did he want to climb it. He said, 'Because it is there.'

Well, space is there, and we're going to climb it, and the moon and the planets are there, and new hopes for knowledge and peace are there.

And, therefore, as we set sail, we ask God's blessing on the most hazardous and dangerous and greatest adventure on which man has ever embarked.

A great speech can be the foundation stone of a nation, or a marriage. A single line can keep us going when there is no other hope. Bearing that incredible power in mind, this is a skill worth learning. Speaking in public with calm assurance – finding the right words under pressure – is vital. It might even save your life.

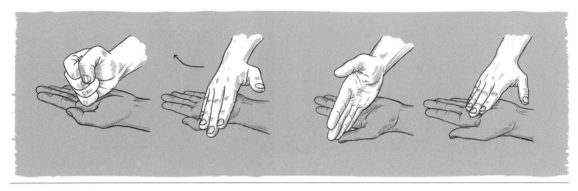

How Many?

These *only* work if you have a group of friends willing to give them a good go before demanding the answer. The best results come from a group who are *determined* to work out what is happening without being told.

In each case, it's vital to say that if someone guesses what is happening, they can whisper it to whoever started and have it confirmed, but they must not reveal it to anyone else or make it obvious. The ideal is to have every person at a dinner table get it, leaving one poor wretch who can't.

## ① 'THIS IS THE POINTING GAME'

Pointing around the group one by one, the leader says, 'This is the Pointing Game, who am I thinking of?'

They wait then for someone to guess.

Someone guesses 'Jack' or 'Dad' and the leader replies: 'No, Susan!' – and starts over. 'This is the pointing game . . .'

The answer comes from whoever speaks first

– *they become the answer*. It is as simple, and as fiendish, as that – and it works beautifully.

## ② HOW MANY?

Whoever knows the game begins with a simple series of gestures. The better you sell the seriousness of this, the better the result.

The gestures are as follows: closed fist on open palm; open palm striking open palm and swept clear, as if wiping dust; one hand brought down on the other like a karate chop; open palm striking open palm and remaining. Use these in any combination – but firmly and seriously.

A typical sequence could go: closed fist, closed fist, wipe, closed fist . . . followed by the question 'How many is that?' Someone will venture an answer.

'Two?'

'No, four.'

Perhaps the second sequence could be a single fist brought down slowly, followed by a single wipe. 'How many?'

'Four?'

'No, two.'

And so on. If someone else wishes to repeat an action for themselves, that is allowed. 'You do one if you want. I'll tell you if you get it right.'

This works in part because it looks like maths. The crowd will drive themselves mad trying to label each gesture as a number, then add and subtract to reach the figure.

The answer is much simpler: it is the number of words said after the gestures.

'How many is that?' – four.

'How many?' – two.

Expectant silence – zero.

'How many do you think that was?' – seven.

---

## 3

## CROSSED/UNCROSSED

This looks so simple it couldn't possibly work. We can only say that one of the authors spent around two hours trying to break the code on a school trip – and had to be told in the end.

You'll need a large spoon or ladle. Establish that if anyone works it out, they mustn't tell the others. That is vital – it's the only thing that can ruin the game. They can continue to take part, showing their knowledge by getting it right each time.

In a ring of people, perhaps lounging on chairs, you pass the spoon from person to person. Whoever knows this has to make it work. He passes the spoon in patterns that others will begin to read and interpret.

For example, he might take the spoon in his left hand, then switch to his right hand before passing it along and saying aloud the word 'Crossed'.

The spoon continues its way around the ring. Each person takes it, trying to guess the code. While they hold it, they say either 'Crossed' or 'Uncrossed' and pass it on. Whoever introduced the game agrees with them that they are right or wrong. Show enthusiasm when they get it right: 'Yes! Crossed! Well done!' or shake your head and look dismayed when they get it wrong. 'Oh no, that's definitely *un*crossed, sorry.'

The answer lies in whether they have their legs crossed or not. Honestly, this should not work. Somehow, it does.

---

## 4

## 'THE MOON IS ROUND'

These are all lateral-thinking games in a way, where the answer is not obvious. They can be intensely frustrating, but among friends, a lot of fun.

This one involves the first speaker drawing a circle in the air while saying, 'The moon is round, has two eyes, a nose and a mouth.'

As the person speaks, he draws a circle in the air for the moon, two dots for the eyes, a line for the nose and a curved smile for the mouth. He then invites the next person to have a go.

They do exactly the same thing, only to have the first speaker say, 'No, that's not it.'

Round the circle it goes, with each person trying to reproduce the same simple design in the air. The host demonstrates over and over, but no one else can draw one he approves.

The secret for this one is that the host clears his throat before drawing each moon. It is amazing how people don't notice this most innocent of sounds. That said, don't make it too obvious.

You may be thinking that if they're in this book, everyone will know the answers to these games. First of all, not everyone will read the book. Secondly, people forget. Try them first on those you know – family or friends – in Cubs, in school, around a dinner table. Or just learn them, so that twenty years from now, on a quiet holiday evening, you can say, 'This is the Pointing Game . . .'

# THE HISTORY OF NAVIGATION

The history of navigation is the history of conquering the unknown, usually at great risk. From ancient times, merchants, soldiers and sailors have followed the North Star during the night and the rising sun during the day. That is the simplest part of finding your way – knowing where you want to go and the direction to take to get there. Knowing where you *are* is much harder.

## THE ANCIENTS

It is possible, even likely, that hard-won knowledge has been lost. In the British Museum, there is a rock-crystal lens found in ancient Assyria, known as the **Nimrud lens**. It is dated to 1000 BC. It might have been used to start fires or as a simple magnifying glass – or combined with another one to make a telescope. We'll never know, though it is interesting that Assyrians described Saturn as being surrounded by a ring of serpents. Saturn's rings are not visible to the naked eye, so either that is a coincidence, or they had some sort of aid to vision – since lost in war and conquest.

Some of the earliest navigation information can be found in the hieroglyphics of ancient Egypt, cut into stone. From their star charts, we know the **Egyptians** were noting the length of the year and the lunar cycle five thousand years ago. As they thought of the sun as a god named 'Ra', they were keen to keep an eye on what he was doing. They were aware of equinoxes, when the length of day and night are equal, and solstices – the longest and shortest days in the year. That understanding of the heavens was learned and structured through a zodiac of symbols (Leo, Gemini, Cancer etc.). They also built lighthouses to show merchant ships the entrance to harbours from far out at sea. However, the Egyptians were not great explorers. They made boats from acacia wood and papyrus, to be used on canals and rivers, or for coastal trade. They were never really sturdy enough to survive the great oceans. Shipbuilding skill is absolutely vital for exploration.

Around the same time, on the other side of the world, the **Polynesians** were spreading from island to island over vast distances. (Their origin is unknown, though some have suggested they may have come from Taiwan or the Philippines.) They too watched the stars at night and understood the constellation we call the Southern Cross, where it points due south – as well as the passage of the sun from east to west. In small boats, they could row and sail for immense distances, reading the sea and winds as they went. They reached New Zealand, Fiji, Tonga and a host of beautiful places, making new cultures there that all share some common ancestry.

The Polynesians used knowledge of currents, the height of the sun, the flight of birds, seedlings seen in the water, types of seaweed and cloud formations over land to find their path. They memorised it all in songs and chants, knowledge that could be the difference between life and death on the deep ocean. These were similar to the songs of Australian Aborigines, used to navigate – or sing – their way across Australian deserts. In the 1960s, Briton David Lewis and Polynesian navigators sailed 1,700 miles from Tahiti to New Zealand using only these ancient techniques.

Around 2000 BC in ancient Greece, the **Minoans** of Crete navigated using the night sky, logging equinoxes and the rise and set of particular stars to reach destinations like Egypt. The Greek author of the *Odyssey*, Homer, lived somewhere around the 12th to the 8th century BC. In Odysseus' classic sea voyage, Homer included advice from a goddess about which stars to use as guides to reach his home.

By 400 BC, the Athenians traded and went to war in great fleets, while in Persia they transported armies. These vessels, called galleys, were mostly powered by banks of oars. Ancient references to the 'white wings' of ships referred to those sun-bleached oars, not sails. Still, the most reliable method of navigation was not to lose sight of the shore. That works reasonably well, but there will always be some who want to see what lies beyond the horizon.

In the 1st century BC, around the time of the birth of Julius Caesar, a Greek ship sank off Antikythera, in the Aegean Sea. It was explored in 1901 and the 'Antikythera mechanism' brought up. Although much corroded, the device had over thirty bronze wheels and gears and appears to have been for navigation. Nothing else like it has been found. In 1st-century BC Rome, Cicero wrote of a device that could predict the motions of the sun, moon and the five planets they knew, but whatever it was, we have only that one, frustrating glimpse.

When the western Roman empire fell, in the 5th century AD, **Vikings** roamed far in small crews, setting sail from countries like Denmark and Sweden and reaching Britain, Greenland, Canada and America – some centuries before Columbus. From the 8th century on, over vast and trackless oceans, they went searching for land. One of their techniques was to keep crows in cages on the decks of their longships. (They also had short ships, which didn't go as far. That sounds like a joke, but it's true.)

They kept the sun behind them in the mornings to go west, following it as it dipped towards the horizon in the evenings. Even so, there were times when they were running low on food and fresh water and desperate for sight of land. On those occasions, they would release one of the crows. The bird would flap madly for height at first, but crows are land birds and they don't like the sight of endless ocean. The crow would fly in vast circles, looking for some hint of green. When the bird saw land, it would break off circling and fly straight – and the Vikings below would follow.

Finding new land is one thing, but for more accurate navigation, a captain needed to know where he was. Enter the **magnetic compass**. This was first introduced to the world by China around 2,500 BC, using a piece of natural magnetised rock. By the 12th century AD, western navigators were using a needle-shaped magnet floating in a bowl of oil and water. A graduated card – the compass rose – was added beneath the needle to indicate magnetic north and other compass points. In those earliest days, it appeared to some to be magic – metal that moved on its own.

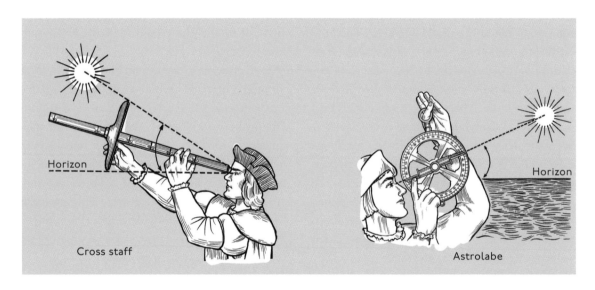

Cross staff

Horizon

Horizon

Astrolabe

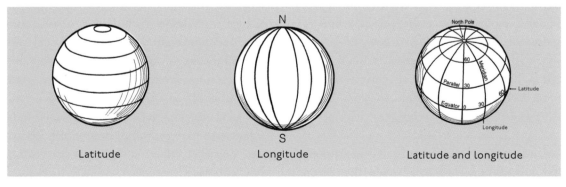

Latitude

Longitude

Latitude and longitude

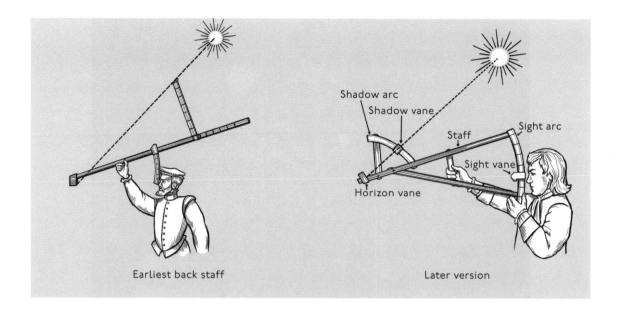

Earliest back staff

Later version

Shadow arc
Shadow vane
Sight arc
Staff
Sight vane
Horizon vane

Direction was a key part, but speed was the other component that would give an accurate location. One of the first techniques was to drop a log from the bow of a ship and time how long it took to reach the stern – a known length. The first accurate estimates didn't come about until the 16th century, with the manufacture of sand-timers. Knots were tied to a thin line with a piece of wood at the end, at intervals of seven fathoms (42 feet). One sailor would drop this log off the stern and call 'Time', while another turned a half-minute sand-glass. The first sailor would count the knots running through his fingers until the second sailor called 'Time' when the sand ran out. If five knots were counted in that time, the ship was making five nautical miles per hour – or five **knots**. This 'heaving the log' was still being used by sailing clippers into the 20th century.

With a fair knowledge of speed and direction, a navigator could estimate his position by what is known as **dead reckoning**. However, as early as

the 12th century, sailors saw that the height of the sun varied depending on where they were – and so the key to navigation at sea was explored. The horizon is the one fixed point that is always present for a ship. As soon as there were tools and methods that could make use of this fact, navigation took off.

**Latitude** is how far north or south you are from the Equator. It was described in the first *Dangerous Book*. The essence of finding it is that the height of the sun at noon from the horizon changes depending on where you are on the earth's surface. If you can measure the height of the sun at noon, you will then know your latitude. Adjustments have to be made for the season, as the earth's tilt affects the result.

One of the earliest ways of doing this was the **cross staff**, or Jacob's staff. Some variation of it was known to ancient Greek and Middle Eastern seafarers and came to western Europeans around the 13th and 14th centuries. It used a moving slide or multiple rods to get a height of the sun at

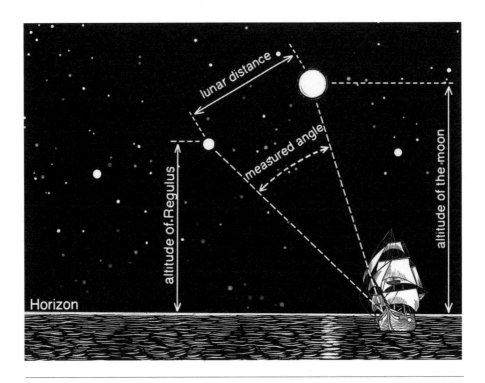

lunar distance

measured angle

altitude of Regulus

altitude of the moon

Horizon

Sighting on a known star

noon. Unfortunately, it required the user to stare directly at the sun, which was uncomfortable and dangerous. Another invention in use at the time was the mariner's **astrolabe**, or 'ring', which was held up to the sun and the angle to the horizon measured. This is basically a mechanical protractor with a moving arm to measure the angle. These systems worked, and with the compass and the log, were the key tools used to explore and map our world.

A major improvement was the **English quadrant** or **back staff**, invented by navigator John Davis in 1595. It was easier to use than the cross staff and astrolabe, and measured the angle of the sun's shadow, so that no one had to stare directly at the sun. It was a revolution in accuracy and was used for over 200 years. John Davis was the English explorer who discovered, charted and landed on the Falkland Islands in 1592. The log book for that horrendous voyage was used by Samuel Taylor Coleridge as the basis for his poem 'The Rime of the Ancient Mariner'.

In 1699, Isaac Newton created the **octant**, or 'reflecting quadrant' – a quantum leap in accuracy from the back staff. Although he gave the details to Edmund Halley (of Halley's Comet fame), they were not published until after Halley's death. By then, another Englishman named John Hadley had invented the sextant in 1730. As with so many things, it was an idea whose time had come. The name 'octant' means an eighth, as it covers 45 degrees, or an eighth of a circle. Using shades, the sun's height above the horizon could be measured. A telescope provided the original

Sextant in use

sighting line, but this was often replaced with a metal point, like a gunsight.

From 1767, the **Nautical Almanac** was published, which included accurate lunar angles from key stars. From that point, it was possible for a navigator to take a sighting on a known star, another on the moon and observe the angle between them. Consulting the table to find the Greenwich time *at which the angle occurs* gives the correct time at zero longitude – the position of Greenwich in London. That time could then be related to local noon – and actual longitude established.

The best instrument for these lunar and star sightings was that improvement on the octant – the **sextant**. It is still in use today to take star and sun sightings, as a navigation back-up when power fails. In combination with a watch, it is extremely accurate and doesn't run out of batteries. The process of using a sextant to measure the angle between a celestial object – usually the sun or a star – and the horizon is called 'taking a sight' or 'shooting' the object. It is also possible to take a sight of an object on land and then use trigonometry to calculate the distance it is away. The sextant became the most

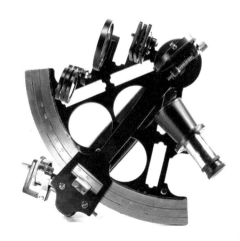

vital tool of navigation in the British navy of the 18th and 19th centuries. The name comes from the Latin for one sixth of a circle – sixty degrees.

The particular genius of a sextant is that by use of mirrors, it can show a twin image, adjustable by the user. First the horizon is set, then the arm released and the half-image brings down the sun to the horizon. The angle can then be read and latitude calculated or read from tables.

**Longitude** is how far east or west you are from the Greenwich meridian. It is explained in the first *Dangerous Book*. The earth rotates on its axis west to east, one day being the time taken to complete a full revolution. Because of this rotation the longitude position east or west of Greenwich – zero degrees longitude – can be measured in time as well as by an angle in degrees. One hour of time is equal to 15 degrees of longitude. Or, in every four minutes, the earth rotates through one degree of longitude. So a person standing 15 degrees east longitude (towards the sunrise) will be one hour ahead of Greenwich Mean Time, while a person standing 15 degrees west longitude (towards the sunset) will be one hour behind Greenwich Mean Time. Therefore, by knowing what time it is at the Greenwich meridian and comparing that with the time where you stand, you can calculate your line, or meridian, of longitude. Where your longitude line crosses your latitude line is your position on the surface of the earth.

If you don't have a latitude or any reliable position line, you can measure with your sextant the heights of several stars, planets and the moon. Where all these position lines cross is where you are on the earth. The calculations are basic spherical trigonometry, which you may learn at school. Because the earth turns like a ball in space, longitude is divided into 360 degrees of a circle, each degree being made of 60 'minutes', each minute being made of 60 'seconds'. All the lines of longitude come together at the North and South Poles and are furthest apart at the Equator. There, one minute of longitude is measured as one nautical mile and equals 6,080 feet (a land mile is 5,280 feet). This is why big-scale maritime and aeronautical distances are measured in nautical miles, not kilometres.

Historically, every city, town and village timed its midday when the sun was at its highest point above its cathedral or church or town hall, and local clocks were set to that. Midday in Edinburgh and Cardiff, both some 4 degrees longitude west of London, is measurably several minutes later than in London. It wasn't until train timetables had to be aligned all across the United Kingdom that the nation first kept exactly the same time. Other countries followed the British example, and it was agreed that all time around the world would be measured from the Greenwich longitude at the Greenwich Observatory. A good exercise is to work out what the exact time differences for midday used to be between London and Edinburgh, Cardiff and Belfast.

Yorkshireman John Harrison played a very important role in the longitude story. He developed a watch – the Harrison model number 4 – which was accurate even at sea with the roll and pitch of a vessel. It was based upon balancing springs and an oscillating wheel. In 1761 this watch made a nine-week voyage from Britain to Jamaica, and lost only five seconds.

## GLOBAL POSITIONING SYSTEM

The first satellite navigation system came about as a result of America launching satellites into near orbit of earth. It uses the same basic idea as star sights. If a line can be established from the navigator to a far-off object, the navigator's bearing – angle – can be worked out. If another sight is taken, or three or four, a more and more accurate position can be calculated. The modern GPS system went live in 1994, with twenty-four Navstar satellites in geostationary orbit around the world. It is an amazing system. There are now thousands swinging around in the vastness and cold of space. A car GPS system could easily be in contact with eight or nine satellites and so gain a very precise position. The system has even been used for self-driving cars to navigate, in combination with radar and cameras.

There is also a Russian Global Navigation System ('GLONASS'), and other systems are in development.

## MARS

There are no satellites in orbit over Mars, though there could be in the near future. Reaching the red planet requires our rockets to 'look back', taking the correct bearing from a sighting of earth behind. It's tempting to point out how similar this is to a cross-staff sighting, at least in principle. Mars Lander missions do not even have cameras to look ahead and see Mars approaching. The whole journey is done with bearings on home. 'Deep Space Network' antennas on earth keep track of the lander and constantly 'tell' it where it is by way of radio signal. Earth and Mars are both moving through space, so the rocket has to be aimed not at Mars, but where Mars will eventually be. That is a pretty impressive feat of mathematics.

For the most part, the mobile Mars laboratories we have landed on the surface had to do so responding independently to angle and speed, adjusting as they went. The distances were just too great to command from Earth. That said, we have also lost one on the surface when it failed to deploy its solar power panels, so it doesn't always go well.

When it comes to navigating a vehicle over the surface of another planet 150 million miles away, extreme care has to be taken. The one-way signal time delay is around thirteen minutes, which means it will take almost half an hour to realise the machine is heading off a cliff and then stop it or put it into reverse. The reality is a combination of remote commands and autonomous commands, where the Mars Rover is told to head for a particular landmark and then left mostly to its own devices. Progress is very slow indeed, as if it tips over, that's it – until future colonists turn it the right way up again, forty or fifty years from today.

As humans, we have always wanted to see over the next hill. We have explored a great deal of our planet, though much of the ocean floor and some flooded caves are still unmapped. Beyond our green and blue ball are planets we might mine or colonise, like Mars, but beyond those are entirely new horizons. At the time of writing, NASA has identified over a hundred planets that should have similar qualities to Earth. They are a long way off, but so was Australia, once.

# CASTING IN CLEAR RESIN

It is worth pointing out that the materials in this chapter are pretty unpleasant. You're going to need adult supervision. We used clear casting polyester resin, which came with these warnings:

---

Harmful if inhaled.
Causes serious eye irritation.
Causes skin irritation.
Causes damage to organs through
prolonged or repeated exposure.

---

You have been warned. If you go ahead with this, it's a good idea to choose a warm, sunny day and an extremely well-ventilated area. We put rubber gloves on and did it in the kitchen with all the windows open. Later on, when we were ignoring the safety instructions, we did it in a small workshop with no ventilation and no gloves. One of us can no longer do the seven times table, so this is not recommended.

That said, people do this for a hobby and it's amazing stuff. If you've ever seen an insect held in a square of clear plastic, this is how it was done. Casting resin is available in hobby shops or online. Ours came in a pack that included rubber gloves, wooden stirring sticks, plastic mixing cups, hardener and the resin itself. You'll also need a mould. Tupperware works, though silicon moulds are best – rectangular or bowl-shaped. The ideal is a perfectly smooth shape. It took us a while to embed coins – the resin cracked on two attempts and gave off extraordinary heat. With 1%

hardener, it neither discoloured nor cracked, but it took almost ninety minutes to grow thick enough to support the coin. As a rule, this isn't meant to be a hot reaction – the mould can be held in the hand throughout. If it gets hot, you've probably put too much hardener in.

## YOU WILL NEED

- 1kg tin of clear polyester resin (35fl oz)
- MEKP catalyst
- A measuring syringe (up to 5ml)
- Wooden lolly sticks
- Plastic or cardboard mixing cups
- A rectangular mould
- Silicon release spray
- Wet-and-dry sandpaper (up to 2000 grit)
- Toothpaste

The idea is simple: empires may rise and fall, but a plastic cube is for ever. If you have a small item you'd like to keep – or give as a gift – this will preserve it for eternity. The father to one of the authors (and grandfather to the other two) used to grow runner beans in his back garden. Some of these beans will be planted, so the circle of life continues. Two were set in resin, to see how it all worked.

As a general rule, we try to keep costs down, on the grounds that boys don't usually have £20 or £30 to hand. There is no way around spending money here, but one tin of the stuff will allow you to make eight or ten casts, depending on the size. The catalyst is methyl ethyl ketone peroxide. Check to see if it comes with a measuring device, such as a syringe, or has a top that will allow you to count drops. The ratio of resin to catalyst is a maximum of 100:2. That worked fine with small volumes, but when we mixed above 200ml, it needed 1% hardener to dry clear.

We sprayed a quick burst of silicon into a plastic mould bought online, then allowed it to dry. Then we mixed hardener with a cupful of resin, measuring everything carefully. You have plenty of time, so stir and pour slowly to avoid bubbles as much as possible. Bubbles are the enemy. You'll have chances to take them out later, so don't panic if you see a few.

We poured the mixed resin into the container to about halfway. If you've mixed too much, there's nothing more you can do with the remainder, so put it outside where it can dry – and get a second disposable cup.

How long it takes for the resin to grow firm enough to support your item depends on the percentage of hardener and the temperature of the room. We noticed the bubbles tend to rise in clusters and can be scooped out with a wooden lolly stick onto an old cloth or paper napkin without too much trouble. This is worth doing.

In the first attempt, we put our beans in too early, after around thirty minutes. They sank, though it had an interesting side effect. Coating them in liquid plastic before their second full immersion appeared to help with air bubbles. We did a similar thing later with a used shotgun cartridge, filling it full of spare resin so that its final immersion

would not be spoiled by bubbles coming out of the empty tube.

After forty to forty-five minutes, our 2% mix resin had become firm enough to support the beans. We placed them on the surface, and mixed an identical batch of resin and hardener to pour over the beans, filling the mould to the top. In this way, the object will appear to float in the cube and not drift to the bottom. It works really well and the seam between layers is not obvious.

The second layer will obviously take the same sort of time to grow firm – but leave it a lot longer than that. Put the mould on a shelf for twenty-four hours. Be patient! Until it's completely dry, this stuff takes fingerprints better than the FBI.

If you remembered to spray silicon in first, the block of resin should come out with a few taps from underneath. It shrinks slightly as it dries, so it should pop out fairly easily. If it has dried clear, it might need nothing more than a rub along the edge to clean it up. However, it will probably need a polish. We found that wet-and-dry sandpaper worked. Taping a sheet to the table and keeping it very wet while rubbing the block back and forth slowly removed an imperfect surface. We used grits of 600, 1000, 1500 and 2000. Just as we were despairing it would ever come clear again, we tried toothpaste. A good dollop rubbed on with a cloth is the final stage. Toothpaste is, after all, an extremely mild abrasive.

This part is time-consuming, but polishing something in this way is an entire skill in itself. Take your time, move slowly and without heavy pressure. Check progress regularly. Remember, the result is probably going to exist a century from now. It won't hurt to spend a couple of hours polishing it. You might decide then to cut a piece of felt to go underneath, if you want a paperweight you made yourself.

It took us three attempts to get the coin to work. We bought a convex bowl mould and poured it as before – but 1% hardener is vital. That coin still sank three times and had to be fished out. For that, we wore the rubber gloves. The third try was the charm and it dried beautifully clear, without heat.

If you have something in an unusual shape that you would like to copy – a chess pawn, for example – you could paint it with liquid latex in multiple coats, until you have a thick enough layer to pop out the original piece. Casting resin can then be slowly poured into the latex mould.

Finally, we have to suggest family photos and, of course, dead insects, with the reminder that you'll probably have to coat them in a pre-mix first to avoid leaving big bubbles visible. Ants would be interesting. Aunts, also.

The block with the beans sits on my desk as I write this, while others grow green and red outside.

# FIVE MORE POEMS
# EVERY BOY SHOULD KNOW

## (Or better still, learn by heart …)

In the original *Dangerous Book*, we chose five of the greats: 'If', 'Ozymandias', 'Invictus', 'Vitae Lampada' and 'Sea-Fever'. Such poems, though short, capture grand ideas and great emotions. There are few things more impressive than having half a dozen lines memorised from one of those – or one of these.

## THY SERVANT A DOG –
## HIS APOLOGIES

by Rudyard Kipling (1865–1936)

Master, this is Thy Servant. He is rising eight weeks old.
He is mainly Head and Tummy. His legs are uncontrolled.
But Thou hast forgiven his ugliness, and settled him on Thy knee . . .
Art Thou content with Thy Servant? He is very comfy with Thee.

Master, behold a Sinner? He hath done grievous wrong.
He hath defiled Thy Premises through being kept in too long.
Wherefore his nose has been rubbed in the dirt, and his self-respect has been bruised.
Master, pardon Thy Sinner, and see he is properly loosed.

Master – again Thy Sinner! This that was once Thy Shoe,
He hath found and taken and carried aside, as fitting matter to chew.
Now there is neither blacking nor tongue, and the Housemaid has us in tow.
Master, remember Thy Servant is young, and tell her to let him go!

Master, extol* Thy Servant! He hath met a most Worthy Foe!
There has been fighting all over the Shop – and into the Shop also!
Till cruel umbrellas parted the strife (or I might have been choking him yet).
But Thy Servant has had the Time of his Life – and now shall we call on the vet?

[*praise]

Master, behold Thy Servant! Strange children came to play,
And because they fought to caress him, Thy Servant wentedst away.
But now that the Little Beasts have gone, he has returned to see
(Brushed – with his Sunday collar on –) what they left over from tea . . .

Master, pity Thy Servant! He is deaf and three parts blind,
He cannot catch Thy Commandments. He cannot read Thy Mind.

Oh, leave him not in his loneliness; nor make
him that kitten's scorn.
He has had none other God than thee, since
the year that he was born!

Lord, look down on Thy Servant! Bad things
have come to pass,
There is no heat in the midday sun, nor health
in the wayside grass.
His bones are full of an old disease – his
torments run and increase.
Lord, make haste with Thy Lightnings and
grant him a quick release.

Kipling was one of the greats – a superb poet and
author. I'm sure he wrote these lines for fun, but as
well as the humour, in the last two verses there is
a compassion and understanding to make any dog
owner pause – and remember.

## BREAK, BREAK, BREAK

by Alfred Lord Tennyson (1809–1892)

Break, break, break,
   On thy cold grey stones, O Sea!
And I would that my tongue could utter
   The thoughts that arise in me.

O, well for the fisherman's boy,
   That he shouts with his sister at play!
O, well for the sailor lad,
   That he sings in his boat on the bay!

And the stately ships go on
   To their haven under the hill;
But O for the touch of a vanished hand,
   And the sound of a voice that is still!

Break, break, break,
   At the foot of thy crags, O Sea!
But the tender grace of a day that is dead
   Will never come back to me.

This is a study of grief. If you have ever known
loss, you'll feel the sadness and longing in the
third verse. Tennyson was a marvellous Poet
Laureate – the official poet of the nation.
Though he died in 1892, his words are loved by
millions today.

## HORATIUS – FROM LAYS OF ANCIENT ROME

by Thomas Macaulay (1800–1859)

There are seventy verses in this entire lay, or bal-
lad. When he was at Harrow school, Winston
Churchill memorised them all and could recite
them. Based on true stories from ancient Rome,
they were written while Macaulay was in India in
the 1830s.

In this part, the young city of Rome is under
attack. The enemy vanguard (the front ranks)
are surging towards a single key bridge over the
river Tiber, made yellow-gold by the setting sun.
Horatius, a brave captain, steps forward to defend
the narrow span, determined to give his people
time to cut the bridge down.

XXVI
But the Consul's brow was sad,
   And the Consul's speech was low,
And darkly looked he at the wall,
   And darkly at the foe.
'Their van will be upon us
   Before the bridge goes down;

And if they once may win the bridge,
  What hope to save the town?'

XXVII

Then out spake brave Horatius,
  The Captain of the Gate:
'To every man upon this earth
  Death cometh soon or late.
And how can man die better
  Than facing fearful odds,
For the Ashes of his fathers,
  And the temples of his Gods.

XXIX

'Hew down the bridge, Sir Consul,
  With all the speed ye may;
I, with two more to help me,
  Will hold the foe in play.
In yon strait path a thousand
  May well be stopped by three.
Now who will stand on either hand,
  And keep the bridge with me?'

XXX

Then out spake Spurius Lartius;
  A Ramnian proud was he:
'Lo, I will stand at thy right hand,
  And keep the bridge with thee.'
And out spake strong Herminius;
  Of Titian* blood was he:
'I will abide on thy left side,
  And keep the bridge with thee.'

[*Pronounced '**Tish**-uhn' – an area of Italy]

L

Was none who would be foremost
  To lead such dire attack:
But those behind cried 'Forward!'

And those before cried 'Back!'
And backwards now and forward
  Wavers the deep array;
And on the tossing sea of steel,
  To and fro the standards reel;
And the victorious trumpet-peal
  Dies fitfully away.

LV

But with a crash like thunder
  Fell every loosened beam,
And, like a dam, the mighty wreck
  Lay right athwart the stream:*
And a long shout of triumph
  Rose from the walls of Rome,
As to the highest turret-tops
  Was splashed the yellow foam.

[*across the river]

LXIV

And now he feels the bottom;
  Now on dry earth he stands;
Now round him throng the Fathers
  To press his gory hands;
And now, with shouts and clapping,
  And noise of weeping loud,
He enters through the River-Gate,
  Borne by the joyous crowd.

LXX

When the goodman mends his armour,
  And trims his helmet's plume;
When the goodwife's shuttle merrily
  Goes flashing through the loom;
With weeping and with laughter
  Still is the story told,
How well Horatius kept the bridge
  In the brave days of old.

The complete poem is well worth a read, for the rolling rhythm alone. For those who are interested in such things, the line 'For the ashes of his fathers and the temples of his Gods' was my choice for the title of my first published book on Julius Caesar as a boy. The publishers pointed out that there would be no room on the cover for anything else, so we settled on *The Gates of Rome* instead.

## THE TYGER

by William Blake (1757–1827)

Tyger Tyger, burning bright,
In the forests of the night:
What immortal hand or eye,
Could frame thy fearful symmetry?

In what distant deeps or skies
Burnt the fire of thine eyes?
On what wings dare he aspire?
What the hand, dare seize the fire?

And what shoulder, & what art,
Could twist the sinews of thy heart?
And when thy heart began to beat,
What dread hand? & what dread feet?

What the hammer? what the chain,
In what furnace was thy brain?
What the anvil? what dread grasp,
Dare its deadly terrors clasp?

When the stars threw down their spears
And water'd heaven with their tears:
Did he smile his work to see?
Did he who made the Lamb make thee?

Tyger Tyger burning bright,
In the forests of the night:
What immortal hand or eye,
Dare frame thy fearful symmetry?

The spelling, of course, is rather old-fashioned. The punctuation is erratic. Yet this poem speaks across generations. Blake was born and died in London, but he lived for a while in Felpham in Sussex, where his cottage is still preserved. He was once thrown out of a pub that stands today in the same road, for fighting with a soldier. Blake is most famous for 'Jerusalem', but his sense of awe at the world comes across here. It captures the sheer wonder of encountering beauty and power.

## AN ARUNDEL TOMB

by Philip Larkin (1922–1985)

Side by side, their faces blurred,
The earl and countess lie in stone,
Their proper habits vaguely shown
As jointed armour, stiffened pleat,
And that faint hint of the absurd –
The little dogs under their feet.

Such plainness of the pre-baroque*
Hardly involves the eye, until
It meets his left-hand gauntlet, still
Clasped empty in the other; and
One sees, with a sharp tender shock,
His hand withdrawn, holding her hand.

They would not think to lie so long.
Such faithfulness in effigy
Was just a detail friends would see:

A sculptor's sweet commissioned grace
Thrown off in helping to prolong
The Latin names around the base.

They would not guess how early in
Their supine stationary voyage
Their air would change to soundless damage,
Turn the old tenantry away;
How soon succeeding eyes begin
To look, not read. Rigidly they

Persisted, linked, through lengths and breadths
Of time. Snow fell, undated. Light
Each summer thronged the grass. A bright
Litter of birdcalls strewed the same
Bone-riddled ground. And up the paths
The endless altered people came,

Washing at their identity.
Now, helpless in the hollow of
An unarmorial age, a trough
Of smoke in slow suspended skeins
Above their scrap of history,
Only an attitude remains:

Time has transfigured them into
Untruth. The stone fidelity
They hardly meant has come to be
Their final blazon, and to prove
Our almost-instinct almost true:
What will survive of us is love.

[*Pre-baroque – the simpler styles of clothing,
    carving and architecture before the 17th and
    18th centuries]

'Supine' means lying face up. 'Prone' means face
down. 'Unarmorial age' – an age when chivalry
and heraldry are in the past, a world the earl

and countess would hardly recognise in all its
wonders. 'Skeins' is usually threads. It might refer
to a grain in the stone. He means the visitors blur
the edges of the tomb, rubbing the personalities
away, as if they are like drifting smoke, rising up to
leave just stone behind.

This is a favourite, worth reading aloud. Larkin
struggled with faith and sometimes despair, yet the
last note has been a comfort to many who read
this poem. The tomb he describes, with husband
and wife holding hands in stone, can be seen in
Chichester Cathedral, in the south of England. It
is worth a visit.

Some poems are made to be said aloud. The lines
become part of us, to be called forth in moments
that need them. It might be an instant of regret,
when you wish to go back and undo a bad day,
but then you remember 'The Moving Finger
writes; and, having writ, / Moves on: nor all thy
Piety nor Wit / Shall lure it back to cancel half
a Line . . .' It might be a desire for forgiveness,
and the thought that 'Twixt the saddle and the
ground, mercy sought and mercy found', twixt
meaning 'between'. In other words, hope for
forgiveness even to the final moments, even as
you are falling from a galloping horse. It could
be the intense sadness of this line by W.B. Yeats:
'Man is in love and loves what vanishes, / What
more is there to say?' or Wordsworth's joy at
seeing 'A host of golden daffodils'.

Poetry is an attempt to communicate emotions
through words. It is a sort of wonder, and we
include five poems here because a life with no
poetry at all would be less than one with these.
That's just the truth of it.

# FAMOUS BATTLES

## CUNAXA AND THE TEN THOUSAND – 401 BC

When Prince Cyrus of Persia fell out with his older brother Artaxerxes, he launched a wild plan to take the imperial throne from him. His brother's army was vast – some sources put it at over a million men under arms. Now, Cyrus could not possibly gather enough Persian soldiers to defeat so many, but he had a secret weapon – the elite hoplite soldiers of Greece. These were the men who had stood at Thermopylae and Marathon, destroying Persian armies. Cyrus understood they had no equal in the world as warriors. In secret, he brought ten thousand of them together – Spartans, Athenians, Corinthians, Thebans, the best of the best, from all over central Greece. In those days, that heartland was sometimes called 'The Dance-floor of Ares' – the Greek god of war.

Cyrus formed his army from a hundred thousand Persians loyal to him and the ten thousand Greek mercenaries. He knew speed was important. If his brother heard what he was planning, the entire Persian army would be turned out to face him. Yet an army of over a million men takes months to bring to the field. It was Cyrus' plan to race east from the Greek coast of Turkey, into what is today Syria and Iraq, before his brother even heard he was on the march. Prince Cyrus avoided the royal road that stretched over a thousand miles and instead struck out across country with his forces, going as fast as they could.

Unfortunately for the young prince, his brother was warned. Spies had reported the unusual troop movements, and one of the Persian lords was suspicious of Cyrus and told the king. King Artaxerxes of Persia summoned his soldiers. Cyrus and his Greeks were marching into a trap.

Cyrus was approaching the city of Babylon when his scouts reported a vast number of armed men on the march, stirring huge dust clouds. With every step it became clearer that his brother had brought out the entire Persian army.

Prince Cyrus knew he couldn't win against so many. His entire army was smaller than one of his brother's wings – and they were the same Persian soldiers. Man for man, he had lost before he could even begin. Yet he still had one chance. He knew that if he could strike his brother down, Cyrus would become king in that instant. His brother had no children. Cyrus was still officially the heir to the throne. If Artaxerxes fell, Cyrus would command his entire army and the battle would be won.

On horseback, Cyrus launched his personal guard of a few hundred across the face of the imperial army, heading straight for his brother's position. At the same time, he ordered the elite Greek force to attack. It was a wild throw, an insane attempt to win it all in one charge.

The Greek ten thousand crashed into the Persian lines. They found no one with the skill to stop them, so they were swallowed up and roamed almost freely in the midst of the Persian host.

Astonishingly, Cyrus battered his way through the king's guards and dealt King Artaxerxes a blow that knocked him from his horse. Cyrus had won – but in that instant, one of the Great King's men threw a spear that struck the young prince in the face, smashing his cheek and jaw. He was dazed and shaken and as he tried to recover, Artaxerxes staggered to his feet. The Great King approached Cyrus on foot and killed him. The Persian army began to cheer that the battle was over.

Meanwhile, the Greeks were far from their own side and blinded by dust and the chaos of a vast battlefield. They had no idea Cyrus had fallen, nor even where they were. They could hear cheering, but they didn't know if Cyrus had won or lost. It took hours for them to be told the news, and by that time the Persian regiments had pulled back. The ten thousand found themselves in a somewhat difficult position. There they were, Greeks in a foreign land, with an angry Persian king and a million of his men.

The Greek force pulled back to their camp, where another ten thousand camp followers had been hoping for victory. In dismay at the bad news, they began to pack up, ready to go home.

That evening, the Persian king sent messengers to invite the Greek generals under truce to a dinner, to discuss the future. They went to his camp, but he broke the truce and killed them at the table. King Artaxerxes believed the Greek soldiers would surrender immediately without their leaders. He sent new messengers to the camp to tell them to lay down their arms. If they had, it is unlikely we would ever have heard what became of them.

A young man stood up then, in the Greek force. His name was Xenophon, an Athenian. He spoke for some time, reminding the other soldiers that the Persians had betrayed them once and would again, no matter what promises were made. No one wanted to surrender and so the Greeks asked Xenophon to lead them, with a Spartan named Chirisophus. Xenophon immediately marched them north, trying to get to the border of Persia. The Greeks knew they would be attacked the whole way, but if they were to be killed, they preferred to die fighting than in meek surrender.

The Persian king was amazed when he heard the Greeks had just marched away, refusing his imperial demands. He sent an army after them and kept them under constant attack. The Greeks fought back, but they marched on the whole time. They had ten thousand camp followers to protect – men, women and children – as well as their own lives.

They crossed mountain ranges and rivers, fighting crag to crag, and surviving ambushes and traps and attacks by archers and cavalry. In snow, they went blind and suffered from frostbite and starvation. It helped that they were the supreme warriors of the age. When it came to hand-to-hand fighting, they were extraordinarily skilful.

After more than a year, they reached the shores of the Black Sea, where there were some Greek settlements. They had come thousands of miles and when they saw the sea for the first time, they shouted, 'Thalatta! Thalatta!' – 'The sea! The sea!' The 'ten thousand' had fought their way out. Though they were bearded and ragged, they had scorned a Persian king and the largest army on earth.

---

( 2 )

## BRUNANBURH – AD 937

In some ways, Brunanburh is the foundation stone of a nation, yet it has been almost completely forgotten. It deserves to be better known.

Eighth-century Britain

In the early 10th century, the problem for the fledgling kingdom of Wessex was almost constant attack from Vikings – from Scandinavia, from Ireland, from Norsemen in northern France. Kings, like everyone else, lived short lives, and whenever one of them died, the wolves all around Britain would expect weakness, launching brutal raids for plunder, slaves and land.

Wessex was a kingdom in southern England that eventually grew to rule the entire country. It was ruled by King Alfred the Great – the only king ever given that name. After being crowned king in AD 925, his grandson, King Æthelstan, conquered the last of the Viking strongholds two years later. He is best known as the first king of England, but he also went into Scotland, known then as the kingdom of Alba. King Constantine of Scotland swore an oath as 'subregulus' (under-king) to Æthelstan. Æthelstan had already won the loyalty of the Welsh, so should really be known as the first king of Britain. On his own coins and royal charters, he is described as 'Rex Totius Britanniae' – king of all Britain. However, his was to be a short reign.

In AD 939, King Constantine of Alba joined with a Viking who had settled in Ireland and called himself King of Dublin – Anlaf Guthfrithson. With supporting forces from King Owen of Strathclyde, the trio formed and landed an army large enough to challenge the High King of Britain himself.

The Battle of Brunanburh is recorded in the *Anglo-Saxon Chronicle*, the key record from the 9th to the 12th century. It is sometimes the only source for events and kings of this period, so reading a modern translation of this brief Wessex text can make an expert out of anyone.

> 'This year Æthelstan and Edmund his brother led a force to Brunanburh and there . . . slew five kings and seven earls.'
>
> Anglo-Saxon Chronicle

Little is known of the actual battle, except that the *Chronicle* records it as the most savage in all history to this point. The location has been lost, though it had to be near the west coast, perhaps somewhere just south of Liverpool. We know the Vikings used bows, berserkers and the shield line, but it was not enough to overcome the forces of the High King. Æthelstan had his own Viking berserker as his personal bodyguard – a fascinating monster of a man called Egill Skiallgrimmson. They fought hand-to-hand all day against the invaders, with great slaughter, until those men finally broke and ran back to their ships. They did not need half as many ships for the retreat as they had needed to arrive. Constantine fled to Scotland, crushed by the loss of his son and heir on the battlefield that day. Anlaf slunk away to Dublin – having lost thousands of men.

This was the classic victory of a battle-king. Æthelstan had been challenged by a group of lesser lords – and fought them himself in the lines. His men remained steadfast and the invaders were broken. It would not be the last time Danes and Irish Vikings came, of course, but this victory allowed Wessex and England to thrive for a brief time – just long enough to form a national identity and, through that, a nation.

Over a century later, in 1066, more Vikings known as Norsemen, or Northmen, would sweep up from northern France and be met at the Battle of Hastings by a different and less lucky king. The age of Anglo-Saxon kings would not end there, as the lines were married together. Queen Elizabeth II can trace her line back and back: through the Tudors, through York and Lancaster – all the way to William of Normandy, King Æthelstan and King Alfred the Great. ③

## TOWTON – 29 MARCH 1461

Towton remains the bloodiest battle ever fought on British soil – taking the crown from Brunanburh. Fifty to eighty thousand men met on 29 March and fought all day, giving no quarter. The death toll was appalling – well over

BATTLE OF TOWTON, 1461.

twenty thousand, which is a similar number to British losses on the first day of the Somme in 1916. The difference is that at the Somme, over four hundred years later, machine guns and rifles existed. At Towton, those deaths were either from the longbows that had utterly destroyed the French at Crécy (1346), Poitiers (1356) and Agincourt (1415), or worse, in hand-to-hand fighting – hand-axe and falchion sword and poleaxe (a combination of hammer and spike or axe). Skeletons from the site commonly show multiple mortal wounds – men hacked to death in an unbelievably savage frenzy.

To understand the brutality, you need to go back to the Great Ruins chapter, to Sandal Castle, where the Duke of York and Earl Salisbury were killed in December 1460. The Duke of York's younger son Edmund had also been killed as he tried to escape, the boy murdered by Lord Clifford of the Lancaster side. The three heads had been impaled on spikes in the city of York – a very public humiliation.

Just three months later, the two sons of those murdered men had gathered an army. Both young men were raw with grief and rage – far, far beyond forgiveness. Nothing demonstrates the personal nature of Towton better than the fact that they fought on, in the dark and snow.

Leading them was Edward, Duke of York, having inherited the title from his father. He was accompanied by Richard, Earl Warwick – the man known to history as the Kingmaker. Warwick had declared Edward king in London, to cheering crowds, before setting off to meet the House of Lancaster in battle. The new King Edward IV was eighteen years old and six foot four – a Goliath or an armoured tank on a battlefield in an age when most men were five foot five to five foot eight.

The House of Lancaster was technically the ruling house in England. King Henry VI was a weak man, supported by a French wife. Yet he was king. At this moment, England had two kings – and that had to be settled. King Henry was no leader, certainly not in battle. He was never more than a pawn for more powerful men. In command of Lancaster were the Duke of Somerset and Earl Percy of Northumberland, along with the same Lord Clifford who had personally killed Edward IV's younger brother at Sandal.

The force met first at Ferrybridge, a key crossing of the river Stour. Lancastrian forces under Lord Clifford destroyed the bridge and were making their way back to the main force when York approached and began to rebuild it. Clifford hung back until darkness came. He had archers with him and decided to spring an ambush while the forces of York slept. It was successful and his men spent every shaft they had, delighted with the slaughter. York had to pull back and his craftsmen struggled to finish enough of the bridge to allow King Edward IV to cross and engage the man whose banners he had recognised – the killer of his brother.

At the same time, Edward sent his uncle racing downriver to a shallow crossing. These men ran miles there and back in armour. Clifford didn't see them coming until they were almost upon him and his men scattered. It began to snow in heavy whiteness, so that Clifford and his men became lost. He signalled to someone, blind and confused. That man was of York and he killed Clifford, dragging him from his horse.

When King Edward rode across the river at last, he was taken to the body, to see Clifford dead. There was still no mercy in him. Rejoined by his uncle's forces, he gathered his entire army and marched on. The following morning, York and Lancaster met in heavy snow, blind to one another. They exchanged a slaughter of arrows, then fell to it, with frozen hands.

Towton has a hill, leading down to a river. It is dangerously steep and many of the fighting men tumbled down the snowy slopes to the river below, where they drowned. They fought all day, until every man was exhausted – and still Edward commanded the field. Darkness fell and he fought on, until at last the forces of Lancaster had no more fight in them and they broke. Many were killed as they trudged away, too tired even to defend themselves. The fields were covered in the dead and the river ran red for days afterwards.

The twists and turns of the Wars of the Roses are many, but this was the worst battle. If you visit Towton today, especially in winter, it is not difficult to imagine the horror of that day, born in loss and rage.

When the battle was over, the very first thing Edward and Warwick did was ride into the city of York and take down the heads of their fathers and Edward's brother. It must have been an extraordinary moment, in silence, while the snow fell still.

# THE SUMMER MEAL

In Italy, it tends to be the women who do most of the cooking, while the men can produce a good sauce and a signature dish. One of the authors once spent a fun afternoon with an Italian businessman, making garlands of sausages of the sort cartoon dogs used to steal from cartoon butchers. The ingredients were: minced pork, lots of red wine, salt, pepper and fennel – encasing them in camel intestine as they came out of the mincer. (Yes, we wondered about that as well, but they are fantastic for sausages.) It was, frankly, a joyous experience, turning 80lb of pork into an enormous number of sausages.

It seems obvious to us that every boy or young man should be able to prepare and serve a few simple dishes. Not only will it impress future girlfriends (oh son, more than you know), it is enormously satisfying. Developing key dishes that you really like is a good way to end up eating them every now and then. You are more likely to get a nice lasagne if you can make one yourself.

The aim here is not just to follow a recipe, but to become so familiar with it that you can do the whole thing without looking. There are high temperatures involved, so you'll need to bring a little common sense, oven gloves and possibly adult supervision. Do not put your head in the oven to see what is going on in there.

## THE STARTER

### INGREDIENTS

- Large slicing tomatoes – sometimes known as beef tomatoes
- Mozzarella – one ball per two people
- Fresh basil
- Salt, pepper, balsamic vinegar and olive oil

Mozzarella is cheese from buffalo milk. It comes in a watery liquid, so the first thing to do is drain it – two seconds, nothing tricky.

Slice the mozzarella balls – roughly as thick as a slice of bread. Three slices per plate – each mozzarella ball to feed two guests.

Wash and slice the tomatoes. Put two or three thick slices on each guest's plate and add a large sprig of basil. The basil will be eaten. Green, red and white are the colours of the Italian flag, so this is a very Italian starter. Drizzle on balsamic vinegar and olive oil and serve. The guests will add salt and pepper to taste.

(An alternative starter is a drizzle of oil and balsamic vinegar on a saucer, with crispy fresh bread to dip into it. This is a surprisingly delicious combination.)

## THE MAIN COURSE: LASAGNE

### INGREDIENTS

- Five tins of Cirio peeled plum tomatoes
- Olive oil
- Garlic clove
- 3lb (1.2kg) minced beef
- Basil leaves
- 1½oz (35g) butter
- 6 heaped teaspoons plain white flour
- About 10fl oz (300ml) milk
- 8–10oz (225–280g) Cheddar cheese
- 14oz (400g) cooking mozzarella
- 5–6oz (140–170g) Parmesan cheese
- Philadelphia cream cheese
- Pasta lasagne sheets
- Garlic salt and salt

### STAGE ONE: GETTING EVERYTHING READY

See what you have in your kitchen already and buy the bits you don't have. If you can, get hold of two foil catering roasting dishes as well – one to go in the freezer. The four main parts are cheese, beef, tomato and pasta sheets. This might seem complicated, but cooking is essentially a craft like any other. It's a pleasure to be able to do.

First, make a tomato sauce. (This is a variant of *the* Italian sauce that goes with pasta – learn to make this and you will never starve.)

Open all the tins of peeled Italian plum tomatoes. Chop them up into a thick paste with a knife and fork in a big mixing bowl. This takes five minutes or so. If you have a blender, you can use it to puree the tomatoes. (That results in a smoother and more spreadable tomato paste, but we wanted a version that didn't need powered equipment.) Add a little bit of water to the empty tomato tins, rinsing it around from one to the other, pouring the last of the tomato into the mixture. Put the cans into recycling.

Add 1½ or 2 tablespoons of olive oil to a large saucepan.

Cut the ends off a single clove of garlic. Peel off the skin and cut into five or six slices.

Turn on the gas to a high heat under the saucepan. Add the garlic slices to the oil. Let the oil heat up.

(If you happened to be making the classic Italian tomato pasta sauce, you would add Supercirio thick tomato paste to the garlic and oil. Lasagne doesn't need such a thick sauce, so we'll skip that here. Remember it, though. Tinned tomatoes, tomato paste, oil, garlic, add salt to taste – and that's the magnificent heart of a thousand Italian dishes, right there.)

Back to lasagne. When the oil starts to bubble around the garlic after about a minute, add the tomatoes. Be careful with this as hot oil will spit.

Stir the mixture with a wooden spoon. Bring it to the boil on a high heat, then as soon as it's boiling, turn the heat down to a simmer. Rest a saucepan lid on the sauce, but don't cover it completely or it will go watery. Leave to simmer for around 30 minutes. Tomatoes change taste as they cook, so don't put salt in until the end, or you'll end up overdoing it.

To cook the minced beef, put a frying pan on a high heat with no oil. When the pan is hot, add all of the beef in one go, breaking it apart with a fork. It has its own oils, so it will quickly create juices. Stir with a wooden spoon until all the meat is lightly browned. This takes about 10 minutes. In the meantime, stir the tomatoes every now and then, so they don't burn.

Once the minced beef has browned and is simmering, sprinkle over one teaspoon of garlic salt and one teaspoon of normal salt. Mix in well, then turn off the heat and leave to cool. Congratulate yourself. This is going pretty well so far. Remind yourself that pride goes before a fall. Take a deep breath and carry on.

## BÉCHAMEL SAUCE

A white sauce made from milk, flour and butter. This is a vital part of the creaminess of a good lasagne. Begin by melting the butter in a small saucepan.

While the butter melts, add salt to the tomatoes. Tastes differ, obviously, but it will be around a teaspoon in pinches, stirring and tasting as you go. Remember, you can always add more salt, but you cannot take it out. Put a few leaves of basil into the tomato sauce.

Back to the béchamel sauce: add the flour to the melted butter, stirring it into a thick paste. On a low heat, add the milk, bit by bit, to the paste, stirring briskly until it forms a smooth batter or sauce, adding more milk as you go.

Turn off the heat on the tomato sauce after 30 minutes and leave to stand. It should have thickened. Add half a teaspoon of garlic salt to the white sauce. Stir in and turn off the heat. Leave to settle.

Grate the Cheddar cheese, ready to be sprinkled. Cut the cooking mozzarella into small cubes. Grate the Parmesan cheese. (Grate more than you need – you can always put it on toast.)

Put the cheese in separate bowls to be snatched up as necessary. You are now ready to begin the second stage – building the lasagne.

## STAGE TWO: BUILDING THE LASAGNE

Assemble everything you need on a single surface: the tomato sauce, the frying pan of beef, the béchamel saucepan, the three cheeses and a pot of Philadelphia, the garlic salt, salt, pepper and the lasagne pasta sheets.

Spoon a couple of ladles of tomato sauce into the first foil dish and spread it around to the corners to cover the whole bottom. Lay the lasagne pasta sheets on top, overlapping slightly. If your foil dish has rounded corners, snap off the corners of those sheets

to make them fit. The aim is to make an unbroken sheet, so feel free to break them lengthways or halfway along until you have covered the entire base.

Smear another couple of ladles of tomato sauce, being careful to spread to the edges of the pasta sheets. If you see a slice of garlic clove, you might want to take it out, depending on whether you like garlic or not.

With a different ladle or big spoon, sprinkle a layer of minced beef. Be generous, but it doesn't have to cover everything. Either use a slotted spoon or tilt the frying pan to avoid picking up too much juice as you go.

Sprinkle cheese liberally: Cheddar, Parmesan and the mozzarella cubes. All three will cover the minced beef beneath. Add around two teaspoonfuls of Philadelphia, spread around in three or more gobbets.

Drizzle the béchamel sauce, around two tablespoons' worth. Season with salt and pepper – a sprinkled pinch of both across the surface of the layer. That is the layer, done.

Now place another two layers in the same pattern: pasta, tomato, minced beef, cheeses, Philadelphia, sauce, salt and pepper.

To finish: a top layer of pasta, with tomato dribbled onto it, then sprinkled Parmesan.

For clarity, the entire sequence is: first layer – tomato, pasta, beef, cheeses, S&P; second layer – pasta, tomato, beef, cheeses, S&P; third layer – pasta, tomato, beef, cheeses, S&P; top layer – pasta, tomato, Parmesan. In all, there are four layers of pasta and three layers of beef. This should fill a typical foil dish and will feed six people.

The ingredients here are just enough to make two standard catering foil dishes (12in × 9in × 2in deep). The reason for that is that a lasagne can be frozen. At some point in the future, perhaps when you are unwell, or when no one wants to cook, a lasagne is a pretty amazing thing to pull out of a freezer. So eat one – and freeze one. You'll always be grateful that you did.

Cover the dish in foil before putting it in the oven (or the freezer), Gas Mark 6 for around 40 minutes. Serve with the simplest green salad in existence.

## THE SIMPLEST GREEN SALAD IN EXISTENCE

Wash and slice an iceberg lettuce – or any sort of lettuce. Tablespoon of olive oil, two tablespoons of lemon juice, sprinkle of salt. Mix together and serve.

## THE DESSERT: TIRAMISU

Tiramisu means 'pull me up' – a dish made with coffee to end a meal and liven up the guests. This most famous of Italian desserts also happens to be very simple to make, so is perfect for our purposes. We are not trying to be master chefs here. Our aim is for readers to make a half-decent meal from scratch. Pleasingly, both the tiramisu and the lasagne can be made beforehand and kept in the fridge. Only the starter needs to be cut fresh.

### INGREDIENTS

*   Three eggs
*   Five large tablespoons of caster sugar
*   500g of mascarpone
*   About one pint (568ml) Espresso coffee (ten espresso cups. You can use instant coffee if you have to)
*   Two packets of sponge fingers – enough for two layers of a serving dish. (Shape of dish is not important, but it should have a couple of inches of depth. Savoyardi biscuits are the best, but supermarket sponge fingers work perfectly well. We bought two packs of 28 and used 20 to make each layer, 40 in all)
*   Drinking chocolate powder
*   A pinch of salt

Note: As with any dessert dish that contains raw eggs, it should not be served to pregnant women.

Separate three yolks from the whites, by tipping them back and forth in the shell. You'll need both yolks and whites, but at different times. Pour the sugar and the egg yolks into a mixing dish. Whisk together until thick. An electric whisk is faster.

Now whisk the egg whites in a separate bowl with a pinch of salt, until stiff – five minutes with an electric whisk, ten by hand.

Add the mascarpone to the egg yolk mixture, stirring it into a thick paste. Don't work it too hard – you don't want it to become runny. Just fold it all together until it's a uniform pale yellow.

Stir in the fluffy egg whites mixture. You don't want to lose all the fluff, so stir slowly until you have a smooth surface.

Pour the espresso coffee into a wide bowl and allow it to go cold. You are now ready to build the tiramisu. Think of it as a lasagne with sponge fingers and coffee. Don't think of it like that. That sounds terrible.

Spread a layer of the thick cream on the base of the serving bowl – about a third of the mixture. Take each sponge finger and dip one side in the coffee for a count of four, until it is soaked, then hold above the coffee to drain for another count of four. Dip . . . one, two, three, four . . . Lift, one, two, three, four . . . Turn it over and lay it in the dish. Continue with each sponge finger in the same way until you have filled the whole layer.

Spread on another layer of the cream, the second third of the mixture, then fill in a second layer of sponge fingers. According to the Italian family recipe we used, you should lay the second layer across the sponge fingers of the first.

Finally, spread on the last of the cream and sprinkle chocolate powder over the top. Put it in the fridge for four hours minimum. You can leave this overnight if you want. Serves eight. This is a truly lovely dessert. Variations include using raspberry juice or sweet lemon instead of coffee. Enjoy chilled, on a warm summer evening.

# BRITISH BIRDS

There are hundreds of bird species to be seen in Britain. Just about everyone recognises blackbirds, robins, sparrows, gulls – and the red kites that have bred very successfully since being reintroduced. This is a brief guide to the ones you might come across in a garden or on a walk.

1. **BLACKCAP**. A warbler. Only the males show the black mark.
2. **NIGHTINGALE**. Famed for its song. Fairly rare, but can be found in the south, particularly around Sussex and Suffolk.
3. **GOLDFINCH**. Red, black and yellow flashes. Small songbird, found all over.
4. **SISKIN**. Smaller than a sparrow. Found across the UK, a type of small finch. Predominantly yellow, but males have a black crown.
5. **LINNET**. Small songbird with a fondness for flax or linseeds, from which linen – and the linnet – take their names.
6. **REDPOLL**. Another ancient finch variety, with red marking on its head.
7. **SKYLARK**. Speckled brown farmland bird. If you've ever walked across muddy fields in Britain, you've heard it sing.
8. **GREENFINCH**. About the size of a sparrow, green or yellow. Can be seen in gardens.
9. **BLACKBIRD**. One of the most common birds in the UK. Males have a gold beak and black eyes with a gold ring around them. Females are brown and lightly spotted. When one of the authors was a young boy, he found a dead blackbird and dissected it with the kitchen breadknife – and never told his parents.
10. **SONG THRUSH**. Speckled brown. The mistle thrush is a variety that country wisdom held was the last bird still in the air when a storm was coming. A brave bird, then, or a mad one.
11. **STARLING**. Glossy, dark green metallic feathers. Used to be very common, but less so now.
12. **BRAMBLING**. Similar to a chaffinch in size, but orange-chested and speckle-winged.
13. **BULLFINCH**. Round little bird, with a short bill. Both male and female have black caps, but only the male has that deep rose underneath. The females tend to be lighter coloured.
14. **CHAFFINCH**. A classic of British gardens where there are seeds. Reddish head and body, with bands of white and black on the wings.
15. **YELLOWHAMMER**. Bright yellow head and forked tail. Slightly larger than a chaffinch.
16. **MAGPIE**. Aggressive, noisy, not much loved, but rather attractive with its black and white colours. They are clever and curious birds.
17. **JAY**. Smaller than a pigeon, with a distinctive blue band on the wings. A lover of acorns.
18. **JACKDAW**. Smallest member of the crow family in Britain. Distinctive grey head and bright blue eyes. They pair for life and are perhaps the cleverest of all birds. They can be tamed and taught tricks.
19. **ROBIN**. The beloved bird. Sings all winter and is both brave and curious enough to approach gardeners wherever they turn over soil, looking for worms.
20. **PEREGRINE FALCON**. The king of birds. The fastest raptor on the planet, these are not common, but can sometimes be seen hunting over fields.
21. **RED KITE**. Once common, these died out and were re-introduced. They've spread well and are now a common sight, flying in lazy circles.

These are the ones you are most likely to see. As with cloud formations or trees, it should be part of living in a country that you know the names of what you find around you.

# SHOTGUNS

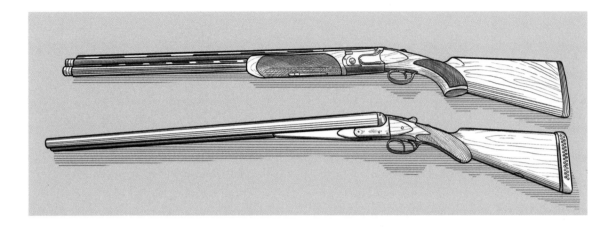

Rifle barrels have a spiral cut along the inside. This is called 'rifling' and it spins the bullet as it passes – giving stability that leads to immense accuracy and range. A shotgun – a gun that fires shot – has no rifling. It fires small metal balls along a perfectly smooth barrel, expanding out to distances of 40–100 yards. That expanding cone of shot makes it a lot easier to hit a fast-moving target, such as a pigeon or pheasant. You would have to be a first-class sniper to hit a flying bird with a rifle, but a shotgun is the perfect tool for the job. In America, they are incredibly common. Like pick-up trucks, everybody has one. Italy is one of the biggest manufacturers of shotguns, with huge companies such as Beretta. They are still made in the UK as well – an ancient business that produces some of the best shotguns manufactured today. New prices range from around £400 up to the tens of thousands. Yet the second-hand market is alive and kicking. It is possible to spend a couple of hundred pounds on a perfectly safe and serviceable second-hand shotgun.

Before you can own a shotgun in the UK, you'll need to apply for a shotgun licence. There are around a million and a half shotguns privately owned in the UK. Applying to own one is not a difficult process, though it does take time and will cost around £80 at the time of writing. The application form can be found on the UK government website. It's not a bad idea to print it out twice, keeping one as a rough copy before sending in the best one to the shotgun licensing unit of your local police force.

FORM 201 – 2017 - 1

**APPLICATION FOR THE GRANT OR RENEWAL OF A FIREARM AND/OR SHOTGUN CERTIFICATE**

PLEASE READ THE NOTES CAREFULLY (PAGES 12-15) BEFORE COMPLETING THE APPLICATION FORM

You may type your responses except where your signature is required. Otherwise, please use black ink and write in **BLOCK CAPITALS** throughout, except when signing. A continuation sheet is provided at page 6 for further information.

I am applying for (tick each box which applies)

- **Firearm certificate** ☐ Grant ☐ Renewal     • **Shotgun certificate** ☐ Grant ☐ Renewal

Do you wish to apply for a shotgun certificate which will expire at the same time as your firearm certificate? ☐ Yes ☐ No

| PART A: Personal details. | PART B: Personal health & medical declaration |
|---|---|
| 1. Gender ☐ Male ☐ Female | If necessary, continue on page 6<br>Important: Read notes 4-12 before completion. |
| 2. Title ......... | |
| 3. Surname ......... | 10. Have you ever been diagnosed with or treated for any of the medical conditions in note 5? |
| 4. Forenames (state all) ......... | ☐ Yes (Please provide details)   ☐ No |
| 5. If you have at any time used a name other than that given in answer to questions 3 and 4 please complete below: | |
| Previous surname(s) ......... | |
| Previous forename(s) ......... | 11. Details of your GP or GP practice |
| 6. Home address ......... | a. Name ......... |
| | b. Address ......... |
| a. Postcode ......... | |
| b. Home tel number ......... | c. Postcode ......... |
| c. Mobile number ......... | d. Tel number ......... |
| d. Home E-mail ......... | E-mail ......... |

As well as your personal details and address, you'll be asked for details of your GP. He or she will be asked if you have a history of psychiatric illness. A policeman will also visit your house to interview you. This should not be a worry. In 2018, police issued over a thousand shotgun certificates to those under sixteen – some as young as eight. The police apply a rule of thumb that there has to be a good reason for a shotgun licence application to be denied. If you have a criminal record for violence, that would probably count as a good reason.

There is no minimum age for using a shotgun, though you do have to be eighteen and above to own one – and those of fifteen and under need to be accompanied by an adult of twenty-one and over. With the support of a responsible parent, it is quite possible to use a shotgun safely – and to learn a fascinating skill. After all, shotguns are used in rural areas all over the UK, to control vermin and shoot game birds. Or you might prefer to visit a clay-pigeon site, where remotely operated clay discs can be sent spinning into the air for you to shatter. Any weapon is potentially dangerous, of course. A shotgun is also a simple, rugged tool that can be a joy to use and own. The licences are valid for five years and can be renewed without any fuss for around £50.

Finally, you'll need to buy a gun cabinet and install it somewhere secure – which usually means bolted to a brick wall. The police visitor will be able to advise on the best location. Gun cabinets are made of heavy steel and have complex locks that are difficult to open. Your shotguns should be stored in one whenever they're not in use.

There is no restriction on where you can store shotgun cartridges, beyond the simple common sense of not leaving them where they can be dropped onto a hard floor. You will need to show a shotgun certificate when buying cartridges. These are sold by any gun shop and the most common size is a box

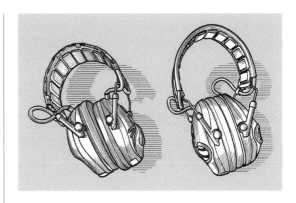

of twenty-five 1oz (28g) shells. You could very easily shoot a hundred at a clay-pigeon session.

Over time, you'll need to get a bag to carry cartridges, but your first purchase after the licence and the gun itself should be a good pair of earphones. Shotguns are loud. If you shoot one a hundred times, you'll need ear protection. There are many brands on the market, from simple earplugs to noise-cancelling powered ones.

## TYPES OF SHOTGUN

In the UK, there are three main types on sale:

1. **SIDE-BY-SIDE** – barrels arranged in parallel. This is the older style, with two elegantly curved triggers, usually one behind the other. Each trigger fires a different barrel, which might seem complicated but actually feels completely natural. Spent cartridges have to be removed by hand. Versions are still available with hammers that can be pulled back manually, but most cock (ready to fire) as the gun is closed.

2. **OVER-AND-UNDER** – barrels sit atop one another. This is by far the most popular shotgun design. Mechanically they are heavier

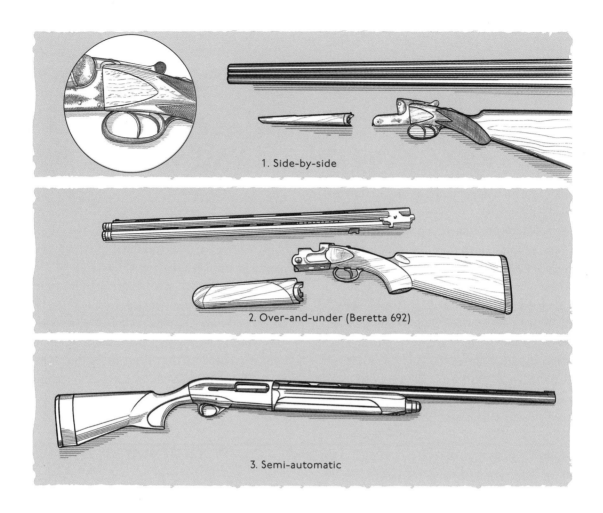

1. Side-by-side

2. Over-and-under (Beretta 692)

3. Semi-automatic

and more complicated than older side-by-sides. They have a single trigger, which resets after the first shot, to be ready to fire the second barrel. They also have an ejector mechanism that spits used cartridges high into the air when the gun is broken. We like both these types, so it's a matter of personal choice which you prefer. The best option would be to go to a gun range and pay for a lesson with both types before buying.

3. **SEMI-AUTOMATIC** – the only one that will take three cartridges at a time, the legal maximum in the UK. 'Semi-automatic' means

it resets after a shot to fire again. Side-loading, these are popular with game-shooters as they can be reloaded with little physical movement.

Within those three types, there is a world of variety. Left- and right-handed guns, intricate decoration, different barrel lengths, weights, materials – and costs. 'Chokes' are a way of restricting the barrel and so shaping the cone of shot, which affects the range. Shooting magazines devote entire articles to chokes.

The other common term you'll hear is 12 bore or 12 gauge, or perhaps 16 gauge or 20 gauge. The

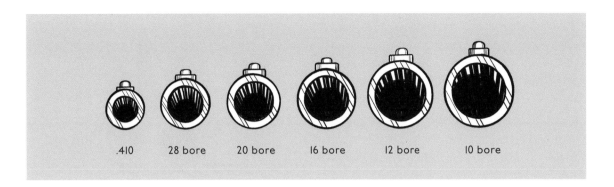

.410      28 bore      20 bore      16 bore      12 bore      10 bore

word 'bore' refers to the diameter of the barrels and comes from single-ball muzzle-loading long guns. A '12-bore' barrel would take a ball that was a twelfth of a pound of lead, rammed down on top of gunpowder and wadding. As a result, 12-bore or 12-gauge shotguns tend to fire a greater weight of shot than smaller ones. They are by far the most popular size, though smaller shooters sometimes prefer a 16- or 20- bore gun. Children starting out are often given a single-shot .410 (.41 of an inch across) – the smallest size of barrel.

## TYPES OF CARTRIDGE

Lead is still the most common type of shot – the first to be made in shot towers, where liquid metal was allowed to drop into a vat of cold water far below. This technique was discovered in 1782 by William Watts, a Bristol plumber, and used for around two hundred years. (It is a pleasant thought that the word 'plumber' comes from 'plumbum' – the Latin for lead – as Roman artisans worked with lead pipes.)

There is also shot made from steel and various other metals – usually chosen in an attempt to reduce the amount of lead being scattered around the landscape. (The absolute ideal would be gold shot, as it is heavy, chemically inert and doesn't pollute. Sadly, gold is also really expensive.)

For a standard 12-bore shotgun, clay-pigeon loads of ⅞oz to 1oz (24/28g), No. 7 or No. 8 ball size are common. Speed is around 1290 fps (feet per second). These are smaller shot balls, which don't penetrate or travel too far.

For live pigeon, 1⅛ oz (32g) at No. 6 size of ball and a cartridge 2½ inches long is ideal – with a muzzle velocity of 1375 fps. No. 5 ball, 3in cartridges of 1¼oz (36g) can be used for high pheasants or even geese. (In America, loads can be right up to 2⅛ oz (60g), to shoot turkeys.)

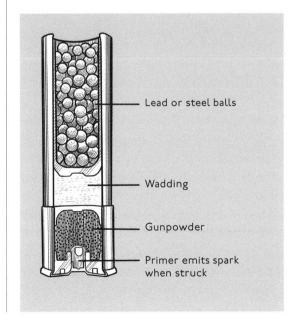

Lead or steel balls

Wadding

Gunpowder

Primer emits spark when struck

Each shotgun barrel is 'proofed', i.e. tested, with a range of shot to make sure it can handle it. It's worth discussing the most suitable ball and cartridge weight and length for the task with the owner of a gun shop or a range. Some ranges insist on cartridges with degradable fibre wadding, for example, preferring them to plastic. They are experts and they are willing to advise. Don't be afraid to ask. You're not expected to know everything and you'll pick it up as you go along.

## SAFETY

Shotguns are mechanical things, made of metal and wood. They need to be kept clean and oiled to remain safe. They should never be pointed at another person – whether loaded or unloaded. Learn never to swing the barrel across anyone else, even if you are certain there are no cartridges in the gun. When carried outside a slip or sleeve, you will 'break' the gun and rest it on a forearm, or over a shoulder. In that way, anyone nearby will know it cannot be fired.

When passing a shotgun to someone, it should be stock first, with the gun broken, so they can see it is empty. The same applies when taking it out of a sleeve. Break the gun and check it is not loaded, with the barrels pointing down. As a rule of thumb, always treat a shotgun as loaded until you're certain it isn't – and then treat it as loaded anyway. Blowing your foot off, or worse, the foot of someone else, is the sort of event that shapes a life – or ends it. It is possible to use a shotgun safely with just a little care and common sense. If you are not sure, ask someone who knows. In our experience, they are delighted to explain, with no sense of judgement whatsoever.

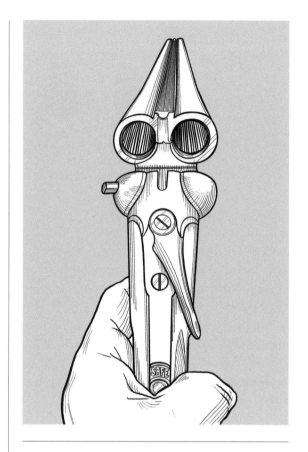

'Broken' gun

When you have a licence, a shotgun, headphones, cartridges and a bag for them, you'll want to see if you can shoot. We suggest visiting a clay-pigeon range and getting a few lessons. Like any other skill, shooting can be learned and improved through practice. If you'd prefer to go after live prey, ask at a local gun shop. There'll be a willing farmer or a shoot of some kind near you.

Compared to, say, tennis, shooting is more expensive to start, but not too bad after the initial costs. Finally, using hand-to-eye coordination to lead a target and hit it is one of the most ancient human skills, which can also be a lot of fun.

# FORGOTTEN EXPLORERS

Human beings have always wanted to see what lies over the next hill. The history of the world is one of increasing horizons – of Cortez climbing a peak in Panama and seeing the vast Pacific ahead of him, or Drake climbing the same peak and vowing to take an English ship to plunder the Spanish, or John Cabot landing in Newfoundland in 1497. With crude tools, these explorers mapped rivers, coasts and the deep oceans, so that those who came after could go further and with less peril. Behind them came traders and builders and families willing to scrape a farm from a clearing in the wilderness. Yet over time, memories fade. Some stories are forgotten, while others are lifted up and burnished. Here are a few of the lost names – and a few who are still famous. They all made a mark.

### SIR MARTIN FROBISHER
### (c. 1535–1594)

Yorkshire captain who tried three times to search for the fabled North-West Passage – a route north from Britain across the top of the world to the Pacific and Asia. (Airlines tend to fly close to the Pole heading from London to New York today as it's the shortest arc.) He discovered a vast sheltered bay on Baffin Island off the coast of Canada. Frobisher Bay is over 140 miles long (over 230km). In later life, he played a role in Drake's fleet that went out to engage the Spanish Armada in 1588. Frobisher died in 1594, from a wound incurred while storming a Spanish fortress.

### SIR FRANCIS DRAKE
### (c. 1540–1596)

As well as more famous exploits against the Spanish, Drake was the first Briton to circumnavigate the world (and the first expedition leader to return home alive – Magellan died halfway round). He mapped and navigated the then unknown west coast of America, right up to Canada. Drake Bay in Costa Rica is named after him, as is Drake Passage, between Antarctica and Cape Horn. Appropriately, this great piratical hero was buried at sea, off the coast of Panama.

### JOHN DAVIS
### (c. 1550–1605)

Like Frobisher and Drake, Davis attempted to find the North-West Passage. It meant heading north into frozen latitudes, searching and mapping each small bay and inlet in case that was the one that led across the roof of the world. The Davis Strait that runs by Greenland is named after him. He also named Cape Walsingham after Queen Elizabeth I's spymaster. Later on, Davis commanded the *Black Dog* against the Spanish Armada in 1588, one of the master captains under Drake. In 1592, Davis discovered the then uninhabited Falkland Islands. They were formally claimed by England in 1596. Davis sailed with Sir Water Raleigh on more than one expedition and was killed by Japanese pirates in 1605. He was also the inventor of the back staff, a navigation device used for 200 years.

### HENRY HUDSON
### (c. 1565–1611)

Hudson also tried to find a way to Japan and China from England via the North Pole. His later explorations led to the Hudson Bay, Strait and River being named after him. His discoveries formed the basis of the original English claim to what would become Canadian territory. In 1670, King Charles II granted a Royal Charter to the Hudson's Bay Company – specifically 'the Governor and Company of Adventurers of England trading into Hudson's Bay'. That company still trades today.

### WILLIAM DAMPIER
### (1651–1715)

Explorer, navigator and pirate, who circumnavigated the world three times and explored much of the coast of northern Australia, collecting specimens of plants and animals, as well as mapping and charting. He was dismissed from the Royal Navy for cruelty, but when war broke out with Spain, Dampier found ship again as a privateer. On one expedition, a captain under Dampier's command marooned seaman Alexander Selkirk for complaining about a ship's seaworthiness. Selkirk became the inspiration for the story *Robinson Crusoe*. Dampier is mentioned in *Gulliver's Travels* as a master navigator and his scientific approach influenced those who came after him.

### SAMUEL WALLIS
### (1728–1795)

Cornish captain, Royal Navy. He circumnavigated the world in 1766 in HMS *Dolphin*. After passing through the Strait of Magellan at the tip of South America, he sailed on to Tahiti in the Pacific. His lieutenant planted a flag and formally claimed the island for King George III. Wallis named another Polynesian island after himself, though it is a French possession today. The ship's goat survived the circumnavigation and went on to complete a second with Captain Cook on *Endeavour*.

### SIR JAMES CLARK ROSS
### (1800–1862)

Ross began his career looking for the North-West Passage in 1818, with his uncle. Ross also plotted the position of the magnetic North Pole in Canada. However, he is best remembered for his exploration of the Antarctic continent around the South Pole. Mapping a vast section of coast, he named Victoria Land, Admiralty Sound and two extinct Antarctic volcanoes: Mount Terror and Mount Erebus, those last names taken from his expedition ships. The Ross Sea and the forbidding Ross Ice Shelf in Antarctica are named after him.

### SIR JOHN FRANKLIN
### (1786–1847)

A rich and varied career took him from being a midshipman in Nelson's navy to Arctic exploration and, on the other side of the world, a stint as Governor of Tasmania. Franklin Square is named for him there, as is the Franklin River on the west coast. In 1845, Franklin went on his last voyage, in the same two ships that had taken Sir James Clark Ross to Antarctica – the *Terror* and the *Erebus*, refitted with steam engines. His entire expedition vanished in the Arctic – a mystery that gripped Victorian

England. Later reports suggested he and his men starved to death over two years of being locked in ice. Though both ships were strong-hulled, they became icebound and were eventually crushed. Franklin was remembered in statues as a hero by the Victorians, but his star has faded almost completely. The wrecks of his ships were located in 2014 and 2016.

### CHARLES DARWIN
### (1809–1882)

Best known for his *Origin of Species* and theory of evolution. Darwin's famous voyage aboard HMS *Beagle* bears a closer look. It lasted from 1831 to 1836 and took in the island of Cape Verde in the Atlantic, where he discovered seashells high in the cliffs; Argentina, where he found massive fossil bones; and Chile, where he witnessed an earthquake. He collected specimens in the Galapagos Islands, off Ecuador, then went west to Australia, where he visited the Blue Mountains, near Sydney. He was astonished at the astonishing variety of species and collected dozens that had never been recorded before. From Australia, HMS *Beagle* went on to Cape Town in South Africa before returning home. Those five years of exploration, mapping and collecting gave him what he needed to form the theories and write the books for which he is best known. The city of Darwin in Australia is named after him, as is Charles Darwin Walk in the Blue Mountains. There are three navigable passages around or through the tip of South America. The Strait of Magellan is to the north and the open-ocean route is Drake Passage. Between them lies the route taken by a 26-year-old Darwin: the Beagle Strait, or Beagle Channel.

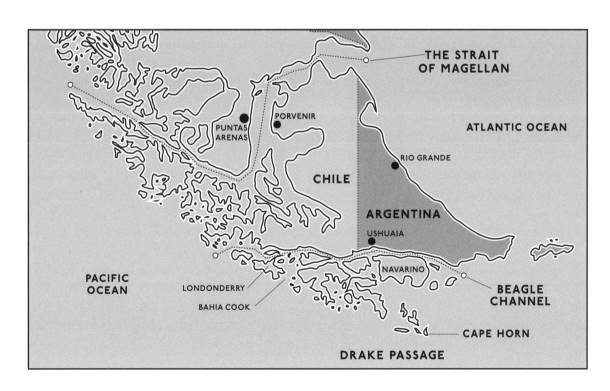

# HOW TO WIRE A PLUG AND
# MAKE AN INSPECTION LAMP

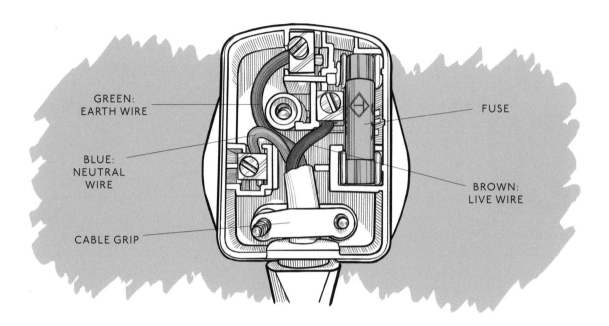

GREEN:
EARTH WIRE

BLUE:
NEUTRAL
WIRE

CABLE GRIP

FUSE

BROWN:
LIVE WIRE

If you've travelled almost anywhere, you may have noticed that plugs used in Britain are different from the ones used abroad. Both America and the countries in Europe tend to use two-prong plugs with no earth wire and no fuse. How can the humble UK plug survive in the 21st century? Luckily, it's a much better design. The UK plug has a longer earth prong, which has to be inserted before the other two can be. It also has two of the three prongs part-covered in insulation so as to reduce the chance of a shock as it is removed or if a plug is loose. Finally, the main wire is held in a plastic grip, which does a terrific job – but if huge force is exerted, the blue neutral and brown live wires are designed to pull out before the earth, keeping the whole thing earthed and as safe as possible. 'Health and Safety' has a bad name when it's used as an excuse not to do something – but good design is a joy.

For a circuit to work, electricity has to be able to flow all the way around. The simplest example needs only a battery, a bulb and two wires – one to the bulb and one from it to complete the circuit. The earth wire is in case something goes wrong – basically, live current should 'earth' or 'run to earth' along a copper wire more easily than through you. The human body has a resistance of around 1,000 ohms and electricity tends to take the easiest route. A brief shock is unlikely to kill you, as it happens, though a prolonged one certainly would. One of the authors put his finger into a live lamp socket in the dark a few years back, expecting there to be a bulb in it. It felt almost exactly like being bitten.

To avoid that, UK plugs use a simple fuse – a weak part, designed to blow the circuit before anything more serious happens. One end is attached to the live prong of the plug, the other to the live wire, so that the fuse forms a bridge across that bit of the circuit. They are usually made of clay, with a very thin wire running through. The thickness of the wire gives the resistance, though they are designated in amps or amperes: 3A, 5A and 13A are the main ones. Lamps will be 3 or 5 amps. Any heater will be 13A. It is important not to put a 13A fuse into a 3A circuit. You want it to be the weak point and blow quickly, before something is set on fire.

---

NOTE: Amps are the units for current, volts are the units for voltage and resistance is measured in ohms. The relationship between them is: Current = Voltage/Resistance. The classic analogy is to think of current as the flow rate, voltage as water pressure – and resistance as the pipe size.

---

The neutral wire is blue in the UK and it attaches to the prong on the left in the picture. You can remove a little of the plastic sheath with either a hobby knife or a pair of wire strippers. The bare metal wire goes into the slot and you'll need a flat-head screwdriver then to tighten the screw down onto it. The same goes for the brown live wire, by the fuse, and the earth, which is always green, or green and yellow. It can be a bit fiddly getting them all to fit.

The main wire exits the plug under a plastic cuff with two more screws that can be tightened onto it. Refitting that cuff is usually a pain if removed completely, so it's best to insert the main wire underneath the cuff, then attach the three smaller wires. It's a simple system, but we believe it's the best in the world. Also, it's a pleasure to be able to do this. A lot of modern plugs arrive fully sealed in plastic, with all the wiring hidden. That's a shame. If you can take a plug off and replace it, you'll have a better understanding of how it works – and that is never a bad thing.

## MAKING AN INSPECTION LAMP

UK law on lamps only require an earth when there is exposed metal. If it's a plastic lamp holder, you only need a two-core flex – the blue and brown wires. We could suggest these inspection lamps are available from any hardware shop and online, but the truth is, when we were kids, we raided parts to make this sort of thing. In our house, broken electrical items always had their plugs cut off before they were thrown away – plugs are useful. The same goes for old lampholders and electrical wire. They're worth cutting and keeping.

Attach the plug to one end, making sure the screws have all been tightened and there are no loose wires. The lampholder will look something like this:

You can buy attractive metal ones, but then legally and for your safety, you'll need to attach the earth cable – in the plug and to a separate connection in the brass lampholder.

It's important to hold the main cable steady. These lampholders usually come with some kind of plastic grabber to prevent the cable from slipping. This is important, so don't just skip it; the main cable needs to be held securely. If you don't have one, you can use duct tape, obviously.

Feed the outer cover onto the wire and wiggle the wire gripper to roughly where you want it – you can't put them on afterwards.

Attach the live and neutral wires. It doesn't matter which is which on a bayonet lamp. If you have a screw-in or Edison lampholder of the sort more common in America and in European countries, you'll have to get the wires the right way round, but the socket will be clearly marked.

There will also be some sort of plastic hook as part of the lampholder. This is to wind the brown and blue wires through before they exit, so that any sudden tug will pull against the hook and not where the wires have been screwed in. Leave enough wire to do this. It's a clever design feature.

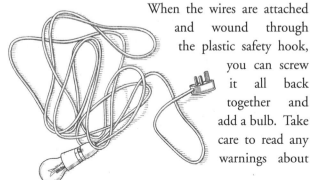

When the wires are attached and wound through the plastic safety hook, you can screw it all back together and add a bulb. Take care to read any warnings about

maximum wattage. If it says 60W maximum, a 100-watt bulb will create too much heat.

That's it – a workshop lamp, perhaps. It can be draped over something, or held in the hand. The bulb is vulnerable to being dropped, of course. Most shop-bought ones will come with a metal cage to protect the bulb.

## JUMP LEADS

As a final thought: jump leads, or jumper cables. The ones you can buy are almost always too short. We bought thick copper welding cable and some grippy crocodile-clip things when we came across them in a hardware shop. At ten feet long, they are the best jump leads we have ever come across, still going strong after many uses, years later. When you connect two car batteries with these, one wire attaches positive terminal to positive terminal, then the second attaches 'negative to negative' – being very careful with the last one, which can weld itself to the wing if you drop it.

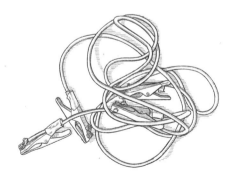

Never forget the old joke: What's black and crispy and hangs from a lampshade? A bad electrician. If you're not sure, ask.

# HOW TO WRITE A THANK-YOU LETTER

There is an old custom in Ireland, to bow the head briefly in prayer when saying 'Jesus' – particularly when saying the line from the Ave Maria, or Hail Mary, that ends with '. . . the fruit of thy womb, Jesus'.

In christening services, where babies are dedicated to the Church, parents and godparents are asked to make some stirring oaths:

'Do you reject Satan and all his works?'

'I do', they reply.

'And all his empty promises?'

'I do' – and so on.

Now, it happened that one morning a priest noticed an old lady in the pews was bowing her head every time she heard 'Satan'. Surprised by this, he waited until the service was over and approached her.

'I couldn't help notice, madam, that you bowed your head, not just for the name of Jesus, but for Satan as well.'

The lady smiled and replied, 'Yes, father. You see, I am very old. I could go at any time.'

'But why "Satan"?' the priest went on.

'Well, father, politeness costs nothing – and you never know.'

An old lady wondering if she's going to spend eternity in heaven or hell is not exactly a side-splitter, perhaps, but it makes the point: politeness costs very little, but it can mean a great deal. Going out of your way to say 'thank you' – and 'sorry' – is often the right thing to do and, frankly, makes life run more smoothly. Such things are the oil in the wheels.

It is, of course, necessary to consider your audience. When we visited Yorkshire, we discovered people there were used to much shorter introductions. In shops, by the time we'd reached the end of 'Excuse me, I'm sorry to trouble you. I wonder if you can tell me . . .' they were serving another customer. There is such a thing as too flowery.

A thank-you letter, then, can be quite simple. Even a couple of lines on notepaper, sent in a stamped envelope, is evidence that it was important to you. This is an often underrated aspect. Yes, obviously, an email is fine in many circumstances. No, you don't want to send a formal thank-you letter to the electricity company, saying how thrilled you were to receive their bill. Still, most people don't realise the impact of taking the time to do this. It proves you value the person you send it to. That can be a powerful thing.

What follows is a template for writing a letter, with some basic comments on structure. There are, of course, different styles and approaches. They are what we call 'incorrect' approaches. This is what is known as the 'correct' way to do it.

First, a short and simple example with some notes included:

In a handwritten letter, put commas after road, town etc. Typed letters don't need them. Postcode – not always necessary.

42 Dangerous Avenue,

Perilous Village,

Kent.

ME15 6JQ

14 February 2020

Centred in handwritten letters.
On the left in typed.

Dear Clive,

       Thank you for coming to lunch.

It was lovely to see you and we had a wonderful time. A good lunch is one

of life's rewards, as my father used to say. This was one of those times.

'Faithfully', after Dear Sir/Madam; 'Sincerely' after Dear Mr Jones.
Just 'Yours' is warmer, so can be used for letters to friends, or as a
catch-all. If you must have more warmth, use 'Love'.

Yours,

John Smith

Note: First line begins underneath the last couple of letters and the comma of
'Dear Clive,'. In a typed letter, everything but the address can be on the left.

If you know someone well, you can still begin a letter with something like 'Dear David'. Emails are less formal, so often begin with 'Hi' or 'Hello'. It is also true that even banks and utility companies sometimes begin a letter with your first name, as if you have known them for years – a sort of forced chumminess that feels like someone sitting down next to you with the whole train carriage empty.

Unfortunately, it has always sounded pretentious to introduce yourself as 'Mr XXX' – especially if that isn't your name. That would just be odd. So you introduce yourself as Todd Martin, but should then be addressed as Mr Martin. 'Master Martin' still exists on passport applications and the like, for those under eighteen, but is only rarely used. It is also unlikely that you'll want to end a letter with 'I remain, Sir, Your obedient Servant', as used to be common in the 19th century.

So much for structure. You include your address in hope of a reply, though it's never required – if people begin thanking others for thank-you letters, it will never end. You include a date to keep track of correspondence – and personally, if you have access to a printer, we think it's a good idea to photocopy the letters you send. This can be vital when dealing with companies and business correspondence, but it doesn't hurt to keep a record of thank-yous either.

The last bit of advice is just common sense, really. If a thank-you note is a postcard, with 'Thank you for coming' on it and a scribbled signature, you won't feel the sender has made any effort at all – and in this case, effort is key. So, yes, get a pad of writing paper. Yes, get a fountain pen and some ink. No, it's not the 18th century, but people haven't evolved since then either. They will appreciate you taking time to acknowledge them.

This will all be useful in the whole love-letter arena as well, by the way. Be careful with poetry there. The grandfather of the authors wrote, 'You are the last of all the charmers. Your hair is yellow like bananas' – and never lived it down. That is all we have to say on that subject.

42 Station Close,
Even Closer,
Trainscoming.
TRAIN!
12 November 2024

Dear Rosemary,

Before I leave, I wanted to say how much I appreciated your support and advice when I was starting out. I honestly don't think I could have survived without your help. I look back and wince when I think of how I argued in the beginning, of all the storms and chaos you endured while I struggled to find a place. Somehow, you were always patient and kind — and you showed me how important that was. I hope you know how much of a good influence you were. I'll try to 'pass it on', as you always say I should. If it matters — and I hope it does — I owe you a great deal. Thank you for your kindness, Rosemary. I will remember my time in the old gang with enormous fondness.

Yours,

Tim Driver

# FIVE GREAT MATHEMATICIANS

Mathematics is the attempt to understand and express the underlying laws of the universe. Since the first man wondered how he might measure the height of a cliff without having to climb the blasted thing, there has been a certain purity associated with it. Those who are good at maths are often good at chess, music and bridge. They are also good at persevering, because no one ever said maths was easy. There is a certain joy in the perfection of its forms, but the truth is, not everyone will see that, and it would be a strange world if they did. Most of the modern world owes its existence to mathematicians. From calculating triangles in ancient Greece, to working out an interception path for the International Space Station, maths underpins all we do.

**PYTHAGORAS** is our first, a name known to all. He was born in ancient Greece in the 6th century BC and lived till he was around seventy-five, an impressive age for the period. He was noted in his life for his handsomeness and long hair. He believed he had lived several previous lives and described them with eerie accuracy. To test his claim that he had been a Phrygian named Euphorbus, son of Panthous, he was taken to the temple of Hera and told to point to the shield of Euphorbus, where it hung among many others. He pointed to it without a hesitation. Pythagoras is said to have used the letter Y ('upsilon' to the Greeks) as a personal symbol – to show virtue departing from vice. He was an early believer in the idea that illness was caused by bodily imbalances and not angry deities. Pythagoras argued that society could and should be moral, and saw virtue in abstinence from both meat and alcohol.

**EUCLID** was also born in ancient Greece, around 325 BC. He taught in Alexandria, Egypt, when he was in his twenties and thirties – around 300 BC. Euclid was born into that extraordinary flowering of democracy, plays, philosophy and mathematics that created the modern world and influenced Rome, Britain, Europe, America – and the world beyond.

For centuries in Britain, geometry was known simply as 'Euclid', because it involved the study of his *Elements* – the books that begin with the mathematical definition of a point, then a line, then a triangle, a square and so on, to great complexity. Euclid's *Elements* was known to Cicero in Rome, as well as every scholar and intelligent adult up to the 20th century, when it was finally supplanted by

other books based on its teachings. It is difficult to imagine a more influential mathematician through all human history than Euclid – or Eukleides, to give him his proper name.

**ISAAC NEWTON** (1642–1726). 'Nature, and Nature's laws lay hid in night. God said, Let Newton Be! and all was light.' Alexander Pope, 1730

Isaac Newton was foremost among a cluster of great men like Edmund Halley, Christopher Wren and Robert Hooke. Members of the Royal Society, they met in coffee shops and discussed thorny problems of maths, architecture and physics. It was Halley who published Newton's *Principia* at his own expense, understanding that Newton was an extraordinary mind. That book was an astonishing leap forward in mathematics and physics. From it come the famous 'Three Laws of Motion', originally written in Latin.

1. An object persists in its state of rest, or uniform motion in a straight line, unless it is compelled to change that state by forces acting on it.
(A rock moving through space, for example, will go on for ever, until it hits something.)

2. The greater the mass of an object, the greater the force needed to accelerate that object. Force = mass × acceleration.

(To calculate the amount of force needed to push a car from stationary, for example.)

3. For every action, there is an equal and opposite reaction.

(So to push a rocket or a rowing boat forward, we need to push in the opposite direction.)

All men are, to some extent, a product of their age – and stand on the shoulders of those who went before them. Yet even so, Isaac Newton may be the greatest thinker humanity has ever produced. He wrenched physics onto a new path for the next three centuries. He *amazed* Halley – and Halley was the man who understood mathematics and the movement of planets well enough to predict a comet that would be named after him, though it appeared only after his death.

The story of Newton seeing an apple fall in his garden and coming up with a theory of gravity is actually not a legend. It was told to the French writer Voltaire by Newton's own niece, a Mrs Conduitt. It happened in his family garden in Lincolnshire. The version where the apple hit him on the head is a later invention.

Newton was a restless genius, with a thousand fascinations, from the light spectrum to operating *on his own eye* to understand how it worked. He was the first great of the scientific age and influenced all those who came after him. Interestingly, he died in the gap between the Julian Calendar year and the Gregorian Calendar year, so can be said to have died in 1726 or 1727. In the same way, we might give thanks for imperial measurements as well as metric, for leap days, for both Fahrenheit and Centigrade. Such things reveal the nature of the chains we have flung around the world.

**ALBERT EINSTEIN** (1879–1955). 'I am convinced that *He* [God] does not play dice.'

Einstein's first great work was in realising that Newton's *Principia* was incomplete – that there were aspects of the universe that were not covered by Newtonian mechanics, such as the speed of light. Einstein worked in the Swiss Patent Office for some years, and in 1905 published four papers on physics that would change the world and lead to his theory of general relativity, a better understanding of light – and the equation $E = mc^2$. (The energy released from an atom is equal to the mass of the atom, multiplied by the speed of light squared.) He would win the Nobel Prize in 1921 for his work on the photoelectric effect – his early work. He had moved rapidly on, realising that light could be related to both space and time, seeking a general theory that would explain the entire universe. His equations predicted that the universe would be expanding – as has proven to be the case.

(Interestingly, if a watch is synchronised with another on the ground and then the first is taken up in a jet fighter and flown at great speed, they will not be synchronised when they return. The fast one will have experienced time moving more slowly. This is a simple, observable proof that Einstein was right, but still amazing.)

As a Jew, Einstein had to leave the Germany of his birth, where violence was beginning to spiral into what would become World War II. He went to America, and his equations would be the foundation of the atomic bomb that helped to end the war. A lifelong pacifist, Einstein worked to limit the spread of such weapons ever after.

He became not only the most famous scientist of the 20th century, but also the face of science itself, with his unruly hair and humour. Like Newton before him, his life was a landmark in physics and mathematics.

**STEPHEN HAWKING** (1942–2018). Hawking went first to Oxford, where he coxed a rowing team and was considered a bit of a daredevil – and an extraordinary genius by the physics department. In 1963 he was given two years to live when he contracted motor neurone disease. A debilitating condition, it led to muscle weakness and a slow withdrawal of physical function until he was almost completely paralysed. Yet his mind was untouched and technology allowed him to communicate aloud, long after he had lost the original power of speech.

After Oxford, Hawking held the post of Lucasian Professor at Cambridge, as Isaac Newton had done before him. He is considered the greatest theoretical physicist since Einstein, and produced work on both gravitational theory and the attributes of black hole radiation – or Hawking–Bekenstein radiation, as it is known.

In the 1970s, Hawking formulated laws for black holes and went on to study quantum gravity and mechanics. In 1988, he published his book *A Brief History of Time*, which sold ten million copies and did a great deal to popularise physics to a new audience. He lost a bet that the Higgs boson would never be found – and supported Peter Higgs for the Nobel Prize in Physics when it was. Throughout his life Hawking revised and improved his work as discoveries were made, like Einstein before him. He was the very essence of a scientist. Despite the complete failure of his body, he endured, worked and married twice. He died in 2018 and is buried in Westminster Abbey, close by the tombs of Charles Darwin and Isaac Newton.

As with the others in this chapter, Hawking benefited from the work of those who went before – and his work will influence and inspire those who come after. There are not many like these five. Perhaps the wonder is that there are any at all.

# THE BEST PAPER AEROPLANE
# IN THE WORLD – TAKE TWO

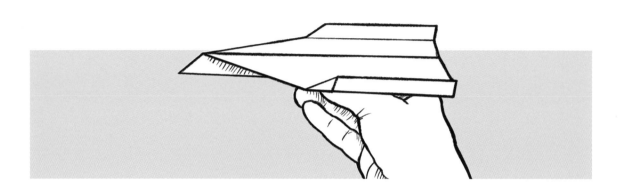

L ife can be strange, sometimes. Shortly after the original *Dangerous Book* was published, one of the authors was walking down a street when he saw a father making a paper plane with his son. A wry smile may have taken place – the author was, after all, an expert on paper planes. Not world-renowned, obviously, but he had published an actual book with a design that really worked. Some smugness was involved – until he watched the thing fly and realised that the design in the first book was only the *second*-best paper plane in the world.

I spoke to that father and explained why I had to have the paper plane in question. There was a scuffle – details need not concern us here. The result is the design for this chapter. It is, simply, astonishing.

It begins in exactly the same way as the first one.

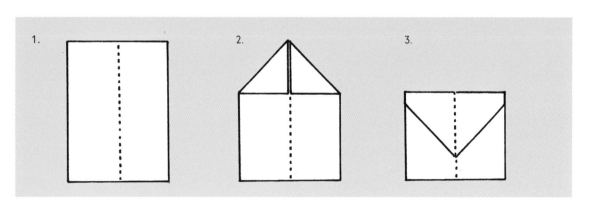

1. Fold a sheet of A4 paper lengthways.

2. Fold two corners in to the spine.

3. Fold the point down the page, leaving around an inch, so it looks like an envelope.

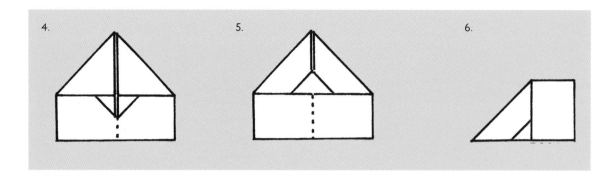

4. Fold down two corners again, leaving a triangle poking out.

5. Fold up the triangle to secure the folds.

6. Fold it back along the spine, with the triangle on the outside. So far – the same as the last time.

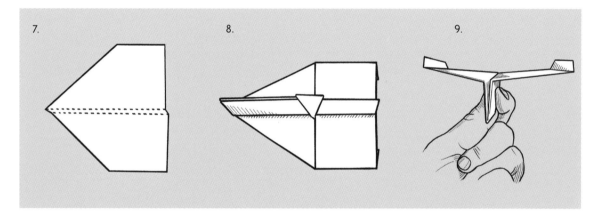

7. Fold one wing parallel with the main body, making the fold roughly the height of the triangle. We found a slightly thicker body worked better.

8. Complete the fold for the second wing. Fold out flat.

9. Add slight upward parallel folds at the wingtips. It should look like the diagram.

Launch flat and watch it go. It flies far too well for indoors, so make a half a dozen and go outdoors.

# THE TWELVE CAESARS

Gaius Suetonius Tranquillus, best known as just 'Suetonius', was a Roman scholar, lawyer, nobleman and historian. He was born around AD 70 and worked as Minister for Correspondence (letters and records) for Emperor Hadrian. As a result, Suetonius had extraordinary access to the archives of the period. His most famous work, known in English as *The Twelve Caesars*, is a record of the first men to follow Julius Caesar. Rome was a literate society, but a great deal of what we know about these early emperors is down to this single man writing in dusty archives.

With constraints of space, what follows can be no more than bare bones. The original is filled with personal detail that brings the Caesars back to life in all their glory – and all their horrors. Some details of the original, not included here, are not for young eyes. Still, we hope these sketches give a flavour of a republic that became a great empire. If nothing else, it will allow you to learn the first twelve Caesars in the correct order.

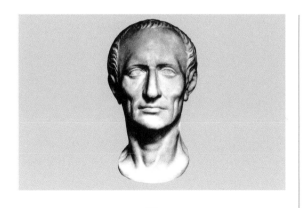

## 1
## GAIUS JULIUS CAESAR
### (c. 100–44 BC)

Ruled the Republic. The best of them all. Julius Caesar lost his father at the age of fifteen. He married Cornelia, the daughter of a consul, shortly afterwards and had one child, named Julia. As a result, young Caesar fell out with the consul's political rival and had to leave Rome for military service.

Caesar saw his first action in the east, where he won the right to wear a wreath for acts of bravery in storming a fortress. He returned to Rome and trained as a lawyer, learning rhetoric. He lost a key case and set sail for Rhodes while trouble died down. He was captured by pirates and kept prisoner while his friends raised a huge sum to free him. He told his captors he would find them and have them crucified, which they found amusing in such a young man. He was eventually freed, raised a fleet and did exactly what he had promised.

When Caesar returned to Rome, he was made tribune, a powerful position. He spoke well in public and was becoming known to the common people of Rome – the plebeians. He was given a posting in Spain, where he saw a statue of Alexander the Great and wept, because by the same age Alexander had conquered the world. When Caesar returned to Rome, he was at the heart of politics, a man on the rise. He borrowed fortunes and staged a lavish gladiatorial event. With the support of the plebeians, he was becoming a hard man to refuse. He won the post of Pontifex Maximus – head of religious observance in Rome and a title still held by the Pope today.

His first wife died young and Caesar stood for the first time as consul – joint leader of Rome. He married Calpurnia, daughter of a consul – and betrothed his own daughter to Gnaeus Pompey, another senior senator. Meanwhile, Caesar chose Gaul as his area of special interest, a land then unconquered. He was made governor of Gaul for nine years, which brought him power, influence and such vast fortunes as to devalue gold in Rome by a third. He crossed the river Rhine and briefly invaded Britain. He was called back to Rome by a tide of troubles there and stood as consul once again. He spent gold like water, winning over men and women of power with astonishing generosity. When he was baulked or stopped, he brought legions from Gaul into Italy that were loyal only to him. He crossed the river Rubicon with them to threaten Rome – an act forbidden by Roman law. A civil war followed against Gnaeus Pompey, ending in a battle between Roman forces at Pharsalus in Greece. Pompey escaped to Egypt, where Caesar pursued him. When Caesar crossed to Alexandria, he was handed Pompey's head and ring. Rather than see a Roman civil war crash across Egypt, the courtiers had executed him. Caesar wept, for a great man brought low.

In Egypt, he met Cleopatra and intervened to return her to power over her younger brother and the court. He headed back to Rome and on the way crushed an army so quickly he declared, 'I came, I saw, I conquered' – or *Veni, vidi, vici*. The 'V' is pronounced as a 'W', so it would have sounded a lot like 'Weeny, weedy, weaky', which is a very old joke.

In Rome, he accepted more powers and titles. He was made 'Dictator for Life' and given the right to be worshipped as a god. He set about immense building schemes, remaking the city and the dominions of Rome. He was never formally an emperor, but there were no limits on his power.

In the year 44 BC, on 15 March – the day known as 'the Ides' in the Roman calendar, he was assassinated by a group of senators. They were led by Marcus Brutus – a great friend of Caesar. Suetonius reported Caesar saying, 'You too, my son?' to the younger man, when he saw Brutus was one of the assassins. Shakespeare later rendered it as '*Et tu, Brute?*'

In the centuries after that single life, the very name 'Caesar' came to mean 'king'. The Russians had 'czars' up to the beginning of the 20th century, just as the Germans had a 'kaiser' – which is not far from the original pronunciation of Caesar. Julius Caesar was born to a republic, but he remade the entire world around him.

## (2)

## AUGUSTUS CAESAR
## (63 BC – AD 14)

Ruled Rome for forty-one years. Official title: 'Princeps' – or first in Rome. When Julius Caesar was killed, he had been in the midst of a thousand plans. Suddenly he was gone – and his great-nephew

Octavian worked with Consul Mark Antony to hunt down and destroy the assassins. Of the men who murdered Julius Caesar, not a single one died a natural death. In the end, Brutus threw himself on his sword rather than be captured.

Aged around eighteen, Octavian was Julius Caesar's official heir, having been adopted by him. He had lost his father aged just four and in some ways Caesar had been a second father to him. When he defeated the last of the assassins, Octavian had their heads sent to Rome to be thrown at the feet of Julius Caesar's statue.

Octavian would not accept Mark Antony or anyone else ruling Rome at his side. In the end, he took a fleet to Alexandria, where Mark Antony and Cleopatra were together. Octavian ordered Mark Antony to commit suicide. Cleopatra killed herself with the bite of a poisonous asp rather than be captured. Octavian also executed the son of Caesar, then aged around seventeen, showing a ruthlessness that would become the hallmark of the emperors to follow him. In some ways, *The Twelve Caesars* is a story of gold mingled with lead – until all the gold has gone.

Augustus is a title meaning 'Noble'. As 'Augustus Caesar', or 'Emperor Augustus', Octavian ruled Rome for decades. He was the consolidating force that was desperately needed after civil war – and, probably more than his great-uncle Julius, he is the reason Rome lasted as long as it did. Augustus reformed the army, renamed a month after himself, rebuilt Roman cities and established the laws and rules of Rome for forty years of *Pax Romana* – a golden era. He used the title of 'Imperator' – a military leader. He was never formally an emperor, though he is usually considered the first.

Augustus was happily married to his wife Livia into old age. She had been briefly married before and when Augustus felt himself failing, he adopted a child of her first marriage as his heir. Together, they sent an announcement to the legions and nations of the empire that they should accept Emperor Tiberius. On his deathbed, Augustus prepared the final words 'I found Rome in clay; I left her in marble', but then whispered to his wife, 'Have I played my part?' She told him he had, and he died.

## 3

## TIBERIUS CAESAR
### (42 BC – AD 37)

Emperor AD 14–37. The story of Tiberius is of a man ruined by power. His father died when Tiberius was just nine. His mother married Augustus Caesar and gained unlimited wealth and authority for her two sons.

Tiberius married and had a son of his own, but was then forced to divorce his first wife and marry Augustus' daughter Julia – a better political match. He hated his new wife. Although he had been made consul and tribune for five years, Tiberius returned all his public offices, left the new wife and took ship to Rhodes, where he lived a simple life. It was the sort of simple life that requires a large staff, unlimited funds and the power of life and death over the locals. For example, Tiberius expressed an idle thought that he might visit the sick on Rhodes, to bring them comfort. In response, his staff dragged ill and dying locals out of their houses and arranged them on the street for their master to inspect.

After seven years, Tiberius returned to Rome. Augustus had two heirs, Gaius and Lucius. When they died, Tiberius was formally adopted as son and heir. At around the same time, his brother died. Tiberius was made to adopt his brother's children as well – among them one who would be called Germanicus and one Claudius. Tiberius was then given command of legions to pacify Germany. Three legions were lost, but Tiberius came out of the war with new credit and honours even so.

When Augustus finally died, Tiberius was fifty-six. He began modestly enough, at least in public. He vetoed the suggestion that September should be renamed Tiberius. He even gave some powers back to the senate, but always as a gift from his hand. Then once again he left Rome suddenly, spending years and fortunes throwing ever more degrading and violent parties on the island of Capri, while the empire began to fall apart. He became a monster in his old age and was utterly amoral – without guilt. He did not bother to attend his mother's funeral and he let her body rot, unburied. He had two of his grandchildren put to death rather than allow them to be honoured. He held executions every day and every crime, no matter how trivial, became punishable by death. He died, eventually, aged seventy-seven, having ruled for nearly twenty-three years. Unloved, unmourned, he was a stain on history. Worse, he created the man who would follow him – the most famous tyrant of them all.

---

4

## GAIUS CALIGULA (AD 12–41)

Emperor for just four years. Though his name would one day be a byword for madness, the little boy nicknamed 'Caligula', or 'little boot', for wearing a miniature legionary uniform, was the product of Tiberius' cruelty. Gaius saw his father Germanicus poisoned, his two brothers executed and his mother Agrippina starve herself to death rather than serve Tiberius. As great-nephew and adopted son to Tiberius, Gaius was one of very few of Tiberius' relatives to survive that brutal reign. What chance did he have of a normal life? Or even a reign marked by ordinary decency and restraint? Caligula was not born a monster. No, he was made one.

After the horrors of his childhood, Caligula was summoned to the island of Capri aged nineteen, where he saw tortures and executions daily. He became at least as savage and cruel as Tiberius himself. He is said to have considered murdering Tiberius for his crimes. Caligula was certainly present for the old emperor's death – and may have ordered him poisoned or smothered. If that is true, it can only be said that Tiberius earned his own end.

From that point, Caligula's reign was one of obscene expense, games, races and circuses for the people – and punishments or execution for anyone who displeased him. He could be incredibly generous or childishly ruthless, depending on how he felt at any given moment, so that he terrorised all Rome. He preyed on men and women alike – having brides carried back to his own home on their wedding day, having crowds beaten with clubs and causing riots. He could never kiss a woman on the neck without whispering, 'And this beautiful throat will be cut whenever I please.' In short, he enjoyed causing sorrow and pain – and there are examples so awful they could not be included here. History is always stranger and more terrible than fiction – because of tyrants like Caligula.

After a reign just shy of four years, he was killed by men of his own Praetorian Guard, cut down at the age of twenty-nine. His wife and daughter were killed at the same time, though the last was a complete innocent. So great was the terror Caligula inspired that for weeks afterwards, men went in fear that it was all some great trick to root out the disloyal and that he would appear again to terrify them, laughing all the while.

5

## CLAUDIUS (10 BC – AD 54)

Emperor for thirteen years, AD 41–54. Tiberius' brother Drusus had a surviving son named Claudius – brother to Germanicus and therefore Caligula's uncle. Claudius had suffered some damage as a child. He was short-sighted and had a slobbering mouth. He walked with a limp, had a stammer and was slightly deaf. In all, he was a meek sort of man and easily overlooked, which kept him alive through the insanity of Caligula's reign. While Caligula was being murdered, Claudius hid himself behind some curtains, but his feet were seen by a soldier. Once again, his meekness saved him and he was proclaimed emperor there and then at the age of fifty. He would turn out to be the man Rome desperately needed after years of chaos.

Claudius survived various attempts on his life – one by an assassin hiding in his bedroom. He had a talent for survival, though at times he fell back into old habits and let others speak harshly to him, just as he had learned to endure when Caligula ruled. He was no tyrant, in comparison. Claudius was rather a clever and patient man.

He is best remembered as the emperor who invaded Britain. (Julius Caesar had been the first to try it, on two occasions, in 55 and 54 BC.) Gaul had long been conquered and could act as a staging post for a massed assault on the white cliffs. In AD 43, Claudius joined his legions as they crossed, subduing British tribes in the south and building forts and roads. So began the Roman occupation of Britain that would last until AD 410, three hundred and sixty-seven years.

At home, Claudius staged panther hunts and gladiatorial games, including re-enactments of British battles and sea battles on a lake, with two dozen oared triremes. He married four times, fathering a son he named Britannicus. The last marriage was to his own niece, Agrippina the Younger. She was a descendant of Augustus and a political match. Her son by a previous husband was therefore Claudius' great-nephew – Nero. Claudius adopted him, as was common practice.

Claudius tried hard to be popular, surrounding himself with favourites and spoiling them with lavish gifts. Yet he was capable of spite and bad temper, so that those who fell out of favour might find themselves under arrest and heading for execution before they realised what had happened. On one occasion, Claudius executed thirty-five senators and 300 of their followers for having displeased him. Roman law had always been harsh in its punishments, but in that capriciousness, that cruel whim, we can see the influence of Caligula – and Tiberius before him, still sitting over them all like a spider.

Aged sixty-three, Claudius may have been poisoned by his wife, but it is not known for sure. Death came quickly and without warning in those far-off days: it was not always summoned. After his death, his adopted son Nero became emperor.

6

# NERO (AD 37–68)

Emperor for fourteen years, AD 54–68. Nero's grandparents were Germanicus and Agrippina – the pair adopted and treated so horribly by Tiberius. Nero was the last descendant of Augustus – and therefore Julius Caesar – to rule Rome. His mother,

Agrippina the younger, was one of Caligula's tragic sisters and a survivor of the reigns of Tiberius and Caligula himself. It would be astonishing if she had not been damaged by all she had seen and endured.

Nero was sixteen when Claudius died. He was acclaimed by the Praetorian Guard as Claudius' successor and he delivered the funeral speech. Like Tiberius, Nero began modestly and with dignity, exercising on the Campus Martius field outside the city and racing chariots. As with those who came before him, he could be extraordinarily generous, showering those around him with gifts and luxuries, from titles, pearls and live birds, to slaves and estates.

Nero was no empire-builder and there was no expansion of territory under his rule. He loved music – both singing and the lyre, an early harp-like instrument. He also loved to act and sing on stage and performed often, employing vast numbers of men to applaud him.

However, greed and cruelty were always in him, and there was no one to curb his excesses. Nero simply enjoyed violence and would stab men in the street as they passed by, just for fun. He robbed Roman shops and sold all he had stolen. Those were the early days – his wild youth – which grew worse and worse as each year passed. He poisoned his only possible rival, Britannicus, administering the fatal dose himself.

Once more, poor Rome was terrorised by a maniac, just as bad as Caligula had been. Nero spent gold at such a rate it seemed he would beggar even the richest city in the world. He never travelled unless it was with a thousand carriages and with every mule shod in silver. He began immense building projects, using slaves and prisoners to complete the work.

Eventually, he was bankrupt – and began to steal from the families of Rome with new death duties of five-sixths of their estate. He fell out with his mother and had her stabbed to death. The guilt of that haunted him for the rest of his life, so that he saw her bloody face wherever he looked. Yet he also murdered his aunt and hundreds of others. In short, he was a man of terrifying and ready violence. The only strange thing is that Caligula is better known.

Nero is best remembered for ordering his servants to set Rome on fire. They carried burning torches through the streets and the city, and no one dared interfere. The city burned for a week and Nero was delighted by it. He did not 'fiddle while Rome burned', as violins had not been invented, but he did sing and may have strummed a lyre.

In the end, the people of Rome rebelled. Some soldiers tried to take him alive, but he stabbed himself before they could capture him, aged thirty-one. He was the end of the line of Julius Caesar, though it had been rotted from within by Tiberius. Pleasingly, no one has ever used the name Nero chose for April – Neroneus.

---

⑦

# SERVIUS SULPICIUS GALBA
## (3 BC – AD 69)

First in the 'Year of the Four Emperors'. Ruled AD 68 – Jan 69. By this time, the name 'Caesar' had become a vital part of ruling Rome. Though Servius Galba was merely a governor and senior military officer at the time Nero died, he took the name 'Augustus Caesar' as a declaration of intent. Galba was descended from consuls – and from one of the assassins of Julius Caesar.

Galba was stern, hook-nosed and extremely fit. He had been a close friend to Emperor Claudius. By the time of Nero's worst excesses, Galba had held many senior roles in Spain and Africa and was semi-retired. It was the discovery of Nero's order for his own assassination that had stung Galba to act against the emperor. Quietly, he began to organise an army rebellion. It coincided with the collapse of support for Nero in Rome, and Galba was able to march right in. His timing was extremely fortunate, but he was best known for ruthless military discipline and his sudden appearance was not at all popular with the citizens of Rome.

It is not surprising that Galba was a poor peacetime leader – not every general has the touch for it. The surprise is that he failed to honour his promises to the soldiers who had raised him up. He angered even the famed Praetorian Guard by dismissing many from service and failing to pay bonuses. Galba was warned of treachery. He agreed to wear a thick linen vest under his robe, but it would not be enough. In the end, the trap was well laid. News reached him that a colleague named Marcus Salvius Otho had taken command of the Praetorians. Galba sent for legionaries and rushed to the Forum, where the trap was sprung. Cavalrymen charged as soon as he appeared and cut him down. He was seventy-two years old and had reigned for just seven months.

in Rome, but in command of Roman legions in Germany, another military commander had his own following: Vitellius. When they advanced on Italy, Otho marched north to the Alps to meet his forces. His legions lost a brief battle and Otho decided to commit suicide rather than counter-attack. He wrote letters in camp, slept well and stabbed himself in the morning.

---

8

## MARCUS SALVIUS OTHO (AD 32–69)

Second in the 'Year of the Four Emperors'. Ruled AD Jan–April 69. Otho was from an established Roman household – his father had once uncovered a plot against Claudius and been rewarded for his loyalty. Otho himself was one of Nero's friends, though of better quality than most. He fell out with Nero over a woman and was exiled for ten years, which probably saved his life. As soon as Galba began to gather his rebellion against Nero, Otho joined him. Galba became emperor and Otho was in a good position to succeed him when Galba adopted a son.

Otho had crushing debts. He had hoped to escape his creditors by becoming emperor. Instead, he saw it getting further away. He put together a quick plan to have Galba killed and himself proclaimed emperor. Such a betrayal meant very little to one who had known both Caligula and Nero. It was Otho who sent cavalry to kill Galba. He had promised fortunes to his supporters and they were loud in their praise. That night, he claimed to have seen Galba's ghost, and woke screaming and tangled in his blankets.

Otho was not the only one who saw how they might snatch the title of emperor if they acted quickly and ruthlessly. Otho may have been first

---

9

## AULUS VITELLIUS GERMANICUS IMPERATOR AUGUSTUS (AD 15–69)

Third in the 'Year of Four Emperors'. Ruled eight months of AD 69. Vitellius was either the descendant of an ancient noble house or of freed slaves. Some things are not known. His father had been consul three times and was a famous flatterer of more than one emperor, though he was accused of treason in the end and died shortly afterwards. Aulus Vitellius spent part of his youth on Capri with Tiberius, just as Caligula had done. The old monster's shadow hangs over all these men.

After that first influence, it should not be a surprise that Vitellius did well in the courts of Caligula, Claudius and Nero. Vitellius knew how to flatter from his father and won all sorts of titles, including governor of Africa. He had a limp from a chariot crash in which Caligula had been the driver. He spent fortunes to keep up his position and ran up massive personal debts. When Galba made him governor of Lower Germany, Vitellius had to put his family in an attic and rent out his own house to get enough money to reach his new post. He also pawned a pearl from his mother's earring.

By the time he reached the legions in Germany, they were already fed up with Galba. Vitellius had a light touch – and the wisdom to cancel the brutal punishments of Galba's army rules. Before news even arrived of Otho killing Galba and ruling in Rome, the delighted soldiers had proclaimed Vitellius as their choice for the new emperor. They presented him with a sword that had belonged to Julius Caesar and carried him around the camp on their shoulders. Fortune had raised Vitellius beyond his wildest dreams.

When Otho committed suicide, that war was over almost before it had begun. Vitellius marched through Italy and right from the start, there were signs of Nero and Caligula in his manner. Poor Rome, to have raised another tainted man.

Vitellius had himself elected consul for life and became a wonder of gluttony, eating three or four banquets each day and making himself vomit to keep going. Vitellius devoured all Rome had to offer, a man lost in his own selfish pleasures.

In cruelty, he resembled Nero or Caligula. When a friend with a fever asked for water, Vitellius added poison to it. He had old creditors summoned and murdered before his eyes, as well as anyone else who displeased him. However, like Otho before him, there was another claimant to the empire: Vespasian.

While Vitellius burned a group of enemies alive in a temple, legions loyal to Vespasian marched on the city. As they entered, the last of his supporters fled. He strapped on a belt with gold pieces sewn into it and jammed himself in a cupboard in his father's house. The soldier who found him demanded to know where Vitellius was. Another one recognised him, however. Vitellius was dragged along the road and killed, his body thrown into the river Tiber.

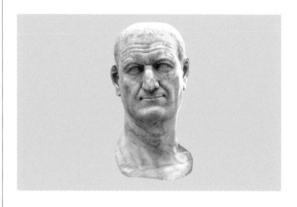

## 10

# VESPASIAN (AD 9–79)

Last in the 'Year of the Four Emperors'. Ruled Rome from December 69 to 79. Vespasian was five when Augustus died. He was a senator during the reign of Caligula and senior commander of the British invasion force under Claudius. Vespasian married early and had two sons and a daughter. His wife and daughter died, but the sons, Titus and Domitian, survived. With Nero ruling Rome, Vespasian lived quietly. When he did come into contact with Nero, he offended him by falling asleep during a song recital and was dismissed from court. As you can imagine, Vespasian was lucky to escape with his life.

After a long period in exile, this capable man was appointed to restore order in Judaea, where the Jews had rebelled and captured a legion eagle. He fought alongside his son Titus, on campaign there. News came of the deaths of Nero, Galba and Otho, with the unworthy Vitellius ruling in Rome. Vespasian was by far the better man. He showed others a letter from Otho, calling on him to save Rome from Vitellius. We cannot know if it was a forgery, of course, but it helped his cause. Vespasian sent some forces ahead and began to make his own way to Rome. He had no way of knowing how weak Vitellius' position had become. Before Vespasian even reached the city, Vitellius had been killed and thrown in the river. The city and the legions were sick of tyrants like Nero and Caligula. Finally, they found a ruler worth the name.

Vespasian's father had been a customs officer and banker in Switzerland. The son brought a similar care and discipline to administrating the empire. Unlike those before him, he was not in favour of gaudy displays of wealth, and he set about making Rome run efficiently and well. He allowed new owners to take over derelict buildings – of which there were many – and rebuilt many more. He reformed the senate and did so not with savagery or whimsy, but the steady hand of a fundamentally decent man. He did not murder innocents or steal their wives. How Rome must have breathed in relief! Yet the city was almost bankrupt after so many upheavals. Vespasian sold almost anything, from the freedom of slaves to pardons for the guilty. He promoted men to wealthy positions so he could squeeze gold out of them. He spent the money he raised on pensions, teachers and buildings.

After ten years as emperor, Vespasian had put the city to rights. He died of illness just before his seventieth birthday. His son Titus became emperor after him, in the first peaceful handover of power since Augustus. Vespasian was granted the right to be worshipped as a divinity.

### 11

## TITUS FLAVIUS VESPASIAN (AD 39–81)

Same name as his father, though usually referred to as 'Titus'. Like his father, Titus added the name 'Caesar' later on. Ruled Rome AD 79–81. Titus was forty when his father died and he became emperor. As well as campaigning in Germany and Britain, he had fought alongside Vespasian in Judaea and been left in charge there when his father raced home. As a child, Titus had been present when Nero poisoned Claudius' son, Britannicus. They had been good friends and Titus never forgot him. He remained loyal to his father and refused to play the games that had brought Rome so close to destruction before. He and his father liked each other, and Vespasian trusted him completely in the administration of Rome. In that role, Titus was quick and ruthless to dispose of enemies, determined to keep his father safe.

When he became emperor himself, he was restrained and honest. He sponsored gladiatorial games, which he loved, and used the public baths in Rome, mingling with the common people. He responded well to disasters, such as another eruption of Vesuvius, providing funds and support, even to the point of stripping his own mansions.

He was also ruthless with informers, a practice he detested. Titus was made Pontifex Maximus and swore not to take life, saying he would rather die.

The only fly in the ointment for the good older brother, was the foolish younger brother – Domitian. He was a wild young man and always plotting. Yet Titus refused to execute him and made it clear that Domitian was his heir. Sadly, Titus died of a fever at the age of just forty-one, in his father's house. Rome mourned the loss of a good man, all the more remarkable for his rarity.

— 12 —

## DOMITIAN (AD 51–96)

The last of the Twelve Caesars. Ruled AD 81–96. Domitian was one of those Vitellius had tried to burn alive in a temple, just before his father Vespasian arrived in Rome. Domitian managed to escape in a group of priests, disguised as a worshipper of Isis. Unlike his brother Titus, Domitian took to being the son of an emperor with indecent glee. He had many affairs and was jealous of any success Titus enjoyed. His father and Titus seemed to understand one another, while Domitian glowered behind them at public events.

On the death of Vespasian, Domitian plotted to succeed him, but the older Titus was the clear choice and he was frustrated, claiming their father's will must have been altered. Two years later, when Titus became ill, Domitian began acting as emperor even before Titus was dead.

Domitian was a tall and handsome man, but also stupid, bad-tempered, spiteful and envious. He caught and impaled flies as a game in his free hours. He staged chariot races for the people as well as mock battles, wild beast hunts and gladiatorial contests. He scattered gifts from his own hand and rebuilt or raised temples in the city. He also ordered military campaigns, justified or not, leading expeditions in person. Such things increased his status with the people and the legions – and allowed him to make a public procession in Rome, which he enjoyed. He was his father's son, however, and came down hard on bribery and corruption, stamping out a great deal of it from public life.

Domitian had many senators executed, some at the first hint of conspiracy, though others were out of the sort of petty viciousness we have seen before. Little by little, Domitian grew in cruelty. He invented tortures and amused himself by dining with men who did not know he had already ordered them to be executed.

When his funds were low, he manufactured accusations that allowed him to confiscate property from wealthy senators, so that they went in terror of his eye falling on them. A careless word or the lies of an enemy might bring Domitian's soldiers to the door. There was no point appealing for mercy – there was none to be had. Domitian began to refer to himself as 'Lord God' and renamed October 'Domitianus', which no one ever used again.

A superstitious man, Domitian had long feared a particular day in his future, when visions described his death. Just as Julius Caesar had his own death linked to the Ides of March, Domitian believed he would die in the fifth hour. When that time came, he asked aloud what hour it was. His terrified servants told him it was the sixth. Relieved, he went to his bedroom, where he was stabbed by five assassins hiding there. He died aged forty-four and had reigned for just under fifteen years. The senate had his images and shields torn down, and did their best to obliterate the records of his reign.

The Suetonius record ends there. He had too much sense to continue up to Hadrian, who might have objected to such a frank style describing his own achievements. For your interest, here is a short list of those emperors who came after Domitian:

Marcus Nerva

**MARCUS NERVA (AD 30–98).** An old man, elected by the senate. Oversaw the capture of Domitian's assassins. Reign: AD 96–98.

**TRAJAN (AD 53–117).** Born in Spain, a great ruler. The empire grew to its largest extent. Reign: AD 98–117.

**HADRIAN (AD 76–138).** Builder of walls on the English edge of empire. Long rule and stable – a benevolent dictator. Reign: AD 117–138.

**ANTONINUS PIUS (AD 86–161).** Builder of the Antonine Wall in Scotland. Peaceful reign. Succeeded by his adopted sons. Reign: AD 138–161.

**MARCUS AURELIUS (AD 121–180) AND LUCIUS VERUS (AD 130–169).** Co-emperors: Aurelius ruled from AD 161 to 180, with Verus up to AD 169. Long and stable reign.

**COMMODUS (AD 161–192).** Ruled alongside his father from AD 177 to 180 and then alone until AD 192.

Commodus

Marcus Aurelius and Commodus mark the end of the golden age of Rome. After that came a Year of Five Emperors – a complex and tricky affair. Slowly, the empire pulled back and back from its conquered regions – back from Britain, from Germany, back and back until the *Pax Romana* was ancient history. Yet not forgotten. The first twelve Caesars are a tragedy, a line corrupted by the foul old spider named Tiberius. We can only wonder what might have been if Augustus had chosen another to be emperor after him.

# JUMPING PAPER FROG

The youngest contributor to this book – who is ten – learned this design from a friend at school. It jumps surprisingly far for something powered just by folds, but it is also a pleasantly complex thing to make from a single piece of paper. For those who enjoyed the first *Dangerous Book*, it has a very similar fold to the water bomb. If you can do that, you can do this.

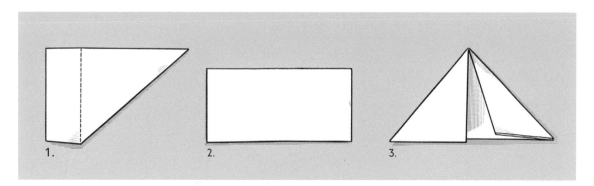

1. Make a sheet of A4 into a square: fold over a triangle until the edges meet. Tear off the rectangle.
2. Fold the square in half, to make a rectangle.
3. Bring each corner in, pressing each fold firmly. Open out to a rectangle, turn it round 180° and fold in the other corners. (These folds are just to make the next step easier.) Open out to a rectangle again.

4–6. This is the trickiest fold – the one we did for the water bomb in the first book. If you've pre-creased the diagonals, it should go smoothly enough.

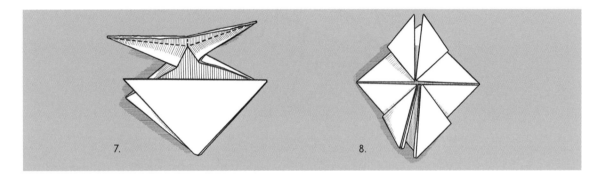

7. Do the same on the other side, so that you have a smaller square.

8. Fold each of the triangle flaps on itself, towards a point.

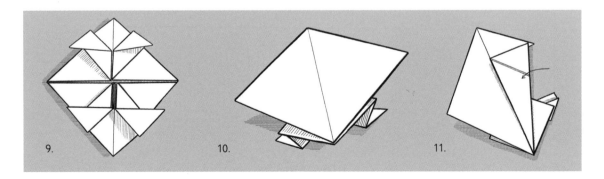

9. Fold each of those triangles across itself, to make little legs.

10. Turn it over. This is what it should look like.

11. Fold in both sides in long triangles, like a kite shape. Crease every fold firmly. The neater the folds, the better this will work at the end.

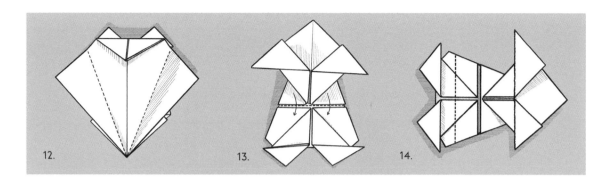

12. Fold down the top and then fold those triangle sides over it. This is the rear of the frog.

13–14. The final part is making the 'spring' folds. There is a natural folding place in the middle of the underbelly. First fold the frog on itself, as if it was trying to touch its toes. Then fold roughly along this marked line in the opposite direction. The idea is to make knees, or a concertina, as shown in the next picture.

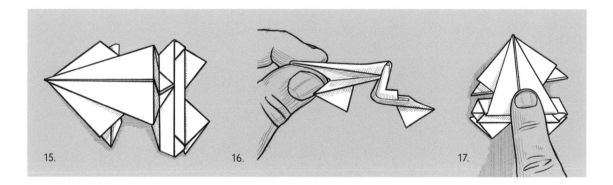

15. View from above.

16. View from the side.

17. Press finger on it. Drag back and watch it leap.

As with the water bomb, this might seem difficult at first, so make a dozen of the things. Difficulty is not a reason to avoid something. In fact, difficulty is a good reason to make yourself expert at something others can't do. After a while, you'll be able to show someone else how to make one – and have races. They are cute little devils, these frogs. You might try painting them, using green paper, or drawing eyes on them.

# EXTRAORDINARY STORIES –
# PART THREE: VICTOR GREGG

Born in 1919, Victor Gregg spent his first years in the East End of London, working to support his mother and make ends meet. He left school at fourteen and was on a factory milling machine the following week, before moving on to a range of other jobs, working for grocers or looking after racing cars, washing glasses – or keeping an eye out for the police. He was a hard and scruffy young man, looking for something. He found it when he signed up for the Army in 1937. Gregg joined the 1st Battalion Rifle Brigade on his eighteenth birthday, expecting to serve a term of twenty-one years. His first posting took him by ship and overland to sleepy Meerut in India, then part of the British Empire.

With war looking likely, he and his regiment were sent to the considerably less sleepy Palestine – as Israel was then known. It had been a British-run 'protectorate' since World War I. It's fair to say this was not a universally popular arrangement, and the work involved hunting down anyone trying to blow up railway lines or snipe at British troops.

On September 1939, war was declared. The Rifle Brigade had been retraining as a mechanised unit and were moved to Cairo in Egypt. North Africa would become one of the most savage theatres of the war.

Gregg's first experience of action was an attack on their position by Italian planes. He also saw the first planes brought down on both sides. He and his regiment were moved up to the border of Libya, where the Italians were based. The London riflemen fought hand to hand with Italian soldiers, all while London was being bombed at home.

After five or six months in the desert, Gregg was pulled back to regroup and counter-attack Italian forces. Although outnumbered ten to one, the British group drove them off and pursued ten thousand through the desert night as they rejoined the main Italian forces – around 250,000 men. Gregg's group used guns they had dismantled and remounted from a crashed Hurricane fighter plane.

Between Benghazi and Tripoli in Libya, British regiments engaged armoured Italian units, destroying tanks and harassing forces many times greater in size and firepower. Gregg's battalion fought with bayonets when they were almost overrun. The Italians eventually surrendered after brutal fighting and Gregg's platoon was sent back to Cairo on leave. Meanwhile in North Africa, the Italians had been replaced by Rommel's Afrika Korps – elite German regiments who would prove a far more ruthless adversary.

Gregg was briefly posted to South Africa, escorting prisoners of war to Durban. In a ship crammed with Italian prisoners, he went through the Suez Canal and on to the Madagascar Strait. He enjoyed the extraordinary hospitality of South African families. Six weeks later, in October 1941, he was back in Egypt. A month after that, he was involved in a tank battle at Sidi Rezegh, with over a thousand tanks and twenty thousand men on the field. The British fought Rommel's tank regiments to a bloody standstill. They prepared to withdraw at dawn – and found Rommel had just beaten them to it and retreated. British forces then shadowed and harassed the Germans for five hundred dogged miles. At last, new orders came. Gregg and his group were told to head for Cairo, for five days' leave.

Having impressed an officer with his ability to navigate in featureless desert, Gregg agreed to be transferred to the Long Range Desert Group as a driver, dealing with the Bedouin tribesmen and taking wounded men to safety through thousands of miles of occupied territory. The LRDG was made up of British, New Zealand and Australian regiments, with men chosen from the sort who could operate on their own in small units and cause trouble behind enemy lines – early commandos. Gregg spent some months in that work, before new orders broke up the unit and he was sent back to his old battalion. Shortly afterwards, Gregg saw a friend killed in an explosion – a brutal event.

To combat Rommel's feared Afrika Korps, Prime Minister Winston Churchill appointed Lieutenant-General Montgomery, known as 'Monty'. He assumed command of the Eighth Army and organised a massive push of men and armour to break the German hold on North Africa – at El Alamein, in October 1942. Gregg was back with his mates and given the privilege of going in ahead of infantry and tank regiments: protecting engineers as they cleared minefields under fire.

In flare-lit darkness, and under mortar and machine-gun attack, Gregg advanced with eleven armoured carriers to shield the engineers. His vehicle was hit and a track was blown off, though no one was hurt. The battle raged around them, with tanks destroyed and men killed, all while Allied forces advanced on German lines. Gregg's battalion engaged German infantry and the tanks of the 21st Panzer Division, with the Italian Trieste Division alongside. They repelled wave after wave of attacks with machine-gun fire, briefly pausing when a white flag went up and the Germans asked to collect their wounded. This was allowed.

When hostilities began once more, Gregg's battalion faced a line of twenty tanks and armoured cars, with infantry attacking in support. They destroyed them with anti-tank guns and machine-gun fire. Despite the decency of allowing them to collect their wounded men, it was kill-or-be-killed and a fight to the death against a determined and ruthless enemy.

Wave after wave of attacks followed as the Germans tried to break the Allied positions and drive them off. The forces with Gregg were slowly whittled down, though they would not retreat. It was with huge relief that they greeted a hundred British tanks coming up in support – only to see forty of them destroyed by anti-tank weapons from the German side.

A last great surge came – thousands of German and Italian infantry pushing forward. On Gregg's side, guns became too hot to touch, and when the bullets were gone it came down to bayonets and knives. A desperate order brought an artillery barrage down on friend and foe alike, bringing the attack to an end.

Rommel was driven right back across North Africa and Libya, losing all he had gained. El Alamein was a key battle of 1942, facing the best veteran soldiers Germany had – and beating them. It was a crucial battle for British morale, to know it could be done.

At Battalion HQ, the men were told about a new Parachute Brigade being formed. Having volunteered, Gregg journeyed to Palestine to learn how to jump out of planes. After that training, he went by ship to Taranto in Italy – where he was warmly welcomed by local residents. He and his new battalion travelled overland to Foggia and fought through a German rearguard force in the area. His unit covered over two hundred miles on foot, driving north through the Italian countryside. Eventually, they were picked up and taken home, to Liverpool. In London, he met a lady who would become his wife, married her and went back to his duties.

On 6 June 1944, the Allies (including America) landed on the beaches of Normandy and began to roll up German forces, against massive, entrenched and fanatical opposition. It was incredibly hard, and Gregg's battalion was called up, then told to 'stand down' more than once, as opportunities were discarded and new plans made. London was under constant attack from flying bombs and the new and massive V2 rockets. The war was far from over and only seemed to be growing more savage each day. In September, Gregg was told about Operation Market Garden – he and hundreds of others were to be dropped in Holland, to form a bridgehead of Allied troops. It was thought that there were no large German forces in that area. Their task was to capture the bridge at Arnhem.

The forces that parachuted down or landed in heavy gliders immediately encountered units of German soldiers who were resting – including two elite Panzer divisions. There was hand-to-hand fighting from the first moments, but as soon as the German tanks started up, the Allies were in serious trouble.

Gregg had made it safely down with his group, only to face rocket-propelled mortars, machine-

Dresden

gun fire – and tanks. He and his companions withdrew into woods, while those who had reached the bridge were under constant attack. German artillery opened up wherever Allied troops were seen. They hung on for two days under fire, with terrible casualties, while running out of bullets and anything to eat. Gregg had to fight once more, with machine-gun and bayonet charges against an unrelenting enemy. He and his dwindling group pulled back to Oosterbeek for another four days under constant attack. The Germans surrounded them with mortars and poured on shell after shell. Gregg's unit had no food for two days and water only from puddles. They were down to their last bullets when they broke out and tried to go across country. Gregg was captured two days later and taken as prisoner back to the town of Arnhem. With hundreds of other captured soldiers, he was sent by train to a German prisoner-of-war camp known as Stalag VI-B.

A month later, the prisoners were given the opportunity to work, and Gregg and six others preferred that option to doing nothing. He was taken to a work camp in Saxony, and from there to farms and to shovel coal and snow. Cut off from any news of the war, he began to store food and formulate a plan to escape, with three others. On New Year's Eve, they agreed they would slip away while clearing snow.

The four of them reached a railway line and laid low until the following day when they set off again. They spent a second night under a bridge and headed on at dawn, trying to reach the border with Czechoslovakia. They were captured just a few miles from it and Gregg was returned to work in the same camp. As punishment, he and another of the escapees were put to work first in a sauerkraut factory, then clearing the rubbish pits of houses in the city of Dresden. Taking a bike, Gregg made another attempt to escape, but was knocked off by a passing lorry and returned once more to the camp. He was initially made to clear cesspits as a punishment, but the local German factories were desperate for labourers so Gregg and another man named Harry were sent to a soap factory.

Soap is usually made from fats, but these were in short supply at this stage of the war, so the main ingredient was pumice powder, an abrasive volcanic dust. Gregg's job was to fill wheelbarrows with the stuff, then pour it into an enormous mixer. It began well enough, but his companion had noticed sacks of cement were also stored there – a grey powder that looked a lot like the pumice dust. He and Gregg agreed to mix them up for the last batch.

When the power was turned on the following day, the factory machines jammed. A fire began and the entire factory burned down. Gregg and Harry were arrested for sabotage and taken to a prison in Dresden. There, they mingled with more than a hundred Allies and discovered that about thirty of them were taken out and executed each day. Gregg and Harry were to be shot the following morning.

That night, the firebombing of Dresden began. It took place in February 1945, a bombing campaign of relentless and total aggression, designed to break the will of the German people and end the war. The RAF dropped thousands of tons of high explosives and incendiaries all night and then the Americans came over all day. The centre of the city of Dresden was annihilated – and the prison wall where Gregg waited to be executed was blown out.

Harry was killed in the explosion of rubble. Gregg was battered and half-deaf – but alive and with a chance to go free. He walked out into the firestorm of Dresden and saw horrors beyond description.

Gregg joined emergency workers trying to help, overcome by the savagery he witnessed. The centre of the city was a furnace by then, too hot to enter. They were driven back and back, and as the second day passed, he thought of escaping before he could be picked up and sent once again to be executed. He began to wander away and found himself among the leading edge of Allied Russian troops entering the area. Blistered and dazed, he spent six or seven weeks with the Russian army and left Dresden behind.

The war came to an end when the Germans surrendered in May 1945, but Gregg was still with the Russian forces and witnessed more brutality against the civilian population before he finally found his way back to a British position and was sent across the Channel. He arrived at last in London, where he made his way home to his wife and his baby son.

It is difficult to imagine the trauma and suffering endured by this man – and millions like him. Wars do more damage than is ever known or told. The author was delighted to meet Victor Gregg briefly when he came to do a talk about his experiences. He does not call himself a hero, but he is one.

We recommend the book of his wartime experiences and the life afterwards: *Rifleman*, written with Rick Stroud, as well as *Dresden – A Survivor's Story*. A donation has been made in Victor Gregg's name to Help for Heroes.

# MORE QUOTES FROM SHAKESPEARE

The first *Dangerous Book* included thirty Shakespearean lines, most of which are known across the world. Because of his unique talent and influence, however, we barely scratched the surface. As the MEP and public speaker Daniel Hannan likes to say, 'Nothing escapes Shakespeare' – no part of human endeavour, small or glorious, lacks its expression in his works. His best lines ring with truth. Yet his greatest work is in longer pieces, where he had room to develop ideas and concepts. It is hard to read a hundred lines from any of his plays without suddenly grasping some wisdom never known before. If, in your entire life, you read only a Complete Works of William Shakespeare, you would *still* be an educated man.

1.  Be not afraid of greatness: some are born great, some achieve greatness, and some have greatness thrust upon them.

    *Twelfth Night*, Act 2, Scene 5 (Malvolio)

2.  Hear my soul speak.
    The very instant that I saw you did
    My heart fly to your service.

    *The Tempest*, Act 3, Scene 1
    (Ferdinand, speaking to Miranda)

3.  The first thing we do, let's kill all the lawyers.

    *Henry VI, Part 2*, Act 4, Scene 2
    (Jack Cade's rebellion in London.
    A line of simple frustration)

4.  I will do such things—
    What they are, yet I know not;
    but they shall be The terrors of the earth.

    *King Lear*, Act 2, Scene 4
    (The king driven to incoherent rage)

5. That one may smile and smile
   and be a villain.

   *Hamlet*, Act 1, Scene 5

6. Doubt thou the stars are fire,
   Doubt that the sun doth move,
   Doubt truth to be a liar,
   But never doubt I love.

   *Hamlet*, Act 2, Scene 2
   (A letter from Hamlet to
   Ophelia, read by Polonius)

7. What a piece of work is a man! How noble in reason, how infinite in faculty, in form and moving how express and admirable, in action how like an angel, in apprehension how like a god – the beauty of the world, the paragon of animals! And yet to me what is this quintessence of dust?

   *Hamlet*, Act 2, Scene 2
   (Spoken in grief by the young Hamlet)

8. How far that little candle throws his beams –
   So shines a good deed in a naughty world.

   *The Merchant of Venice*, Act 5, Scene 1
   (Portia speaking)

9. Cowards die many times before their deaths;
   The valiant never taste of death but once.

   *Julius Caesar*, Act 2, Scene 2
   (Spoken by Caesar himself)

10. But man, proud man,
    Dressed in a little brief authority,
    Most ignorant of what he's most assured,
    His glassy essence, like an angry ape,
    Plays such fantastic tricks before high heaven
    As makes the angels weep.

    *Measure for Measure*, Act 2, Scene 2
    (Isabella speaking in exasperation)

11. Come, we burn daylight.

    *Romeo and Juliet*, Act 1, Scene 4
    (Mercutio to Romeo)

12. Suspicion always haunts the guilty mind.

    *Henry VI*, Part 3, Act 5, Scene 6
    (Gloucester speaking)

13. Here will be an old abusing
    of God's patience and the King's English.

    *The Merry Wives of Windsor*, Act 1, Scene 4
    (The character of Quickly, warning
    about a tiresome guest)

14. A man whose blood
    Is very snow-broth; one who never feels
    The wanton stings and motions of the sense

    *Measure for Measure*, Act 1, Scene 4
    (Lucio describing a man with
    ice-water in his veins)

15. The course of true love
    never did run smooth.

    *A Midsummer Night's Dream*,
    Act 1, Scene 1 (Lysander to Hermia)

16. The brain may devise laws for the blood,
    but a hot temper leaps o'er a cold decree.

    *The Merchant of Venice*,
    Act 1, Scene 2 (Portia speaking)

17. Come kiss me, sweet and twenty.

    *Twelfth Night*, Act 2,
    Scene 3 (Sung by the Clown)

18. O for a Muse of fire, that would ascend
    The brightest heaven of invention.

    *Henry V*, first line of the Prologue.
    (Calling for greatness and inspiration)

19. Nothing in his life
    Became him like the leaving it. He died
    As one that had been studied in his death
    To throw away the dearest thing he owed
    As 'twere a careless trifle.

    *Macbeth*, Act 1, Scene 4
    (Discussing how the Thane of Cawdor met
    his death without show of fear)

20. All the perfumes of Arabia will not sweeten
    this little hand.

    *Macbeth*, Act 5, Scene 1
    (Lady Macbeth, driven mad by guilt and the
    memory of blood on her skin)

21. How sharper than a serpent's tooth it is
    To have a thankless child.

    *King Lear*, Act 1, Scene 4
    (Spoken by Lear himself)

22. O, beware, my lord, of jealousy.
    It is the green-eyed monster
    which doth mock
    The meat it feeds on.

    *Othello*, Act 3, Scene 3
    (Iago speaking to Othello)

23. I have touched the highest
    point of all my greatness,
    And from that full meridian of my glory
    I haste now to my setting. I shall fall
    Like a bright exhalation in the evening,
    And no man see me more.

    *Henry VIII*, Act 3, Scene 2
    (One of his least-known plays, but this is a
    beautiful speech, made by Cardinal Wolsey,
    on hearing the king has turned against him)

24. Had I but served my God with half the zeal
    I served my King, He would not in mine age
    Have left me naked to mine enemies.

    *Henry VIII*, Act 3, Scene 2
    (Wolsey in despair, knowing
    he will not survive)

25. My salad days,
    When I was green in judgement.

    *Antony and Cleopatra*,
    Act 1, Scene 5 (Spoken by Cleopatra,
    looking back on better times)

26. Age cannot wither her, nor custom stale
    Her infinite variety.

    *Antony and Cleopatra*, Act 2, Scene 2
    (Enobarbus explaining why Antony will
    never put Cleopatra aside,
    even to please Caesar)

27. Though this be madness,
    yet there is method in't.

    *Hamlet*, Act 2, Scene 2
    (Polonius, sensing Hamlet's
    apparent madness is not real)

28. If you prick us, do we not bleed? If you tickle
    us, do we not laugh? If you poison us, do we
    not die? And if you wrong us, shall we not
    revenge?

    *The Merchant of Venice*, Act III, Scene I
    (Poor, tormented Shylock, driven to spite)

29. Uneasy lies the head that wears a crown.

    *Henry IV, Part 2*, Act 3,
    Scene 1 (Spoken by the king,
    who cannot sleep – used now to refer to the
    cares and worries of those in authority)

30. This story shall the good man teach his son.

    *Henry V*, Act 4, Scene 3
    (The St Crispin's Day speech
    before the Battle of Agincourt)

It's well known that Shakespeare added a vast number of phrases to the English language – and in translation, to every other language. A few lie above, such as the 'green-eyed monster' of jealousy, or the 'salad days' of youth. Some have been altered over the years, so that Polonius' line is better known as 'There's method in his madness'. Here are some more that did not exist before Shakespeare.

'wear my heart on my sleeve', 'send him packing', 'vanish into thin air', 'neither here nor there', 'in a pickle', 'what the dickens', 'as good luck would have it', 'it's a wise father that knows his own child', 'all that glisters is not gold', 'laid on with a trowel', 'with bag and baggage', 'it is meat and drink to me', 'I'll not budge an inch', 'thereby hangs a tale', 'out of the jaws of death', 'a sorry sight', 'all of a sudden', 'dead as a doornail', 'pure as the driven snow', 'with bated breath', 'it was Greek to me', 'fair play', 'heart's content', 'in stitches', 'lily-livered', 'halcyon days', 'the weakest goes to the wall', 'a charmed life', 'more fool you', 'pound of flesh', 'short shrift', 'the be all and end all', 'neither rhyme nor reason', 'the game is afoot', 'wild goose chase', 'more in sorrow than in anger', 'brevity is the soul of wit'. . .

. . . and on that last, we'll draw the curtain. There is not space enough for all.

# MAKING AN IGLOO

The tricky thing here is making an igloo from the sort of snowfall we get at most two or three times a year in Britain – and sometimes not at all, outside of Scotland. If you are in the Arctic and can cut bricks of snow from a permanently compressed layer, you have a pretty fair advantage.

For our garden one, we needed a plastic box to cram with snow and form the blocks. Ours was about eighteen inches by twelve and had its first life as an Ikea drawer for clutter. A pair of them will allow you to get a rhythm going for two people, with one always being filled and the other being added to the wall.

In the Arctic, where an igloo might be a matter of life and death, they begin by cutting a deeper floor, so that the base sits lower than the snow all around them. In that way, the door out leads up and lets less of the howling gale in. That wasn't possible here, either.

The key to this is a spiral – and cutting the door at the end. Begin with a single line of blocks, as below.

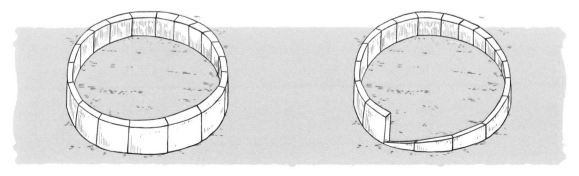

When that first ring is complete, use a saw to cut four of the blocks back, as you see in the second picture. Build on that rising line, layer by layer. This makes a tight structure.

A second way involves using a long knife or a machete to cut an incline angle across the top of that first ring, so that the next rings lean in slightly. The spiral worked well for us in a snow-filled garden, without that.

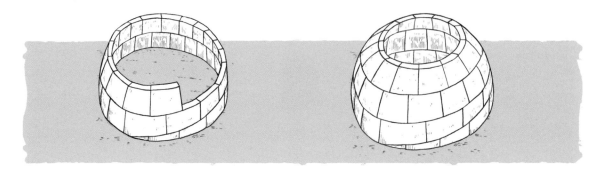

Continue the spiral, two or three layers more, depending on the size of your blocks. By this point, you need a minimum of two people – one to create the blocks and one to stand inside and pack them into the rising walls.

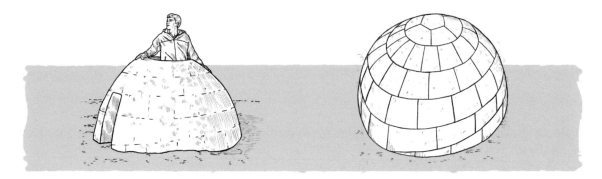

We cut our door before putting on the final blocks – but the point remains the same. It's much easier to cut it from a solid wall than to form it as you go.

The final blocks are obviously smaller, leaving the smallest hole possible – ideally the size of a single block. Cut it to fit with a knife or saw and gently drop it on top.

Our igloo was small and we weren't expecting to spend a night in there. A larger one designed for long stays might need holes bored in the sides to prevent $CO_2$ build-up. As with the bow and arrow in the last book, the aim wasn't to produce the world's best igloo, but to provide the basic ideas for the sort of igloo it's possible to make in a garden. Photos of good ones can be sent to the publishers.

# BRITISH PRIME MINISTERS

From left to right: William Gladstone, Winston Churchill and Margaret Thatcher

A thousand years ago, kings like Alfred the Great and Æthelstan were advised by a council known as the Witan. The Witan exercised real power, such as choosing which of two brothers should be king, regardless of who was older. With the Plantagenet kings of the 11th and 12th centuries, power resided more and more in the king and his lords. Kings believed they were appointed by God – given a 'divine right' to rule. Many people even thought they could cure skin diseases with the touch of a royal hand.

The king's council still existed, composed of lords and knights and men of the counties, but it had little power. That changed with education, printing and fortunes made in trade. Representatives in Parliament began to feel that they should do more than simply agree to whatever the king wanted. It came to a head with King Charles I and a civil war was fought, essentially between parliamentary democracy and the right of noblemen to rule as they saw fit. It is hard, today, not to support the cause of Oliver Cromwell and that 17th-century Parliament.

After the execution of Charles I, Cromwell led the country as 'Lord Protector' for a time, though he refused a crown. When he died, there was a vacuum. The old ways had gone, but the new ways had barely been bedded in. Parliament asked the son of Charles I to become King Charles

II, which turned out to be an ideal compromise, oddly enough. Yes, the king had returned, but the power of Parliament had been demonstrated – and the modern democratic age had begun.

Though he had many illegitimate children born outside marriage, Charles II lacked legitimate ones who could inherit. He was succeeded by his brother James, as King James II of England and Ireland (and VII of Scotland), the last Catholic monarch in Britain. His Catholicism was too much for Protestant England. When James produced an heir, a group of nobles asked a Protestant relative, William of Orange, to take the throne in the peaceful handover that became known as the 'Glorious Revolution' of 1688 – another key date in the primacy of elected representatives over a monarch. James fled, and both William of Orange and his wife Mary had certain rights and obligations set out in what would become the English Bill of Rights – a vital democratic document, given royal assent in 1689. It remains on the statute books today and continues to have legal force.

William and Mary ruled together, then William alone. They had no children, so Mary's sister Anne, another daughter of King James II, became the first queen of Great Britain. Despite many miscarriages, she too was unable to produce an heir and was succeeded by George I – a descendant of King James I (and VI of Scotland). He came over from Hanover – a region that would one day be part of Germany when that country was created in the 19th century. It was during George I's reign that Parliament assumed more power over a growing populace, which required a cabinet of ministers – and a leader to guide and order their discussions. That man was Sir Robert Walpole and he is considered the first prime minister, though the term was not used in his day. He was a Whig – a member of a political faction strongly opposed to absolute rule and in favour of 'constitutional' monarchy – a monarch who might be loved or revered, but who had extremely limited powers.

1. **ROBERT WALPOLE.** Served 1721–1742 and holds the record for the longest-serving PM. He was made an earl a few years before his death and so established the House of Lords as the retirement home for old prime ministers. His twenty years as first minister to King George were peaceful and prosperous, as much the result of his wit and wisdom as any other factor.

2. **SPENCER COMPTON**. 1742–1743. Whig. Died in office, having exhausted himself.

3. **HENRY PELHAM**. 1743–1754. Whig. PM during the Catholic Jacobite rebellion of 1745. A man of great integrity and decency.

4. **THOMAS PELHAM HOLLES**. 1754–1756. Whig. The man who became the 1st Duke of Newcastle was in government alongside his brother Henry Pelham for thirty years. The brothers were both powerful and decent men, whose lives served the country rather than their own status. Resigned in 1756, when the Seven Years' War (Britain's favourite war of all time) started badly.

5. **WILLIAM CAVENDISH**. 1756–1757. Whig. Secured more funds for the Seven Years' War. Mishandled the trial and execution of Admiral Byng, who was executed for 'failing to do his utmost' against the French. As the French writer Voltaire said, having observed the event, 'In this country, it is good to kill an admiral from time to time, in order to

encourage the others.' ('Pour encourager les autres' – 'to encourage the others' – is a phrase worth knowing.)

6. **THOMAS PELHAM HOLLES.** 1757–1762. Whig. Returned when Cavendish stepped down.

7. **JOHN STUART.** 1762–1763. First Scottish prime minister. First Tory in the role. Negotiated the Treaty of Paris that ended the Seven Years' War.

8. **GEORGE GRENVILLE.** 1763–1765. Whig. Creator of the Stamp Act that led to unrest in the American colonies and cries of 'No taxation without representation' – a call for a say in their own affairs that would eventually lead to independence in 1776.

9. **CHARLES WATSON-WENTWORTH.** 1765–1766. Whig. Disliked by King George III and his own cabinet, resigned in 1766.

10. **WILLIAM PITT (THE ELDER)** – so called to distinguish him from his son. 1766–1768. Whig. Best known for his wartime political leadership during the Seven Years' War (1756–1763) that won India and Canada for Britain rather than France. A decent and honourable man.

11. **AUGUSTUS FITZROY.** 1768–1770. Whig. Not the most able of fellows, in a Parliament of great talents. Stepped down as abruptly as he stepped up.

12. **FREDERICK NORTH.** 1770–1782. Whig. PM for the American War of Independence.

Related to the diarist Samuel Pepys. Lost America, but he did prevent the Spanish taking the Falkland Islands, so not a complete disaster.

13. **CHARLES WATSON-WENTWORTH.** March–July 1782. Whig. Brief return. Died in office, of influenza.

14. **WILLIAM PETTY.** 1782–1783. Whig. Became PM after the death in office of Charles Watson-Wentworth. Irish-born. Oversaw the peace with America.

15. **WILLIAM CAVENDISH-BENTINCK.** April–December 1783. Whig. Merely warming up for a better role later on.

16. **WILLIAM PITT (THE YOUNGER).** 1783–1801. Tory. PM at the age of twenty-four. PM during the start of the French Revolution and rise of Napoleon. PM for Nelson's Battle of the Nile. Pitt was a solid hand on the tiller when the world was aflame. A good friend of William Wilberforce, the man who pressed for the abolition of slavery.

17. **HENRY ADDINGTON.** 1801–1804. Tory. Poor speaker. Ousted by Pitt for his handling of the war with France.

18. **WILLIAM PITT (THE YOUNGER).** Second time as PM. Tory. 1804–1806. Died in office, but lived to witness Nelson's victory at Trafalgar. Pitt never used the role to enrich himself. He died with enormous debts – and the country agreed to pay them all for valorous service.

19. **WILLIAM GRENVILLE**. 1806–1807. Whig. Son of No. 8, George Grenville. First cousin of William Pitt the Younger – a well-connected man.

20. **WILLIAM CAVENDISH-BENTINCK**. No. 15 again, for longer this time. 1807–1809. Tory. The longest gap between periods of being PM in history. An ancestor of Queen Elizabeth II.

21. **SPENCER PERCEVAL**. 1809–1812. Tory. Served well until shot dead in the lobby of the House of Commons in 1812. The only prime minister to have been assassinated.

22. **ROBERT JENKINSON**. 1812–1827. Tory. Best known as Lord Liverpool. (With a few notable exceptions, we've avoided titles here, as many were given later as a reward for service.) A capable man. Oversaw the short war of 1812 with America, which was clearly a draw. America still believes they won that one, as does Canada. Britain was more concerned with beating Napoleon.

23. **GEORGE CANNING**. 1827. Anglo-Irish Tory. Died in office after just a few months, the shortest term of all. Canning would have been PM before, but was wounded in a duel, so Spencer Perceval became PM instead. Canning detested the idea of any kind of European superstate, believing the nation state was the perfect and most honourable form of government. Good man.

24. **FREDERICK JOHN ROBINSON**. 1827–1828. Tory. Took over on Canning's sudden death, but could not command enough authority and resigned after 131 days.

25. **ARTHUR WELLESLEY, DUKE OF WELLINGTON**. 1828–1830. Tory. The victor of Waterloo and guarantor of freedom from tyrants. First and foremost a military man, he said of his first cabinet meeting, 'An extraordinary affair! I gave them their orders and they wanted to stay and discuss them!' Passed the Catholic Emancipation Act. When he was unpopular, mobs threw stones at his house in Hyde Park, breaking the windows. He had iron shutters put up and carried on, which revived an old nickname: 'The Iron Duke'.

26. **CHARLES GREY**. 1830–1834. Whig. Best known – as Earl Grey – for having a tea named after him. The story goes that one of Grey's servants saved the son of a Chinese diplomat when the unfortunate young man fell into a canal. As a reward for saving the life of his son, the diplomat sent Grey a parcel of the tea usually only drunk by the imperial family in China. Grey sent it to Twinings tea company and they created the blend that became known as Earl Grey.

27. **WILLIAM LAMB**. July–Nov 1834. Better known as Lord Melbourne. Whig reformer who was not popular with King William IV – father to Queen Victoria. The king dismissed Melbourne after just a few months – the last PM to be dismissed by a monarch.

28. **ARTHUR WELLESLEY, DUKE OF WELLINGTON**. Nov–Dec 1834. Tory. Very brief caretaker period as PM, after Wellington refused to form a government, preferring to favour Robert Peel.

29. **ROBERT PEEL**. 1834–1835. 1834 could be known as the Year of Four Prime Ministers, but it isn't. The first Conservative PM, Peel is most famous for creating the first professional police force, known as Peelers, or Bobbies.

30. **WILLIAM LAMB, LORD MELBOURNE**. 1835–1841. Whig. Much longer stint at the top this time. He was PM for the death of King William IV and the crowning of Queen Victoria in 1837. An extraordinary era begins.

31. **ROBERT PEEL**. 1841–1846. Conservative – a more liberal party compared with the old Tories. Repealed the 'Corn Laws' – import tariffs on grain. A decent and thoughtful man.

32. **JOHN RUSSELL**. 1846–1852. Whig. Failed to handle the Great Irish Famine with any great vision. However, he did arrange funding for teacher-training and passed a Factory Act to reduce work hours to ten a day.

33. **EDWARD STANLEY, EARL DERBY**. Feb–Dec 1852. Conservative. Appointed many new ministers. They were nicknamed the 'Who? Who?' government. That was the elderly and mostly deaf Duke of Wellington's response when he heard their names read aloud.

34. **GEORGE HAMILTON GORDON**. 1852–1855. Conservative. Led a coalition government. Entered the Crimean War, which brought the government down when it was seen to be a disaster.

35. **HENRY TEMPLE**. Better known as **LORD PALMERSTON**. 1855–1858. Whig. One of the great PMs of the 19th century, with Gladstone and Disraeli alongside. Between them, they oversaw the establishment of Britain as the pre-eminent world power – on land and sea, in industry and manufacturing. Palmerston believed a gunboat could solve many problems.

36. **EDWARD STANLEY, EARL DERBY**. 1858–1859. Conservative. Second time as PM. The rule of India was taken over by the Crown from the British East India Company at this time.

37. **HENRY TEMPLE, LORD PALMERSTON**. 1859–1865. Liberal. Second time as PM. Considered the first Liberal PM, though the term is unrecognisable by any modern definition. Nonetheless, he was a humane and intelligent leader. A titan, even on this list.

38. **JOHN RUSSELL**. 1865–1866. No. 32 returned. Liberal. On Palmerston's death, this very elderly and well-respected gentleman became PM for a second time. No mere caretaker, he attempted serious reform and saw his fragile government collapse.

39. **EDWARD STANLEY, EARL DERBY**. 1866–1868. Conservative. Third time in power. Passed the Reform Act of 1867, which extended the right to vote to more of the male working classes.

40. **BENJAMIN DISRAELI**. Feb–Dec 1868. Conservative. After Derby retired on health grounds, Disraeli took the reins for a brief period, but lost the general election that followed. Born Jewish, he became an Anglican in childhood.

**41. WILLIAM GLADSTONE**. 1868–1874. Liberal. Introduced the secret ballot in British voting for the first time – a vital pillar and safeguard of democracy. Up to then, votes were held in public, and bullying and bribery were common. Good man.

**42. BENJAMIN DISRAELI**. 1874–1880. Conservative. In poor health, Disraeli nonetheless enacted some important legislation, such as Public Health Acts and the Royal Titles Act that made Victoria Empress of India and so established the British dominions as an empire. He died in 1881.

**43. WILLIAM GLADSTONE**. 1880–1885. Liberal. Most of his achievements in these years were fairly minor, which is not to say lesser. Sometimes, a good government is one that interferes least in the affairs of its citizens.

**44. ROBERT CECIL, LORD SALISBURY**. 1885–1886. Conservative. Became PM on Gladstone's resignation. He opposed Irish self-rule, which brought him down on a vote, with Gladstone on the winning side.

**45. WILLIAM GLADSTONE**. Feb–Jul 1886. Liberal. A supporter of Irish independence, he was supported in turn by Irish nationalist MPs, who held the balance of power for a time. Gladstone introduced an Irish Home Rule Bill, but it was defeated and took his brief third term as PM with it. In 1885, the term 'Prime Minister' appeared in the parliamentary record known as *Hansard* for the very first time.

**46. ROBERT CECIL, LORD SALISBURY**. 1886–1892. Conservative. 'Whatever happens will be for the worse, therefore it is in our interest that as little should happen as possible.' Good man.

**47. WILLIAM GLADSTONE**. 1892–1894. Liberal. The fourth and last time – a record on this list. Aged 82 as he became PM. Gladstone introduced another Home Rule Bill for Ireland, but saw it defeated in the House of Lords.

**48. ARCHIBALD PRIMROSE**. 1894–1895. Liberal. Never a popular leader, he lost a vote after a year as PM and tendered his resignation.

**49. ROBERT CECIL, LORD SALISBURY**. 1895–1902. Conservative. Back for a third period in office – at a crucial time for Britain. Queen Victoria died in 1901, after what was then the longest reign in British history, surpassed only by Queen Elizabeth II. It was the end of a great era.

**50. ARTHUR BALFOUR**. 1902–1905. Conservative. First PM of the brief Edwardian period. Brought in a Liquor Licensing Act and an Education Act.

**51. HENRY CAMPBELL-BANNERMAN**. 1905–1908. Liberal. The first PM to be officially recorded as prime minister, along with the ancient title held by all PMs of 'First Lord of the Treasury'. His government granted self-rule to the Boer states of South Africa.

52. **HERBERT ASQUITH.** 1908–1916. Liberal. Oversaw the outbreak of hostilities of WWI, when the new country of Germany invaded Belgium, a country Britain had vowed to defend if attacked.

53. **DAVID LLOYD GEORGE.** 1916–1922. Liberal. The first Welsh PM. Took overall command of British Empire forces from Asquith and did well. Britain and her allies won the war in 1918, after a series of crushing victories and lunging advances brought Germany at last to the peace table. Germany was not invaded, though severe penalties were imposed at the Treaty of Versailles.

54. **ANDREW BONAR LAW.** 1922–1923. Conservative. Born in Canada, he is the only PM to have been born outside Britain. He wrote that Britain 'could not act as policeman to the world'. Forced to resign by illness.

55. **STANLEY BALDWIN.** 1923–1924. Conservative. A principled man, he felt he needed a new general election and mandate from the people to introduce the tariffs he wanted. He lost that election.

56. **RAMSAY MACDONALD.** Jan–Nov 1924. First Labour PM and a founder of the party. MacDonald officially recognised the Soviet Union, formed after the Russian Revolution of 1917.

57. **STANLEY BALDWIN.** 1924–1929. Conservative. Winston Churchill was his Chancellor of the Exchequer. Passed the first proper Pensions Act in 1925, for widows, orphans and the elderly.

58. **RAMSAY MACDONALD.** 1929–1935. Labour. Led a fragile coalition 'National Government' of Conservatives, Liberals and Labour. The stock market crash of 1929 led to great poverty.

59. **STANLEY BALDWIN.** 1935–1937. Conservative. Germany was re-arming for war. Churchill pressed to match them, seeing the threat.

60. **NEVILLE CHAMBERLAIN.** 1937–1940. Conservative. Attempted to negotiate a peace with Germany, but failed. Declared war after the German invasion of Poland. Mortally ill, Chamberlain resigned and recommended Winston Churchill to King George VI.

61. **WINSTON CHURCHILL.** 1940–1945. Conservative. Greatest Briton. Gave his all to the preservation of Britain and her allies in WWII.

62. **CLEMENT ATTLEE.** 1945–1951. Labour. The public wanted change and change is what they got, though rationing continued for years.

63. **WINSTON CHURCHILL.** 1951–1955. Conservative. Oversaw some difficult years as Britain tried to recover and find a new place in the world. Lived till 1965 and was given a state funeral. The world watched and cranes dipped all along the Thames as the funeral barge passed.

64. **ANTHONY EDEN.** 1955–1957. Conservative. Lost control of the Suez Canal when it was seized by Egyptian forces. Resigned due to ill-health.

**65. HAROLD MACMILLAN.** 1957–1963. Conservative. Oversaw British development of the nuclear bomb and nuclear power.

**66. ALEC DOUGLAS-HOME.** 1963–1964. Conservative. A period of economic growth. Fought a tight election and lost by a few seats.

**67. HAROLD WILSON.** 1964–1970. Labour. Devalued the pound in 1967. Sent the British Army into Northern Ireland in 1969, where they would remain until 2007.

**68. EDWARD HEATH.** 1970–1974. Conservative. Took Britain into the Common Market, which would become the EU. Oversaw crippling strikes, power cuts and a three-day week.

**69. HAROLD WILSON.** 1974–1976. Labour. Oversaw a difficult period of strikes and unemployment before resigning due to ill-health.

**70. JAMES CALLAGHAN.** 1976–1979. Labour. Worsening industrial relations led to general strikes across the country.

**71. MARGARET THATCHER.** 1979–1990. Conservative. First female PM and first to win three elections in a row. A believer in low tax and small government. A formidable woman.

**72. JOHN MAJOR.** 1990–1997. Conservative. Replaced Margaret Thatcher to win an election in 1992. Began the Northern Ireland peace process and forced through the Maastricht Treaty, creating the European Union.

**73. TONY BLAIR.** 1997–2007. Labour. Continued the Northern Ireland peace process. Created devolved governments in both Scotland and Wales.

**74. GORDON BROWN.** 2007–2010. Labour. Took over when Blair resigned, but lost the next election.

**75. DAVID CAMERON.** 2010–2016. Conservative. Granted a referendum on British EU membership. The result went against him.

**76. THERESA MAY.** 2016–2019. Conservative. Won a snap election in 2017.

**77. BORIS JOHNSON.** 2019– Conservative. Replaced Theresa May when she resigned mid-term.

Over 297 years, that makes 77 periods in office, but only 55 prime ministers. Two were women, both Conservative; 53 were men from Whig, Tory, Labour, Liberal and Conservative parties. It is a period that saw the abolition of slavery, the introduction of pensions, the creation of the NHS, votes for women and working-class men, the Seven Years' War, as well as the Crimean War, World Wars I and II and any number of smaller conflicts. It saw the peaceful rise of constitutional monarchy in Britain, after the turbulence of civil war.

One day, this list will be twice as long, with 150 names on it. No doubt that future will be just as interesting.

# PENCIL CATAPULT

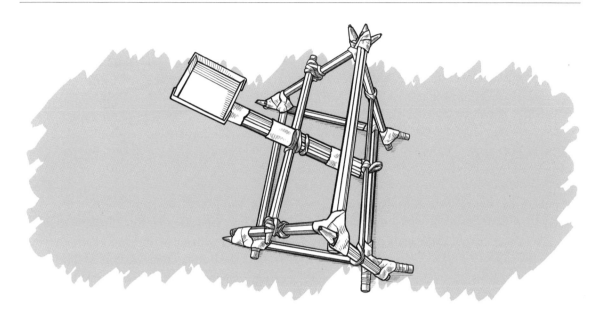

This is fairly easy to make, though fiddly. It requires the sort of things you can find around any office or stationery cupboard. (Note the 'e' in stationery – 'e' for envelopes. Stationary, spelled with an 'a', means 'not moving'.)

### YOU WILL NEED

* A dozen pencils
* A roll of masking tape
* Five ordinary elastic bands
* A bit of cardboard

You can make a version of this with every joint held by an elastic band. We found in practice that all those bands set up stresses that pulled the entire assembly in odd directions – which was incredibly annoying. To construct the basic shapes, masking tape worked best. Before you start, break the tips off the pencils. If they are new and sharp, constantly stabbing yourself with them can get tiresome. It feels like vandalism, but you can always sharpen them again.

1. Construct two triangles, binding the pencils together with tape. Take care with it – you want them to be as similar as possible. We put the rubber ends of the pencils at the bottom to make a sturdy base.

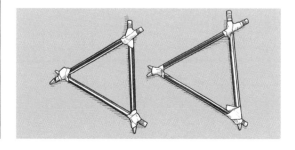

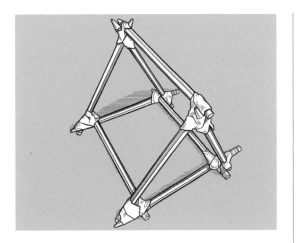

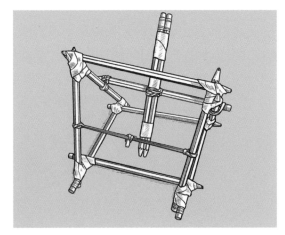

2. Connect the two triangles using another three pencils, securing each one with a thin strip of masking tape. It's not particularly pretty, but it does the trick.

3. Using two elastic bands, connect one more pencil across. This will be the pivot for your catapult bar. It can't be taped as it needs to turn. Get it as straight as you can. In fact, take a moment to fiddle with the whole thing. It's almost finished.

4. Bind two pencils together with strips of masking tape. Tie that pair of pencils to the pivot bar with an elastic band. (Basically, you wind the band around and around until it's tight, then put the loop over the pencil ends to hold it.)

5. Attach a band across for the pencil to push against – the main spring. It isn't easy attaching elastic bands when the pencil ends are attached. We found a simple hitch – seen below – on both sides, then tied in the middle, worked really well. (The double pencil beam doesn't have to touch the spring band until it's time to wind it back.)

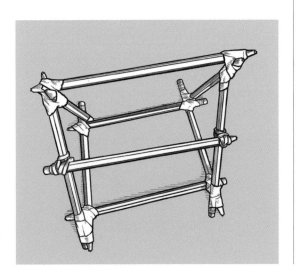

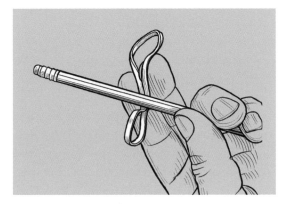

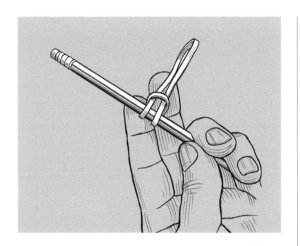

Snip small cuts along the red lines. Fold along the dotted lines. Tape the flaps that result. Use masking tape to attach the basket to the double pencils. Done. This will shoot a ball of masking tape right across a room.

6. Finally, we made a little cardboard bucket from a piece of a cereal packet. One alternative would be to use a plastic spoon, though it has to be long enough to clear the upper bar, while still reaching the band spring below.

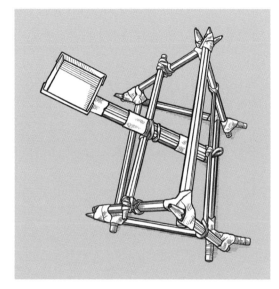

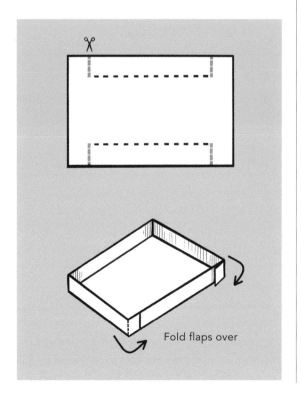

Fold flaps over

# BRITISH SIGN LANGUAGE

HELP

FRIEND

You know more sign language than you think. You can certainly signal 'drink' by raising an invisible glass, or 'telephone call' to someone too far off to hear you. You can also pat your mouth in a yawn to signal boredom, give something the thumbs up or thumbs down, indicate scissors – or that something is crazy by tapping your temple. You can shrug to say you don't know something, or shake your head as a 'no'. If you've ever played charades, you can also signal a book, film or play. All of these are in sign language, exactly as you intend them.

Sign language is something you might learn to communicate with deaf people, obviously, but that's not the only way to use it. While researching this chapter, we discovered a sign can be turned into its opposite by shaking the head and frowning. If you sign 'happy' – flat right palm brushing flat left palm twice towards you – but shake your head and frown, you are signing 'not happy'! Instant sarcasm. It has become a thing in our family to sign 'clever' – a closed-fist thumb dragged across the forehead – then frowning and shaking our heads at one another. In the right place, it can be pretty funny. Sign can be a private language, unless of course you come across one of the 70,000 or so people in the UK who know and use it.

It takes an hour or two to learn the sign-language alphabet. Certainly you can learn to spell your own name in just a minute, then practise it until you can do it anywhere. Or practise signing the letters of 'The quick brown fox jumps over the lazy dog', which has every letter in it. That's our aim here – to give you a few useful words and the alphabet. Whether you go further is up to you, but there is something mesmerising about sign language. As soon as we started learning a few signs, we wanted to know more. Better still, it turned out that the ten-year-old had already learned a few signs from a kid at school and used them to communicate in class – in silence. With no prompting, he signed the two letters 'h' and 'i' as a way of saying, 'Hi, hello.'

Note: These signs are all British Sign Language or BSL. Other countries have developed their own, just as different spoken languages have developed in different nations. They also won't work to communicate with deaf-and-blind people. They are taught the alphabet in capital letters, drawn on their palm with your finger.

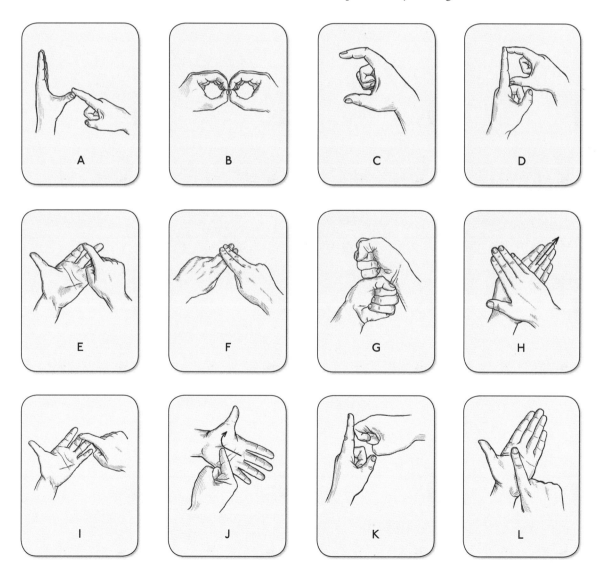

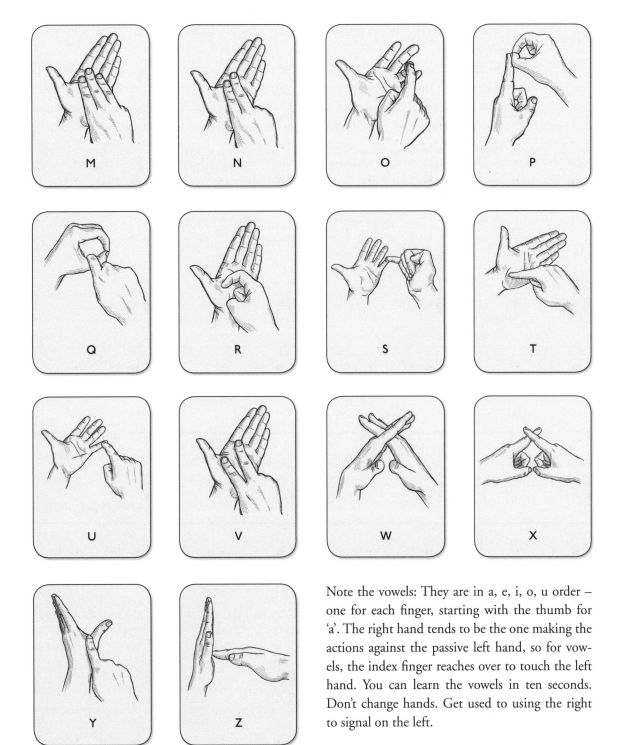

Note the vowels: They are in a, e, i, o, u order –
one for each finger, starting with the thumb for
'a'. The right hand tends to be the one making the
actions against the passive left hand, so for vowels, the index finger reaches over to touch the left
hand. You can learn the vowels in ten seconds.
Don't change hands. Get used to using the right
to signal on the left.

Here are a few other signs we think might be useful. Arrows indicate movement.

These are just a few to get you started. There are some terrific books, but this is also something the internet is really good at. Look up 'BSL signs' and learn a few more. You'll never regret knowing them. That much we can guarantee.

**THANK YOU**

**LOVE**

**DAD**
*(letter 'f' tapped twice)*

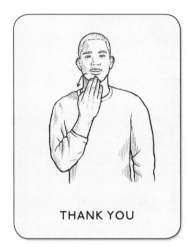

**MUM**
*(letter 'm' tapped twice)*

**SISTER**
*(hook index finger, taps nose twice)*

**BROTHER**
*(two touching fists rubbing up and down together as if milking a tiny cow)*

# FORTY QUOTATIONS WORTH KNOWING

Captain Lawrence Oates (Quote No.32)

The past is the experience of others – and those who learned something interesting in their time on earth often had interesting things to say about it. Memorising these will actually make you a better person, through a sort of osmosis of wisdom.

1. Nothing in the affairs of men is worthy of great anxiety.

   Plato (429–347 BC)

2. Let me not then die ingloriously and without a struggle, but let me first do some great thing that shall be told among men hereafter.

   Homer, Book 22 of the *Iliad*
   (before 87th century BC)

3. It is indeed desirable to be well-descended, but the glory belongs to our ancestors.

   Plutarch (AD *c.* 46–120)

4. And I am convinced that every man of you would rise up and tear me down from my place if I were for one moment to contemplate parley or surrender. If this long island story of ours is to end at last, let it end only when each one of us lies choking in his own blood upon the ground.

   Winston Churchill (1874–1965), speaking in 1940, after a disastrous beginning to World War II

5. She's the sort of woman who lives for others –
   you can always tell the others by their hunted
   expression.

   C.S. Lewis (1898–1963),
   *The Screwtape Letters*

6. I'm not conceited. It is just that I have a
   fondness for the good things in life . . .
   and I happen to be one of them.

   Kenneth Williams, actor (1926–1988)

7. The reasonable man adapts himself to the
   world; the unreasonable one persists in trying
   to adapt the world to himself. Therefore, all
   progress depends on the unreasonable man.

   George Bernard Shaw,
   Irish playwright (1856–1950)

8. A nation can survive its fools, even the
   ambitious, but it cannot survive treason from
   within. An enemy at the gate is less formidable,
   for he is known and carries his banners openly.
   But the traitor moves freely among those within
   the gate, his sly whispers rustling through the
   alleys, heard in the halls of government itself.

   Marcus Tullius Cicero,
   Roman statesman (106–43 BC)

9. Men fight for liberty and win it with hard
   knocks. Their children, brought up easy,
   let it slip away again, poor fools. And their
   grandchildren are once more slaves.

   D.H. Lawrence, author (1885–1930)

Kenneth Williams (Quote No.6)

10. It is enough to live one hour in a free country,
    answerable only to ourselves, governed by the
    laws that raised us to greatness.

    Titus Josephus, Roman-Jewish
    scholar (AD 37–100)

11. All the stories I would like to write persecute
    me. When I am in my chamber, it seems as
    if they are all around me, like little devils,
    and while one tugs at my ear, another tweaks
    my nose, and each says to me, 'Sir, write me,
    I am beautiful.'

    Umberto Eco, author (1932–2016)

12. Ask the powerful five questions:
    1. What power have you got?
    2. Where did you get it from?
    3. In whose interest do you exercise it?
    4. To whom are you accountable?
    5. How can we get rid of you?

    Tony Benn, MP (1925–2014)

13. Let me give you my vision: a man's right to work as he will, to spend what he earns, to own property, to have the state as servant and not as master.

Margaret Thatcher, prime minister (1925–2013)

14. With government as with medicine, its only business is the choice of evils. Every law is an evil, for every law is an infraction of liberty.

Jeremy Bentham, philosopher (1748–1832)

15. Man that is born of a woman is of few days, and full of trouble. He cometh forth like a flower, and is cut down: he fleeth also as a shadow, and continueth not.

Book of Job, King James Bible

16. Freedom is the sure possession of those alone who have the courage to defend it.

Pericles, Athenian statesman (*c.* 495–429 BC). Used on the Bomber Command memorial in London

Tony Benn (Quote No.12)

17. Give me liberty to know, to utter and to argue freely according to my conscience, above all other liberties.

John Milton (1608–1674). Inscribed on the outer wall of the Chicago Tribune newspaper offices

18. Lost to a world in which I crave no part, I sit alone and commune with my heart: Pleased with my little corner of the earth, Glad that I came, not sorry to depart.

Originally Catullus (*c.* 84–54 BC), rewritten by D.H. Lawrence. Inscribed in stone in Ravello, on the Amalfi Coast of Italy

19. Rise early, work late, strike oil.

The formula for success of billionaire J. Paul Getty (1892–1976)

20. And in the end, when the life went out of him and my hands could work no more, I left from that place into the night and wept – for myself, for life, for the tragedy of death's coming. Then I rose, and walking back to the suffering-house, forgot again my own wounds for the sake of healing theirs.

Anonymous Emergency Room doctor

21. The whole Mediterranean – the sculptures, the palms, the gold beads, the bearded heroes, the wine, the ideas, the ships, the moonlight, the winged gorgons, the bronze men, the philosophers – all of it seems to rise in the sour, pungent taste of these black olives between the teeth. A taste older than meat,

older than wine.
A taste as old as cold water.

Lawrence Durrell, novelist (1912–1990),
from *Prospero's Cell*

22. On turning over in my mind the contents
of your last letters, I have put myself into
great agony, not knowing how to interpret
them, whether to my disadvantage, as you
show in some places, or to my advantage, as I
understand them in some others, beseeching
you earnestly to let me know expressly your
whole mind as to the love between us two.

Love letter from King Henry VIII to Anne
Boleyn, his second wife

23. The Schleswig-Holstein question is so
complicated, only three men in Europe have
ever understood it. One was Prince Albert,
who is dead. The second was a German
professor who became mad. I am the third
and I have forgotten all about it.

Lord Palmerston (1784–1865)

24. Annual income twenty pounds, annual
expenditure nineteen pounds, nineteen shillings
and sixpence – result, happiness. Annual
income twenty pounds, annual expenditure
twenty pounds and sixpence – result, misery.

Charles Dickens (1812–1870), from *David
Copperfield*, slightly rewritten

25. And the lord said unto John, 'Come forth
and receive eternal life,' but John came fifth
and won a toaster.

Anonymous, included because
it made us laugh

26. It was involuntary. They sank my boat.

President John F. Kennedy (1917–1963), on
being asked how he became a war hero

27. There is plenty of time to win this game, and
to thrash the Spaniards too.

Sir Francis Drake (1540–1596), on being
interrupted in a game of bowls with the
news that the Spanish Armada fleet was
approaching

28. To his dog, every man is Napoleon. Hence
the constant popularity of dogs.

Aldous Huxley, author (1894–1963)

29. To no man will we sell, or deny, or delay,
right or justice.

Clause 40 of the Magna Carta (Great
Charter), sealed by King John in 1215

30. I pray you, Master Lieutenant,
see me safe up, and for my coming down,
let me shift for myself.

Sir Thomas More (1478–1535),
spoken while ascending a rickety
old scaffold to be beheaded

31. I do not know what I may seem to the
world, but as to myself, I seem to have been
only like a boy playing on the seashore and
diverting myself in now and then finding

a smoother pebble or a prettier shell than ordinary, whilst the great ocean of truth lay all undiscovered before me.

Isaac Newton (1642–1727)

32. I am just going outside, and may be some time.

Captain Lawrence Oates (1880–1912). These were his last words as he removed himself as a burden on Captain Scott and the others, and headed out into the blizzard to die alone. His body has never been found.

33. Fain would I, but I dare not: I dare, and yet I may not; I may, although I care not, for pleasure when I play not.

Flirtatious lines by Sir Walter Raleigh (1552–1618) ('fain' means roughly 'like to')

34. This burning of widows is your custom; prepare the funeral pile. But my nation has also a custom. When men burn women alive we hang them, and confiscate all their property. My carpenters shall therefore erect gibbets on which to hang all concerned when the widow is consumed. Let us all act according to our national customs.

General Sir Charles Napier (1782–1853), responding to the suggestion that even as Governor of India, he should not interfere with the custom of burning widows alive on their husband's funeral pyre. His statue is in Trafalgar Square.

35. When I was a boy of fourteen, my father was so ignorant I could hardly stand to have the old man around. But when I got to be twenty-one, I was astonished at how much he had learned in seven years.

Mark Twain (1835–1910)

36. Moderation, the noblest gift of Heaven.

Euripides (485–406 BC)

37. Thou wilt find rest from vain fancies if thou doest every act in life as though it were thy last.

Marcus Aurelius Antoninus (AD 121–180)

38. Beware the peddlers of rights. They wish to turn you into someone who is simultaneously privileged and 'victimised': whiny, narcissistic, noisy, demanding, chronically unhappy, and of little use to themselves or other people. Instead . . . sort yourselves out. Shoulder your responsibilities. Make yourself useful to others. Find the heaviest burden you can bear and bear it stoically, forthrightly and admirably.

Jordan Peterson (born 1962). Canadian author and academic

39. England has saved herself by her exertions, and will, as I trust, save Europe by her example.

William Pitt (1759–1806), on the Napoleonic Wars

40. A little learning is a dangerous thing.

Alexander Pope (1688–1744)

# QUESTIONS ABOUT THE LAW –
# PART TWO

1. Does the death penalty still exist?
2. What rights do you have in a police station once you're under arrest?
3. How and when can you legally use force in self-defence?
4. Who has the right to enter your home and when?
5. What happens if you're maliciously targeted by the police?

---
( 1 )

## DOES THE DEATH PENALTY STILL EXIST?

The death penalty existed in the UK for many centuries and its abolition took several decades to finalise across all British territories. As recently as the Victorian era (1837–1901), offences for which you could hang included: being in the company of gypsies for a month, impersonating a Chelsea Pensioner and being out at night with a blackened face. On pronouncing a death sentence, the judge would put a black cloth over his wig, signalling the seriousness of the moment. He would then say some variant of the following:

> The sentence of this Court is that you be taken from this place to a lawful prison, and thence to a place of execution, and that you be hanged by the neck until you are dead, and that your body be afterwards buried within the precincts of the prison in which you were confined before your execution. And may God have mercy on your soul. Amen.

Capital punishment for murder was suspended in Great Britain in 1965 by a private member's bill in Parliament – the Murder Act. The final executions in England took place on 13 August 1964. Gwynne Owen Evans was hanged at Manchester's Strangeways Prison at the same time as Peter Allen was hanged at Liverpool's Walton Prison, both having admitted their involvement in the brutal killing of John Alan West only four months earlier. Thus, no one person can be described as the last person to hang in England.

The last person sentenced to death in the UK was in Northern Ireland, where the death penalty was not abolished until 1973, with the introduction of the Emergency Provisions Act. In the same year, nineteen-year-old Liam Holden was sentenced to death for killing a British soldier during the height of the Troubles. His sentence was commuted in July 1973 and he was eventually released after serving seventeen years. It wasn't until much later, in 2012, that Holden's conviction was quashed on appeal after secret MoD papers came to light that supported his original claim that he had been illegally detained by the British Army (rather than the police) and subjected to waterboarding before he confessed.

The final executions anywhere on British territory took place in Bermuda in 1977. The death penalty was finally completely abolished for any offence in the UK in 1998 (although, interestingly, in the overseas British territory of the Turks and Caicos Islands, the death penalty remained technically on the statute book as a punishment for treason and piracy until October 2002).

The adoption of the 13th Protocol of the European Convention of Human Rights, which came into effect in 2004, prevents the UK from reintroducing the death penalty in any circumstances while it remains part of the convention. Although theoretically this could change in the future by British withdrawal from the ECHR, it is almost inconceivable that anyone will ever face execution on British soil again.

— 2 —

## WHAT RIGHTS DO YOU HAVE IN A POLICE STATION ONCE YOU'RE UNDER ARREST?

If you find yourself in police custody having been arrested for an offence, you have a number of basic rights:

- You are entitled to free and independent legal advice.
- You can call someone to tell them where you are.

- The police must give you access to medical care if you feel unwell.
- All detainees must be given regular meals and access to the toilet.
- If you are a foreign national, you must be given access to an interpreter.
- You must be given a notice telling you about these rights.
- You can ask to see the rules the police must follow (PACE 'Codes of Practice').

If you are under eighteen, the police must try to contact your parent, guardian or carer. You are entitled to an 'appropriate adult' who will come to the station to help you and be present during the interview process. Their role is to aid communication and also to advise you about obtaining legal advice if you are unsure.

— 3 —

## HOW AND WHEN CAN YOU LEGALLY USE FORCE IN SELF-DEFENCE?

The law on self-defence is one of the oldest and most well-developed areas of UK law. The principle goes back further than medieval times and is enshrined in the common-law principle that a person who is attacked may defend himself by using 'reasonable force' to repel the attack. The common-law principle of self-defence extends to defending other people and also to the defence of property. There is also a statutory defence in the Criminal Law Act 1967 for self-defence in prevention of a crime and assisting in the arrest of offenders.

There is a common misconception that a person who is attacked is under a duty to retreat before using force. There is no such duty imposed by the case law. It could be argued that in some situations retreating would be likely to encourage an attacker and that the best mode of defence is to stand your ground. However, it may be compelling evidence that a person was indeed acting in self-defence if he or she first attempted to disengage and withdraw. If, for example, a person chose to stand and fight when there was a clear avenue of retreat available, then a jury may conclude that the subsequent force used was *unreasonable*.

One of the most famous quotes dealing with reasonable force comes from the case of *Palmer-v-R* (1971), in which Lord Morris said this:

> If there has been an attack so that defence is reasonably necessary, it will be recognised that a person defending himself cannot weigh to a nicety the exact measure of his defensive action. If the jury thought that in a moment of unexpected anguish a person attacked had only done what he honestly and instinctively thought necessary that would be the most potent evidence that only reasonable defensive action had been taken . . .

This means that reasonable force is not an exact science and that the law allows for a margin of error. However, if the force is of an entirely more serious nature, then it will not be reasonable. For example, if a man attacked you with a knuckle-duster and in response you ran him down in your car and killed him, then that would not be reasonable or necessary force in the circumstances.

One of the most famous cases of recent times that tested the principle of 'reasonable force' was that of Tony Martin, who was convicted of the murder of a sixteen-year-old traveller who had broken into his house in order to burgle it. Martin was a bachelor living at the farmhouse

he had inherited from an uncle, whose property had been targeted on numerous occasions by members of the travelling community (although the precise number of break-ins is unclear). On 20 August 1999, Fred Barras (16) and Brendon Fearon (29) broke into Martin's property. The prosecution later alleged that Martin was lying in wait for them with a 12-gauge Winchester pump-action shotgun, and opened fire on them in the stairwell of the property. The prosecution's case rested heavily on the fact that the shot that killed Barras was fired at his back, as he was apparently attempting to escape from a window. They argued, therefore, that Martin's actions could not have been self-defence, and even if they were, the force used was unreasonable in the circumstances. The case became a media sensation due in part to the notion of the 'castle doctrine', which is the idea that you can use deadly force to protect yourself inside your own home. This principle does not exist as such in UK law. Rather, the principles of self-defence apply generally whether or not you are in your own home at the time, although your avenues of retreat may be significantly reduced so as to make the use of force more likely.

---

④

## WHO HAS THE RIGHT TO ENTER YOUR HOME AND WHEN?

### THE POLICE

The police have various powers under the Police and Criminal Evidence Act 1984 (PACE) to enter a person's home. Section 17 gives them the power to force entry in order to: execute an arrest warrant, arrest someone for an indictable offence, recapture a criminal they believe to be unlawfully at large, or save life or limb and/or prevent serious damage to property. Apart from the last scenario, the police must have reasonable grounds to believe the person they are seeking is on the premises before they are able to enter.

Section 18 PACE confers a power to enter and search any property 'occupied or controlled' by a person who is under arrest, in order to search for evidence relating to the offence for which they have been arrested or similar related offences. This can include a person's parent's house, even if they do not live there all the time.

## SEARCH WARRANTS

Search warrants are court orders issued by a magistrate or judge which confer a power for entry, usually on a law-enforcement agency or regulator, to search for evidence of a crime. The agency applying for a search warrant must satisfy the court that there are reasonable grounds for believing an offence has been committed, that there is material on the premises that is likely to be relevant evidence (which is not legally privileged) and that it is not practical or possible to obtain the evidence another way.

## OTHER AGENCIES

Agencies that have powers of search and entry are numerous and include Her Majesty's Revenue and Customs (HMRC), the Serious Fraud Office (SFO), the Financial Conduct Authority (FCA) and the intelligence services. However, if MI5 decide they need to enter your home, then you'll probably never find out about it anyway.

## BAILIFFS

There are certain myths around who can force entry into your home. For example, there are a number of restrictions on what bailiffs can and can't do. A certified bailiff (as opposed to a debt collector) can only force entry into your home if you owe certain types of debt, for example unpaid tax to HMRC or unpaid court fines to HMCTS (Her Majesty's Courts and Tribunals Service). Although rare, if refused entry, in these limited circumstances a bailiff can return with a locksmith to gain entry to your home. They will be looking for goods that can be sold in order to satisfy the debt if you do not agree to pay. Otherwise, bailiffs are only allowed to try to gain entry into your home between 6 a.m. and 9 p.m. and can only enter through open doors or windows. You should therefore keep your doors and windows locked to prevent entry and only talk to them through the door. If they refuse to leave or are physically threatening, you can report them to the police.

## TV LICENSING

TV Licensing agents have even less power than bailiffs. They have no more right to enter your home than a door-to-door salesman does, unless of course you agree to let them in. In order to be able to enter your home, they would require a search warrant issued by a magistrates' court, which would require evidence to support the belief that the home was receiving TV broadcasts without a licence (which in practice is very difficult to establish). TV Licensing refuse to disclose the number of warrant applications made each year, perhaps because they are statistically very low. However, they could rely on a householder's own admission at the doorstep as evidence to obtain a warrant or prosecute. In the event that one simply ignores the threatening letters and refuses to engage with them, it is very unlikely that TV Licensing would ever obtain the necessary warrant to enter your home without your permission.

---

(5)

## WHAT HAPPENS IF YOU'RE MALICIOUSLY TARGETED BY THE POLICE?

As a rule, 'a kind word turneth away wrath' – it pays to be polite. Beginning a conversation with 'How can I help, officer?' helps put you on the side of the angels. Try to remember that policemen and policewomen deal with aggressive, angry people every day. They are doing an incredibly difficult job that is not often appreciated even by those they protect.

In the event that you are wrongly arrested or maliciously prosecuted for an offence you haven't committed, you can take legal action against the police and sue for damages. You can even claim for false imprisonment if you were never arrested or suspected of an offence but were held somewhere by police when they had no right to keep you there.

In one of the largest payouts of its kind, ex-policeman Sultan Alam was awarded over £800,000 in compensation seventeen years after he was the victim of a police 'fit-up'. Alam was set up by his colleagues in Cleveland police force after he sued for racial discrimination, and wrongly served eighteen months in custody for conspiracy to steal motor parts. His conviction was overturned in 2007 and Cleveland police later admitted misfeasance in public office and malicious prosecution. The shocking sequence of events started with Alam's fellow officers leaving a Ku Klux Klan poster on his desk, and culminated in a full-blown conspiracy among at least four officers to frame Alam. The officers involved were cleared in criminal court but one later made admissions in disciplinary proceedings.

Our sense is that there was a time when our parents and grandparents had a pretty good idea where they stood in reference to the law – and yet somehow that confidence has slipped away in the decades since. Laws change, of course, which is part of it. It becomes our duty to keep up with those changes.

One trivial example came a few years ago, when one of the authors was summoned to a police station after his dog attacked another dog. He chose to be accompanied by a solicitor, who listened quietly while the police suggested an official caution. The solicitor then pointed out that one dog attacking another wasn't actually an offence. If the dog in question had attacked a person it would have been more serious, but the law accepts that dogs sometimes go for other dogs. The policemen completely dropped their suggestion of a caution. Now, it would not have resulted in a criminal record, though that caution would have remained on file – in this case, wrongly. Had the solicitor not been there to point that out, the author would have accepted the caution. Instead, he apologised to the other owner, paid their vet fees and made a donation to a charity of their choice.

Churchill said democracy was the worst of all systems, except for all the others. In a way, the law is a little like that. It was conceived to defend the often powerless individual from a powerful nobility or state, while attempting to punish deserving criminals. It is practical, rather than strictly moral, but for all its flaws, its existence gives us a better chance at justice than anything else that might exist.

*Our questions were answered by Daniel Martin, partner in a law firm. He provided both his time and expertise with enormous generosity. Thank you.*

*For more detail than space allows here, we also recommend* How the Law Works *by Gary Slapper.*

# ELASTIC-BAND GUN

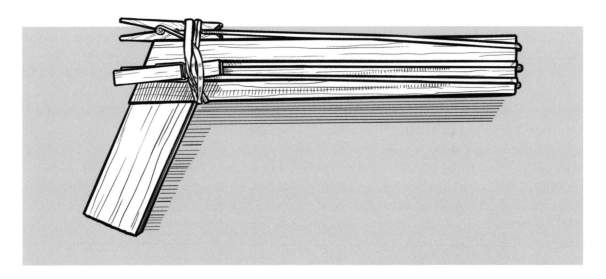

This is a simple, low-skill design – the sort of thing you can rough out with a few bits of scrap pine, a tenon saw and an electric drill. You will also need three wooden clothes pegs, sandpaper or an electric sander, some good wood glue and, of course, some elastic bands.

We began by digging out a piece of pine from an offcuts box. You'll want something with roughly the dimensions of a pistol, but with a longer barrel to stretch the elastic bands. Ours was 1¾in × 1in (44 × 25mm) – and 11½in (29cm) long. If we were making it for smaller hands, we'd adjust, so don't get too hung up on exact measurements for this one.

For the look we wanted, we set a 30-degree angle on a sliding bevel, then gripped the scrap wood in a vice and used a tenon saw to cut a piece off the end.

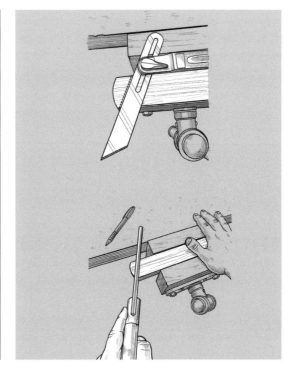

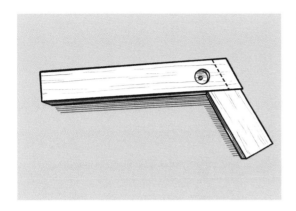

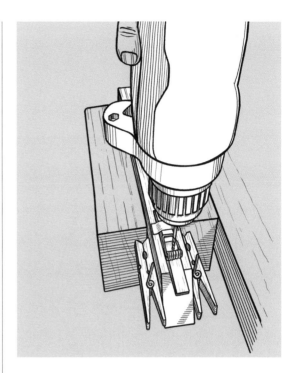

The nice thing about a sliding bevel is that you can set an angle – and then use it over and over without having to measure everything again. We cut a hilt piece at the same angle, aiming for something with a nice rake, a bit like a Beretta pistol.

Wood glues like Gorilla Glue are terrific these days. However, we prefer a belt-and-braces approach, so we put a single screw down from the barrel into the hilt piece as well as gluing them. If you do this, remember to 'countersink' the screwhead – use a countersink drill bit to widen the hole so the screw can sit flush. This is surprisingly important in this case.

Take the first of your three wooden clothes pegs – and slide it apart gently. You are going to attach one piece to the gun body, then slide the other half back on. Place the first bit by eye: parallel to the barrel, with a little of the tail sticking out. The idea will be to release an elastic band while gripping the hilt, so adjust for your hand size as necessary. Your thumb will work the 'triggers'.

Dab on some glue, then hammer a small wire tack through the body of the peg. If it splits (and two of ours did), you might need a tiny drill bit and a pilot hole for the tack. Hold the peg in place with a bit of Sellotape. Ideally, find someone who knows how to do this.

The combination of nail and glue will hold it very securely. Once the tack has been hammered in, slide the second half of the clothes peg back on.

You'll need to lift up the metal spring to do this. Repeat on both sides – and on top of the gun.

Finally, you'll need three pegs sticking out of the end of the gun for the elastic bands. The idea is to make a three-shot pistol.

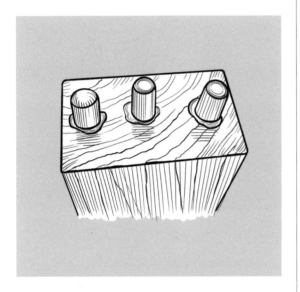

To do this, put the barrel in a vice and drill three holes. If you want them all to be the same depth, use a little bit of masking tape on the drill bit and then drill to it each time. Now, you might have to use a bit of imagination here. You need three roughly equal stubs of pine. We used an old artist's paintbrush. We cut three bits off the handle and rounded them on an electric sander held upside down in the vice. The old artist was furious, but otherwise it worked pretty well. You could also buy some pine dowel rod.

On first use, we found the clothes pegs would slip during loading, firing off elastic bands with no warning. Luckily the solution was a simple one – we wrapped three elastic bands around the pegs,

holding them closed until they were deliberately triggered. Not pretty, but it worked.

Overall, this was easy to make, and fun to use. Obviously, you should avoid shooting someone with

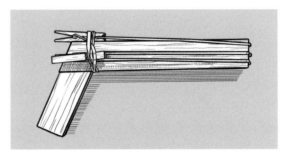

it – and take care not to shoot yourself as well. Range depends on the elastic bands and the enhanced grip of the clothes pegs.

Finally, you might consider spraying it. Black or dark blue would work well for the body – and if you cut a simple stencil shape out of card, you could spray through it to add a small skull-and-crossbones in white. Just a suggestion.

# MAKING A CUP OF COFFEE

Children don't drink coffee, obviously. Both coffee and tea contain caffeine, which is a stimulant – it makes the heart beat faster. It's also pretty bitter, as drinks go. However, many adults do drink coffee and so you might find this interesting. It isn't a definitive guide. That would take entire chapters on blends, beans and roasts. These are just a few facts, opinions and guidelines you might find useful one day.

Coffee is grown in around fifty countries, usually on or near the Equator. Brazil is the main producer by far, followed by Colombia. When one of the authors went to Brazil, he spoke to a coffee plantation owner – and mentioned that in his experience, Italian coffee was the best. The plantation owner smiled and said that might be because the Italians had the oldest relationship with his business. The representatives of Illy, Lavazza and Pellini were all given first choice of the coffee harvest each year. Once they had taken the best beans, the big American chains came in and took the rest. It's also interesting to note that the 'Italian Roast' is the highest temperature for coffee beans: 245°C (472°F). The beans then are so dark they're almost completely black.

Coffee begins as a flowering bush that produces red, cherry-like fruits. There are two main species – *Coffea arabica* and *Coffea canephora*, more usually known as *Coffea robusta*. Arabica beans

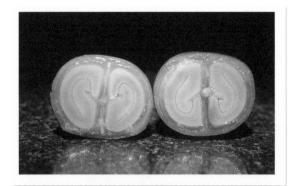

Top left: cross section of coffee bean, above left: Bialetti, right: coffee beans, natural through to roasted

are considered higher quality as they are less bitter. However, Robusta beans have almost twice as much caffeine. Many coffees use blends of the two, though some still see virtue in claiming to be 100% Arabica.

Inside each red berry is a pair of green seeds, separated by pale pith. Both varieties need a hot climate and heavy rain to thrive. They are still usually picked by hand and then either dried in the sun or soaked and washed to separate the berries from the seeds. The seeds tend to go yellow-brown when they are dried, but the most important part of the process is the roasting.

Coffee beans have been roasted in iron pans held over a fire for at least five hundred years – and possibly much longer. It is possible to roast green beans in a home oven, but they have to be rotated regularly or they'll burn. Industrial roasters usually have some sort of tumbler mechanism to keep them turning.

The great variety of coffee bean types is much more to do with the roasting temperature than any blend of beans. The lowest temperature is around 200°C (380–400°F). Those are pale brown in colour. After the roasting process, the beans are shiny and hard. They can be ground up at this point. That dust of 'coffee grounds' is sold in tins around the world, with no other ingredients.

In Italy, coffee is drunk in the mornings, up to noon – rarely later. It is often drunk standing up at a bar, as a quick pick-me-up. Espresso coffee there is a very small amount of very strong coffee. It is served in a small cup and is no more than a few sips. You might prefer a frothy cappuccino or an Americano, which is an espresso with extra hot water. Whichever you choose, there is no better coffee in the world, we believe. The Italians really do get the best beans.

Bars and restaurants often use enormous machines. They take deep spoonfuls of the coffee, jam it into a holder and dribble hot water through into tiny cups. The result is the espresso or cappuccino we know and love. It's not at all easy to replicate a busy coffee machine at home. The closest you'll come is some form of percolator. To 'percolate' is to bubble or filter through. An idea can percolate through a society over time. In this case, a percolator boils water until it bubbles up through coffee.

We recommend coffee companies like Illy for reasons of taste. We did know one well-travelled lady who always swore by Douwe Egberts. However, as with all things, you'll have to discover which brand you like.

Accepting that Italians named most coffees and tend to know what they're doing in this area, we would also recommend an Italian percolator company: Bialetti. Their six-cup coffee-maker has a recognisable logo of a man with a large nose holding up his hand. Note: We receive no money for this recommendation. They just work.

You fill the bottom part with water to the level of the valve and add coffee to the internal holder, filling it completely. Screw the parts of the coffee-maker together and put on a medium heat for around ten minutes – or until the coffee bubbles up. Pour out into small cups. Add sugar to taste, or a splash of milk if the coffee is bitter. Remember to clean it afterwards. In our opinion, there is a lovely, old-fashioned mechanical simplicity to these coffee-makers. They clunk and fit together beautifully.

Instant coffee begins with the black liquid you have just made in your Bialetti. It is then flash-frozen, then slowly rewarmed while all moisture is removed, leaving just granules. Adding water to it undoes that process. It's valued for its speed, but the truth is, it's not as good as a cup of fresh coffee from a percolator – and *that* won't be as good as the cup they serve in a beach bar on the Amalfi Coast.

# POLISHING BOOTS LIKE THE BRITISH ARMY

## This chapter is formed from the personal experiences and recollection of a veteran of the Royal Corps of Signals

'Shiny shoes, shiny mind!' I have never really understood that statement. I first heard it in the early 1990s when my training sergeant screamed it at me. In those days, my Army life consisted of a circular process: preparation for inspection, inspection, recovering from the inspection.

When it comes to clothing or kit inspections, it's all about creases and boots. In normal life, boots you can see your face in are not a requirement, but this was not normal life. Every Army corps, regiment and unit has evolved its own method for producing the perfect shine, to a lesser extent the Navy and Air Force. The equipment and methodology below is the one I was taught. It will raise eyebrows, and create argument, but as far as I am concerned it is absolute.

I suppose a good starting question would be: Why do boots need to be so shiny? As well as the regular inspections, there are obvious occasions when only perfectly shiny boots will do: ceremonial parades such as Remembrance Parade and funerals, for example. On such occasions, scuffed or dull boots would be disrespectful.

Less obvious are the secondary benefits of the activity: 'bulling' or polishing boots takes time, lots of time. Believe it or not, I have had some of the best nights of my life packed around a square table in my eight-man room, sitting with my fellow soldiers, bulling, joking, swearing, laughing, fighting, supporting and ultimately building the kind of friendships that last a lifetime.

'Ammo boots', or 'Boots, ankle, General Service (BGS)', are the favoured ceremonial boots.

Benefiting from having iron-studded leather soles which make a quite outstanding noise on impact, they also have the advantage of being entirely useless outside of ceremonial activities, not a comfortable wear, and a similar ride to ice-skates. Yet in the right market, a good pair of bulled ammo boots have an offensively high street value.

Allowing a trainee soldier to wear ammo boots would be far too kind for the Army Apprentices College in Harrogate. No, I was stuck with the standard-issue assault boot, with softly dimpled leather uppers that were not at all conducive to a perfect shine. Their surface is more like the standard leather shoe of civilian life. Ammo boots came later.

Now, the process of creating a deep mirror-like shine is both long and laborious, but it is the only way to achieve the result you want. The average British soldier has an incredible aptitude for saving time and effort. For example, when in 'long-sleeved order' (wearing a woollen jumper) in the early spring heat, soldiers have been known to cut the shirt underneath off at the shoulders. What remains is essentially a large olive-green dog collar. Not only is it cool, but it saves time ironing. So when it comes to polishing a boot, every possible shortcut has been tried. Floor polish, furniture polish, paints of every type, patent leather, felt-tip pens – none of them work.

---
## YOU WILL NEED
---

- Two tins of Kiwi black boot polish/parade gloss: one is for cleaning your boots with brushes, the other for the shine. Other boot polish is available but just doesn't work.
- A stick of beeswax
- Two boot brushes: one to polish on, one to polish off

- A toothbrush for cleaning the treads, a nailbrush for removing dirt
- A bulling rag: either an old yellow duster your nan might have, or a Selvyt (pronounced silvette, originally a jewellery-polishing cloth)
- Some water
- A camping stove
- A heat gun/paint stripper gun or burner
- A black Sharpie pen

---
## METHOD
---

First things first, the boots need to be clean, incredibly clean, as any grit or ground-in mud will render any bulling useless.

For day-to-day life, applying polish to the boot, leaving it for a few minutes to dry and gently polishing off will give a sufficient shine. Also, a very impressive shine on the toecaps and heel can be achieved without the use of beeswax. Just skip the 'Applying Beeswax' section below.

---
## APPLYING BEESWAX
---

It's worth mentioning why we use beeswax, or Carnauba wax. The required result is a solid surface, without dimples in the leather. Beeswax has a very low melting point, but when hardened in multiple layers it will fill the dimples in.

There are two main application methods. Some heat the shoe and the stick of wax and rub the stick on the hot shoe, then use a hot spoon to mould the wax into the leather. Others heat the wax in a mess tin, then 'paint' it on the shoe.

I am very much in the school of heating the shoe and wax stick. I have always found that painting the melted wax creates a mess on the exposed sole of the shoe and the welts (the leather rim sewn around the edge of a shoe upper, to which the sole is attached), which will need attention with a penknife to remove.

To ensure the boot leather does not dry out completely and the shape is retained, fill the boot with damp sand or damp newspaper, making sure the laces are out and eyelets are kept together with metal sandwich bag ties. If you use sand, you can remove it with a spoon – and then rinse the boot out under a tap to get the last grains.

Using the heat gun, apply direct heat to the leather. Make sure it does not burn, just gently heats up. Test this by rubbing the stick of wax on the leather – it should immediately coat the area and shine (though that shine will not last). Continue this over the boot, focusing on the area between the toecap and the bottom eyelet, where the toes bend. Remember there is little point in applying wax above the ankle as your trousers will cover that part of the boot.

Once the beeswax is cold and hardened, the sand/paper inserts can be removed. You are going to be holding these boots for a while and any weight reduction will be appreciated later. As a benchmark for polishing, we spent four hours a night for a week preparing our boots for our pass-out parade.

## APPLYING THE POLISH, OR 'BULLING'

Once you have a couple of layers of beeswax on the boot and have removed any drips or ripples by applying some heat, you are ready for some polish. Pour some tap water in the lid of your second parade gloss tin. You will be dipping the bulling rag in and out for the duration of the bulling.

Wrap the Selvyt cloth around your index and middle fingers, ensuring the pads of your fingers have a covering of cloth without creases. Dip the cloth into the water, then into the polish, collecting a blob the size of your little fingernail. The trick here is to rub the polish into the boot in a small circular pattern, one section at a time. Once a dull shine appears, pare down the amount of polish to a smudge on the damp rag and widen the circles. Get comfortable, because the more layers of polish and the longer you take, the deeper the shine will become.

Once satisfied with your efforts – and once the shine in both boots matches – carefully and loosely lace the boots. If there is wear on the eyelets, use the Sharpie pen to colour them in. Don't forget to dry the polish lid, as tiny pieces of rust will scratch a bulled boot.

Bulling boots is almost certainly an exercise in futility. The effects of the ceremony, marching out to parade, marking time, changing step, halting and marching back takes its toll, especially on boots without a beeswax layer. After the day is over, it only takes a brief glance at the cracks, creases, scuffs and mild explosions of polish to realise the circular process of preparation for inspection, the inspection itself and recovering from the inspection.

That said, there is almost always a right and wrong way to do things. This is the British Army method and is the right way. It might also give you a sense of what you have to do to really polish a pair of shoes in civilian life.

Mount Nyiragongo

1. How many active volcanoes are there?
2. How many satellites orbit the earth?
3. How deep can we go?
4. How do we generate electricity?
5. What is the universe made of?

( 1 )

## HOW MANY ACTIVE VOLCANOES ARE THERE?

The answer is around 1,500, but because of their nature, no one can say for certain. Volcanoes lie dormant for decades or even centuries, then blow up with enough violence to destroy entire cities. Here are a few of the most active as of 2018 – sampled from around a constantly erupting world.

1. Mauna Loa/Kilauea volcanoes on Hawaii. Hawaii's volcanoes have been erupting since the 1980s, adding to the land with molten lava that solidifies when it comes into contact with the sea. The trouble is that magma – molten rock – can eat its way through to the surface in great fissures, destroying homes and putting lives in danger. Hawaii itself was formed by five enormous volcanoes out of the sea.

2. Mount Etna, Italy. Europe's tallest active volcano. It has erupted almost continuously throughout recorded history. Vesuvius near Naples is more famous and can be walked up.

3. Mount Yasur, Vanuatu. Located on a tiny Pacific island, Yasur is part of the 'Pacific Ring of Fire' in which 75 per cent of the world's

volcanoes are located. It has been active for a thousand years or more.

4. Volcán de Colima, Mexico. A regular erupter since the 16th century. Very active in 2017.

5. Mount Nyiragongo, Democratic Republic of the Congo, Africa. Topped by a permanent lava lake.

6. Mount Erebus, Antarctica. Discovered by Sir James Ross – see Forgotten Explorers – and named after his ship. Lava lake. Included here because hardly anyone knows there is an active volcano in Antarctica. The other one – Mount Sidley – is dormant.

---

② 

## HOW MANY SATELLITES ORBIT THE EARTH?

By 2018, there were around five thousand, but three or four will be added to that number every single day for the next few years – and realistically that daily launch number is only likely to rise. Some of them fail, of course, in the most hostile environment we have ever encountered. A percentage 'degrade' or fall back into lower orbit, usually burning up on entering the atmosphere. Others go completely dead and can't be contacted, so just continue on at immense speeds for ever. They are still tracked, so danger from them is minimal, but the main protection for future endeavours is still simply scale.

The surface area of the earth is 197 million square miles (510,064,000km$^2$). However, if you take off from the surface, you create a sphere with a much larger surface area, using this equation: surface area of a sphere = $4\pi r^2$. (Notice that the surface area equation increases by 4 times pi (22/7 as a guide) times the radius *squared*. In other words, even a small increase in radius makes the surface area shoot up.)

The earth isn't a perfect sphere so we'll have to round up to show how it works. Say the distance from the centre of the earth to the shell (the radius) is 3,960 miles (approx. 6,300km). The surface area of the sphere would be $4 \times \pi \times 3,960^2$ = 197 million square miles. So far so good.

If you boosted a satellite to orbit at around 12,000 miles – where we have placed a shell of GPS satellites – you increase your radius to 15,960 miles, which gives a surface area on a new sphere of: $4 \times \pi \times 15,960^2 = 3.2$ *billion* square miles. Four times the original radius, but seventeen times the surface area of the sphere. That is a lot of space.

---

③

## HOW DEEP CAN WE GO?

An adult snorkeller with flippers on can probably manage 20 feet down (6 m) in clear water, as long as he or she knows to hold their nose and blow slightly on the way down. It's probably worth pointing out that you shouldn't try this unless you are experienced and confident – and never alone either.

Scuba divers take air with them, so can go much, much deeper. For recreational divers, depths of 40 feet (12m) are normal, with 130 feet (40m) as a limit. Experienced divers have gone much, much deeper, however – down to 1,090 feet (332m). That record, set by Ahmed Gabr, took a team of thirty people and months of training. Beyond that, the pressure on the human body is brutal. To go further, we need to be encased in steel.

A 'diving bell' is actually an ancient device. Alexander the Great's tutor Aristotle described men descending beneath the sea with a chamber that retained air – in the 4th century BC. It wasn't until the 18th century that British engineer John

Left: Bathyscaphe *Trieste*. Bottom left: DCV1 *Deepsea Challenger*

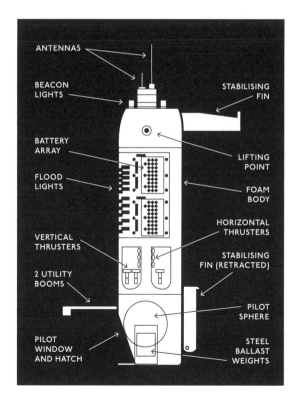

ANTENNAS

BEACON LIGHTS

STABILISING FIN

BATTERY ARRAY

LIFTING POINT

FLOOD LIGHTS

FOAM BODY

HORIZONTAL THRUSTERS

VERTICAL THRUSTERS

STABILISING FIN (RETRACTED)

2 UTILITY BOOMS

PILOT SPHERE

PILOT WINDOW AND HATCH

STEEL BALLAST WEIGHTS

Smeaton worked out how to pump air down to a bell. They are still used today to transport divers from the surface down to deep-water work, such as underwater welding on oil rigs.

In 1960, the *Trieste* bathyscaphe ('deep ship') reached the bottom of 'Challenger Deep' – the deepest part of the Mariana Trench at 35,787 feet or 10,901 metres down. Swiss national Jacques Piccard, son of the *Trieste* designer, Auguste Piccard, and US Navy diver Don Walsh were the first to reach the lowest point on earth. In 2012, film director James Cameron (*Titanic*) touched down at the same crushing depth in DCV1 – the *Deepsea Challenger* Vehicle. There will be others in the future, but it has to be an achievement up there with climbing Mount Everest for the first time. No one can go deeper.

---
4
---

## HOW DO WE GENERATE ELECTRICITY?

The British scientist Michael Faraday was the first to discover electricity could be generated by rotating copper wire through a magnetic field. (An electromagnet, such as the sort used in scrapyards to pick up old cars, is the same principle in reverse – electricity is run through the wire and the magnetic field activates.) Most electrical generators still rely on this basic principle, while electric motors rely on the process in reverse to produce mechanical movement from electricity. Faraday must have a claim to creating the most useful invention of all time.

For an electric motor to generate nice, clean electricity, turbines have to turn a mass of copper around a magnetic core. A number of fuels can be used to make this happen. Water made into steam from the heat of burning oil or coal works well. Water itself can be used in hydroelectric dam set-ups. It's particularly good as it produces no emissions, though the start-up costs are enormous. Sadly, there are few places in the world where the geography supports hydroelectric turbines. (Australia has over 120 of them, though, producing terawatts of electrical energy.)

Nuclear power – or heat produced by a sustained nuclear reaction – is an excellent method of producing electricity using steam, turbines and magnets. The downside there is that it leaves radioactive waste that will be dangerous for thousands of years. (The ideal would be to boost it out of the atmosphere and point it at the sun, but no one wants to take the risk of a vehicle blowing up mid-launch and scattering radioactive dust over a continent or two.)

Wind power lends itself to electricity generation as it involves a turning turbine at the start point. Each turbine includes magnets, and electricity is produced as long as they turn. Unfortunately, they don't always turn and are immensely expensive to produce, maintain and decommission. Wind power probably isn't the answer.

Tidal turbines show promise, as do solar panels. Each method of generating electricity has drawbacks, such as sea-corrosion problems or huge inefficiency. We're still waiting for better ways of storing electricity. At the moment, the best we have are the batteries in mobile phones. They last only a few hundred charging cycles before degrading. The world waits for a better battery – if we could build up safe and reliable stores of electricity, it wouldn't matter half as much how we produced it.

---
5
---

## WHAT IS THE UNIVERSE MADE OF?

It's possible to conceive of forces so vast and powerful as to break the laws of time and the universe – inside a black hole, for example, or watching a clock in an exam hall. Yet we do have a pretty good sense of the elements that make up the universe. Each one differs from the next by a single electron whizzing around each atom – and changing its properties completely.

Hydrogen is the simplest atom we have encountered – the building block of the universe and, along with helium, the source of our sun's energy.

At the core of a hydrogen atom is a single proton, a particle with a positive charge. Around that proton is a single electron, with a negative charge. That empty 'shell' allows hydrogen to bond with many other elements, making it extremely reactive – and explosive. The other main

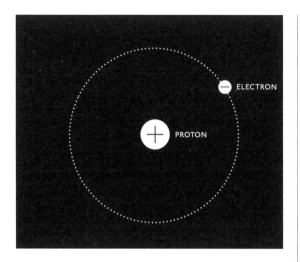

type of subatomic particle is a neutron, which carries no charge. There are more rarely occurring forms of the hydrogen atom that have either one or two neutrons. They are deuterium and tritium – isotopes of hydrogen. (An isotope always has the same number of protons, but neutrons will vary.)

The 'atomic number' of hydrogen is 1 – the number of protons in the nucleus. Note that there will always be the same number of electrons as protons.

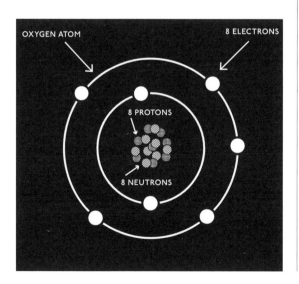

An oxygen atom has eight protons and eight neutrons, with eight electrons in two shells around the core – arranged 2, 6. Its atomic number is 8.

If hydrogen and oxygen are combined, the result is an extraordinary substance known as 'water'. The chemical symbol for water is $H_2O$, which means two hydrogen atoms combine with each oxygen atom into a new molecule. As far as we know, water is vital for life, so this is a key chemical reaction.

We arrange elements like hydrogen, oxygen, iron and gold into the Periodic Table. 'Periods' here refers to groupings of similar properties. These days, the gaps have been filled and the only new elements tend to be radioactive substances that appear and vanish in fractions of a second during violent reactions.

Hydrogen and helium are only one proton/electron apart, but helium is extremely stable and has far more in common with neon, argon, krypton, xenon and radon than it does with explosive hydrogen. Note that after lead – written as 82 Pb (for 'plumbum', the Latin word) – the real atomic heavyweights are all radioactive. That means they 'decay', giving off neutrons, protons, electrons or photon energy. The three kinds are called alpha, beta and gamma radiation. Beta and gamma can be very dangerous. Radium (atomic number 88), for example, discovered by Marie Curie, was responsible for her death. In the early 20th century, radium was painted on watch dials for its healthy glow at night. Unfortunately, the young women who painted the dials were exposed to high levels and many died as a result. However, most things are radioactive to a degree. We refer to the ordinary radiation found in granite, or bananas, or people, as 'background' radiation. It's both unavoidable and mostly harmless.

If there *are* new elements out there in the

# Periodic Table of the Elements

Atomic Number → | 1
H ← Symbol
Name → Hydrogen ← Atomic Weight
1.008

| 1 IA | | | | | | | | | | | | | | | | | 18 VIIIA |
|---|---|---|---|---|---|---|---|---|---|---|---|---|---|---|---|---|---|
| 1 **H** Hydrogen 1.008 | 2 IIA | | | | | | | | | | | 13 IIIA | 14 IVA | 15 VA | 16 VIA | 17 VIIA | 2 **He** Helium 4.002802 |
| 3 **Li** Lithium 6.94 | 4 **Be** Beryllium 9.0121831 | | | | | | | | | | | 5 **B** Boron 10.81 | 6 **C** Carbon 12.011 | 7 **N** Nitrogen 14.007 | 8 **O** Oxygen 15.999 | 9 **F** Fluorine 18.998403163 | 10 **Ne** Neon 20.1797 |
| 11 **Na** Sodium 22.98976928 | 12 **Mg** Magnesium 24.305 | 3 IIIB | 4 IVB | 5 VB | 6 VIB | 7 VIIB | 8 VIIIB | 9 VIIIB | 10 VIIIB | 11 IB | 12 IIB | 13 **Al** Aluminium 26.9815385 | 14 **Si** Silicon 28.085 | 15 **P** Phosphorus 30.973761998 | 16 **S** Sulfur 32.06 | 17 **Cl** Chlorine 35.45 | 18 **Ar** Argon 39.948 |
| 19 **K** Potassium 39.0983 | 20 **Ca** Calcium 40.078 | 21 **Sc** Scandium 44.955908 | 22 **Ti** Titanium 47.867 | 23 **V** Vanadium 50.9415 | 24 **Cr** Chromium 51.9961 | 25 **Mn** Manganese 54.938044 | 26 **Fe** Iron 55.845 | 27 **Co** Cobalt 58.933194 | 28 **Ni** Nickel 58.6934 | 29 **Cu** Copper 63.546 | 30 **Zn** Zinc 65.38 | 31 **Ga** Gallium 69.723 | 32 **Ge** Germanium 72.630 | 33 **As** Arsenic 74.921595 | 34 **Se** Selenium 78.971 | 35 **Br** Bromine 79.904 | 36 **Kr** Krypton 83.798 |
| 37 **Rb** Rubidium 85.4678 | 38 **Sr** Strontium 87.62 | 39 **Y** Yttrium 88.90584 | 40 **Zr** Zirconium 91.224 | 41 **Nb** Niobium 92.90637 | 42 **Mo** Molybdenum 95.95 | 43 **Tc** Technetium (98) | 44 **Ru** Ruthenium 101.07 | 45 **Rh** Rhodium 102.90550 | 46 **Pd** Palladium 106.42 | 47 **Ag** Silver 107.8682 | 48 **Cd** Cadmium 112.414 | 49 **In** Indium 114.818 | 50 **Sn** Tin 118.710 | 51 **Sb** Antimony 121.760 | 52 **Te** Tellurium 127.60 | 53 **I** Iodine 126.90447 | 54 **Xe** Xenon 131.293 |
| 55 **Cs** Caesium 132.90545196 | 56 **Ba** Barium 137.327 | 57 - 71 Lanthanoids | 72 **Hf** Hafnium 178.49 | 73 **Ta** Tantalum 180.94788 | 74 **W** Tungsten 183.84 | 75 **Re** Rhenium 186.207 | 76 **Os** Osmium 190.23 | 77 **Ir** Iridium 192.217 | 78 **Pt** Platinum 195.084 | 79 **Au** Gold 196.966569 | 80 **Hg** Mercury 200.592 | 81 **Tl** Thallium 204.38 | 82 **Pb** Lead 207.2 | 83 **Bi** Bismuth 208.98040 | 84 **Po** Polonium (209) | 85 **At** Astatine (210) | 86 **Rn** Radon (222) |
| 87 **Fr** Francium (223) | 88 **Ra** Radium (226) | 89 - 103 Actinoids | 104 **Rf** Rutherfordium (267) | 105 **Db** Dubnium (268) | 106 **Sg** Seaborgium (269) | 107 **Bh** Bohrium (270) | 108 **Hs** Hassium (269) | 109 **Mt** Meitnerium (278) | 110 **Ds** Darmstadtium (281) | 111 **Rg** Roentgenium (282) | 112 **Cn** Copernicium (285) | 113 **Nh** Nihonium (286) | 114 **Fl** Flerovium (289) | 115 **Mc** Moscovium (289) | 116 **Lv** Livermorium (293) | 117 **Ts** Tennessine (294) | 118 **Og** Oganesson (294) |

| 57 **La** Lanthanum 138.90547 | 58 **Ce** Cerium 140.116 | 59 **Pr** Praseodymium 140.90766 | 60 **Nd** Neodymium 144.242 | 61 **Pm** Promethium (145) | 62 **Sm** Samarium 150.36 | 63 **Eu** Europium 151.964 | 64 **Gd** Gadolinium 157.25 | 65 **Tb** Terbium 158.92535 | 66 **Dy** Dysprosium 162.500 | 67 **Ho** Holmium 164.93033 | 68 **Er** Erbium 167.259 | 69 **Tm** Thulium 168.93422 | 70 **Yb** Ytterbium 173.045 | 71 **Lu** Lutetium 174.9668 |
|---|---|---|---|---|---|---|---|---|---|---|---|---|---|---|
| 89 **Ac** Actinium (227) | 90 **Th** Thorium 232.0377 | 91 **Pa** Protactinium 231.03588 | 92 **U** Uranium 238.02891 | 93 **Np** Neptunium (237) | 94 **Pu** Plutonium (244) | 95 **Am** Americium (243) | 96 **Cm** Curium (247) | 97 **Bk** Berkelium (247) | 98 **Cf** Californium (251) | 99 **Es** Einsteinium (252) | 100 **Fm** Fermium (257) | 101 **Md** Mendelevium (258) | 102 **No** Nobelium (259) | 103 **Lr** Lawrencium (266) |

universe, they would shatter our understanding of how atoms are constructed. Of course, the history of science suggests that this could very well happen.

Mass creates gravitational effects – it's how we know where black holes are when they swallow even light. Some of these effects have been observed that cannot be explained without a great deal more matter in the universe than we can see. The current name for this hypothetical substance is 'dark matter'. If it exists, it would be very different from the matter we understand. We can say with almost perfect certainty that new particles, even entire new systems of understanding, are waiting to be discovered.

# EXTRAORDINARY STORIES –
# PART FOUR: HUNTING A KING

'Where their king is, God knows.'
*Weekly Intelligencer*, a news sheet (1651)

In 1660, a ship brought King Charles II back from France to England. Its name had been changed from the *Naseby*, celebrating a Parliamentary victory in the Civil War, to the *Royal Charles*. Its figurehead of Oliver Cromwell had also been discreetly removed.

The diarist Samuel Pepys was on board. As they crossed, he listened to the king tell the story of how he had survived being hunted across ten English counties, nine years earlier. Pepys

was fascinated. He went on to interview all the surviving characters, producing a complete record of those extraordinary six weeks of 1651.

As the oldest son of King Charles I, the young prince played a part in the battles of the Civil War as soon as he was able. He was present at the battle of Edgehill in 1642, aged just twelve. Prince Charles and his brother James had to hide in a barn that day to avoid capture. Three years later, his father sent him to command forces in Wales and the west of England. It would be the last time they ever saw each other. When the forces of Parliament and Cromwell were triumphant in 1648, the prince escaped to France by way of Jersey, a Royalist stronghold.

In January 1649, King Charles I was taken to London for trial. He would not recognise the authority of the court that tried him, so refused to plead. From France, his son and heir sent a single sheet of paper to Parliament, left blank with his name at the bottom. They could have put anything to it – he would have signed away all he had in the world in exchange for freeing his father. Instead, fifty-nine of them signed a death warrant. The forces of Parliament beheaded King Charles I and declared kingship abolished. Cromwell and his dour Puritans had the Royal Seal broken with hammers. The new Commonwealth Seal read, 'IN THE FIRST YEAR OF FREEDOM, BY GOD'S BLESSING RESTORED'.

Those were heady times for the victors, when men like the poet John Milton supported them in the creation of a new kind of state, a new government. It would not be a gentle one, however. New offences of immorality would earn the death penalty. The iron grip of Puritan discipline began to close on the country.

Cromwell took his 'New Model Army' to Ireland and then into Scotland, as well as putting down rebellions in England. He and his men earned a reputation for utter ruthlessness. His self-belief was total and a string of victories only confirmed his view that God was on his side. In Scotland, his professional soldiers defeated twice their number at Dunbar, losing only twenty-eight men for the enemy's 3,000 dead and 10,000 captured. Afterwards, Cromwell said, 'God made them as stubble to our swords.'

As an exile in France, Prince Charles was tempted to try a scheme to regain the throne he would have inherited. His mother was a French princess and she persuaded him to land in Scotland, where he could be crowned king, then come south into England, gathering Royalists as he went. It was madness – a triumph of desperate hope over reality. Time and expense might eventually have withered Cromwell's armies, but in that year of 1651 he was the pre-eminent soldier in England, with men who believed they were unbeatable.

Prince Charles gambled everything on that wild chance at the throne. Just eighteen months after his father's execution, he landed in Scotland and made his way to Scone, where he was crowned King of Scotland, aged just twenty-one. An army of Scots gathered to support him. In London, as news spread of his return, Parliament whipped up popular feeling against the 'traitor' prince.

Charles marched south, but no great Royalist uprising materialised to support him. His Scottish army was an unpopular presence in England and very few Royalists came to join them as he made a base in the city of Worcester. One supporter who did come was a Lord Talbot, accompanied by sixty cavalry and the wonderfully named Major Careless.

Cromwell joined forces with two other senior officers to form an army of almost 40,000. It was one of the largest forces ever to stalk the fields and roads of England as it converged on Worcester in August 1651. At the same time, the Parliamentary Council sent orders to all towns and officials, to close roads, passes and ports. None of the Royalists would escape. Cromwell intended to make an end of Charles and his supporters in one fell swoop.

On 3 September, Charles climbed to the top of Worcester Cathedral to view the enemy forces. He must have despaired at the numbers. Out there in the morning mists were men who had signed his father's death warrant and witnessed his execution. Still, his father had been resolute to the end and young Charles would not yield.

When fighting began, Charles led from the front and broke a cavalry regiment with a charge, before his men were driven back by superior numbers. Cromwell's soldiers were well trained, with high morale. Yet the Royalists fought for their lives – and for their king. Cromwell said later that it was 'as stiff a contest for four or five hours as ever I have seen'. One key moment came when 3,000 Scots in reserve decided to quit the battlefield rather than support a doomed cause.

Charles fought until there was no hope left. His men blocked streets in a rearguard action that allowed him to escape. He rode out with a rabble of battered and wounded men into the gloom of evening. At 6 p.m., he was on the run, with Cromwell's men hunting him.

Major General Thomas Harrison was among the first on the trail of the escaped king. For a time, he believed Charles had to be lying among the dead. Thousands of Royalists had been slaughtered at Worcester. They had to be searched. Harrison also knew he could end it all quickly if he found the king alive. Charles had already been named traitor by Parliament. There would be no need for a trial if they could catch him.

A mile out from Worcester, Charles halted with the weary men who had come out with him. He knew then that he would be hunted – and that he had a better chance in a smaller group. He ordered his men to scatter and went on with just a few. One of those was Charles Giffard, who owned a house to the north – known as Boscobel ('beautiful forest'). It was an isolated place and Charles headed there. On the way, the plan changed to take him to another property even further from the road, known as 'Whiteladies'.

At Whiteladies, Charles endured his hair being cut and coal dust rubbed into his skin. He was given peasant clothes and crude shoes. There was nothing they could do about his height of six foot and two inches.

Five Penderel brothers lived in those woods around Boscobel and Whiteladies – more a community than a single home. They helped Charles with his disguise. At dawn, he set out with just Richard Penderel, carrying a woodsman's heavy bill for chopping wood. They named the king 'William Jones' and tried to get him to walk bent over to hide his height as Richard Penderel led him into the woods.

Parliamentary troops arrived at Whiteladies just hours later. Though they were over twenty miles from Worcester, they were following reports of a force of Royalists that had been seen heading in that direction. Such was their efficiency, every house would be searched for fugitives.

Charles wanted to reach London, but Parliamentary forces were everywhere. It was impossible to move around the country without permissions from local magistrates and the right papers. Those who were challenged on the road and found to be without them would be arrested and held for questioning. Instead, Charles agreed to try for the Welsh border, on foot and in the dark. He and Richard Penderel set off that evening across wild country. It wasn't long before the king's feet were raw and bleeding. At one point, he collapsed and refused to go on, but his companion persuaded him to continue.

In the small hours of the morning, they encountered a miller who shouted, 'Rogues! Rogues!' Penderel and Charles had to wade through a freezing brook to escape him. They reached the river Severn, but every quay and boat was being watched by Parliamentary forces. Wales was known to be a hotbed of Royalist sympathies and Major General Harrison had poured soldiers into the area to capture anyone trying to cross. The pair hid in a hay barn for a day, but there was no way over to Wales and so they turned back and reached Boscobel on 5 September. By then, Major William Careless was also concealed there, hiding from Parliamentary soldiers. He wept when he saw Charles alive.

Major Careless thought soldiers would search Boscobel and recommended a huge oak not far from the house to hide in. He and Charles climbed it using a ladder, taking bread, cheese and beer with them. In the branches, the exhausted young king fell asleep across the leg of his companion.

The soldiers of Parliament's New Model Army were still searching. They reached Boscobel and turned out every room and chest. More men roamed through the woods, passing right beneath the oak where Charles slept. Major Careless remained still for such a long time his leg went numb and he began to slip. He had to wake the king by pinching him before they both pitched to the ground. The Penderel brothers – and one sister – distracted the search parties and the king went undiscovered. That evening, Charles and Careless returned to Boscobel – to grim news. A reward had been put on the king's head of £1,000 – a vast sum for those days.

With Parliamentary forces still searching the area, Charles and the Penderels decided to move to another safe house of Royalists: Moseley Hall. They went in darkest night, armed to the teeth with blades and pistols, with the king sitting on an old horse in the centre. There, Charles met Father Huddleston, a Catholic priest; the Whitgreave family, and one of his own escaped officers, Henry Wilmot. It was something of a miracle that Wilmot had avoided arrest, as both he and his horse were richly dressed.

Behind them, Parliamentary soldiers searched Boscobel again. More arrived at Moseley Hall and beat up the owner when he tried to delay them long enough for Charles to hide. The soldiers had no idea Charles was close by and left it at that. Yet it was clear the hunt was only heating up. A Royalist colonel named John Lane was trusted with the news. He brought fresh horses and accompanied Charles through the night.

A second disguise followed. Charles's skin was darkened with walnut juice and he was given the clothes of a manservant. His new name was 'William Jackson' and he would move across country as the servant of Jane Lane, sister to Colonel Lane. Jane had a pass to Bristol to visit a pregnant cousin – the key to the new plan.

The small group travelling to Bristol included Henry Lascelles, Jane's cousin, as well as her sister Withy and Withy's husband. Only Lascelles and Jane knew the identity of her groom. Jane's horse had a double saddle and Charles rode in front of her. Up ahead of them all, Charles' friend Henry Wilmot still refused to wear a disguise. He had relented enough to carry a hawk on his arm and be accompanied by spaniels. If challenged by Parliamentary soldiers, he said he would claim he was a gentleman out hunting.

When the horse carrying Jane Lane and Charles threw a shoe, they had to stop at a village blacksmith. Charles engaged the blacksmith in talk of the recent battle at Worcester. They both agreed that Charles Stuart was a rogue and should be hanged.

Jane, Charles and Henry Lascelles parted ways with Jane's sister and brother-in-law, passing through checkpoints to reach a new safe house, Long Marston. Still in disguise, Charles was sent to help in the kitchens. He nearly gave the game away when he couldn't use a mechanical kitchen device, but kept his nerve.

Charles II in disguise aided in his escape by Jane Law

From there, the small group travelled to Cirencester and reached Chipping Sodbury by 12 September. When Charles was recognised at Abbot's Leigh, he admitted his identity to a loyal man and moved on. All around them, the hunt continued, with the reward waiting on word of his whereabouts.

Jane's cousin suffered a stillbirth and Charles had to concoct a fake letter to call Jane away. They set off once more, moving south to Dorset. Charles knew he would be safe with the Royalist Wyndham family in Trent House, reaching it on 17 September. The owner wept on seeing Charles alive. While there, another old friend sent Charles £100 in gold pieces while Wyndham scouted Lyme Regis for ships crossing to France. He found a captain willing to take two anonymous gentlemen (Wilmot and Charles) across the English Channel for £50.

Meanwhile, the hunt grew frenzied. Parliamentary newsletters described every rumour of Charles's whereabouts and repeated that anyone who helped him would be executed for treason. Known Royalists were tortured to reveal the whereabouts of the young king. Ten thousand had been captured at Worcester and every prison was full while the countryside was still being combed for stragglers, more desperate with every day that passed. Kept in appalling conditions, they were beaten and starved. Some of the prisoners were indentured as prison-workers. Two thousand were sent to Ireland or the New World – America and the West Indies. Not a day passed without corpses being cleared away. Meanwhile, Cromwell returned to London to wait for news.

On 22 September, Charles set off from Trent House to Charmouth to be picked up by ship. He posed as servant to Juliana Coningsby, a cousin of the Wyndhams. Francis Wyndham went with him, as well as Wilmot, Wilmot's servant and a servant named Harry Peters.

Peters went ahead into Charmouth with money to secure rooms. Charles and Wilmot came in later, but there was no sign of the ship they'd been promised. There had either been a mix-up or the down-payment had not been paid.

While waiting, Charles' horse threw a shoe. The local blacksmith remarked on a couple of their horses having forge marks of Worcester smiths. He said nothing more, but reported them the moment they were gone. Charles barely made it out of town before Parliamentary soldiers were searching his rooms and riding out after him. Any report of a tall, dark-haired young man was followed up immediately.

Charles rode with Wyndham and Wilmot to Bridport – only to find it stuffed with 1,500 New Model Army soldiers, waiting to cross to Jersey, still a Royalist stronghold. It would have looked suspicious if they'd turned around and ridden away, so they stayed a night in a good tavern in the centre of town, surrounded by men who would have arrested and executed them all if their identities had become known. As groom, it fell to Charles to take the horses to the stables of an inn, where he chatted with the ostler who looked after the horses, trying hard not to seem nervous.

The following day, they learned the captain on whom they'd pinned their hopes had refused. The risks were too great.

In despair, Charles turned his horse towards Trent House once again. Barely an hour later, a troop of Parliamentary soldiers reached Bridport, looking for the party of Royalists with Worcester marks on their horseshoes. When they heard the party had left, they spread out to search local homes.

While Charles rested, Wilmot and Harry Peters sounded out a Colonel Robert Philips about carrying a 'gentleman in distress' out of the kingdom. When he was reluctant, they revealed the gentleman's identity. Philips was loyal to the king and found a suitable ship in Southampton, only to see it commandeered by Parliamentary forces. Cromwell's men were efficient. They suspected Charles was in the area – and therefore that he would be after a ship. Soldiers poured into that part of the country, searching for him. Parliament sent warnings to every port and customs office on the south coast to be on the lookout for the fugitive king.

Charles moved on. Sussex seemed a better bet, and he and Wilmot made their way across country. They stopped for a few hours at Stonehenge, alone and ancient. Charles was fascinated by its mysteries. After that, Charles stayed with the Hyde family at Heale for several days, hiding in a priest-hole.

On the Sussex coast, Wilmot had an old friend named Colonel George Gunter. Wilmot apparently kissed his cheeks when Gunter agreed to help find them a boat. By 8 October,

Gunter had arranged for two anonymous passengers to be collected by Captain Nicholas Tattersall at Brighton, some eighty miles along the coast.

Gunter met the king near Winchester, leading the small group to a house owned by Thomas Symonds. Though he was a Royalist, they did not trust the owner with the identity of the guest they protected. Symonds was drunk and peered suspiciously at Charles, saying, 'Here's a Roundhead.' Gunter agreed that he was indeed a Puritan and that the young man should go to bed to let them drink. Wilmot then matched their host glass for glass all night.

The following day, they carried on through Sussex, passing Arundel Castle and the village of Bramber, which was full of soldiers. As they rode on through Bramber, thirty or forty horsemen came barrelling out. The game was clearly up and the king's small group halted in the road, only to be ordered out of the way as the soldiers rode through. They had not been recognised after all. The riders were off hunting down another rumour of a tall gentleman in the area.

Wilmot sent Colonel Philips to London to arrange funds to be sent to Rouen in France. Meanwhile, Charles, Wilmot and Gunter reached Brighton and a tavern, where they met Captain Nicholas Tattersall. Astonishingly, Tattersall recognised the king. Despite his short hair and darkened skin, it seemed Charles was not as well disguised as he'd hoped. To further embarrass him, the innkeeper suddenly kissed his hand.

Sensing the opportunity of a lifetime, Tattersall used his knowledge to increase his fee to £200, the value of his ship. He asked for a banker's bond to seal the deal – a piece of paper as good as money. Charles told him firmly that 'a gentleman's word is as good as a bond.'

They retired to their rooms, but at 2 a.m., Charles was woken and taken by road to a creek, where a sixty-ton coal-ship called the *Surprise* rested in the mud. Wilmot and Charles went on board to wait for the tide to raise them up. Tattersall kissed Charles's hand, and when the tide rose at 7 a.m. they set off. Behind them, soldiers arrived in Brighton, looking for a dark young man of six foot and two inches.

Tattersall was clearly a very sharp bargainer. He had Charles convince the crew to take him to France, with a story about being on the run from debts. In that way, Tattersall hoped to protect himself from any future accusation, so he could claim he had never known it was the king.

The *Surprise* crossed the Channel without incident and Tattersall anchored off the French coast, waiting for the tide to turn and take him in. They sighted another ship then, and both the crew and Charles feared piracy or the tireless hunters of Parliament. He and Wilmot decided not to wait and took the ship's boat, rowing themselves in. The *Surprise* retrieved its anchor and continued on its normal route.

Charles and Wilmot arrived on the French coast, exhausted and filthy. The Rouen money order had reached a banker and so they had funds again. The two weary young men hired a coach and set off for Paris. It was not long before the news of their safe deliverance was reported in England.

Seven years after the Battle of Worcester, Oliver Cromwell died. His Commonwealth could not survive without him and it was not long before Parliament asked Charles to come home as king. It might have seemed as if the Royalist side had won the Civil War, but one key event was not easily forgotten. When the old king had stood against the people, they had beheaded him on a London green. It was true his son had returned to be king

in turn. It was true that the body of Cromwell was dug up, put on trial, found guilty of treason and then hanged, drawn and quartered, with pieces scattered across the kingdom. Yet the pre-eminence of Parliament – and the democratic principle – had been established in blood. The throne of England was restored, but it was not quite the same. In the end, it was a very English compromise.

The period of Charles II's return is known as the Restoration. Puritan laws that had closed theatres were abolished and the king spent lavishly on his court. King Charles II presided over an extraordinary collection of great minds: Isaac Newton, Sir Christopher Wren, Edmund Halley and Samuel Pepys, to name just a few. His reign also saw disasters such as the Great Plague of 1665 and the Great Fire of London in 1666. Yet he always looked back on the six weeks he had spent on the run for his life as one of the happiest times he had known.

He rewarded everyone who had helped him, usually with pensions for life or even to their descendants. Jane Lane was given £1,000 a year for life, a portrait of the king, a gold watch and a lock of his hair. Wilmot was made Earl of Rochester, though his hard-drinking roistering life caught up with him and he died two years before the Restoration of 1660, aged just forty-five. His son became a fixture at the Restoration court, as wild a man as his father had been and even more so.

The 'Royal Oak' near Boscobel that had sheltered the young king was ravaged by souvenir hunters when the story became known. Acorns were taken from it and a descendant of that great tree grows there still.

*Adapted from* To Catch a King: Charles II's Great Escape *by Charles Spencer, published by William Collins*

The last six – and two extra ones that drove the authors mad.

---
(13)

## THE BOUNDING HOUNDS

Here are four dogs, one at each corner of a field exactly 100 metres square. The dogs all run a hundred metres in 10 seconds. But the four dogs always run towards the dog directly in front of them when they start and keep on running straight for that dog, till they catch it. So all four dogs run in a curved path and all will eventually meet in the middle of the field.

The question is, how long will that run take?

---
(14)

## WAG ONS ROLL

My dad was a shunter in a department store. He would watch for someone stealing anything and then go up to them and say, 'You shunter done that!'

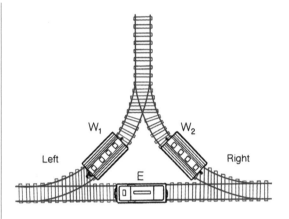

Here we have a rail junction network. There is a shunting engine (E) and two freight wagons – W1 and W2. But the wagons are in the wrong place. The top junction space (J) can take the engine or a wagon only, at any one time. How can the engine shunt the two wagons so they swap places and he can return to his start position?

Surely there shunt be any problem?

---
(15)

## DON'T BREAK ANY EGGS

Sally sells eggs. They are so fresh, the hens haven't missed them yet. I'm not yolking. The other day she had an amazing time selling her eggs. She only had five customers all day, but they all behaved in a very similar fashion.

First Anne came and bought half Sally's eggs, plus half an egg.

Then Betty turned up and bought half of the eggs left and half an egg.

Then Cathy came round and purchased half the remaining eggs and half an egg.

Then along came Daisy and she took half the eggs remaining, plus half an egg.

Finally, Erica arrived and bought half the eggs left, plus half an egg.

Now Sally went home, all sold out, tired, wide eyed and eggless.

In the whole day no one had broken an egg. So how many eggs did Sally arrive with?

---

## 16

## THE CANOEIST'S CLEVER HAT TRICK?

A canoeist goes canoeing in his canoe – on a river that flows at a steady speed of 5 mph. He is wearing a hat, and then he is not, for unbeknown to him, as he starts to paddle upstream, his hat falls off his head and into the river.

After rowing exactly 5 minutes upstream, at 3 miles per hour, he feels the sun on his head and realises his hat has gone and that it must have fallen into the river. His hat floats, so assuming he can turn the boat around instantly, rowing at the same speed, how long will it take him to row back to his hat?

Flow at 5 mph

---

## 17

## HOW TO BECOME UNTIED

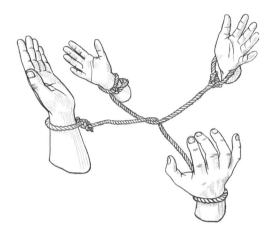

For this party trick, you need two pieces of string around one metre long. Tie each end to a volunteer's wrists to form a pair of handcuffs. But do it so the strings link one person to the other, as in our picture. The question now is, can each release themselves from the other? The answer is yes. But how? (Sliding the loops off the wrist is too easy and not the right answer.)

---

## 18

## CASTING A CLOUT, WITHOUT REMOVING YOUR OVER-CLOUT

There is an old saying: 'Ne'er cast a clout till May be out.' This has nothing to do with people clouting each other. It means don't shed your warm outer garments until June, because summer doesn't really begin till then.

This is an old party trick that always amuses, but is hardly ever tried these days. It's all to do with casting

as it would running along the edge of the field – exactly 10 seconds.

## WAGONS ROLL

1. The engine goes left, picks up W1 and shunts it down and across the bottom to the far right of the whole junction.
2. It unhooks and then shunts W2 into the junction J.
3. The engine then backs down to the main line, moves left and up the left side, hooks up W2 and pulls it down left and across to the bottom centre.
4. It then unhooks, goes left, up the left side to J, then comes down right, hooks up and drags W1 to the right side position.
5. It then unhooks, goes to J, down the left side, then right.
6. It hooks up W2, drags it left and then up to the left side position.
7. It then unhooks and returns to the original bottom centre position – job done!

your inner clout. Get a young volunteer, wearing a sleeveless jumper, to then put on an adult's jacket over the top, so they are double wrapped.

Now, the question is, can they cast the under-clout without removing the over-clout, or coat?

## ANSWERS

## THE BOUNDING HOUNDS

It will take exactly 10 seconds before the dogs all meet. Each dog starts by running along the edge of the field, but it has to take a curved path, always heading for the dog directly in front of it. So each dog is always running towards a line square to the line they are taking. The speed at which they are closing the gap does not vary. So each dog will take exactly the same time to reach the one it is chasing

## DON'T BREAK ANY EGGS

Sally arrived with 31 eggs.
Anne bought half the eggs plus half an egg, or 16 eggs, leaving 15.
Betty bought half the eggs plus half an egg, or 8 eggs, leaving 7.
Cathy took half the eggs plus half an egg, or 4 eggs, leaving 3.
Daisy bought half the eggs plus half an egg, or 2 eggs, leaving 1.
Erica then took half that egg, plus half an egg, and Sally had sold out.

## THE CANOEIST'S HAT TRICK

Surprisingly, assuming he always rows at the same stroke speed, it will take the canoeist the same time to row back to his hat as he took rowing away from it – 5 minutes. The speed of the river is not important and you can ignore the passing bank of the river. Imagine he is on a carpet of river. That it is moving is irrelevant. He will cover the same distance in the same time, whichever way he is going.

## HOW TO BECOME UNTIED

As they are tied together, you could wait for the tide to go out? Rubbish. But it is possible for them to free themselves. Take the middle of one string to form a loop and pass it up through the wrist hole of the other volunteer. Now slip the loop over their hand and withdraw it. They are both now as free as can be – and there might still be time for a swim before the tide goes out?

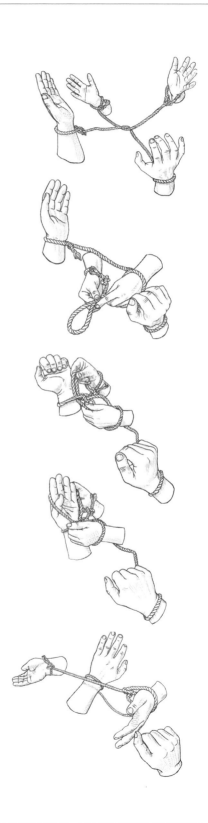

---

(18)

## CASTING A CLOUT

It is amazingly easy to take off the under jumper while not taking off the jacket. Here's how. First clasp their two hands together. Now pull the outer jacket over their heads so it lies on their arms in front of them. Now take the sleeveless jumper forward and over their heads too. Now put the outer jacket back over the head to its original position. The sleeveless jumper is now lying on their arms.

With a little effort you can pass it down one arm-hole in the outer jacket and slip it over the hand, and then draw the whole thing up again and down the other arm-hole. Job done!

I haven't space here, or I would tell you how to take your jeans off over your head. That's a great trick, but it will have to wait till next time. Goodbye!

As a postscript, we thought we'd include two devilish questions. No answers are attached. Read on at your peril.

1.  Three men went to a restaurant and enjoyed a meal. The bill came to £10 each – £30 in all – which they paid and left. The manager of the restaurant then realised they'd been overcharged by £5. An honest man, he sent the waiter after them. Halfway down the street, the waiter called to the men, but he was a less honest man and he decided to say they'd been overcharged by just £1 each. He paid each man £1 and kept £2 for himself. Now, each man paid £10 and had £1 refunded: £9 each, or £27 in total. The dishonest waiter kept £2, so £29 in all. Where did the other £1 go?

This last one is not exactly a puzzle, but an idea that has bothered one of the authors for years. We know it contains a flaw – it must do, or nothing could move. We've even listened to patient explanations on more than one occasion and are still none the wiser.

2.  If a fly travelling east strikes the windscreen of a train travelling west, the fly's direction is reversed. It is impossible to reverse direction along a straight line without slowing, then, briefly, coming to a halt. The fly is in contact with the train at the moment it reverses direction, during which it must halt – so why doesn't the fly stop the train?

Answers on a postcard . . . to the authors, care of HarperCollins Publishers.

# STRENGTH EXERCISES
# EVERY BOY SHOULD DO

The simple truth is this: if you do the exercises in this chapter every day of your life, you will suffer fewer injuries, fewer heart problems and less lower back pain than if you don't. We asked a professional fitness instructor who specialises in body mechanics for this list. It could very easily change your life – and, of course, your physique.

For each one, concentrate on doing it right. Slow and correct is much better than fast and sloppy. Focus on the technique, especially when you are getting used to them.

Perform 10–15 repetitions of each exercise, in two or three sets (groups). You have done enough when you can't finish a repetition properly. If you can't manage these straight off, begin with a smaller number and add one to it each day until you can. You should aim to spend 20–60 minutes on your workout.

Hand weights: as with all things *Dangerous Book*, we prefer to avoid expense. If you don't have weights, make your own with pairs of water bottles filled with water or sand and small stones. If you can perform around six repetitions well with your chosen weight, it's right for you.

Finally, you should try to 'engage your core' – that is bear down and lock your stomach muscles for *all* these exercises. The core is the band of muscles all around your stomach and lower back. A strong core will benefit you in many ways.

## ( 1 )
## SQUATS

You should feel this in your thighs and buttocks. Begin with feet hip-width apart, with your weight evenly over your feet. Hinge at the hips, dropping your bottom back, as if reaching for a seat that is being taken away. Keep your upper body lifted and straight, with eyes front. Lower with control, keeping heels down. Hold a second, then push up to stand.

Arms can rise to shoulder height as you squat – or rest on your hips so that the elbows point forward.

## 2

## OVERHEAD PUSH

Feel this one in the shoulders and upper back. The idea is to raise your arms over your head, straight and parallel to your ears – *without* arching the back or allowing the ribs to stick out. Standing for this is harder than sitting as you need to stabilise and balance the body to push.

With weights, stand with hands a little wider than shoulder-width apart. Palms face forward. Push the weights from the top of the chest overhead, arms slightly in front of the head. Lower slowly, with control.

## 3

## PRESS-UPS

Feel it in the chest and arms. Hands a little wider than the shoulders, elbows are at right angles as you lower. Four kinds, in increasing difficulty – all useful.

i.   On all fours. Pull belly button towards your spine (engaging core muscles in stomach). Bend from the hips as you bend the arms and lower the body, then push up. Maintain the core pull as you complete the dip and raise.
ii.  On your thighs. Core locked and taut.
iii. On your toes. Plank position needs good core strength before you move to this.
iv.  Hot hands. This can be performed at any stage to add variety. Lower the body. As you push up, pull one elbow back, lifting the flat palm off the floor. Maintain taut core muscles and place the hand down as you ready for the next dip. Alternate the elbows as you repeat.

(In British tae kwon do classes, those who are sixteen and above are required to complete press-ups on their knuckles. That's not necessary here, but is interesting to know.)

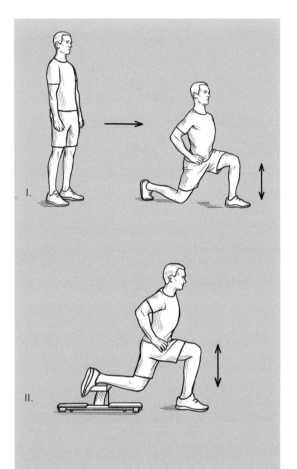

## LUNGES

Feel it in the thighs and glutes.

i. One leg forward, lower with the knee bent to 90 degrees over the ankle, pointing in line with the toes, foot flat on the ground. The back leg is behind, with the knee dropping under the hip and the heel off the ground. The weight of the body is mainly on the front leg. Main body is upright throughout. Complete a set on one side, then move to the other.

ii. Single leg lunge with one foot on a stair. Rest top of foot on stair step behind and use front leg to lower and raise the body.

iii. Step up onto a stair – and knee lift. This is good for runners and to maintain balance.

iv. Take leg back down into the lunge and repeat.

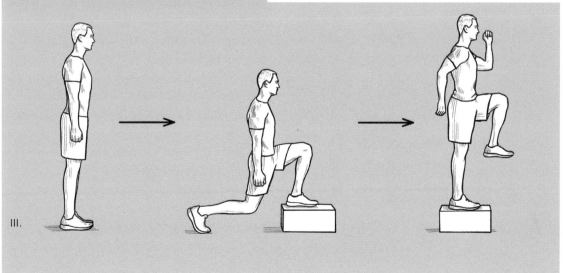

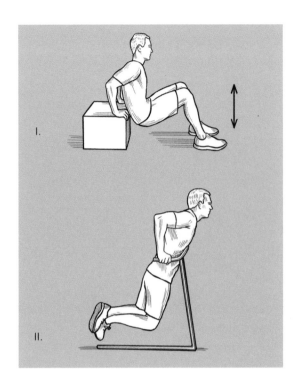

## DIPS

Upper body. Place your hands on a step or parallel bars. The body remains vertical. Lower the body by bending the elbows to 90 degrees. The shoulders should not drop below the elbows. Push back up without locking the elbows.

i. Use a step with the feet on the floor, knees bent. Progress to straight legs.

ii. Use parallel bars – if you can find something suitable. With the body off the floor, using all your bodyweight.

## PULL-UPS

Upper body. If you don't have a bar at home, you can usually find something suitable in a local park. Hold a bar that is firmly attached, with your hands shoulder-width apart and overhand. (So you can see your knuckles.)

Pull your shoulders back and down. Engage your core while pulling your body up, focusing on the muscles of the upper body. Bring your chin just above the bar, then slowly lower down to straighten the arms. If you can't manage a complete pull-up, get used to your weight by hanging from the bar until you drop. Wider hand grip is harder. Underhand grip, with palms towards you, focuses more on the arms than the back.

## SQUAT JUMPS

For lower body and heart cardio. As the squats, but with added power. Lower and jump up to leave the floor. Arms up.

## MOUNTAIN CLIMBERS

Sometimes called 'The Spiderman'. Good for the whole body and heart. Begin with plank position: shoulders over wrists, stabilise the shoulders and core. Belly button pulled towards spine, body locked. Bring alternate knees in towards the shoulder without lifting the hips. The more flexible you are, the further the knees will come in. The faster you move, the more the heart rate increases.

## 9

## SQUAT THRUSTS

Good for whole body and heart. From a squat position, place hands on the floor. Thrust/jump both legs backwards together until they are straight and you are in a plank position. Jump back into squat. Repeat. See how many you can do over thirty seconds, then forty, then sixty.

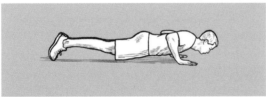

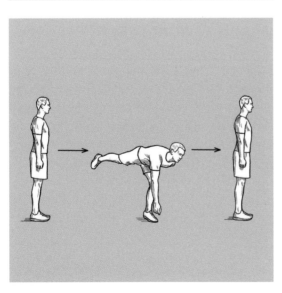

## BURPEES

Whole body and heart. Do not try this after a meal.

i.  Stand, squat, jump legs out to plank, jump legs into squat and jump up to original position.

ii.  As above, but once in a plank, perform a press-up.

What order? Feel free to mix these up to suit the time you have available – or get up a little earlier. You can put together a HIIT (High-intensity Interval Training) regime by performing heart/cardio in between the strength exercises.

Alternate upper and lower body, or perform upper body one day, lower body another.

Finally, add a useful balance: Stand, pivot from the hips to lift one leg behind you and touch your opposite foot, then pivot to stand up again. Repeat on the other side.

The first *Dangerous Book* listed a number of brilliant books, from Roald Dahl to Stephen King. Now, we didn't list every book worth reading, so there is room here for a second try.

These are all excellent. Some will be too old for you – like the Hornblower ones, or *The Reality Dysfunction* perhaps. They are still worth including. Boys become young men, after all – and young men need great books. If you want to play it safe, get one or two from a library and read the first twenty pages

or so. It's long been our belief that if an author hasn't hooked you in twenty pages, you probably won't enjoy the rest. Openings that punch you in the chest are not the only way to start a book, of course. The Patrick O'Brian books that begin with *Master and Commander* are wonderful, gentle books, more concerned with life on board ship in the Napoleonic Wars than gripping the reader from the first page. Leave those until you are thirty or so. Until then, enjoy a few of these. You won't be disappointed.

### 1. THE SECRET DIARY OF ADRIAN MOLE AGED 13¾ BY SUE TOWNSEND

The funniest series of books I have ever read – the only ones that made me weep with laughter on a crowded train. I read the first when I was around the age of Adrian Mole. Wonderful, warm and hilarious. Go on to *The Growing Pains of Adrian Mole* and *The True Confessions of Adrian Albert Mole*. There are others, but you'll find them on your own.

### 2. DIARY OF A WIMPY KID BY JEFF KINNEY

These are beloved of the ten-year-old, who has read the whole series with enormous relish.

### 3. HORRIBLE HISTORIES BY TERRY DEARY

These are also much loved. With titles such as *Rotten Romans* or *Measly Middle Ages*, they are short, punchy and funny.

### 4. USBORNE ILLUSTRATED ADVENTURE STORIES

'The Count of Monte Cristo', 'The Prisoner of Zenda', 'Don Quixote', 'The Three Musketeers', 'The 39 Steps'. Simplified versions for younger children, these are well written in a single volume.

### 5. USBORNE ILLUSTRATED CLASSICS FOR BOYS

Another favourite of the ten-year-old – to read himself or to have read to him. Single volume with six stories: 'Robin Hood', 'Gulliver's Travels', 'Moonfleet' and so on.

### 6. GANGSTA GRANNY BY DAVID WALLIAMS

Hugely successful for a reason. Funny, touching books.

### 7. MY GYM TEACHER IS AN ALIEN OVERLORD BY DAVID SOLOMONS

Funny adventure about superpowers, aliens and gym teachers.

### 8. BALL OF CONFUSION BY JOHNNY BALL

As we have included some problems provided by JB in this book, it makes sense to recommend one of his collections. Non-fiction, puzzling fun.

### 9. MR GUM BOOKS BY ANDY STANTON

Writing humour is difficult. These are completely bonkers and well worth a look. Aged ten to twelve or thereabouts.

### 10. ARTEMIS FOWL BY EOIN COLFER

Highly enjoyable tales of a boy genius, his bodyguard and encounters with Captain Holly Short of the supernatural world. Great fun.

### 11. THE SPLIT INFINITY TRILOGY BY PIERS ANTHONY

Also, his *Incarnations of Immortality* series. Piers Anthony is an incredibly prolific fantasy author, so it isn't always easy to know where to start. If you like the first three – *Split Infinity*, *Blue Adept* and *Juxtaposition* – you'll enjoy the Immortality series that begins with *On a Pale Horse*. They are wonderful.

### 12. THE LIVESHIP TRADERS TRILOGY BY ROBIN HOBB

Begin with *Ship of Magic*, then *The Mad Ship* and *Ship of Destiny*. Epic fantasy, with fantastic characters and plotting. You won't be disappointed. Hobb is one of the greats.

### 13. JIM BUTCHER'S DRESDEN FILES

More the adult end, these – long fantasy series set in modern-day Chicago. Try *Storm Front*. If you enjoy that, there are over a dozen or more. One of life's little pleasures is discovering a decent backlist.

### 14. THE TIME TRAVELLER'S GUIDE TO MEDIEVAL ENGLAND BY IAN MORTIMER

For those who might prefer a little non-fiction, this book is brilliant. It is a detailed and easy-to-read study of the period, as you might see it if you travelled back. Look out for others in the series.

### 15. THE NIGHT'S DAWN TRILOGY BY PETER F. HAMILTON

These are big books, but Hamilton can really write. The first one is called *The Reality Dysfunction*. They are science fiction on the epic tech scale, mingled with Al Capone.

### 16. THE FIRST FAST DRAW BY LOUIS L'AMOUR

L'Amour was a terrific writer of westerns. This is a good example of his style – and a short one at 120 pages. If you like it, there are dozens more. I enjoyed *The Man from Skibbereen* and *The Walking Drum* in particular.

### 17. GILES KRISTIAN'S LANCELOT

If you want tales of King Arthur, this one is brilliantly written, with a touch of David Gemmell in the style. A stand-alone novel. Well worth getting.

### 18. TEGNÉ, WARLORD OF ZENDOW BY RICHARD LA PLANTE

I loved this as a kid, but then I am a complete sucker for anything involving martial arts. It's a gripping tale of the art of the Empty Hand.

### 19. THE DESTROYER BOOKS BY SAPIR AND MURPHY

If you like the first few, there are well over a hundred. There was a film made of them, called *Remo: Unarmed and Dangerous*.

### 20. THE MISENCHANTED SWORD BY LAWRENCE WATT-EVANS

One-off classic adventure fantasy – better plotted than most.

### 21. THE HORNBLOWER BOOKS BY C.S. FORESTER

Historical fiction. The first is *Mr Midshipman Hornblower*. Terrific, exciting series set in the Napoleonic Wars.

### 22. PETER POOK BOOKS

Most are out of print, though you can find them online or in second-hand bookshops. Along with Sue Townsend and Jerome K. Jerome (*Three Men in a Boat*), the Pook books are the other leg of a top-three funny series. Try *Playboy Pook* as a flavour. They might seem a little racy, but they are actually rather innocent and decent books.

### 23. TO YOUR SCATTERED BODIES GO BY PHILIP JOSÉ FARMER

Perhaps it says more about us that we like books that involve historical characters alongside epic fantasy. One of the authors loved this when he was around twelve or fourteen. There are a few more in the series to enjoy if you like the first.

### 24. ALEX RIDER SERIES BY ANTHONY HOROWITZ

We hadn't read these when the first *Dangerous Book* came out. They're brilliantly done, in a young Bond style. Can be read to ten-year-olds, though the chapters are a bit long for night-time stories. Otherwise, suits up to sixteen. Exciting, clearly written adventures. Instant classics.

# THINGS THAT DIDN'T GO IN

The rule for both the original *Dangerous Book* and this one was simple: if we couldn't make it work, it couldn't go in. In the first one, for example, we wanted to include a simple telegraph machine to send Morse code. After three days of trying, all we had was a jumble of balsa wood, batteries and wires. We had only six months to write the book, so that chapter had to be abandoned. Please note, we know it's possible to buy them, or for an electrical engineer to make them. We could probably have made a better bow, for example (though the arrows were fantastic), but we chose to operate at somewhere around the level we managed as kids. It had to be simple – and generally either cheap or free.

For this book, we couldn't use the Flour Bomb Tin. The first failure was years ago, but this time we went about it with a lot more care – and it still wouldn't work.

The basic idea is sound. Flour is a fairly unreactive substance. However, if it can be sprayed into the air, the surface area becomes so vast that even flour can be made to flare. Using a tin, a bit of garden hose taped to a hole and a candle stub, the idea was to jam the lid on, blow flour through the hose and see the lid blow off. Did not happen. What did happen was that after carefully tapping flour into the hose, we forgot to block it as the lid went on – so received a blast of blowback and instant clown face. Sadly, that turned out to be the best bit. With the lid off, we managed a few brief flares of flour as the dust passed over the candle flame. It was never enough to blow the lid off, however. We even tried cornflour, which is much finer, so should have a greater surface area. Nothing. Same small flare; no bang. It's probably possible under laboratory conditions – the theory is sound. Yet we couldn't make it work, so it didn't get a chapter.

In the knots chapter in the original *Dangerous Book*, we had to take one knot out. If you ask a man to list famous knots, he'll probably come up with the 'hangman's noose' – the sort of thing you see used in cowboy films to hang someone from a tree. It's grisly but fascinating, so we learned how to make one and were intending to include it in the book. The problem was that once you've made the noose, the first thing you think of doing is putting it over your head. I did that and said to my brother, 'Look! This is what it must have felt like to stand on a chair or sit on a horse, waiting to be hanged.' It gave me a cold shiver. I then went to take it off.

There are two bits of rope that exit the hangman's noose. One of them loosens the noose, the other tightens it. I pulled the wrong one. It was then tight against my throat – and, crucially, hidden from view under my chin, so I couldn't see which bit of rope to pull to loosen it. They both looked identical and I'd lost track of which was which while I was fiddling with it. So I said to my brother, 'Quick – I've tightened it. Pull the other rope.' And, of course, he pulled the one to tighten it again. Before we finally got that noose off, I was turning a very nice shade of blue. We decided not to put that one in the book, because there's dangerous and there's actually suicidal.

In the chapter on setting things in clear resin, we thought it would be a brilliant idea to put an unfired shotgun cartridge into the resin, perhaps with a little square of card saying 'Break in Case of Emergency' – or something like that. By fluke, we put too much hardener into one of the test moulds and

discovered that if you do, it can become too hot to hold in the hand. The idea of putting a shotgun cartridge into an enclosed mould and then effectively baking it in an oven doesn't bear thinking about.

When one of the authors was a kid, he took all the heads off a box of matches and put them into a long pen cartridge. When he held a lit match to the end, it worked as a sort of firework. He got away with it once, but there was some burning of a thumb and we suspected this might lead to horrific injuries. We do not recommend it now. Remember, if you blow your fingers off, you can't write to complain.

We also had a look at recreating an 'electric honeycomb effect', which seemed to be something we might produce with just a pan of oil and an electrical supply. Sadly, the electrical supply had to be very high voltage indeed – up to ten kilovolts. That would have meant specialist equipment, which is where we usually draw the line. A chapter on making a chess set didn't go in for the same reason – it needed a lathe, and a lathe is too rare a piece of kit.

. . . and that's about it. From the beginning to the end, from making a treehouse in the garden of in-laws, to checking these chapters for typos and errors, this has been an extraordinary privilege. We had no idea there were so many people out there who cared about the same things. That discovery has been a great joy.

Best wishes,

Conn Iggulden        Cameron Iggulden        Arthur Iggulden

# IMPERIAL AND METRIC MEASURES

## LINEAR MEASURES

- 1 **MILE** = 8 furlongs = 1,760 yards = 5,280 feet = 1.609 kilometres (km)
- 1 **FURLONG** = 10 chains = 220 yards = 201 metres (m)
- 1 **CHAIN** = cricket pitch = 22 yards = 66 feet = 20 metres
- 1 **YARD** (yd) = 3 feet = 0.9144 metre / 1 metre = 3ft 4in 3 metres = 10 feet, near as makes no odds.
- 1 **FOOT** (ft) = 12 inches = 0.3048 metre
- 1 **INCH** (in) = 25.4 millimetres (mm)

## SQUARE MEASURES

- 1 **SQUARE MILE** = 640 acres = 259 hectares
- 1 **ACRE** = 10 square chains = 4,840 square yards = 0.405 hectare = 70 paces by 70 paces when pacing out a field
- 1 **ROOD** = ¼ acre = 1,210 square yards = 1,011 square metres ($m^2$)
- 1 **SQUARE YARD** (sq yd) = 9 square feet = 0.836 square metre
- 1 **SQUARE FOOT** (sq ft) = 144 square inches = 9.29 square decimetres
- 1 **SQUARE INCH** (sq in) = 6.45 square centimetres ($cm^2$)

## CUBIC MEASURES

- 1 **CUBIC YARD** = 27 cubic feet = 0.765 cubic metre ($m^3$)
- 1 **CUBIC FOOT** = 1,728 cubic inches = 0.028 cubic metre
- 1 **CUBIC INCH** = 16.4 cubic centimetres

## CAPACITY MEASURES

- 1 **BUSHEL** = four pecks = 64 pints = 8 gallons = 36.4 litres (l)
- 1 **PECK** = 2 gallons / 16 pints = 9.1 litres
- 1 **GALLON** (gal) = 4 quarts / 8 pints = 4.55 litres
- 1 **QUART** (qt) = 2 pints = 1.14 litres
- 1 **PINT** (pt) = 20 fluid ounces = 4 gills = 0.57 litre
- 1 **GILL** = 5 fluid ounces = 0.14 litre
- 1 **FLUID OUNCE** (fl oz) = 1.8 cubic inches = 0.03 litre

## WEIGHT

- 1 **TON** = 20 hundredweight = 2,240 pounds = 1.016 metric tonnes
- 1 **HUNDREDWEIGHT** (cwt) = four quarters = 112 lb = 50.80 kilograms (kg)
- 1 **QUARTER** = 2 stones = 28 pounds = 12.70 kilograms
- 1 **STONE** = 14 pounds = 6.35 kilograms
- 1 **POUND** (lb) = 16 ounces = 7,000 grains = 0.45 kilogram
- 1 **OUNCE** (oz) = 16 drams = 28.35 grams (g)
- 1 **DRAM** = 27.3 grains = 1.772 grams
- 1 **GRAIN** = 0.065 gram

The Last Word
From *The Boy's Own Paper*, Christmas 1903

'One word about smoking. You never will be a perfect man if you smoke. Smoking debilitates and enfeebles the body and all its chief organs, and it weakens heart and brain. The mind of a smoking boy is in a condition of chaos, and he will never be much good in the world. The smoking boy cannot look forward to either a long or happy life. Now ponder on the things I have told you today. There is much food for thought in them. Do the best for yourself, and you will thus be in a position to assist others. Remember this – that in this world, we must live for each other, and the selfish man is in the end the most miserable of all. If God has given you a good constitution, and you ruin it or fail to keep it in working order, you are sinning against nature – and neither doing your duty to your King nor your country. With these last lines I must say goodbye for the present, wishing you a Happy Christmas and a wholesome good New Year.'

Dr Gordon Stables, Royal Navy

# PICTURE CREDITS